Gender and Elections

Sixth Edition

The sixth edition of *Gender and Elections* offers a systematic, lively, multifaceted account of the role of gender in the electoral process through the 2024 elections. This timely, yet enduring, volume strikes a balance between highlighting the most important developments for women as voters and candidates in the 2024 elections and providing a more long-term, in-depth analysis of the ways that gender has helped shape the contours and outcomes of electoral politics in the United States. Individual chapters demonstrate the importance of gender in understanding and interpreting presidential, congressional, and state elections; voter participation, turnout, and choices; the role of social movements in elections; the participation of Black women and Latinas; the political history and success of LGBTQ+ women; the support of political parties and women's organizations; and candidate strategy. Without question, *Gender and Elections* is the most comprehensive, reliable, and trustworthy resource on the role of gender in electoral politics.

Richard L. Fox is Dean of the Bellarmine College of Liberal Arts and Professor of Political Science at Loyola Marymount University. His research examines how gender affects voting behavior, state executive elections, congressional elections, and political ambition. He is coauthor of *It Takes More Than a Candidate: Why Women Don't Run for Office* (2025), *American Politics: A Field Guide* (2023), *Women, Men & US Politics: Ten Big Questions* (2017), and *Running from Office: Why Young Americans Are Turned Off to Politics* (2015). His articles have appeared in the *Journal of Politics*, *American Journal of Political Science*, *American Political Science Review*, *Political Psychology*, *PS*, *Women & Politics*, *Political Research Quarterly*, and *Public Administration Review*.

Kelly Dittmar is an associate professor of political science at Rutgers-Camden. She is also a scholar and Director of Research at the Center for American Women and Politics (CAWP) at the Eagleton Institute of Politics at Rutgers University. Her research focuses on gender and American political institutions. She is the coauthor of *A Seat at the Table: Congresswomen's Perspectives on Why Their Representation Matters* (2018, with Kira Sanbonmatsu and Susan J. Carroll) and author *of Navigating Gendered Terrain: Stereotypes and Strategy in Political Campaigns* (2015). At CAWP, Dittmar manages national research projects, helps to develop and implement CAWP's research agenda, and contributes to CAWP reports, publications, and analyses.

Susan J. Carroll is Professor Emerita at Rutgers University. Formerly a senior scholar at the Center for American Women and Politics, the Eagleton Institute of Politics, Rutgers University, she is coauthor of *A Seat at the Table: Congresswomen's Perspectives on Why Their Presence Matters* (2018, with Kelly Dittmar and Kira Sanbonmatsu) and *More Women Can Run: Gender and Pathways to State Legislatures* (2013, with Kira Sanbonmatsu). Earlier books include *Women as Candidates in American Politics* (2nd edition, 1994), *Women and American Politics: New Questions, New Directions* (2003), and *The Impact of Women in Public Office* (2001). Carroll also has published numerous journal articles and book chapters focusing on women candidates, voters, elected officials, and political appointees in the United States.

Gender and Elections

SHAPING THE FUTURE OF AMERICAN POLITICS

Sixth Edition

Edited by

Richard L. Fox
Loyola Marymount University

Kelly Dittmar
Rutgers University

Susan J. Carroll
Rutgers University

Shaftesbury Road, Cambridge CB2 8EA, United Kingdom

One Liberty Plaza, 20th Floor, New York, NY 10006, USA

477 Williamstown Road, Port Melbourne, VIC 3207, Australia

314–321, 3rd Floor, Plot 3, Splendor Forum, Jasola District Centre, New Delhi – 110025, India

Cambridge University Press is part of Cambridge University Press & Assessment, a department of the University of Cambridge.

We share the University's mission to contribute to society through the pursuit of education, learning and research at the highest international levels of excellence.

www.cambridge.org
Information on this title: www.cambridge.org/highereducation/isbn/9781009680202
DOI: 10.1017/9781009680240

When citing this work, please include a reference to the DOI 10.1017/9781009680240

First published 2006
Second edition published 2010
Third edition published 2014
Fourth edition published 2018
Reprinted 2018
Fifth edition published 2022
Sixth edition published 2026

Cover image: Top photo: Saul Loeb/AFP/Getty Images; Bottom photo: Brendan Smialowski/AFP/Getty Images

A catalogue record for this publication is available from the British Library

Library of Congress Cataloging-in-Publication Data
Names: Fox, Richard L., 1967– editor | Dittmar, Kelly, 1984– editor |
Carroll, Susan J., 1950– editor
Title: Gender and elections : shaping the future of American politics /
Richard L. Fox, Kelly Dittmar, Susan J. Carroll.
Description: 6th edition. | New York : Cambridge University Press, 2026. |
Includes bibliographical references and index.
Identifiers: LCCN 2025054973 | ISBN 9781009680196 hardback |
ISBN 9781009680240 ebook
Subjects: LCSH: Women – Political activity – United States |
Elections – United States | Voting – United States | Women political
candidates – United States | Sex role – Political aspects – United States |
Hispanic American women – Political activity – United States | Women,
Black – Political activity – United States
Classification: LCC HQ1236.5.U6 G444 2026
LC record available at https://lccn.loc.gov/2025054973

ISBN 978-1-009-68019-6 Hardback
ISBN 978-1-009-68020-2 Paperback

Additional resources for this publication at www.cambridge.org/genderandelections

Contents

Figures

Tables

Text Boxes

Contributors

Susan J. Carroll is Professor Emerita at Rutgers University. Formerly a senior scholar at the Center for American Women and Politics, the Eagleton Institute of Politics, Rutgers University, she is coauthor of *A Seat at the Table: Congresswomen's Perspectives on Why Their Presence Matters* (2018, with Kelly Dittmar and Kira Sanbonmatsu) and *More Women Can Run: Gender and Pathways to State Legislatures* (2013, with Kira Sanbonmatsu). Earlier books include *Women as Candidates in American Politics* (2nd edition, 1994), *Women and American Politics: New Questions, New Directions* (2003), and *The Impact of Women in Public Office* (2001). Carroll also has published numerous journal articles and book chapters focusing on women candidates, voters, elected officials, and political appointees in the United States.

Erin C. Cassese is a professor in the departments of political science and communication at the University of Delaware. Her research focuses on voter psychology, with an emphasis on the role of gender in American political campaigns and elections. She is a coauthor of *Abortion Attitudes and Polarization in the American Electorate* (Cambridge University Press Elements Series, 2025) and her scholarship has appeared in journals such as *Politics & Gender*, *Political Behavior*, and *Political Psychology*.

Rosalyn Cooperman is a professor of political science at the University of Mary Washington. Since 2004, she has served as principal investigator for the Convention Delegate Study, a survey of Democratic and Republican party delegates. Her research focuses on the role that political parties and women's campaign finance networks play in supporting women candidates. Her articles have appeared in journals such as the *American Political Science Review*, *Journal of Politics*, and *Party Politics*. She is presently working on a project that evaluates women's service in the Virginia General Assembly.

Kelly Dittmar is an associate professor of political science at Rutgers-Camden. She is also a scholar and Director of Research at the Center for American Women and Politics (CAWP) at the Eagleton Institute of Politics at Rutgers University. Her research focuses on gender and American political institutions. She is the coauthor of *A Seat at the Table: Congresswomen's Perspectives on Why Their Representation Matters* (2018, with Kira Sanbonmatsu and Susan J. Carroll) and author *of Navigating Gendered Terrain: Stereotypes and Strategy in Political Campaigns* (2015). At CAWP, Dittmar manages national research projects, helps to develop and implement CAWP's research agenda, and contributes to CAWP reports, publications, and analyses.

Richard L. Fox is Professor of Political Science at Loyola Marymount University. His research examines how gender affects voting behavior, state executive elections, congressional elections, and political ambition. The coauthor of *Women, Men & US Politics: Ten Big Questions* (2017), his other books include *Running from Office: Why Young Americans Are Turned Off to Politics* (2015) and *It Still Takes a Candidate: Why Women Don't Run for Office* (Cambridge University Press, 2010). His articles have appeared in the *Journal of Politics, American Journal of Political Science, American Political Science Review, Political Psychology, PS, Women & Politics, Political Research Quarterly*, and *Public Administration Review*.

Yueshan Long is a doctoral student in the department of political science at the University of Delaware. She holds BAs in economics and business English from the Northeast Normal University and an MA in American studies from Beijing Foreign Studies University. Her research focuses on obstacles to women's political incorporation and women voter political behavior in the United States.

Gabriele Magni is Assistant Professor of Political Science at Loyola Marymount University. During the academic year 2023–24, he was also a visiting scholar at the Russell Sage Foundation. His research examines public opinion, voting behavior, and political representation, with a focus on LGBTQ+ politics and immigration. His work has appeared in journals such as the *American Political Science Review, American Journal of Political Science, Journal of Politics, British Journal of Political Science*, and *Comparative Political Studies*. Gabriele is currently working on a book that explores the experiences of LGBTQ+ political candidates in the United States. He has written op-eds for the *Washington Post*, *Politico*, and *The New Republic*, and his scholarship has been covered by outlets such as the *New York Times*, *Washington Post*, *FiveThirtyEight*, *Fox News*, *NBC News*, *ABC News*, *TIME*, *Al Jazeera*, *USA Today*, Associated Press, and Reuters.

Celeste Montoya is a professor in women and gender studies and political science at the University of Colorado Boulder. Her research focuses on gender and race in American and European politics. She has written extensively on intersectionality as it pertains to social movements, public policy, and political representation and is the author of *From Global to Grassroots: The European Union, Transnational Advocacy, and Combating Violence against Women* (2013) and coeditor of *Gendered Mobilizations and Intersectional Challenges* (2019).

Anna Sampaio is a professor of ethnic studies and political science, and Chair of the Ethnic Studies Department, at Santa Clara University, with specializations in immigration, Latina/o/x politics, race and gender politics, intersectionality, and transnationalism. She is the author of *Terrorizing Latina/o Immigrants: Race, Gender, and Immigration Politics in the Age of Security* (2015), which won the 2016 American Political Science Association award for Best New Book in Latina/o/x Politics. She is currently coeditor of the Intersectionality book series at Temple University Press (with Julia Jordan-Zachery and Celeste Montoya) as well as coeditor of *Transnational Latino/a Communities: Politics, Processes, and Cultures* (2002, with Carlos Vélez-Ibáñez). Her research has appeared in a wide range of research centered and public-facing settings, including the *International Feminist Journal of Politics*, *Latino Decisions*, *NACLA*, *New Political Science*, *Politics Groups and Identities*, *Political Research Quarterly*, *PS: Political Science and Politics*, *The Gender Policy Report*, and the *Washington Post*. Her current book project, *Latina Political Participation and Activism in the US*, examines the history of Latina political engagement in the United States, with particular attention to the experiences of Mexican American, Puerto Rican, and Cuban American activists in the nineteenth and twentieth centuries.

Kira Sanbonmatsu is Professor of Political Science at Rutgers University and Senior Scholar at the Center for American Women and Politics (CAWP) at the Eagleton Institute of Politics. Her research interests include gender, race/ethnicity, parties, public opinion, state politics, and money and politics. She is the coauthor of *A Seat at the Table: Congresswomen's*

Perspectives on Why Their Presence Matters (2018), written with Kelly Dittmar and Susan J. Carroll, and *More Women Can Run: Gender and Pathways to the State Legislatures* (2013), written with Susan J. Carroll. She is the author of *Where Women Run: Gender and Party in the American States* (2006) and *Democrats, Republicans, and the Politics of Women's Place* (2002). Her articles have appeared in such journals as *Politics, Groups, and Identities* and *The Journal of Women, Politics & Policy*. She coedits the CAWP Series in Gender and American Politics at the University of Michigan Press with Susan J. Carroll.

Jamil Scott is an assistant professor at Georgetown University. Her work focuses on how race and gender identity matter for the behavior of political elites and the mass public. Her work has been published in journals such as *Politics, Groups and Identities, American Politics Research, Politics & Gender*, and *Journal of Race and Ethnicity Politics*. She is currently working on a book-length manuscript that explores Black women's path to state legislative office.

Acknowledgments

This volume had its origins in a series of three roundtable panels at professional meetings in 2002 and 2003 focusing on how women fared in the 2002 elections. Several of the first contributors to this book were participants on those roundtables. As we gathered at these professional meetings, we began to talk among ourselves about a major frustration we faced in teaching courses on women and politics, campaigns and elections, and American politics. We all had difficulty finding suitable, up-to-date materials on women candidates, the gender gap, and other facets of women's involvement in elections, and certainly none of us had been able to find a text focused specifically on gender and elections that we could use. We felt the literature was in great need of a recurring and reliable source that would first be published immediately following a presidential election and then updated every four years so that it remained current.

At some point in our early discussions, we all looked at one another and collectively asked, "As the academic experts in this field, aren't we the ones to take on this project? Why don't we produce a volume suitable for classroom use that would also be a resource for scholars, journalists, and practitioners?" In that moment *Gender and Elections* was born. We are enormously grateful to Barbara Burrell for organizing the first of our roundtable panels and thus identifying and pulling together the initial core of contributors to this volume.

We produced the first volume of *Gender and Elections* in the immediate aftermath of the 2004 presidential election and updated and expanded the volume in the second, third, fourth, and fifth editions following the elections of 2008, 2012, 2016, and 2020, respectively. Gratified by the positive response the book has received over the years, we are pleased to provide this sixth edition, which includes up-to-date information through the 2024 elections as well as some new chapters and contributors to reflect the changing times. We hope to continue to revise and publish new editions following future presidential elections.

As we approached the 2024 elections and a possible sixth, we had to navigate Sue's retirement. We begged her to say on board, and she reluctantly agreed to stay on but only to help with the Introduction. Sue is saying she cannot possibly help with a seventh edition, but we will keep on her to return. Her insights are invaluable and her legacy in the field of gender and politics is immeasurable. In this sixth edition we also reluctantly said goodbye to some long-term contributors – Dianne Bystrom, Susan A. MacManus, and Wendy G. Smooth – whom we cannot thank enough for all they have meant to this collective endeavor over the years. Although we are sad to lose them, we are very pleased to welcome a number of new contributors – Erin C. Cassese, Yueshan Long, Gabriele Magni, and Jamil Scott – all of whom bring renewed energy, scholarly expertise, and fresh perspectives to this edition. In addition to our new contributors, we would like to thank those contributors who have stayed on for multiple editions, engaging each new cycle with the intellectual curiosity, creativity, and expertise that makes this volume so rich.

This book would not have been possible without the assistance of the Center for American Women and Politics (CAWP) at Rutgers University and its various staff members. In particular, Debbie Walsh, director of CAWP, has embraced and encouraged this project and been supportive in numerous ways. The data team, led by Chelsea Hill, has been invaluable in providing information about women and politics, and several contributors have relied on data they compiled. We are also incredibly grateful to Kiana Karimi, research associate at Loyola Marymount University, who was essential in preparing our chapters for publication.

Finally, we would like to thank Melanie McFadyen, senior editor, who greatly assisted in helping bring the sixth edition to completion. We also are grateful to Sara Doskow and Maggie Jeffers, editors for the fifth edition. We thank Robert Dreesen, our editor for the third and fourth editions, and Ed Parsons, our editor on the first two editions, for their support in both launching and sustaining this project over the years.

RICHARD L. FOX, KELLY DITTMAR, AND SUSAN J. CARROLL

Introduction

Gender and Electoral Politics in Contemporary US Politics

Twenty years ago, we published the first edition of *Gender and Elections: Shaping the Future of American Politics*. Our goal for that volume, and the four additional editions that have followed, was to offer critical and timely analysis of the role of gender in the electoral process. It has been our aim to produce an updated volume after every presidential election year. A foundational premise for the book is that readers must be presented with key theoretical foundations and historical developments in order to understand how elections are gendered in the United States. This is especially true in light of the dramatically evolving and shifting role of gender in elections in the past two decades. The sixth edition of *Gender and Elections* aligns with our original goals while also representing evolution in the analytical scope and approach of research related to gender and elections. This edition is published after two decades of progress – and backlash against it – for women and politics.

In 2005, when the first edition of this volume was published, women held 15 percent of congressional seats, were 23 percent of state legislators, and held eight of fifty governorships. No woman had yet secured a major-party nomination for US president, and 38 percent of people believed that Americans were not ready to elect a woman president.[1] Since then, the number of women in Congress has nearly doubled and women are now one-third of state legislators. Almost half of the fifty-one women who have *ever* served as governors through 2025 have entered office since 2005. At the presidential level, this period includes the election of the first woman vice president of the United States as well as the first two nominations of women to be major-party nominees for US president.

---

[1] Gallup poll, PollingReport.com, September 2006, www.pollingreport.com/politics4.htm

Women have achieved other notable milestones in the past two decades of US politics.[2] US Representative Nancy Pelosi became the first woman Speaker of the House and served in that role for eight years. The first Native and Muslim women were elected to the US Congress, the first Latina was elected to the US Senate, and the first Latina and Asian women were elected as governors during this period. Women made record gains in congressional and state legislative representation, particularly in the 2018 election. In the same year, Nevada became the first state to have a majority-woman state legislature; since then, the number of women legislators has surpassed the number of men in four other states. Finally, the past twenty years have witnessed the first openly LGBTQ+ women elected as governor and to the US Senate, as well as the first openly transgender women elected to state legislatures and the US Congress.

The gains for and achievements of women candidates and officeholders are not the only markers of gender progress in US politics. Public perceptions of gender and political leadership have evolved in the past two decades. For example, research conducted by Monica Schneider and Angela Bos in 2011 found that women politicians were defined more by their perceived *lack* of traits associated with political leadership than their leadership strengths. In late 2020 and early 2021, Angela Bos joined other researchers to find that women politicians were more likely than a decade earlier to be associated with competence, strong leadership, and integrity while retaining perceived advantages on stereotypically feminine traits like compassion.[3] Scholars continue to debate the persistence and influence of gender and intersectional stereotypes in the evaluation of women candidates and officeholders, with some studies in the past decade showing little negative impact of gender stereotypes on women's political success.[4] But while gendered attitudes confronted by political women may have "grown subtler," Cecilia Mo offers evidence that they "remain consequential" in the electoral process.[5]

---

[2] Center for American Women and Politics (CAWP), Milestones for Women in American Politics, n.d., https://cawp.rutgers.edu/data?tab=Milestones

[3] Monica C. Schneider and Angela L. Bos, Measuring Stereotypes of Female Politicians, *Political Psychology* 35(2) (2014): 245–66; Daphne van der Pas, Loes Aaldering, and Angela L. Bos, Looks Like a Leader: Measuring Evolution in Gendered Politician Stereotypes, *Political Behavior* 46 (2024): 1653–75.

[4] Kathleen Dolan, *When Does Gender Matter? Women Candidates and Gender Stereotypes in American Elections* (New York: Oxford University Press, 2014).

[5] Hyunjung Cecilia Mo, The Consequences of Explicit and Implicit Gender Attitudes and Candidate Quality in the Calculations of Voters, *Political Behavior* 37(2) (2015): 357–95.

Similar evolution is evident in research and practice on gender and intersectional biases in candidate recruitment, institutional inclusion, media coverage, and fundraising that have been historically cited as areas of disadvantage for women and women of color in US politics. In each of these areas, research over the past two decades uncovers both progress and persistent hurdles along axes of gender and race. Some progress has resulted from national gender and racial reckonings spurred by movements like #MeToo and Black Lives Matter, which put pressure on political institutions – and their leaders – to address deeply rooted biases in processes and policies. These movements also mobilized many women to engage more directly in political activism, and some women have translated that activism to candidacy and officeholding.

But just as in the larger arc of US history, progress has not come without backlash. And that backlash has been both leveraged and incited in recent elections. In 2016, Donald Trump tapped into racial resentment on the heels of two terms under the nation's first Black president. Running against the first woman major-party presidential nominee, he also promised voters concerned that society was becoming "too soft and feminine" a return to a more traditional and ultimately more masculine form of leadership. In 2020, he positioned himself in opposition to racial justice protesters. During this period, Trump did not act alone. The backlash he leveraged was fueled by conservative activists, media pundits, and political leaders who claimed that efforts to promote gender and racial equity and inclusion – both inside and outside of politics – had gone too far. Opposition to gender and racial equity efforts only grew between 2020 and 2024, when Donald Trump again focused his presidential campaign – and subsequent presidency – in part on rejecting the existence of and efforts to address systemic discrimination, as well as expansive and inclusive understandings of gender.

As recent electoral history reveals, understanding the role of gender in elections and how gender influences electoral outcomes requires that we apply an intersectional lens – a lens that acknowledges the interplay between gender and race and how these categories highlight overlapping forms of disadvantage.

GENDER AND THE CONTEXT OF THE 2024 ELECTION

The elections of 2016, 2018, and 2020 all marked key milestones for women in US politics. In 2016, Hillary Clinton put over 65 million cracks in the presidential glass ceiling through her historic nomination and win of the national popular vote. Her defeat – and Trump's success – mobilized record numbers of women and contributed to the record numbers of women who ran for and won elective office in 2018. Two years later, women made history again at the presidential level, with a record number of women running for the Democratic nomination and Kamala Harris becoming the first woman vice president. That year, women also continued to mark historic highs in candidacy and officeholding across levels of office. The numbers of women running for elective office dropped in 2022, signaling a decline in momentum in women's electoral progress. And by 2024, hardly any counts for women candidates or nominees – across party, race, and level of office – reached new highs. The results of the 2024 elections for women's representation are best summarized as relative stasis.

At the presidential level, the 2024 cycle began with low enthusiasm and growing discontent. Many voters were particularly dismayed by the inevitable rematch of Joe Biden and Donald Trump, two elderly white men who had dominated presidential politics for the past decade. Donald Trump largely ignored his opponents in the Republican primary, refusing participation in any primary debates and assuming the mantle of Republican presidential nominee well before votes were cast. The last Republican standing to challenge Donald Trump was former South Carolina Governor Nikki Haley. Though she did not come close to beating Trump, Haley was arguably the most successful female Republican to ever run for president. On the Democratic side of things, President Biden faced no serious challenge for the Democratic nomination. He did, however, confront dissatisfaction from many Democrats who felt that it was time for him to cede the stage to a younger generation and feared that he would be unable to defeat Trump. Those fears were highlighted to the broader public when Biden performed poorly in a June 2024 debate against Trump. Biden appeared confused, struggled with recall, and stumbled over words and statements. As pressure mounted for him to drop out of the contest, the prospect of a second woman major-party presidential nominee quickly became real.

Less than a month after the dismal presidential debate performance, Joe Biden announced his withdrawal from the presidential race and expressed his support for Vice President Kamala Harris to become the Democratic nominee. Harris quickly announced that she would seek the nomination and just one month later she formally received it at the Democratic National Convention. Harris's candidacy was unprecedented on multiple fronts. She was the first Black woman and South Asian person to be a major-party presidential nominee. She was also the first presidential nominee in modern US history to earn her party's nomination without her name receiving top billing on primary ballots. And while Harris was part of the presidential ticket that had been waging a reelection campaign for over a year, she was tasked with launching and executing her own presidential campaign, including selecting a running mate, in less than four months.

Despite this expedited calendar, Harris's nomination appeared to reinvigorate the Democratic presidential campaign and progressive voters. The Harris campaign immediately achieved fundraising records and inspired voter mobilization and organizing nationwide. But the heightened enthusiasm was not enough to overcome forces working against the Democratic campaign. Pre- and post-election surveys showed voters' primary concerns were economic, focused on inflation and higher costs on basic needs like food, gas, and housing. Harris, as vice president, was tied to the negative approval ratings of the Biden administration. Beyond concerns over inflation, perceptions that the Democratic administration had done little to curb illegal immigration, mishandled the Israeli–Palestinian conflict, and overspent on the lengthy war in Ukraine also worked against the Democratic campaign. This was a difficult political landscape to overcome.

Aiding the Harris campaign, many voters were also concerned with preserving US democracy, perceiving threats to democratic norms and processes that were most clearly evident in and since the January 6, 2021, insurrection at the US Capitol. Harris warned voters of the risk of returning power to the president who had inspired and defended the insurrection, and who had been accused and convicted of multiple crimes since leaving office. Exit polls showed that voters who rated preserving democracy as a top issue voted overwhelmingly for Harris. Harris's advantage on another issue she made central to her campaign may have been overestimated. Democrats believed that the overturning of *Roe v. Wade* in 2022 and Republican efforts to further restrict reproductive rights would rally voters against Republican candidates at all levels, but the issue turned out to be less broadly determinative in vote choice and election outcomes. Instead, Trump-led opposition to transgender rights and diversity, equity, and inclusion (DEI) efforts proved to be – for some – at least equally motivating against Democratic candidates.

Despite her ultimate defeat, Vice President Kamala Harris ran a historic campaign that further disrupted gendered and racialized norms of presidential leadership. In both her identities and agenda, Harris's campaign starkly contrasted with that of her opponent. While Trump

emphasized and capitalized on white and male grievance in the electorate, Harris embodied the gender and multiracial progress that many of
Trump's supporters perceived as a threat.

From the presidential level down, the 2024 elections showed that gender remains a visible and important influence in US politics, and that it is
intertwined with other influential forces like race and party. This volume
analyzes various aspects of electoral politics, explaining how underlying
gender dynamics are critical to shaping the contours and the outcomes of
elections in the United States. No interpretation of American elections can
be complete without an understanding of the growing role of women as
political actors and the multiple ways that gender enters into and affects
contemporary electoral politics.

THE GENDERED NATURE OF ELECTIONS

Elections in the United States are deeply gendered in several ways. Most
obviously, men dominate the electoral playing field. Despite the progress of
the past two decades, men remained a majority of candidates across all levels of government in 2024. Many of the most recognized behind-the-scenes
campaign strategists and consultants – the pollsters, media experts, fundraising advisers, and those who develop campaign messages – are also men.

Further, while there has been progress in the representation of women
in political media, a 2022 study found that 60 percent of US journalists
covering government and politics were men.[6] It also found that sports is
the only beat more male-dominated than politics. Research has shown that
gains for women in elective office are related to an increase in the number
of women journalists covering politics and that women holding editorial
leadership roles at news organizations yields more bylines for women.[7] In
those media leadership roles, women are still seeking gender parity.

Finally, over the two decades in which we have edited this volume,
the media landscape has shifted significantly. Today, some of the most
influential voices in news come from alternative outlets and platforms,
including social media. A 2024 Pew study found that nearly 40 percent
of US adults under age thirty get their news from social media influencers. And in capturing the diversity among those influencers, they found

---

[6] Emily Tomasik and Jeffrey Gottfried, US Journalists' Beats Vary Widely by Gender and
Other Factors, *Pew Research Center*, April 4, 2023, https://shorturl.at/yMkfM
[7] Nichole M. Bauer, Cana Kim, Kenlea Barnes, Khaleel Ouedraogo, and Elise Strain, Still
a Boy's Club: Women Journalists and Political News Coverage, *Journalism Studies* 25(13)
(2024): 1654–75.

that 63 percent were men.[8] Men also remain the leading voices in political talk radio and podcasts. The most listened to podcast in the United States is *The Joe Rogan Experience*. Rogan's podcast has platformed key figures in the "manosphere" – a network of online spaces and influencers promoting men's rights and, often concurrently, white supremacy and misogyny – and has a distinctly male (80 percent) listenership.[9] In 2024, Donald Trump and JD Vance appealed to voters vis-à-vis these influencers and touted Rogan's endorsement ahead of Election Day.

Men also contribute the largest sums of money to candidates and parties, perhaps the most essential ingredient in American politics.[10] In 2024, men were a majority of the cycle's biggest political donors and they were responsible for nearly two-thirds of all contributions to congressional candidates.[11] Moreover, gender disparities in the sphere of money in politics do not just exist among donors. While many studies prove that women candidates are capable of achieving the same fundraising success as men, it may take more effort for women to do so. Specifically, women continue to be more likely to amass campaign funds from small versus large donations and are less likely than men to fund their campaigns with their own money. Access to donor networks varies across both gender and racial lines, with historic and persistent disparities in wealth and income influencing the gendered and racialized realities of political giving.

Gendered expectations also permeate our political landscape. Citizens have historically preferred leaders who are tough, dominant, and assertive – qualities much more associated with masculinity than femininity in American culture. Masculine demands on candidates and officeholders have proven harder for women to negotiate. Women must both meet masculine expectations of political leaders and appease voters' gender-based expectations that they are more likable, caring, and ethical than their male counterparts. In practice, these disparate expectations have meant that women candidates and officeholders must often spend more time and energy than men in proving their competence and fitness for political roles. Likewise, women are likely to consider how their

---

[8] Galen Stocking et al., America's News Influencers, *Pew Research Center*, November 18, 2024, https://pewresearch.org/journalism/2024/11/18/americas-news-influencers/

[9] James Fitzgerald, Joe Rogan Gives Backing to Donald Trump in US Election, *BBC News*, November 5, 2024, https://bbc.com/news/articles/cp9z2p3vr48o

[10] Open Secrets, Donor Demographics, https://opensecrets.org/elections-overview/donor-demographics

[11] Open Secrets, Who Are the Biggest Donors?, https://opensecrets.org/elections-overview/biggest-donors; Kira Sanbonmatsu, Women, Money, and Politics Watch 2024, CAWP, 2024, https://shorturl.at/39cR3

appearance, messages, and behavior may land differently due to voters' gendered – and racialized – expectations and adjust their approach accordingly. Especially at the highest levels of elective office and among women of color, women are also more likely to combat doubts over their electability in political environments that remain dominated by white men. Political practitioners have pointed to the dual campaigns that women wage to prove not only that they are the best candidate in a given contest but also that they can win, referring to the latter as a "concurrent campaign of belief" to convince voters, donors, and practitioners that their success is possible.[12]

In this and other ways, elections in the United States are gendered in the strategies that candidates employ in reaching out to the general public. Candidates, both men and women, strategize about how to present themselves to voters of the same and opposite sexes. Pollsters and campaign consultants routinely try to figure out what issues or themes will appeal specifically to women or to men. Specially devised appeals are directed at young women and/or men, non-college-educated men, college-educated women, married women, or Black, Hispanic, or white men or women, to name only some of the targeted groups. While researchers have cautioned practitioners to avoid trying for one-size-fits-all appeals to groups of voters, recent elections – including in 2024 – demonstrate the persistence of campaign efforts to segment and appeal to voters on the basis of gender and other demographics.

Finally, a significant gender gap in women's and men's interest in running for office persists in US politics. Across more than two decades, the difference between women and men in their desire to consider becoming political candidates remains virtually unchanged. All the factors that researchers and analysts expected might have changed this reality in recent decades – more women running and serving in top elected positions, greater awareness of women's underrepresentation, and a greater emphasis on candidate recruitment – have not altered the fundamental differences. The gender gap in interest in running for office among a group of potential candidates was sixteen points in 2001, sixteen points in 2011, and eighteen points in 2021.[13] And this gender gap persists across all racial categories. While this gap is complicated and multifaceted, at the

---

[12] Kelly Dittmar, Elizabeth Warren, and Kamala Harris Are Running Dual Campaigns, *CNN*, September 2, 2019, https://shorturl.at/TOHdO

[13] Richard L. Fox and Jennifer Lawless, The Invincible Gender Gap in Political Ambition, *PS: Political Science & Politics* 57(2) (2024): 231–37.

very least it indicates that women and men have different levels of comfort in seeing themselves as candidates for public office. These findings may also reflect the different calculations that women make when considering candidacy and officeholding. In a political landscape where they are still more likely than men to face greater scrutiny over their qualifications, institutional sexism and racism, and harassment that is often distinctly sexualized in nature, it is unsurprising that women may consider other paths to political and policy influence.

In short, when we look at the people, the expectations, the strategies, and candidate experiences of contemporary politics, we see that gender plays an important role in elections in the United States. Even when it is not explicitly acknowledged, it often operates in the background, affecting our assumptions about who legitimate political actors are and how they should behave. And often in the United States, the effects of gender are inextricably intertwined with the effects of race and ethnicity. It is not surprising, for example, that the first nonwhite person elected to the presidency was a man or that the first female major-party nominee was white.

This is not to say, however, that the role of gender has been constant over time. Rather, we regard gender as malleable, manifesting itself differently at various times and in different contexts in the electoral process. In women's candidacies for elective office, for example, there has been obvious change. As recently as twenty-five years ago, a woman seeking high-level office almost anywhere in the United States was an anomaly, and she might have faced overt hostility. Clearly, the electoral environment is much more hospitable now. Over the years, slowly but steadily, more and more women have entered the electoral arena at all levels. And they have exerted their political influence in other areas, such as in media, among political practitioners, and as voters and donors.

Although there are important political differences between women and men in the aggregate, there are also significant differences among women too. The role of gender is not independent of the influences of race, ethnicity, sexuality, social class, and even age/generation. Rather, these categories are mutually constitutive. For example, the experiences of a Black woman in politics are likely to differ from the experiences of a white woman, and the political perspectives of a Latina millennial might vary significantly from those of her senior-citizen grandmother. Diversity among women was certainly evident in the 2024 election, with Black women forming the bedrock of support for Vice President Kamala Harris, while President Trump made gains among Latinas and carried a solid majority of white women voters.

POLITICAL REPRESENTATION AND SIMPLE JUSTICE: WHY GENDER MATTERS IN ELECTORAL POLITICS

Beyond the reality that gender shapes the contours of contemporary elections, it is important to examine and monitor the role of gender in the electoral process because of concerns about justice and the quality of political representation. The United States lags far behind many other nations in the number of women serving in its national legislature. In early 2025, with only 28 percent of members of Congress being women, the United States ranked 77th among countries throughout the world for the proportion of women serving in its national parliament or legislature.[14] Twelve women served as governors across fifty states, and only 33.4 percent of all state legislators across the country were women, according to the Center for American Women and Politics (CAWP).[15]

Despite the relatively low proportion of women in positions of political leadership, women constitute a majority of the voters who elect these leaders. In the 2024 elections, for example, US Census figures showed that 81.5 million women reported voting, compared with 72.8 million men; thus, 8.7 million more women than men voted in those elections. As a matter of simple justice, something seems fundamentally wrong with a democratic system where women are a majority of voters but remain dramatically underrepresented among elected political leaders. The fact that women constitute a majority of the electorate but only a minority of public officials is a sufficient reason, in and of itself, to pay attention to the underlying gender dynamics of US politics.

Beyond the issue of simple justice, however, there are significant concerns over the quality of political representation in the United States. Beginning with a series of studies commissioned by CAWP in the 1980s, a great deal of empirical research indicates that women and men support and devote attention to somewhat different issues as public officials.[16] Although party differences are increasingly more predictive than gender differences, at both national and state levels male and female legislators have been shown to have different policy priorities and preferences.[17]

---

[14]   IPU Parline Global data on national parliaments, Monthly ranking of women in national parliaments, 2025, https://data.ipu.org/women-ranking/?date_month=3&date_year=2025

[15]   CAWP, Women in Elective Office, https://cawp.rutgers.edu/data/levels-office/

[16]   Debra Dodson, ed., Gender and Policymaking: Studies of Women in Office, CAWP, 1991, https://cawp.rutgers.edu/sites/default/files/resources/genderpolicymaking.pdf

[17]   Tracy Osborn, *How Women Represent Women: Political Parties, Gender, and Representation in the State Legislatures* (New York: Oxford University Press, 2012); Jessica Gerrity, Tracy

In two different studies of women in the US Congress, female office-holders have reported feeling a special responsibility to act on behalf of women.[18] More specifically, studies of members of the US House of Representatives have found that women have been more likely than men to support policies favoring gender equity, daycare programs, flextime in the workplace, legal and accessible abortion, minimum wage increases, and the extension of the food stamp program (now known as SNAP).[19] They have also been more likely to advocate for greater spending on women's economic initiatives and for efforts to address violence against women.[20] Congressional studies have also shown that women are more effective in securing federal funding and passing legislation, and that – on average – they propose *more* legislation than men.[21] They have also proven to be more responsive than men to their constituents, including to those with shared identities and on women's issues.[22] Similarly, several studies have found that women serving in state legislatures give priority to, introduce, and work on legislation related to women's rights, health care, education, and the welfare of families and children more often than men do, and that they are more responsive to women's groups.[23]

Political ideology and partisan affiliation are also key axes of difference among women. Recent work at the congressional level has shown that Republican legislators face conflicting pressures of party loyalty and policy responsiveness rooted in their gendered experiences. While moderate conservative women are still more likely to advocate on social welfare and women's rights issues than their Republican male counterparts,

Osborn, and Jeanette Morehouse Mendez, Women and Representation: A Different View of the District?, *Politics & Gender* 3(2) (2007): 179–200.

[18] Kelly Dittmar, Kira Sanbonmatsu, and Susan J. Carroll, *A Seat at the Table: Congresswomen's Perspectives on Why Their Representation Matters* (New York: Oxford University Press, 2018); Susan J. Carroll, Representing Women: Congresswomen's Perceptions of Their Representational Roles, in *Women Transforming Congress*, ed. Cindy Simon Rosenthal (Norman: University of Oklahoma Press, 2002).

[19] See, for example, Michele Swers, *The Difference Women Make: The Policy Impact of Women in Congress* (Chicago, IL: University of Chicago Press, 2002).

[20] Corina Schulze and Jared Hurvitz, The Dynamics of Earmark Requests for the Women and Men of the US House of Representatives, *Journal of Women, Politics, & Policy* 37(1) (2016): 68–86.

[21] Jeffrey Lazarus and Amy Steigerwalt, *Gendered Vulnerability: How Women Work Harder to Stay in Office* (Ann Arbor: University of Michigan Press, 2018).

[22] Lazarus and Steigerwalt, *Gendered Vulnerability*; Danielle M. Thomsen and Bailey K. Sanders, Gender Differences in Legislator Responsiveness, *Perspectives on Politics* 18(4) (2019): 1017–30.

[23] See Osborn, *How Women Represent Women*; and Elizabeth Weiner, Getting a High Heel in the Door: An Experiment on State Legislator Responsiveness to Women's Issue Lobbying, *Political Research Quarterly* online issue (2020): 1–15.

more conservative women are less likely to sponsor legislation on these issues.[24] Because Republican officeholders have grown more conservative over time, the likelihood of alignment among women on these distinctly gendered agendas has declined.

Beyond potential gender differences in policy priorities, women public officials have historically exhibited leadership styles and ways of conducting business that are different from those of their male colleagues. Studies conducted prior to 2000 found evidence that women adopted approaches to governing that emphasize congeniality, cooperation, and facilitation, whereas men tended to emphasize hierarchy and individual decision-making. A more recent study of women members of Congress found that most of them believe they are more consensual and collaborative and more likely to work across party lines than their male colleagues.[25] Another study of women's representation in congressional committees found their presence decreased interruptions and increased focus.[26] And work on women's caucuses demonstrates both the ways in which women collaborate in state legislatures and the constraints on gender-based organizing, including distinct challenges at the intersection of gender and race-based organizing.[27] The partisan polarization in US politics presents hurdles to engaging in the type of cooperation and coalition-building that women officeholders have historically championed. Still, if their tendency to conduct business in more inclusive and communicative ways holds, women's representation may be critical to addressing the especially divisive dynamics in today's politics.

The presence of women among elected officials also helps to empower other women. Barbara Burrell captured this idea well when she wrote: "Women in public office stand as symbols for other women, both enhancing their identification with the system and their ability to have influence within it. This subjective sense of being involved and heard for women, in

---

[24] Michele L. Swers and Danielle M. Thomsen, Understanding the Policy Priorities of Republican Women in the US House of Representatives, *Politics & Gender* 21(2) (2025): 306–332.

[25] Dittmar, Sanbonmatsu, and Carroll, *A Seat at the Table*.

[26] Pamela Ban et al., How Does the Rising Number of Women in the U.S. Congress Change Deliberation? Evidence from House Committee Hearings, *Quarterly Journal of Political Science* 17(3) (2022): 355–87.

[27] Anna Mahoney, *Women Take Their Place in State Legislatures* (Philadelphia, PA: Temple University Press, 2018); Nadia Brown, Christopher J. Clark, and Anna Mahoney, Part of the Club? What Black Women Legislators Can Tell Us about Effective Lawmaking, CAWP, 2024, https://tinyurl.com/bp7ut95h

general, alone makes the election of women to public office important."[28] Recent research demonstrates the benefit of women as political role models for shaping young people's, especially girls', perceptions of who is capable of political leadership.[29] Women officials are also committed to ensuring that other women follow in their footsteps, with many engaged directly in efforts to mentor other women and encourage them to run for office.[30] Their efforts and example seem to work, as research shows a positive relationship between women's high-level political leadership and the emergence of women candidates.[31]

Thus, attention to the role of gender in the electoral process, and more specifically to the presence of women among elected officials, is critically important because it has implications for improving the quality of political representation. Although Republican and Democratic women generally favor different solutions to public policy problems, the election of larger numbers of women to office is more likely to ensure that the diverse perspectives and lived experiences among women are reflected in policy debates, priorities, and outcomes. Electing more women is also likely to lead to enhanced political empowerment for other women and to further disrupt prevailing expectations of who can and should hold political power.

ORGANIZATION OF THE BOOK

This volume utilizes a gendered lens to aid in the interpretation and understanding of contemporary elections in the United States. Contributors examine the ways that gender enters into and helps to shape elections for offices ranging from president to state legislator across the United States. As several chapters demonstrate, gender dynamics – including the prominent role of masculinity – are important for understanding the outcomes of presidential elections. Gender also shapes both the ways candidates appeal to voters and the ways voters respond to candidates. Many women have run for Congress and for state offices; this volume analyzes

---

[28] Barbara Burrell, *A Woman's Place Is in the House* (Ann Arbor: University of Michigan Press, 1996), p. 151.

[29] David E. Campbell and Christina Wolbrecht, *See Jane Run: How Women Politicians Matter for Young People* (Chicago, IL: University of Chicago Press, 2025).

[30] Kelly Dittmar, Rethinking Women's Political Power, CAWP, 2023, https://rethinkingpower.rutgers.edu/

[31] Christina Ladam, Jeffrey J. Harden, and Jason H. Windett, Prominent Role Models: High-Profile Female Politicians and the Emergence of Women as Candidates for Public Office, *American Journal of Political Science* 62(2) (2018): 369–81.

the support they have received, the problems they have confronted, and the reasons for gender and racial disparities in candidacy and officeholding. It also offers evidence of how media coverage influences perceptions of gender and race in US elections. Women face distinctive challenges in electoral politics because of the interaction of their race or ethnicity and gender; this volume also contributes to an understanding of the status of women of color, particularly Black women and Latinas, and the electoral circumstances they encounter.

In Chapter 1, Kelly Dittmar examines the gender, race, and intersectional dynamics of presidential politics, focusing specifically on the dominance of masculinity and whiteness at the highest level of American politics. After providing an overview of concepts key to understanding the presidency as a raced and gendered institution, she presents a history of the pioneering women who have dared to step forward to seek the presidency or vice presidency. Dittmar then evaluates how Kamala Harris, Nikki Haley, and Donald Trump navigated gender and intersectional dynamics on the campaign trail. She analyzes the ways that gender and race influenced the strategies employed by these candidates, media coverage of their campaigns, and public responses to their candidacies. While Dittmar points to areas of progress, she illustrates how a presidential campaign that exploited white and male grievance and reinforced gendered, racialized, and intersectional stereotypes emerged victorious in 2024.

In Chapter 2, Erin C. Cassese and Yueshan Long document gender differences in public opinion and vote choice. They provide evidence of the emergence and trajectory of the gender gap in vote choice over time, including in recent elections. However, they also demonstrate how the influence of gender is varies and depends on other voter characteristics such as race, class, geography, and party. Cassese and Long outline common theoretical explanations for the gender gap and situate the American gap in global perspective. Shifting their attention from cause to effect, Cassese and Long explore how beliefs about women and men voters – including social constructions of key voting groups – shape campaign strategy and political communications. They evaluate the specific appeals to women and men voters in the 2024 presidential election, with particular attention to the influence of the overturning of *Roe v. Wade* in voter mobilization.

In Chapter 3, Celeste Montoya examines the role that gendered mobilization has played in US electoral politics, both historically and in the recent elections. She provides a conceptualization of gendered mobilization that emphasizes the importance of looking at the role that gender (often at the intersection of race and class) plays in a wide array of US social movements. She provides a historical overview that demonstrates the various ways in which gendered mobilizations have influenced the development of US democracy and the evolution of its electoral politics. Montoya focuses specifically on the mobilizations surrounding the 2024 election, outlining the mobilization of the MAGA (Make America Great Again) movement around restricting transgender rights and opposing critical race theory, gender studies, and DEI. She identifies race-gendered mobilization among progressives in 2024 as well, emphasizing the role of intersectional coalitions in advocating for racial justice and reproductive rights among other issues. Gendered mobilization has been a significant part of efforts to expand political participation and representation, as well as those to restrict it. It has shaped party platforms and electoral coalitions. The patterns of the past help explain the current political moment and what may be at stake.

In Chapter 4, Jamil Scott places 2024 election outcomes in the context of the history of Black women in US electoral politics. She begins by evaluating the trends in Black women's representation across levels of office, including changes as a result of the most recent election. Scott then describes Black women's relationship with the Democratic Party, explaining how Black women's support to the party has not been reciprocated in party support of Black women's leadership or in prioritization of their policy concerns. She analyzes gender differences in voting behavior among Black voters, as well as generational differences among Black women voters, with particular attention to the 2024 election. Scott concludes her chapter by offering both historic and contemporary evidence of Black women's crucial role in the fight for democracy. She argues that Black women will continue this fight but questions whether they will look to gender-based coalitions as a fruitful site for engagement.

In Chapter 5, Anna Sampaio provides an intersectional analysis of Latina candidates for national office and Latiné/x voting behavior in the 2024 election. She pays particular attention to how disparities in polling inform our understanding of Latiné/x voters' impact on the presidential election outcome while acknowledging that a widening gender gap among this community of voters was evident across multiple polls. Sampaio describes how gender and racialized messaging were weaponized in campaign communications to aggravate gender differences among

Latiné/x voters. In her analysis of Latina candidates and officeholders, Sampaio places recent gains in historical context while pointing out the stalled progress for Latinas in the 2024 election. The chapter concludes with a discussion of obstacles and opportunities in the future of Latina politics in the United States.

In Chapter 6, Gabriele Magni examines the experiences of LGBTQ+ women running for office at various levels. Tracing the historical evolution of these candidacies from the 1970s to 2024, the analysis shows how the number of LGBTQ+ women running for office has increased over time and how the group has grown more diverse along gender identity, race, and ethnicity. The chapter then explores the challenges that LGBTQ+ women face when running for office, highlighting both similarities and differences with straight, cisgender women as well as male candidates. Subgroup analysis then reveals how transgender women and LGBTQ+ women of color face heightened obstacles. The analysis also shows that, despite the challenges, cisgender lesbian women often perform at least as well as their straight, cisgender counterparts in elections. The chapter concludes with an assessment of the factors that can help increase and improve the political representation of LGBTQ+ women.

In Chapter 7, Richard L. Fox analyzes the historical evolution of women running for seats in the US Congress. The fundamental question he addresses is why women continue to be so underrepresented in the congressional ranks. Fox examines the experiences of female and male candidates for Congress by comparing fundraising totals and vote totals through the 2024 elections. While acknowledging the historic number of women candidates in 2022 and 2024, his analysis also explores the subtler ways that gender dynamics manifest in the electoral arena, examining regional variation in the performance of women and men running for Congress, the difficulty of change in light of the incumbency advantage, and gender differences in political ambition to serve in the House or Senate. The chapter concludes with an assessment of the degree to which gender still plays an important role in congressional elections and the prospects for gender parity in the future.

In Chapter 8, Rosalyn Cooperman examines the role that political parties, women's organizations, and political action committees (PACs) play in the recruitment of women to run for federal office and support of women's candidacies. With a focus on 2024, she describes the structures of the national Democratic and Republican parties and looks at how party organizations assist candidates to run for office. She assesses attitudes about women's political participation from Democratic and

Republican party activists who influence who runs for office, and the issue positions they embrace. She looks at the strategies pursued by women's PACs, candidate training groups, and campaign finance networks to train and fund women candidates. Cooperman finds that the resources available to Democratic women candidates far exceed those available to their Republican counterparts, which holds implications for women as parties compete to capture or expand majority party status in Congress.

In Chapter 9, Kira Sanbonmatsu turns to the often overlooked subject of gender in state elections. She examines the presence and performance of women who ran for state legislatures and statewide executive offices in 2022 and 2024, analyzes the reasons for the underrepresentation of women in these offices, and highlights changes in women's candidacies in recent years. The chapter also investigates the factors driving variation across states in women's officeholding and assesses the status of women of color and LGBTQ+ women as candidates in state elections. Sanbonmatsu also includes an analysis of the role certain issues, particularly abortion rights, play in state elections. Understanding why women have not fared better in the states is critical to understanding women's status in electoral politics and their prospects for achieving parity in higher office in the future.

Collectively, the chapters provide an overview of the major ways that gender affects the contours and outcomes of contemporary elections. While gender is just one of many factors that shape US elections, we believe that ignoring or simplifying its influence yields an incomplete understanding of campaign dynamics, voter decision-making, candidate behavior, and broader social dynamics. Instead of telling one story about gender in US politics, the joint purpose of these chapters is to reveal how underlying gender and intersectional dynamics shape a great deal of what happens in the electoral process in the United States. Each chapter, in some way, illuminates both progress toward women's full integration into the electoral arena and backlash to their political advancement, reminding us that paths to equity rarely come without roadblocks and detours. For many, the 2024 election made clear that progress for women in US politics is not inevitable. Not only was a woman defeated at the presidential level, but women's gains in representation were either minimal or nonexistent across levels of office. Likewise, the election resulted in greater power to those politicians seeking to advance restrictions on efforts to promote diversity and inclusion, LGBTQ+ rights, and initiatives aimed at securing and advancing gender equality. These are policy positions that have often animated the agendas of even the earliest women candidates and policy advocates. Amid this backlash, however, candidates, voters, and other political practitioners pressed for further disruption of a political status quo that has historically privileged men and embraced masculinity. These concurrent – and sometimes conflicting – forces are detailed in the remainder of this volume.

1 Gender, Race, and Presidential Politics

Assessing Persistent Forces in 2024

After 235 years of only male presidents, the United States nominated its second woman to be a major-party nominee for president in 2024. While Kamala Harris was the second woman nominee, she was the first Black and South Asian woman to appear on a general election presidential ballot. In her concession speech, Harris reminded supporters, "On the campaign, I would often say 'when we fight, we win.' But here's the thing … sometimes the fight takes a while. That doesn't mean we won't win." She added, "The important thing is don't ever give up. … And don't you ever listen when anyone tells you something is impossible because it has never been done before."[1]

The fight that Harris and Republican primary candidate Nikki Haley – the other woman running in 2024 – waged was not only to make history as the first woman president of the United States. Their campaigns confronted persistent gender, racial, and intersectional biases in perceptions of presidential leadership, as well as a reinvigoration of white and male grievance that Donald Trump invoked and exploited in 2016 and returned to again in making his case for the presidency in 2024.

The chapter begins with a history of the dominance of masculinity and whiteness in presidential politics. Next comes a review of the women who have waged competitive campaigns for president and vice president, including the two women who sought the Oval Office in 2024. Finally,

Thank you to Tavana Farzaneh, Michaela Merla, and Thu Nguyen for research assistance critical to this chapter's analysis of the 2024 presidential election. Thank you to Melanye Price for her contributions to a previous edition of this chapter that continue to inform its content.

[1] Kamala Harris, concession speech, Washington, DC, November 6, 2024, https://time .com/7173617/kamala-harris-concession-speech-full-transcript/

the chapter evaluates how these women – and the man who defeated them both – navigated and experienced gender and intersectional dynamics on the campaign trail and what it reveals about the salience and role of gender and race in presidential campaigns.

THE PRESIDENCY AS A GENDERED AND RACED INSTITUTION

The fact that nearly all US presidents have been white and male is both an artifact of white supremacist patriarchy and an explanation for why Americans associate white men with fitness for leadership. Political scientist Sally Kenney describes the gendering of institutions as "the ways in which political institutions reflect, structure, and reinforce gendered patterns of power."[2] In other words, gender is a salient axis by which power within institutions is distributed and exercised. Gender is also evident in images, symbols, and language adopted within institutions. Finally, within gendered institutions, gender influences the behavior of and interactions between institutional actors. For example, presidents themselves face expectations of performing masculinity in ways that align with how inhabitants of the office have done the job before them; that said, presidents who navigate gender in ways different than their predecessors can change – instead of reinforce – the "gendered patterns of power" by suggesting a revaluation of traits, expertise, and leadership styles that are less strictly aligned with traditional ideas of masculinity and power.

Gender functions within institutions like the presidency in ways that are both parallel to and interactive with raced processes and practices that can either maintain or disrupt raced patterns of power. Like the role of gender within gendered institutions, racial norms, expectations, and often biases influence the allocation and exercise of power, the language and symbols upheld, and the actions of and interactions between those navigating raced institutions. And, as scholars such as Mary Hawkesworth have described, institutions are commonly raced-gendered, meaning that all of these forces are functioning simultaneously to influence how political institutions function and the distinct experiences of those who are seeking power and influence within them.[3] For nearly all of US history, the processes and practices in US political institutions have reinforced patterns of

---

[2] Sally Kenney, New Research on Gendered Political Institutions, *Political Research Quarterly* 49(2) (1996): 445–66, at 455.

[3] Mary Hawkesworth, Congressional Enactments of Race-Gender: Toward a Theory of Raced-Gendered Institutions, *American Political Science Review* 97(4) (2003): 529–50.

power that advantage masculinity and whiteness. Moreover, the privileging of masculinity and whiteness in presidential politics has benefited white men as candidates, officeholders, and voters and disadvantaged others. While these forces are at play across levels of office, the findings in this chapter are focused on their influence at the presidential level. Before turning to the history of women presidential candidates and the dynamics of election 2024, I outline three critical concepts to the analysis of presidential politics – both historically and in the most recent election. Despite their centrality in the 2024 election, mainstream analyses often simplify or understate the influence of these forces alongside the hyper-partisanship and other factors at play in the most recent presidential contest.

Masculinity

Recognizing the presidency as a gendered institution reveals hurdles to women's presidential power. As Georgia Duerst-Lahti has written, "Masculinity is neither fixed nor uniform."[4] Scholars have relied on typologies of masculinity to better grasp the multiple forms in which it is privileged or expressed. Dominance masculinity prioritizes domination and control.[5] It is also categorized as authoritative and is linked to traits including aggression and decisiveness.[6] Expertise masculinity is tied to a mastery of fields or ideas and, relatedly, high levels of competence.[7] Masculinity has also been categorized as patriarchal – related to dominance, but in relation to women specifically – and toxic – which upholds norms of masculinity that are harmful to both men and women. Finally, instead of recognizing the full spectrum of gender power and expression, masculinity is often viewed and exercised in contrast to femininity, hence proving masculinity means rejecting femininity and, as a result, rejecting women candidates. In recent years, the concept of tonic masculinity has taken hold as a contrast to toxic masculinity; Miles Groth argues that tonic masculinity – which values creativity and care and rejects authority and control as essential – will contribute to "restoring harmony between the sexes."[8]

---

[4] Georgia Duerst-Lahti, Presidential Elections: Gendered Space and the Case of 2012, in *Gender and Elections: Shaping the Future of American Politics*, eds. Susan J. Carroll and Richard L. Fox (New York: Cambridge University Press, 2013), pp. 16–48, p. 37.

[5] Ibid.

[6] Jackson Katz, *Man Enough? Donald Trump, Hillary Clinton, and the Politics of Presidential Masculinity* (Northampton, MA: Interlink Books, 2016), p. 30.

[7] Duerst-Lahti, Presidential Elections; R. W. Connell, *Masculinities*, 2nd edn. (Berkeley, CA: University of California Press, 2005).

[8] Miles Groth, Tonic Masculinity in the Post-Gender Era, *New Male Studies* 10(2) (2021): 49–62.

Presidential campaigns represent a site of contestation over what is masculine and whether or not candidates uphold masculine credentials. As scholar Jackson Katz argues, "Presidential politics has long been the site of an ongoing cultural struggle over the meanings of American manhood."[9] The US presidency, wherein leaders have been characterized as heroes, protectors, and fathers of the nation, has been most aligned with dominance masculinity. Presidential campaign history is replete with examples of candidate efforts to prove their manhood in accordance with stereotypical expectations and apart from stereotypically feminine traits.[10] For example, candidates have used masculine imagery associated with force and war as evidence of their authoritative leadership. Moreover, previous presidential contenders have been attacked for failing to meet masculine expectations and/or appearing too feminine. These emasculation tactics have been adopted by many critics, including presidential candidates seeking to use masculinity as a site for contrast with their opponents.

In each of his campaigns, Trump has engaged in these masculinist tactics and tapped into "hostile sexism" among voters. Hostile sexism includes perceptions that women demanding equality are seeking special favors and that women complaining about discrimination cause more problems than they solve. These beliefs predicted voter support for Donald Trump in election 2016.[11]

Whiteness

Understanding the presidency as a raced institution means revealing the ways it privileges whiteness, which is often rendered invisible as a default racial identity. Naming and defining whiteness is a first step to recognizing how it functions within all institutions, including the presidency. The dominance of whiteness is evident since forty-four of forty-five presidents and forty-eight of fifty vice presidents have been white men (in addition

---

[9] Katz, *Man Enough?*, p. 1.

[10] Ibid.

[11] Jarrod Bock, Jennifer Byrd-Craven, and Melissa Burkley, The Role of Sexism in Voting in the 2016 Presidential Election, *Personality and Individual Differences* 1190 (2017): 189–93; Erin C. Cassese and Tiffany D. Barnes, Reconciling Sexism and Women's Support for Republican Candidates: A Look at Gender, Class, and Whiteness in the 2012 and 2016 Presidential Races, *Political Behavior* 41(3) (2019): 677–700; Brian Schaffner, Matthew Macwilliams, and Tatishe Nteta, Understanding White Polarization in the 2016 Vote for President: The Sobering Role of Racism and Sexism, *Political Science Quarterly* 133(1) (2018): 9–34; Nicholas A. Valentino, Carly Wayne, and Marzia Oceno, Mobilizing Sexism: The Interaction of Emotion and Gender Attitudes in the 2016 Presidential Election, *Public Opinion Quarterly* 82(1) (2018): 799–821.

to Vice President Harris, Vice President Charles Curtis, who served from 1929 to 1933, was Native American on his mother's side). It is also evident in the power dynamics within presidential politics that have deemed white people—primarily men, white cultural referents and practices, and white citizens' experiences and priorities as primary, "normal," and thus privileged in holding, exercising, and benefitting from presidential power.

Institutions dominated by whiteness have often masked racial differences and encouraged those who seek power within them to do the same. For example, scholars have cited Barack Obama's election as the first Black (and nonwhite) president as dependent, at least in part, on his "race-transcendent Black politics," which avoided direct racial appeals and employed a "deracialized" campaign strategy.[12] Melanye Price explains how Obama relied on "race-neutral themes or themes related to aspects of African American history that have become part of America's universal understanding of itself."[13] This attempt to transcend difference is a function of white dominance and may have appeased those concerned about its disruption through Obama's electoral advantage, but Price emphasizes it also "reinforces the existing racial order" where whiteness is privileged.[14] Moreover, while Obama was successful, this approach did not insulate him from race-based scrutiny and racism on the campaign trail and once in office.

The 2016 presidential election exposed how threats to white dominance fueled political behavior. Racial resentment, or believing that minorities seek special favors and denying the existence of racial discrimination and inequity, was a strong predictor of support for Donald Trump.[15] In rhetoric and strategy, Trump capitalized on and likely furthered those feelings among his supporters. From launching his campaign by calling Mexicans immigrating to the United States rapists to continuing to demonize immigrants of color and banning Muslims from entering the country, Trump fostered perceptions of threat from racial minority groups. In the 2020 campaign, Trump demonized racial justice protesters and appeared unwilling to condemn white supremacist groups. By 2024,

---

[12] Valeria Sinclair-Chapman and Melanye Price, Black Politics, the 2008 Election, and the (Im)Possibility of Race Transcendence, *PS: Political Science & Politics* 41(4) (2008): 739–45.

[13] Melanye Price, *The Race Whisperer: Barack Obama and the Political Uses of Race* (New York: New York University Press, 2016), p. 18.

[14] Ibid.

[15] Brian F. Schaffner, Matthew Macwilliams, and Tatishe Nteta, Understanding White Polarization in the 2016 Vote for President: The Sobering Role of Racism and Sexism, *Political Science Quarterly* 133(1) (2018): 9–34.

the backlash to diversity, equity, and inclusion efforts that resulted from racial justice mobilization in and beyond 2020 was in full swing, and ripe for exploitation by politicians.

With Vice President Kamala Harris already holding the second-highest position in US politics and en route to fully disrupting the white, male norm of the presidency, Donald Trump both provoked and exploited racial resentment in his bid to reclaim the presidency in 2024.

Intersectionality

The dominance of whiteness and of masculinity in presidential politics cannot be viewed in isolation from each other. As Jackson Katz argues, the study of presidential masculinity "needs to incorporate a racialized understanding of gender, not to mention a gendered understanding of race."[16] This argument aligns with the fundamental claims of intersectionality, a theoretical framework developed by Black feminists to explain the experiences of Black women at the convergence of multiple systems of oppression.[17] As Wendy Smooth notes, intersectionality is "the assertion that social identity categories such as race, gender, class, sexuality, and ability are interconnected and operate simultaneously to produce experiences of both privilege and marginalization."[18] Applying an intersectional lens to our understanding of presidential politics means challenging single-axis approaches to understanding gendered and raced dynamics as discrete, and instead grappling with the ways in which these dynamics are interacting. It requires recognizing that while race and gender have always organized presidential power dynamics, they were rendered invisible based on the assumption that the race default was white and the gender default was male.[19]

The 2024 presidential election exposes differences in how major-party presidential contenders' intersectional identities inform how they experience and navigate the masculine and white dominance that has characterized US presidential politics to date. Chapters 2, 4, and 5 in this volume

---

[16] Katz, *Man Enough?*, p. 7.

[17] Kimberlé Crenshaw, Demarginalizing the Intersection of Race and Sex: A Black Feminist Critique of Antidiscrimination Doctrine, Feminist Theory, and Antiracist Politics, *University of Chicago Legal Forum* 8(1) (1989): 139–67.

[18] Wendy G. Smooth, Intersectionality from Theoretical Framework to Policy Intervention, in *Situating Intersectionality: Politics, Policy, and Power*, ed. Angelia R. Wilson (London: Palgrave Macmillan, 2013), pp. 11–41, p. 11.

[19] Katz, *Man Enough?*, p. 7; Jane Junn, Making Room for Women of Color: Race and Gender Categories in the 2008 US Presidential Election, *Politics & Gender* 5(1) (2009): 105–10.

also offer more detailed analyses of how voter evaluation and support at the presidential level varies by gender, race, and age.

WOMEN PRESIDENTIAL AND VICE PRESIDENTIAL CANDIDATES

Victoria Woodhull, a newspaper publisher and the first woman stockbroker, was only thirty-three years old when she was nominated for president by the Equal Rights Party in 1872 (see Table 1.1 for a list of women presidential candidates). She was too young to meet the constitutionally mandated age requirement of thirty-five for the presidency, and as an advocate of free love, Woodhull spent Election Day in jail on charges that she had sent obscene materials through the mail.[20] Unlike Woodhull, who made no real effort to convince voters to support her, Belva Lockwood actively campaigned for the presidency for the Equal Rights Party in 1884 and 1888, despite public mockery and even criticism from her fellow suffragists.

Almost a century after Woodhull's run, Republican Senator Margaret Chase Smith of Maine became the first female candidate to have her name placed in nomination for president at a major-party convention, winning twenty-seven delegate votes from three states in 1964. In 1972, Congresswoman Shirley Chisholm of New York, the first Black woman elected to Congress, became the first woman and the first Black person to have her name placed in nomination for the presidency at a Democratic National Convention, winning just over 150 delegate votes. Smith and Chisholm, like their predecessors Woodhull and Lockwood a century earlier, recognized the improbability of their nominations, measuring success in other terms. Smith prioritized normalizing the image of a woman running for executive office, and Chisholm sought to pave the way for women after her, proving that "it can be done."[21]

Despite the presence of women on some minor-party ballots, no woman was nominated to a major party's presidential ticket until 1984, when New York Congresswoman Geraldine Ferraro was chosen as presidential nominee Walter Mondale's Democratic running mate (see Table 1.2 for a full list of women vice presidential nominees). Her candidacy was shaded by questions surrounding her gender, from whether she was schooled enough in military and foreign policy to how she should dress and interact with presidential nominee Mondale. Much attention, too,

---

[20] Jo Freeman, *We Will Be Heard: Women's Struggles for Political Power in the United States* (Lanham, MD: Rowman & Littlefield, 2008).

[21] Shirley Chisholm, *The Good Fight* (New York: HarperCollins, 1973).

Table 1.1 Selected list of women US presidential candidates

	Party Affiliation	Race/Ethnicity	Candidate Details
Victoria Claflin Woodhull (1872)	Equal Rights Party	White	Acknowledged as the first woman to run for US president but did not meet age requirement of thirty-five
Belva Ann Bennett Lockwood (1884 and 1888)	Equal Rights Party	White	First woman to run for US president meeting eligibility criteria
Margaret Chase Smith (1964)	Republican	White	First woman to have her name placed in nomination for president by a major party
Shirley Anita Chisholm (1972)	Democrat	Black	First Black woman to seek a major party's nomination for president and first woman to receive delegate votes at a Democratic National Convention
Patsy Takemoto Mink (1972)	Democrat	Asian American	Withdrew after limited campaign as anti-war candidate concentrated in Oregon
Ellen McCormack (1976, 1980)	Democrat (1976) Right to Life Party (1980)	White	First woman to qualify for federal campaign matching funds and qualify for Secret Service protection (1976)
Sonia Johnson (1984)	Citizens Party	White	Qualified for federal matching funds
Patricia S. Schroeder (1988)	Democrat	White	Ended campaign before primaries
Lenora Fulani (1988, 1992)	New Alliance Party	Black	Qualified for federal matching funds; appeared on ballot in all fifty states
Elizabeth Hanford Dole (2000)	Republican	White	Ended campaign before primaries
Carol Moseley Braun (2004)	Democrat	Black	Ended campaign before the Iowa caucuses
Cynthia McKinney (2008)	Green Party	Black	Appeared on ballot in thirty-two states
Michele Bachmann (2012)	Republican	White	Suspended campaign after the Iowa caucuses
Jill Stein (2008, 2016, 2024)	Green Party	White	Received more than one million votes in 2016 general election

Candidate	Party	Race/Ethnicity	Notes
Hillary Rodham Clinton (2008, 2016)	Democrat	White	First woman major-party nominee for president (2016)
Carly Fiorina (2016)	Republican	White	Withdrew after the Iowa caucuses and New Hampshire primary
Tulsi Gabbard (2020)	Democrat	American Samoan	Suspended campaign in March 2020
Kirsten Gillibrand (2020)	Democrat	White	Suspended campaign before primaries
Kamala Harris (2020, 2024)	Democrat	Black and South Asian	First woman vice president of the United States (2021–24); first Black woman and South Asian person to be a major-party nominee for president (2024)
Elizabeth Warren (2020)	Democrat	White	Suspended campaign in March 2020
Marianne Williamson (2020, 2024)	Democrat	White	Ended campaign before primaries (2020); withdrew from contest in July 2024 after multiple suspensions (2024)
Amy Klobuchar (2020)	Democrat	White	Suspended campaign in March 2020
Jo Jorgensen (2020)	Libertarian	White	First woman to be the Libertarian nominee for president; received more than one million votes in general election
Nikki Haley (2024)	Republican	South Asian	First Republican woman to win a presidential nominating contest; withdrew in March 2024

Note: This list includes all women candidates for US president included by the Center for American Women and Politics (CAWP) at Rutgers University. This is not a comprehensive list of all women who have ever run for president. Instead, it includes all women presidential candidates known to CAWP who meet any of the following criteria: achieved major historic firsts; were named in national polls; achieved prominence by holding significant elected or appointed office; appeared on the general election ballot in a majority of states; and/or became eligible for federal matching funds.

Source: Center for American Women and Politics, Rutgers University.

Table 1.2 List of women nominees for vice president of the United States

	Party Affiliation	Race/ Ethnicity	Nominee Details
Marietta Stow (1884)	Equal Rights Party	White	Acknowledged as the first woman to run for vice president in the United States; running mate to Belva Lockwood
Lena Springs (1924)	Democrat	White	First woman to have her name placed into nomination for vice president at a major-party political convention
Charlotta Spears Bass (1952)	Progressive Party	Black	First Black woman nominee for vice president
Frances "Sissy" Farenthold (1972)	Democrat	White	Finished second in the balloting for the vice presidential nomination, receiving 400 votes, at 1972 Democratic National Convention
Toni Nathan (1972)	Libertarian	White	First woman to receive an electoral vote for vice president
LaDonna Harris (1980)	Citizens Party	Native American	First Native American woman nominee for vice president*
Geraldine Anne Ferraro (1984)	Democrat	White	First woman major-party vice presidential nominee
Emma Wong Mar (1984)	Peace and Freedom Party	Asian American	First Asian American woman nominee for vice president*
Winona LaDuke (1996, 2000)	Green Party	Native American	Received 2.7 percent of the popular vote in 2000, a larger percentage than any other third-party woman candidate for vice president before her
Sarah Palin (2008)	Republican	White	First Republican woman nominee for vice president and second woman major-party vice presidential nominee
Kamala Harris (2020)	Democrat	Black and South Asian	First woman elected vice president; first Black and South Asian woman major-party vice presidential nominee

* These women are believed to be the first vice presidential nominees identifying as Native American or Asian American but limited historical information on lesser-known nominees means that others could have been missed.

Table 1.2 (cont.)

Note: This list includes all women nominees for US vice president included by the Center for American Women and Politics (CAWP) at Rutgers University. This is not a comprehensive list of all women who have ever been vice presidential nominees for any political party. Instead, it includes all women vice presidential nominees known to CAWP who meet any of the following criteria: achieved historic firsts; received more than one percent of the popular vote; and/or received more than 100 votes at a major-party presidential nominating convention.

Source: Center for American Women and Politics, Rutgers University.

was paid to her husband, a trend that continued with female candidates who came after her.

Congresswoman Patricia Schroeder of Colorado prepared to make a presidential bid a few years later. Despite the fact that she raised more money than any woman candidate in US history, Schroeder decided against running before any nominating contests were held in the 1988 presidential cycle. Two-time presidential cabinet member Elizabeth Dole similarly mounted a short-lived campaign for president in 1999 but withdrew from the race in October, before the primaries began. In 2003, Carol Moseley Braun, the first Black woman to serve in the US Senate and a former ambassador to New Zealand, appeared in six televised debates with a group of all-male opponents. Like her recent predecessors, she dropped out of the race shortly before the first primaries and caucuses in January 2004.

Standing on the shoulders of the pioneering women who came before her, former US Senator and First Lady Hillary Clinton launched a campaign in 2008 that was widely perceived as the most viable chance for a woman to become president to date. Holding the front-runner position throughout her first year of campaigning for the Democratic nomination, many observers thought her background, political clout, and wide coalition of supporters made her nomination inevitable. Despite winning nine of the last sixteen primaries and caucuses and nearly eighteen million votes nationwide, Hillary Clinton could not overcome Barack Obama's lead in the delegate count and conceded the Democratic nomination to him on June 7, 2008.

Nearly three months later, John McCain announced his choice of Alaska Governor Sarah Palin as the Republican candidate for vice president. While the Republican ticket was defeated in November, Palin emerged from the 2008 election as one of the most fascinating women on the political scene at the time and made history as only the second woman (after Ferraro) on a major-party presidential ticket.

Minnesota Congresswoman Michele Bachmann officially announced her candidacy for the Republican nomination for president on June 27, 2011. However, as the field of candidates narrowed by half by January 2012, Bachmann was among the candidates edged out due to waning popularity, campaign missteps and disorganization, and insufficient resources.

Four years later, Hillary Clinton and Carly Fiorina competed for major-party nominations, marking the 2016 election as the first presidential election with women running in both the Democratic and Republican party primaries. Republican candidate Carly Fiorina, a former CEO of Hewlett-Packard and well known for being the first woman to head up a Fortune 20 company, entered the 2016 presidential race on May 4, 2015. After finishing seventh in the second primary contest in New Hampshire in February 2016, she ended her presidential bid.

Hillary Clinton announced her second presidential candidacy on April 12, 2015. She entered the race, as in 2008, as the strong front-runner, successfully clearing most of the field before even confirming her bid. While five other candidates entered the Democratic primary race, it was only Vermont Senator Bernie Sanders who challenged Clinton beyond the first caucus votes cast in Iowa. Sanders proved to be a formidable opponent, capturing the support of young people and progressives who sought the antiestablishment "revolution" he promised. Despite significant wins in populous states like Colorado, Michigan, Minnesota, and Washington, Sanders failed to best Clinton in either the popular vote or delegate count. On July 28, 2016, Hillary Clinton became the first woman to ever be nominated as a major-party candidate for US president. In accepting the nomination, she noted the importance of this milestone: "Standing here as my mother's daughter, and my daughter's mother, I'm so happy this day has come. Happy for grandmothers and little girls and everyone in between. Happy for boys and men, too – because when any barrier falls in America, for anyone, it clears the way for everyone. When there are no ceilings, the sky's the limit." Clinton's emphasis on inclusivity over individual achievement was reflected in her campaign's theme: "Stronger Together." In embracing that theme, she created a stark contrast with the campaign of her Republican opponent, Donald Trump, who had emerged victorious from a field of seventeen contenders by capitalizing on race, class, and ideological divides.

In an unexpected result of an extraordinary campaign, Donald Trump won the electoral college vote by seventy-seven votes to become the forty-fifth president of the United States. Importantly, however, Hillary Clinton won the popular vote by nearly three million votes, besting every white male presidential candidate in US history to that date, including Trump. In her concession speech on the morning of November 9, 2016, Clinton recognized the disappointment that many of her supporters, especially women, felt. She said, "I know we have still not shattered that highest and hardest glass ceiling, but some day someone will and hopefully sooner than we might think right now."

Clinton's 2016 defeat – and Trump's success – did not yield a drop in women's political engagement, candidacies, or success. In fact, the 2018 midterm elections set records for women's candidacies, nominations, and wins across levels of office. While these successes were concentrated among Democratic women, they led to record levels of women's political representation in Congress and state legislatures nationwide.[22] It was in this context that six women – Massachusetts Senator Elizabeth Warren, New York Senator Kirsten Gillibrand, California Senator Kamala Harris, Minnesota Senator Amy Klobuchar, Hawaii Congresswoman Tulsi Gabbard, and author Marianne Williamson – launched their candidacies for the 2020 Democratic presidential nomination.[23] They joined a field of twenty-eight Democrats eager to run against Donald Trump, an incumbent with low approval ratings and already mobilized opposition in the electorate. Despite the qualifications, performance, and even popularity of some of these women, they all confronted concerns about a woman's electability in an election year when many Democratic voters were solely focused on who could defeat Donald Trump. After over fourteen months of campaigning, each of the record six women who waged campaigns for the 2020 Democratic presidential nomination had left the race, along with many of their male colleagues. By June 5, 2020, Joe Biden had secured the votes he would need to win the Democratic nomination, ensuring a general election between two white men in their seventies against each other and that 2020 would not be the year that the United States elected its first woman president. It was, however, the year that the nation's first woman *vice* president would be elected.

---

[22] Kelly Dittmar, Unfinished Business: Women Running in 2018 and Beyond, Center for American Women and Politics, 2019, https://womenrun.rutgers.edu/

[23] Marianne Williamson also ran for the Democratic nomination for president in election 2024. She formally announced her candidacy in March 2023 but suspended her campaign by early February 2024; she unsuspended her campaign in late February but left the race by June 2024. She appeared on the presidential primary ballot in only thirty-seven states and territories, receiving no more than 12 percent of votes in any single contest and zero delegate votes.

On January 20, 2021, Kamala Harris was sworn in as the first woman, first Black person, and first South Asian person to be vice president of the United States. Biden tapped Harris – who had previously served in the US Senate (2017–21), as California's attorney general (2011–17), and as district attorney of San Francisco (2004–11) – to be his running mate in August of 2020. While her own bid for the presidency was short-lived the year before, Harris's addition to the Democratic ticket was received positively by many voters eager to see greater diversity – of age, race, gender, and lived experience – in the White House. The Trump campaign and Republican backers quickly shifted the focus of their attacks to Harris, arguing that she – not Biden – would be in charge if the Democrats won. They sought benefit from perceptions that Harris, particularly as a Black woman, was even more "extreme" than Biden, calling her a "monster" who would destroy the country. And the opposition tapped into gender and racial biases in other ways, from circulating rumors that she was sexually promiscuous to raising doubts about her eligibility to become president. These attacks did not ultimately derail the Biden–Harris ticket but resurfaced again in election 2024.

In fact, former South Carolina Governor Nikki Haley – who launched her presidential bid in February 2023 – repeatedly made the claim that "a vote for Biden is really a vote for Kamala Harris."[24] She positioned Harris as her potential Democratic opponent, arguing that Biden would not be able to complete a second term and suggesting that Harris was already in a position of elevated influence. Haley's approach sought to raise doubts about Biden's fitness for office, but it is difficult to believe that her campaign did not also consider the potential electoral benefit of cuing voter biases that would be distinctly tied to the potential presidency of a progressive Black and multiracial woman.

Of course, as a South Asian woman, Haley was subject to some of those same biases from her first campaign for the state legislature in 2004 to becoming the first woman governor of South Carolina – and one of the first two women of color governors nationwide – in 2011. Haley was governor for six years before leaving to serve as US ambassador to the United Nations for two years under President Donald Trump. She launched her campaign for the Republican nomination on February 14, 2023, calling for a "new generation" in the White House and emphasizing

[24] Nikki Haley, It's Time for a Competency Test for Politicians. Here's Why, *Fox News*, May 1, 2023, www.foxnews.com/opinion/time-competency-test-politicians-heres-why

her foreign policy experience, level-headed approach to leadership, and ability to move America past "all of the division and distractions" of modern politics.[25] Over the course of her thirteen-month campaign, Haley had some notable wins. In all five Republican primary debates, she outperformed her male opponents and garnered attention so difficult to capture in a crowded race. By the end of November 2023, she earned the endorsement and financial backing of Americans for Prosperity Action, a super PAC (political action committee) with close ties to conservative billionaire Charles Koch. But neither Haley nor other Republican primary candidates could overcome Trump's solid base of support. Despite refusing to participate in any of the Republican primary debates, Trump consistently led in pre-primary polls and never lost his position as front-runner for the nomination.

Trump also won all but two state primaries and caucuses once they began in January 2024. Haley finished third in Iowa and second in New Hampshire – where she had focused much of her time and resources. While she remained the only opponent to Trump by February 2024, she ended her presidential campaign on March 6, 2024, after being defeated in her home state of South Carolina and in all but one of the state primaries and caucuses held on "Super Tuesday" (March 5, 2024). Though Haley was unsuccessful in stopping Trump's nomination, she did make history by becoming the first Republican woman – and second woman ever – to win a presidential nominating contest; she won two, in Washington, DC and Vermont, before leaving the race. Haley waited to endorse Trump until her July 2024 speech at the Republican National Convention.

Less than a week later, Haley's prediction of a Harris presidency became a more realistic prospect. After a poor performance at the first presidential debate in late June 2024 elicited widespread concern about Biden's acuity and put significant pressure on Biden to drop out of the race, he did so on July 21, 2024. He endorsed his vice president the same day, and Harris formally announced she would seek the Democratic nomination. Harris's expedited campaign began once it was obvious that no one would challenge her for the nomination ahead of or at the Democratic National Convention. Just one month after Biden left the race, Harris became the second woman – and the first Black and first South Asian woman – major-party nominee for president.

<hr>

[25] Nikki Haley, Strong and Proud, February 14, 2023, www.youtube.com/watch?v=ARWLEPf5iaw

From late July through November, Harris revamped the Biden–Harris campaign into the Harris–Walz ticket, engaging in tactics and outreach to better connect with young voters and those less attuned to or feeling alienated from US politics. She benefited from an immediate surge of support and enthusiasm and sought to maintain that energy until Election Day. The Harris campaign outraised and outspent Trump's campaign, promising a "new way forward" that would uphold democracy, reject regressive policies, and promote a politics of progress, positivity, and inclusion. Reminding supporters that "when we fight, we win," Harris and her surrogates hoped to re-engage an electorate whose enthusiasm had been waning before her entry into the race. Despite her success in rejuvenating the Democratic campaign, Harris could not overcome voters' disapproval of the party in power. On November 5, 2024, Trump defeated Harris with just under 50 percent of the popular vote and 312 of 538 electoral college votes.

NAVIGATING THE GENDERED AND RACIALIZED CONTEXT OF ELECTION 2024

The women who ran for president in election 2024 – as well as the man who defeated them – navigated a gendered and racialized environment not wholly dissimilar to the ones confronted by the women presidential contenders who came before them. They faced criticism rooted in gender, racial, and intersectional biases about who is qualified and capable to hold presidential office, and they balanced the potential benefit of celebrating an historical milestone with the dangers of emphasizing identity-based difference. But these women also encountered a political landscape where the progress they would embody if successful symbolized the disruption of whiteness and masculinity that so many voters already perceived as threatening.

In an October 2024 CBS/YouGov survey, 43 percent of American men, versus 29 percent of women, said that efforts in the United States to promote gender equality had "gone too far of late." And 84 percent of men and women who agreed with this statement intended to vote for Donald Trump.[26] Consistent with perceptions of threat to men and masculinity, 73 percent of Republicans told the Public Religion Research Institute in

[26] Anthony Salvanto, Jennifer De Pinto, and Fred Backus, CBS News Harris–Trump Poll Has Closer Look Inside Gender Gap as Candidates Draw Even, *CBS News*, October 28, 2024, www.cbsnews.com/news/trump-harris-poll-gender-gap/

2024 that "society as a whole has become too soft and feminine," up from the 60 percent of Republicans who reported the same in 2016.[27]

In 2024, Republicans were also more likely to report and problematize the existence of racial discrimination against white Americans than to view Black Americans as a target of racial discrimination, with the majority of Republicans rejecting the claim that generations of slavery and discrimination have given white people unfair economic advantages.[28] And reaffirming sentiments of threat to whiteness, 61 percent of Republicans – compared with 13 percent of Democrats – agreed in 2024 that "immigrants entering the country illegally today are poisoning the blood of our country."[29]

The remainder of the chapter examines three areas in which race and gender played out in the 2024 campaign: identity-based messages and tactics, the competition between masculine dominance and feminine disruption, and the exploitation of gender and intersectional bias. It provides evidence of the ways in which Nikki Haley, Kamala Harris, and Donald Trump leveraged – or not – their own and their opponents' gender and racial identities, experienced and exploited prevailing stereotypes, and responded to the gendered and racialized context in which the 2024 campaign was contested.

Identity-Based Messages and Tactics
Identity as Inspiration or Distinction
At her campaign launch event on February 15, 2023, Nikki Haley joked, "I will simply say this, may the best woman win," distinguishing herself from her all-male opponents. Immediately, however, she added, "This is not about identity politics. I don't believe in that. And I don't believe in glass ceilings either."[30] It is not surprising, then, that Haley did not focus on her potential to make history – by breaking the highest, hardest glass ceiling in US politics – during her presidential campaign. While Haley did not emphasize the history-making nature of her candidacy, she did invoke her gender and race to claim it invalidated liberal claims that racism and sexism hold minority Americans back from success. She affirmed,

---

27 Daniel Cox and Robert P. Jones, Two-Thirds of Trump Supporters Say Nation Needs a Leader Willing to Break the Rules, PRRI, April 7, 2016, www.prri.org/research/prri-atlantic-poll-republican-democratic-primary-trump-supporters/; PRRI, Challenges to Democracy: The 2024 Election in Focus, October 11, 2024, https://shorturl.at/RBVSx
28 PRRI, Challenges to Democracy.
29 Ibid.
30 Nikki Haley, presidential campaign launch speech, *Transcripts.CNN*, February 15, 2024, https://transcripts.cnn.com/show/ip/date/2023-02-15/segment/01

"Take it from me, the first minority female governor in history, America is not a racist country."[31] Haley also emphasized something distinctly valuable about her gender identity when she claimed, "To save this country, we need to send a badass Republican woman to the White House."[32] And in distinguishing herself from her male opponents at an August 2023 debate, Haley explained, "I think this is exactly why Margaret Thatcher said if you want something said, ask a man. If you want something done, ask a woman."[33]

Haley's campaign also targeted women voters by leveraging gender-informed messages. For example, a tweet promoting the campaign's first "Women for Nikki" included a video clip of a supporter holding a sign saying, "Sometimes, it takes a woman." And at that event, Haley spoke on the basis of her shared experience with women to claim their superiority in avoiding drama and getting things done.[34] She also included a frequent riff in speeches to inspire girls, promising, "Strong girls become strong women, and strong women become strong leaders" who …"can change the world." On March 4, 2024, two days ending her campaign, Haley posted this line with and inspirational video and the addition, "This one's for all the strong girls out there."[35] Kamala Harris, who was at least one step closer to making history as the first woman president of the US, even more rarely invoked her gender or race in explicit ways while campaigning. In an October 2024 interview with *NBC News*, journalist Hallie Jackson suggested that Harris had been "reluctant" to discuss the historic nature of her candidacy and asked Harris why. Harris responded: "Well, I'm clearly a woman, [laughs] I don't need to point that out to anyone." She went on, "The point that most people really care about is, can you do the job, and do you have a plan to actually focus on them? That is why I spend the majority of my time listening and then addressing the concerns, the challenges, the dreams, the ambitions, and aspirations of the American people."[36] Harris was right to point out that her gender and

---

[31] Nikki Haley, X post, March 3, 2023, 1:10pm, https://x.com/NikkiHaley/status/1631718709583650844

[32] Nikki Haley, speech at Moms for Liberty convention, *C-Span*, June 30, 2023, https://shorturl.at/44o1H

[33] Fox News Republican Presidential Debate transcript, *Rev*, August 24, 2023, https://shorturl.at/sgvsF

[34] Sarah Stook, Campaign Diaries: Nikki Haley (April 10–16), *Elections Daily*, April 10, 2023, https://elections-daily.com/2023/04/17/campaign-diaries-nikki-haley-april-10-16/

[35] Nikki Haley, X post, March 4, 2024, 10:39am, https://x.com/NikkiHaley/status/1764676955343827170

[36] Vice President Kamala Harris interviewed by NBC News' Hallie Jackson transcript, *NBC News*, October 22, 2024, https://shorturl.at/sMofD

racial identities were self-evident; voters not only knew that Harris was a woman of color from simply looking at her, but they also knew that she would be making history if elected.

Still, there are other reasons for Harris's supposed "reluctance" to make more overt mentions of her race and gender, as well as her potential to disrupt the white- and male-dominated roster of US presidents. First, Harris and Haley would likely be accused of "playing the gender/race card" if they spoke too much of their distinct identities on the campaign trail. That critique is loaded with the same resentments and hostilities motivating male and white grievance: that those who are neither white nor male are asking for special favors or treatment in order to get ahead. It also evokes, for some, the idea that a candidate is expecting or assuming voter support on the basis of shared identity. Harris frequently rejected both of these ideas, saying:

> I will never assume that anyone in our country should elect a leader based on their gender or their race, instead that that leader needs to earn the vote based on substance and what they will do to address challenges, and to inspire people to know that their aspirations and their ambitions can and will be achieved through the opportunity to do that.[37]

Consistent with the "race-transcendent politics" that Melanye Price describes, then, it is not uncommon for Black and other racial minority candidates to emphasize how they "transcend difference" instead of amplifying it. In fact, at a *CNN* Townhall in June 2023, Nikki Haley recalled advice from her mother that informed how she lived her life and waged her campaign: "Your job isn't to show them how you're different, your job is to show them how you're similar."[38]

Another reason why neither Haley nor Harris likely talked more often about the history-making nature of their candidacies is because there is no evidence that this would be strategically advantageous. Nearly half of Americans surveyed in August 2024 said that it made no difference to them if the country elected a woman president.[39] And surveys of target voter groups – young men and Black voters – showed that invoking gender and/or racial identity in presidential candidate appeals was

---

[37] Ibid.
[38] Nikki Haley, X post, June 4, 2023, 8:52pm, https://twitter.com/NikkiHaley/status/1665521830516408326
[39] Gary Langer, Harris Leads Trump Overall but Not on Handling of the Economy, *ABC News*, August 18, 2024, https://shorturl.at/qvIaf

less compelling than emphasizing policy differences and, for Black voters, candidates' potential to beat Donald Trump.[40]

However, Harris – like Haley – did not ignore identity in her campaign. From her campaign biography – which described her as "Wife, Momala, Auntie" – to her frequent references to being inspired by her single mother and being an alum of a historically Black college/university, Harris discussed lived experiences and relationships that cannot be separated from her intersectional identities as Black, South Asian, and female. Harris's campaign also made references to the history she could make without Harris making it a primary talking point of her campaign, from merchandise touting "Yes She Can" to surrogates celebrating the value of electing a woman to the Oval Office. For example, Harris's running mate, Tim Walz, told audiences that they could "put that fist through the glass ceiling" of presidential politics.

Just over a week after Biden dropped out of the presidential race, Donald Trump targeted Harris's racial identity at a meeting of the National Association of Black Journalists. He claimed she "happened to turn Black" in recent history, suggesting that she adopted a Black identity for purely political purposes.[41] When asked to respond to Trump's comments, Harris described it as the "same old, tired playbook" and resisted giving the attack further credibility.[42] This instance demonstrated again why Harris and other racial minority candidates may use caution in the ways they navigate their racial identity; Trump and others nearly immediately and frequently found ways to leverage that identity as a line of attack.

While Harris spent little time acknowledging Trump's obviously false and insulting remarks, she did use an opportunity on the *All the Smoke* podcast to shift the burden of understanding multiracial identity to those like Trump instead of it being on multiracial individuals like her. She told the hosts, "I'm really clear about who I am and if anybody else is not, they need to go through their own level of therapy. That's not my issue." She elaborated:

[40] Young Men Research Initiative, YMRI/YouGov Release Poll of Young Men Voters & Views on Presidential Race, YMRI Substack, July 24, 2024, https://shorturl.at/Z3NAv; Lakshya Jain, Harrison Lavelle, Max McCall, and Leon Sit, We Polled Black Voters. Here's What We Found, *Data for Progress*, July 18, 2024, https://shorturl.at/ldT0j

[41] Stephen Fowler, Trump Attacks Kamala Harris' Racial Identity at Black Journalism Convention, *NPR*, July 31, 2024, www.npr.org/2024/07/31/nx-s1-5059091/donald-trump-nabj-interview

[42] Harris and Walz's exclusive joint interview with CNN transcript, *CNN*, August 29, 2024, www.cnn.com/2024/08/29/politics/harris-walz-interview-read-transcript/index.html

Over the years, journalists, some, not most, will want to talk about it, and I say, "Ok, if you want to have this conversation, I'm prepared to have it, but sit down and get comfortable for a few hours if you want to start talking about race in America. You want to talk about the ⅛ rule? You want to talk about what it means and who you are perceived to be and the impact that can have on the rest of your life, regardless of who you are in terms of your God-given capacity, and the rights you do have and should have?" And so, I don't mess with that. I think that other people trying to figure some stuff out and they gotta deal with it.[43]

In likely one of the most candid moments of her campaign, Harris revealed an important truth in understanding the hurdles that candidates who are not white or male confront in seeking an office that has been defined by those identities. While they are expected to explain how their "difference" will impact their candidacy and officeholding, they are simultaneously criticized for appearing to rely on that difference as a credential for their success. And perhaps most notably, they face an electorate, media, and opponents rarely willing or even able to interrogate the nuances of identity and its entanglement with systemic disparities and individual experiences, perspectives, and priorities.

Contrary to Trump's claims, voters were most likely to perceive Harris as Black alone when asked to describe her racial and ethnic background.[44] In fact, Republicans were the most likely to characterize Harris as Black instead of multiracial. These perceptions of identity not only reflect the complexities so often overlooked by voters but also inform the ways in which racial stereotypes would be applied to Harris, most often those associated with Black women.

Identity as Motivating Policy Claims and Expertise

Even when candidates do not invoke their gender and intersectional identities in campaigns, they might frame those identities – and the experiences and perspectives to which they are attached – as adding expertise, motivation, and value to their policy objectives.

Nikki Haley offered multiple examples of this in her presidential campaign. Responding to questions about her stance on abortion access, she told *CNN*'s Dana Bash in March 2024, "The fellas just don't know how to talk about this," adding, "They've got to humanize this issue and stop

---

[43] Vice President Kamala Harris Interview, All the Smoke podcast, September 30, 2024, www.youtube.com/watch?v=bzThwqnQJDY&ab_channel=ALLTHESMOKE

[44] Nathan Chan and Matthew Tokeshi, How Americans Actually Perceive Kamala Harris' Racial Identity, *Good Authority*, August 19, 2024, https://shorturl.at/Wcd2b

demonizing it."[45] That humanization, she implied, came – at least in part – from women's lived experiences. In an earlier interview with *ABC News*, Haley affirmed that her gender gives her a different perspective on reproductive access issues: "I think, for women, while it's personal for men too, for women, we feel it. We feel this for our daughters, we feel this for our sisters, we feel this for our friends." As early as March 2023, Haley talked about a college roommate who was raped and how that experience reminded her of the need to consider abortion access with both respect and compassion. She also discussed her own struggles to become pregnant and reliance on fertility treatments, noting how these experiences affirmed both her pro-life view and her belief that "when you're going through something that hard, you don't want government telling you anything else to get in the way of that conversation."[46]

Haley leaned into her identity as a woman in another policy message pervasive in conservative politics before and during the 2024 election season. From the earliest days of her campaign, she centered attacks on the inclusion of trans women in women's sports, claiming this as "one of the most important women's rights issues of our time."[47] In social media and speeches, she repeatedly featured individual cases where she argued trans women athletes were threatening cis women athletes, going so far as to argue that trans women athletes' inclusion equates to an erasure of cis women – athletes and beyond. Haley talked about threats to her own athlete daughter and even argued, without evidence, that the inclusion of trans women in sports threatened the mental health of cis women and girls. She also included the use of gender-expansive language as another part of the "war on women" and signed Concerned Women for America's (CWA) "Pledge Defending Women." In that pledge, she – and other Republican candidates – promised to "uphold the truth that women are exclusively female" and affirm that "sex is binary is a scientific reality, and all federal agencies will be directed to uphold this fact in every policy and program at home and abroad."[48] CWA titled their release celebrating Haley's support "Woman Presidential Candidate Declares What a Woman

---

[45] Tara Suter, Haley Hits Male Politicians for "Demonizing" Abortion Issue with Talk of Bans, *The Hill*, March 1, 2024, www.yahoo.com/news/haley-hits-male-politicians-demonizing-230851220.html

[46] Sarah McCammon, Presidential Hopeful Nikki Haley Has Shared More of Her Thoughts on IVF, *NPR*, March 1, 2024, https://shorturl.at/c4Dw6

[47] Nikki Haley, X post, April 22, 2023, 3:11pm, https://x.com/NikkiHaley/status/1649853489734987782

[48] Concerned Women for America Communications Team, Woman Presidential Candidate Declares What a Woman Is, August 8, 2023, https://shorturl.at/jtRoy

Is." While unsuccessful, Haley's strategy demonstrates how the identity of "woman" can be weaponized against the expansion of gender rights.

Masculine Dominance versus Feminine Disruption
Toughness and Empathy

The imposition of masculine dominance in presidential leadership can come in multiple modes, including the use of physical or martial force and intimidation. Presidential candidates have historically been expected to demonstrate toughness and strength in addressing military, national security, and foreign affairs to prove their capacity to be commander in chief. Voters have worried that women lack experience and expertise in these areas. As recently as 2023, Pew found that the policy area in which respondents were least likely to believe a woman president would be superior to men was national security and defense.[49] Five years before, they found that 35 percent of respondents believed men in politics are better than women at dealing with national security and defense issues; just 6 percent reported that women were better suited than men at handling these issues.[50] Women candidates have also faced concerns that they will be too "soft" in dealing with US enemies. For example, Geraldine Ferraro, when she was the Democratic nominee for vice president in 1984, was asked on *Meet the Press* if she would be able, if necessary, to push the button to launch nuclear weapons. No man seeking the presidency or vice presidency had ever been asked a similar question on national television. As a result, women candidates have historically taken steps to prove their national defense bona fides and combat perceptions of weakness in taking on any perceived or real enemies of the United States.

Trump has repeatedly reinforced toughness as a masculine standard by which he measured presidential fitness, calling his opponents weak and touting their stereotypically feminine traits as evidence that they are unfit for the Oval Office. Cuing the long-held concerns that women are particularly vulnerable on an international stage, Trump attacked both Haley and Harris as unable to stand up to tough-guy leaders. Of Haley, he said, "She is not presidential timber. I know her very well. She's not tough enough. She's not smart enough. And she wasn't respected enough. She cannot

[49] Juliana Menasce Horowitz and Isabel Goddard, Women and Political Leadership Ahead of the 2024 Election, Pew Research Center, September 27, 2023, www.pewresearch.org/social-trends/2023/09/27/views-of-having-a-woman-president/

[50] Juliana Menasce Horowitz, Ruth Igielnik, and Kim Parker, Women and Leadership 2018, Pew Research Center, September 20, 2018, www.pewresearch.org/social-trends/2018/09/20/women-and-leadership-2018/

do this job." He added, "She's not going to be able to deal with President Xi. She's not going to be able to deal with Putin."[51] Of Harris, he claimed, "She will never be respected by the Tyrants of the World!"[52] Just a week before, *Fox News* host and Trump supporter Jeanine Pirro told viewers, "I can't imagine her sitting in the room with any of the world leaders without them looking at her saying should I be afraid of this woman?"[53] These claims are likely influential to and influenced by perceptions of the conservative electorate that both Trump and Pirro target; in Pew's 2023 survey, nearly one-third of Republicans (and 15% of Democrats) said that having a woman as president would make the United States less respected by the rest of the world.[54] Democrats, especially since Trump's ascendance to presidential politics, appeared more skeptical of tough-guy presidents. Nearly a year after Trump took office, Pew found that 48 percent of Democrats (compared with 20% of Republicans) said that it was a bad thing that society looks up to masculine or manly men.[55]

In a July 2018 Pew poll, 36 percent of respondents argued that the perception that "women aren't tough enough for politics" is a major or minor reason there are not more women in high political offices.[56] And research shows that women of both parties who present themselves as tough and assertive benefit in voter evaluations that they are knowledgeable and strong leaders.[57] Both Haley and Harris made some effort to prove these credentials in the 2024 presidential campaign. For example, they both described themselves as fighters and touted themselves as gun owners. And both women repeatedly challenged Trump to engage them directly in debates, using his refusal as evidence that he would not "man up" or was "running scared."[58]

<hr>

[51] Jack McCordick, "Not Tough Enough" and "Not Smart Enough": Trump Rules Out Nikki Haley as VP, *Vanity Fair*, January 20, 2024, https://shorturl.at/nENnz

[52] Donald Trump (@realDonaldTrump), Truth Social post, August 22, 2024, 11:13pm, https://truthsocial.com/@realDonaldTrump/113009153020753095

[53] Acyn, X post, August 13, 2024, 10:23pm, https://x.com/acyn/status/1823545847071846 660?s=12&t=zJSDDCFmJL33EHyFPSalpw

[54] Horowitz and Goddard, Women and Political Leadership.

[55] Kim Parker, Juliana Menasce Horowitz, and Renee Stepler, On Gender Differences, No Consensus on Nature vs. Nurture, Pew Research Center, December 5, 2017, www .pewresearch.org/social-trends/2017/12/05/americans-see-society-placing-more-of-a- premium-on-masculinity-than-on-femininity/

[56] Horowitz, Igielnik, and Parker, Women and Leadership 2018.

[57] Nichole Bauer, The Effects of Counterstereotypic Gender Strategies on Candidate Evaluations, *Political Psychology* 38(2) (2017): 279–95.

[58] Nikki Haley, X post, February 7, 2024, 1:54pm, https://twitter.com/NikkiHaley/ status/1755304111304585699; Kamala HQ, X post, August 3, 2024, 10:54pm, https://x .com/KamalaHQ/status/1819748584109076836

Haley, who was appealing to a Republican electorate for whom masculine traits hold particular value, was especially overt in her efforts to prove her toughness credentials, telling voters in her announcement speech that taking on foreign and domestic enemies will "require doing some things we've never done – like sending a tough as nails woman to the White House."[59] She also tried to convert a stereotypically feminine aspect of her appearance – her high heels – into a masculine credential for leadership. "I wear heels," Haley noted. "It's not for a fashion statement, it's because if I see something wrong, we're going to kick 'em every single time."

Harris and her surrogates did not ignore voter demands for displays of toughness but also navigated terrain unique to Black women. Research shows that Black women are more likely than white women to be perceived as tough and strong and even less likely to be punished for displaying those agentic traits. However, Black women are also more likely than white women to be viewed as angry, a trait that both violates gender norms and is especially penalized among racial/ethnic minorities.[60] Harris is well accustomed to traversing this terrain, as was evident in highly circulated clips of her in US Senate hearings and in the 2020 vice presidential debate where she was firm but calm, persistent but never reactive or emotive. In 2024, she displayed a similar stoicism when directly or indirectly confronted by Trump and his allies, aware of the ways in which her behavior could or would be interpreted in ways informed by the trope of "angry Black women." In navigating the same terrain, Harris's husband, second gentleman Douglas Emhoff, described her as "tough as they come," but added that Harris is a "joyful warrior," bridging that toughness with a warmth more commonly accepted and expected in women and less reliably attributed to Black women leaders.[61]

Throughout her campaign, Harris pushed for a rethinking of how we measure strength. "I think that there has been a certain backward thinking approach over the last few years," she said, "which is to suggest that the measure of the strength of a leader is based on who you beat down instead of what we know. The true measure of the strength of a leader

---

[59] Haley Launch Speech 2023.

[60] Melissa V. Harris-Perry, *Sister Citizen: Shame, Stereotypes, and Black Women in America* (New Haven, CT: Yale University Press, 2011).

[61] Doug Emhoff, 2024 Democratic National Convention Speech transcript, August 20, 2024, https://shorturl.at/J0TAH; Ashleigh Shelby Rosette, Christy Zhou Koval, Anyi Ma, and Robert Livingston, Race Matters for Women Leaders: Intersectional Effects on Agentic Deficiencies and Penalties, *The Leadership Quarterly* 27 (2016): 429–45.

is based on who you lift up."[62] This approach is consistent with findings from research that distinguish between toughness and strength in analyzing effective strategies for women candidates, arguing that strength is more directly tied to personal character, can be decoupled from toughness, and has surpassed toughness in traits most important to voters.[63] While this research was not conducted at the presidential level, it suggests that women candidates can meet credentials of toughness or strength in less stereotypically masculine ways.

Harris also sought to undermine Trump's claims that he was best suited to take on foreign adversaries, arguing that his admiration for dictators and authoritarians is a source of weakness, not strength. She suggested Trump gets "played" by these leaders due to his obsession with hyper-masculinity and his desire to be viewed alongside these "strong men" leaders. When Harris baited Trump to react at the September 2024 debate by questioning the size of his rally crowds and saying that he was the subject of world leaders' laughs, she demonstrated the fragile ego that she and others described as a liability in ensuring presidential strength. Harris, Haley, and others opposing Trump engaged in other emasculation tactics, including questioning his physical stamina, cognitive ability, and obsession with appearance, in addition to calling him a "small man." These tactics sought to undermine Trump's attempts to make his masculinist case for the presidency. However, they also risk conceding to his contention that masculinity is the primary barometer for presidential fitness.

Marking the presidential contest as a contrast on candidate empathy shifts the focus to an area in which women – and women leaders – have held a perceptual advantage.[64] And while stereotypes of women politicians have evolved in ways that aid in agentic qualities while retaining assumptions of empathy, men politicians have seen little improvement in being perceived as communal or caring.[65] Some studies show an increased demand for empathy among leaders in diverse sectors, but voters in a recent survey on desired presidential traits still rated strength and

---

[62] Vice President Harris Campaigns in Detroit, Michigan, September 2, 2024, www.c-span.org/video/?538081-1/vice-president-harris-campaigns-detroit-michigan

[63] Turning Point: The Changing Landscape for Women Candidates, Governors Guidebook Series, Barbara Lee Family Foundation, 2011, www.barbaraleefoundation.org/wp-content/uploads/Turning-Point.pdf

[64] Alice H. Eagly and Linda Carli, *Through the Labyrinth: The Truth About How Women Become Leaders* (Cambridge, MA: Harvard Business Review Press, 2007).

[65] Daphne van der Pas, Loes Aaldering, and Angela L. Bos, Looks Like a Leader: Measuring Evolution in Gendered Politician Stereotypes, *Political Behavior* 46 (2024): 1652–75.

competence over empathy, and less than half of Republicans see empathy as a very important presidential leadership quality.[66] When Harris recommended voters listen to Trump rallies, she warned them, "You're going to hear conversations that are about himself and all of his personal grievances and what you will not hear is anything about you, the listener."[67] In contrast, Harris uplifted her own empathetic credentials by engaging directly with voters, listening to and affirming their lived experiences, and trying to communicate understanding of voter concerns and struggles. Sometimes she was able to leverage her distinctly gendered, racialized, and intersectional experiences to demonstrate that understanding; for example, she described her role as caregiver to her aging mother as a way to empathize with those emotional and financial hurdles that caregivers – still predominately women – face.

Throughout election 2024, Harris led Trump in voter evaluations of empathy. But on Election Day, voters prioritized a candidate's "ability to lead" over whether or not they "care about people like me." Notably, among those who rated the latter trait as the candidate quality most important to their vote, 72 percent voted for Harris. Among those who prioritized a candidate's ability to lead, 66 percent voted for Trump.[68]

Protection and Trust

Another mode by which Trump has asserted his masculine dominance is by positioning himself as a protector of women (see Chapter 2 in this volume for more on this type of Trump appeal to women voters). He applies what scholar Iris Marion Young terms the "logic of masculinist protection," whereby "the role of the masculine protector puts those protected, paradigmatically women and children, in a subordinate position of dependence and obedience."[69] In addition to claiming that he would protect women from violence and crime, he also leaned into this role in navigating abortion policy debates of the 2024 election. Trump celebrated the overturning of *Roe v. Wade* as one of his proudest accomplishments, but he also confronted a campaign landscape where stories of women's health

[66]   Jamie Ballard, What Leadership Qualities Do Americans Want in a President?, *YouGov*, August 6, 2020, https://shorturl.at/2nETO

[67]   Kamala Harris: The 2024 60 Minutes Interview, *CBS News*, October 7, 2024, www .youtube.com/watch?v=TJys7OVH24E

[68]   Election 2024: Exit Polls, *CNN*, www.cnn.com/election/2024/exit-polls/national-results/ general/president/0

[69]   Iris Marion Young, The Logic of Masculinist Protection: Reflections on the Current Security State, *Signs: Journal of Women in Culture and Society* 29(1) (2001): 1–25.

crises as a result of abortion bans were demanding more nuance of position. Avoiding that nuance by the end of his campaign, Trump returned to his claim of being women's "protector" and discounted the importance of abortion access altogether. He assured women voters that – under his presidency – they would be "happy, health, confident, and free," and "will no longer be thinking about abortion."[70]

The Harris–Walz campaign, and before it the Biden–Harris campaign, sought to undermine this logic in multiple ways. First, in direct response to Trump's claim of protection, Harris said, "I don't think the women of America need him to protect them. The women of America need him to trust them."[71] Her campaign adopted a "trust women" motto earlier in the campaign, asking about Trump and Republicans, "Why exactly is it that they don't trust women?" and affirming, "Well, we trust women." Instead of putting women in a position of dependence on presidential protection, Harris's rhetoric on this issue promoted women's autonomy and rejected the brand of male and masculine dominance that she argued was evident in Trump's and Republicans' positions on abortion and reproductive rights.

Exploiting Gender and Intersectional Bias
Qualifications and Competency

Viewed as apart from the norm of male and masculine officeholders, women are assumed to be less qualified than men to hold public office, even when they have more experience and stronger credentials. Research reveals that the penalty for voter perceptions of candidate incompetence is greater for women than for men candidates.[72] This is consistent with findings from political practitioners, who report that women candidates need to prove themselves while their male colleagues face fewer questions of credibility to lead.[73] It is no surprise, then, that research finds women candidates and officeholders are more qualified than their male counterparts on multiple measures of political experience – an indication

---

[70] Kate Sullivan and Eric Bradner, Trump Says Women Won't Be "Thinking about Abortion" if He's Elected, Casting Himself as Their "Protector," *CNN*, September 25, 2024, https://shorturl.at/k47uZ

[71] Kamala Harris' first solo network interview as 2024 candidate, *MSNBC*, September 25, 2024, www.youtube.com/watch?v=36ovmQj7gbQ

[72] Tessa Ditonto, A High Bar or a Double Standard? Gender, Competence, and Information in Political Campaigns, *Political Behavior* 39(2) (2017): 301–25.

[73] Kelly Dittmar, *Navigating Gendered Terrain: Stereotypes and Strategy in Political Campaigns* (Philadelphia, PA: Temple University Press, 2015).

that women who run for office know that they need to accumulate more credentials to be perceived as equally qualified to male candidates.[74]

Perceptions of intelligence – directly related to competence – are also racialized. Research has consistently shown racial biases whereby Black people are viewed as less intelligent than whites, while Asian Americans are more likely to be attributed with positive intellect.[75] Black women confront this perceived intelligence deficit, even if it is abated somewhat when Black women achieve "elite" status (such as holding elective office).[76] Some research finds that Black women candidates are credited with particular knowledge on civil rights issues, but attribution of broadscale competence is still limited.[77] Scholarship to date on multiracial candidates and officeholders is limited and focuses more on voter perceptions of shared experiences and voter support instead of interrogating how multiracial identity might specifically alter stereotype expectations.[78]

Donald Trump made attacks on Kamala Harris's intelligence and competence central to claims that she should not be president. In countless speeches, interviews, and posts on Truth Social, Trump described Harris as "mentally unfit," "mentally disabled," "mentally impaired," "defective," "stupid," a "moron," a "dummy," a "low IQ individual," and "dumb as a rock." He falsely claimed she – the former attorney general of California – did not pass the bar exam and argued that news outlets conspired to make her look more intelligent than she is.

Questioning her qualifications, Trump called Harris "totally incompetent" and "inept." And, along with many of his surrogates, Trump implied that Harris's political successes to date were not achieved on merit. Within a day of Harris becoming the likely Democratic nominee, US Representative Harriet Hageman (R-WY) described her as,

---

[74] Sarah Fulton and Kostanca Dhima, The Gendered Politics of Congressional Elections, *Political Behavior* 43 (2021): 1611–37.

[75] Rosette et al., Race Matters for Women Leaders.

[76] Jessica Carew, "Lifting as We Climb?": The Role of Stereotypes in the Evaluation of Political Candidates at the Intersection of Race and Gender, Duke University PhD dissertation (2012); Jessica Carew, How Do You See Me? Stereotyping of Black Women and How It Affects Them in an Electoral Context, in *Distinct Identities: Minority Women in US Politics*, eds. Nadia E. Brown and Sarah Allen Gershon (New York: Routledge, 2016), pp. 95–115.

[77] Ann Gordon and Jerry Miller, *When Stereotypes Collide: Race/Ethnicity, Gender, and Videostyle in Congressional Campaigns* (New York: Peter Lang, 2005).

[78] See, for example, Danielle Casarez Lemi, Do Voters Prefer Just Any Descriptive Representative? The Case of Multiracial Candidates, *Perspectives on Politics* 19(4) (2021): 1061–81.

"Intellectually, just really kind of the bottom of the barrel." She added, "I think she was a DEI hire."[79] *Fox News* commentator Larry Kudlow likewise claimed of Harris, "Her whole history is DEI."[80] Other conservative pundits used the sexualized trope of women "sleeping their way to the top" to suggest that Harris's political ascendance could not be credited to competence and hard work. Laura Loomer, a conservative conspiracy theorist who had a close relationship with Trump, made this claim most overtly, posting: "Did you know that Kamala Harris was once an escort and that she got her career started giving blow jobs to successful, rich, black men? She sucked [former San Francisco Mayor] Willie Brown's penis while he was a married man in exchange for political power."[81] While Trump never made such explicit comments, he did share a post on Truth Social that included a photo of Hillary Clinton and Kamala Harris smiling together with the text, "Funny how blowjobs impacted their careers differently …".[82]

Attacks on Harris's intelligence and qualifications drew upon prevalent racism and sexism. Even Nikki Haley, who also described Harris as incompetent and unqualified, argued that some in her party had gone too far in their attacks. Asked why Trump and Vance were performing poorly among women voters in September 2024, Haley told *Fox News*:

> I think that Donald Trump and JD Vance need to change the way that they speak about women. You don't need to call Kamala dumb. She didn't get this far just by accident. She's here, that's what it is. She's a prosecutor. You don't need to go and talk about intelligence, or looks, or anything else. Just focus on the policies. When you call, even a Democrat woman dumb, Republican women get their backs up too.[83]

Haley's criticism was likely related to her own experience. Vivek Ramaswamy, a Republican primary opponent, questioned whether she – a former UN ambassador – needed his three-year-old son to show her

[79] Josh Rultenberg, X post, July 23, 2024, 5:10pm, https://x.com/joshrultnews/status/181 585706381945685O?s=12&t=zJSDDCFmJL33EHyFPSalpw

[80] Aaron Rupar, X post, July 23, 2024, 4:20pm, https://x.com/atrupar/status/1815844530 643452103?s=12&t=zJSDDCFmJL33EHyFPSalpw

[81] Blabette, X post, July 22, 2024, 5:29pm, https://x.com/Blabette_/status/ 1815499372765077775

[82] Michael Gold, Trump Reposts Crude Sexual Remark about Harris on Truth Social, *New York Times*, August 28, 2024, www.nytimes.com/2024/08/28/us/politics/trump-truth-social-posts.html

[83] Tara Suter, Haley: Trump, Vance "Need to Change the Way They Speak about Women," *The Hill*, September 9, 2024, https://thehill.com/homenews/campaign/4869964-nikki-haley-trump-vance-women/

where Israel was on a map.[84] And throughout the primary campaign, Trump referred to Haley as "birdbrain." Responding to these types of attacks on her preparedness for office, Haley often told supporters that "the fellas love to throw things out like that" and warned, "Underestimate me, that'll be fun."[85]

Multiple Harris surrogates, including President Joe Biden and vice presidential nominee Tim Walz, affirmed her qualifications and competence in speeches and communications. As white men benefitting from assumptions of competence, they acted as validators for Harris among voters who might succumb to bias-informed doubts about her preparedness to lead. Former First Lady Michelle Obama also called out the different – and arguably gendered and racialized – standards to which Harris was being held. She told a Michigan crowd, "We expect [Harris] to be intelligent and articulate, to have a clear set of policies, to never show too much anger, to prove time and time again that she belongs. But for Trump, we expect nothing at all – no understanding of policy, no ability to put together a coherent argument."[86]

Hoping to alter those expectations, Harris and her campaign repeatedly targeted Trump's competence to make the case that he – not she – was unfit to be president. They shared clips of Trump rambling at rallies, of him dancing on stage for thirty minutes, and of other instances where he appeared confused and engaged in conspiracy-theorizing. Harris herself urged voters to be attentive to his behavior, telling reporters, "I invite the public to watch Trump's rallies and be the decision-maker on his acuity."[87]

Two dynamics are important in considering the differential impact of these competence-centered attacks in election 2024. First, while voters value competence and qualifications for all presidential candidates, any predisposition to *question* those credentials for women and racial/ethnic minorities – and *assume* them for white men – increases the likelihood that attacks on women's competence will be more effective. At the same time, the evidence of women candidates' and officeholders' overqualifications in comparison with men suggests that Michelle Obama's

[84] NewsNation Republican Presidential Primary Debate transcript, December 6, 2023, https://shorturl.at/WwfZc

[85] Nikki Haley, X post, January 14, 2024, 7:52pm, https://twitter.com/NikkiHaley/status/1746696766789951592

[86] VP Kamala Harris and Michelle Obama in Kalamazoo, Michigan, October 26, 2024, www.youtube.com/watch?v=vaYXybmmfSI

[87] Ian Sams, X post, October 12, 2024, 4:50pm, https://x.com/IanSams/status/1845205501774024836

claim of different standards is true; if men are not expected to meet similarly high standards of competence and qualifications for officeholding, then attempts to undermine those traits may be less electorally damaging to men.

Extremism and Threat

Research shows that Black candidates are perceived as more ideologically liberal than white candidates who hold similar policy positions, particularly among white voters.[88] Likewise, women are often assumed to be more liberal than men in politics, based in part on the continued overrepresentation of women among Democratic voters, candidates, and officeholders. And research on elite Black women affirms that they are viewed as more liberal than white women, white men, and Black men.[89] For many women of color, especially Black women, these beliefs contribute to assumptions that they occupy an ideological extreme. But attacks of extremism are also rooted in history, as Black women have been at the forefront of social movements working to end white and male supremacy. A common response by those in power to threats to upend the status quo is to demonize those motivating change, characterizing them as radical, dangerous, and out of line with the desires and needs of average citizens. For women of color in positions of political power, their very presence in what have for so long been white and male-dominated spaces can be perceived as "radical."

Upon Harris's announcement that she would seek the Democratic nomination in July 2024, the National Republican Senatorial Committee released talking points that described her as "an avowed radical" and claimed, "an endorsement of Kamala Harris is an endorsement of her extreme agenda."[90] Likewise, Trump told reporters, "She's the same as Biden but much more radical. She's a radical left person and this country doesn't want a radical left person to destroy it." Trump and his team made repeated references to Harris as "Comrade Kamala," calling her a Marxist and a "radical left lunatic." In a specific example, Trump appealed

---

[88] Matthew L. Jacobsmeier, From Black and White to Left and Right: Race, Perceptions of Candidates' Ideologies, and Voting Behavior in U.S. House Elections, *Political Behavior* 37(3) (2015): 595–621; Chase B. Meyer and Kaitlin M. Boyle, The Intersection of Race and Party: Voter Perceptions and Candidate Selection in U.S. Senate Elections, *Journal of Elections, Public Opinion and Parties* 32(4) (2022): 918–37.

[89] Carew, How Do You See Me?

[90] Riley Beggin, X post, July 22, 2024, 3:28pm, https://x.com/rbeggin/status/1815469097045692658/photo/2

to anti-trans sentiment in the electorate as a way to further make the case of Harris's extremism. His campaign launched an ad in September 2024 that attacked Harris for supporting gender-affirming health care for federal inmates.[91] According to *Axios*'s Alex Thompson, the Trump campaign spent more on this ad than on any others for the first three weeks of October 2024, and it ranked fourth in expenditures in that period for any ad by any campaign or PAC.[92]

Republican strategists told the *New York Times* that this ad and ones with similar anti-trans messages being used at or below the presidential contest were meant to portray Democratic positions and priorities as extreme and out of step with everyday Americans, more than signaling any specific policy agenda for the right.[93] They calculated that amplifying positions promoting transgender rights would evoke backlash – not only to transgender rights policies but also to the broader expansion of LGBTQ+ rights and evolution of our societal definitions and expectations of gender. Anti-trans sentiment is well documented along party lines.[94] For example, a 2024 Gallup survey found that 72 percent of Democrats but just 11 percent of Republicans reported that they personally believe that "in general it is morally acceptable to change one's gender."[95] Trump tapped this opposition in promoting his own transphobic policy agenda, including a ban on trans women in women's sports, withholding federal funding from schools that recognize transgender identities, and waging a multipronged and government-backed assault on access to and funding of gender-affirming health care and recognition of gender identities different than those assigned at birth.[96]

Notably, the Harris campaign spent little time responding to these attacks, instead presenting their agenda as promoting rights and dignity for all – including trans Americans. When asked about transgender rights in an interview with *NBC News*, Harris responded, "I believe that all people should be treated with dignity and respect, period, and should not be vilified for

[91] Grace Abels, Harris Has Supported Gender-Affirming Care for Incarcerated People, but Trump Ads Need Context, *19th News/Politifact*, October 28, 2024, https://shorturl.at/Swxbo

[92] Alex Thompson, X post, October 22, 2024, 7:05pm, https://x.com/AlexThomp/status/1848863166828363844

[93] Shane Goldmacher, Trump and Republicans Bet Big on Anti-Trans Ads across the Country, *New York Times*, October 8, 2024, https://shorturl.at/illAb

[94] 19th news September 2024 survey re: gender-affirming care.

[95] Megan Brenan, Slim Majority of U.S. Adults Still Say Changing Gender Is Morally Wrong, *Gallup*, June 7, 2024, https://shorturl.at/uHmLx

[96] President Trump's Plan to Protect Children from Left-Wing Gender Insanity, February 1, 2023, https://shorturl.at/GC3em

who they are, and should not be bullied for who they are. And that is a true statement for me my entire career. And that has not changed."[97]

Likewise, Harris did not respond directly to claims that she was extreme or radical. Instead, she engaged in messaging and tactics that emphasized her desire to work across party lines in the protection of democracy, a democracy that she argued was threatened by Trump. She campaigned with Republican leaders and called for unity over division. At the same time, she made the case that Trump was the candidate most threatening to US citizens. She outlined the many ways he undermined democratic norms, attempted to consolidate executive power, and threatened citizen rights – including those to bodily autonomy and reproductive choice. Harris described Trump as a fascist and shared similar warnings from those who were closest to him, including military leaders who served him during his first term of office.

In AP VoteCast's 2024 exit poll, a majority of voters reported being concerned that *both* Trump's and Harris's views were too extreme, with expected differences across party lines. On the issue of transgender rights specifically, over 50 percent of voters said they believed transgender rights had "gone too far," and 85 percent of those voters cast their ballots for Donald Trump.[98] These data demonstrate the myriad ways in which candidates work to invoke fear among voters about their opponents. But among those ways are tapping into racial bias, fears of the "other," and perception of threat to both gender and racial status quos that have privileged white dominance and stereotypical norms of masculinity.

CONCLUSION

Even before the Associated Press officially called the 2024 presidential election for Donald Trump, far-right pundit and white supremacist Nick Fuentes posted to X, "Your body, my choice. Forever."[99] And within days of the election, texts targeting Black youth claiming they had been "selected" to be "house slaves" were reported across the nation.[100] These

---

[97] Hallie Jackson interview 2024.

[98] AP VoteCast: How America Voted in 2024, *Associated Press*, https://apnews.com/projects/election-results-2024/votecast/

[99] Nicholas J. Fuentes, X post, November 5, 2024, 11:19pm, https://x.com/NickJFuentes/status/1854015641218355621

[100] Ayanna Alexander and Matt O'Brien, FBI, Justice Department Investigating Racist Mass Texts Sent Following the Election, *Associated Press*, November 8, 2024, https://shorturl.at/LUhk9

events demonstrate the repercussions of success for a presidential campaign that exploited white and male grievance and reinforced gendered, racialized, and intersectional stereotypes en route to electoral victory.

Many factors were at play in the 2024 presidential election, including hyper-partisanship and a particularly strong loyalty to Trump among Republican voters; voter frustration with the party holding presidential power (Democrats) and blame attribution to Democrats for economic vulnerability and international crises; and the expedited timeline for Harris to launch and execute a presidential campaign. Amid these factors, white and masculine dominance persisted in the presidential politics of election 2024 in both the strategies Trump espoused and the identities he embodies. And while gender and race were not the sole determinants of the presidential outcome, these forces – in the identities of candidates and voters as well as their perceptions on policy and progress – were influential throughout the presidential campaign. Beyond victory or defeat, however, we should not ignore how the 2024 election contributed to progress in presidential expectations. In Haley's emergence as a top contender to take on Donald Trump and Harris's selection as the first Black and South Asian woman major-party presidential nominee, women presidential candidates further disrupted the image of who can and should hold presidential leadership. Both candidates also challenged some prevailing gender and intersectional norms in their messages, strategy, and tactics.

This chapter has only highlighted some of the ways in which gender, race, and intersectional dynamics are part of the complex puzzle of what happened in the 2024 presidential election. But its content should serve as a reminder that these forces have long been at play in US presidential politics, regardless of the identities of presidential contenders.

2 Courting Women Voters

Gender Gaps in Political Behavior and Gender-Based Campaign Appeals

The political relevance of gender in American elections is often framed around the concept of a gender gap among voters. The gender gap is typically reported as the difference between the percentage of men and the percentage of women voting for a particular candidate, and it is used to highlight circumstances where men's and women's preferences diverge. American women won the right to vote in 1920 with the passage of the Nineteenth Amendment. But it was not until the 1980 election, in which the victorious Republican candidate Ronald Reagan received significantly more support from men voters compared with women voters, that the modern gender gap solidified. Since 1980, women have consistently supported the Democratic presidential candidate at higher rates than men. This change has been attributed to a number of factors – for example, women's growing educational attainment and economic independence from men, consciousness-raising efforts by the women's movement in the 1960s and 1970s, and expanding reproductive freedoms.[1] But this leftward shift among women was not unique to the United States – it tracked with global trends reflecting a leftward shift among women voters in advanced industrial societies.

In the four decades that followed, the gender gap has become an enduring feature of the American electoral landscape. In this chapter, we provide some empirical data describing the trajectory of the gender gap over time and complement this data with an analysis of how contest-level

We took over from Susan J. Carroll, who contributed this chapter in previous editions. Thanks for passing the torch to us, Sue! Thanks also to Kelly Dittmar for thoughtful editorial feedback and to Claire Rasmussen for fruitful conversations about the 2024 campaign.

[1] Susan J. Carroll, Women's Autonomy and the Gender Gap: 1980 and 1982, in *The Politics of the Gender Gap: The Social Construction of Political Influence*, ed. Carol M. Mueller (California: Sage, 1998), pp. 236–57.

factors are thought to have contributed to the size of the gap in given election years. We then transition from focusing on a singular gender gap – comparing all men voters to all women voters – to the many and varied gender gaps created by intersecting social and demographic factors such as race, class, geography, and party. This analysis reveals that the role of gender in American elections is more complex than is often conveyed in popular discourse about gender and voting. It also highlights the role certain groups of women – namely college-educated women and women of color – play in driving the singular gender gap in voting behavior.

Next, we turn to common theoretical explanations for the gender gap (e.g., social role theory, growing economic and reproductive autonomy, feminist consciousness) and briefly review the evidence supporting each of these perspectives from the political science literature on gender and political behavior. We look briefly to other political contexts in order to situate the American gap in global perspective and gain a sense of whether it is a uniquely American phenomenon or a reflection of a more universal gender difference in orientations toward the political world.

We then change gears to explore how beliefs about women voters – whether backed by evidence or not – shape political communication. Political candidates rely on social constructions of various groups defined at least in part by gender (e.g., suburban women, white working-class men) in their campaign messaging, and these social constructions often show up in the way the media describes key voting groups as well (e.g., suburban women as swing voters). Our discussion focuses on how these images of men and women voters connect to broader expectations about the things men and women want from government and why they want them. To the extent that these expectations are based on common gender stereotypes, political candidates may overlook the nuanced preferences of women voters and appeal to an overly narrow set of policy issues. The chapter concludes with a discussion of the impact of the Supreme Court's decision in *Dobbs v. Jackson Women's Health Organization* on the 2024 election, a gender issue that was particularly salient this election cycle.

EMERGENCE OF THE GENDER GAP IN AMERICAN ELECTIONS

The 1980 presidential election sparked renewed interest in the electoral power of women. Though shifts in women's partisanship and vote choice began earlier (in the mid 1960s), gender issues including the Equal Rights Amendment, abortion rights, and affirmative action were particularly salient in the 1980 campaign, with Republican Ronald Reagan and

Table 2.1 The gender gap in voting, 1980–2024

Election	Winning Candidate	Women Voting for Winner (%)	Men Voting for Winner (%)	Gender Gap
2024	Donald Trump (R)	45	55	10
2020	Joe Biden (D)	57	45	12
2016	Donald Trump (R)	41	52	11
2012	Barack Obama (D)	55	45	10
2008	Barack Obama (D)	56	49	7
2004	George W. Bush (R)	48	55	7
2000	George W. Bush (R)	44	54	10
1996	Bill Clinton (D)	55	44	11
1992	Bill Clinton (D)	45	41	4
1988	George H. W. Bush (R)	50	57	7
1984	Ronald Reagan (R)	56	62	6
1980	Ronald Reagan (R)	47	55	8

Source: CBS/*New York Times* Exit Polls, 1980, 1984, 1988; Voter News Service, 1992, 1996, 2000; Edison Media Research and Mitofsky International, 2004, 2008; Edison Research 2012, 2016, 2020, and 2024.

Democrat Jimmy Carter staking out distinctive positions on women's rights.[2] Post-election analysis suggested many women viewed Reagan as a strong proponent of traditional gender roles who would roll back some of the changes ushered in by the efforts of the women's and civil rights movements.[3] Given the outcome of the election and the persistence of the gender gap in support for the Democratic Party and its candidates moving forward, political scientists have pointed to this election as a critical juncture for partisan polarization on gender issues.[4]

The percentage of men and women voting for the winning presidential candidate since 1980 is provided in Table 2.1. Across these twelve elections, the average gender gap is 8.58 percentage points. There is some variability across election years, ranging from a low of four percentage points in support for Bill Clinton in 1992 to a high of twelve percentage points in support for Joe Biden in 2020. These differences speak to the influence of contest-specific factors in shaping women's vote choices.

[2] Karen M. Kaufmann, The Gender Gap, *PS: Political Science & Politics* 39(3) (2006): 447–53.

[3] Jane J. Mansbridge, Myth and Reality: The ERA and the Gender Gap in the 1980 Election, *Public Opinion Quarterly* 49(2) (1985): 164–78.

[4] Daniel Q. Gillion, Jonathan M. Ladd, and Marc Meredith, Party Polarization, Ideological Sorting, and the Emergence of the US Partisan Gender Gap, *British Journal of Political Science* 50(4) (2020): 1217–43.

As the example of the 1980 election shows, contest-specific factors influencing the size of the gender gap can include things such as candidates' position-taking and the salience of policy issues related to women's rights. Candidate characteristics themselves can matter, too. When one of the major-party nominees is a woman, as was the case in 2016 and 2024, media coverage of the campaign is often focused on whether women voters will turn out at higher rates or even cross party lines to vote for a woman candidate. This expectation is referred to as a "gender affinity effect."[5] Despite predictions of a historic gender gap in 2024 due to Kamala Harris's candidacy, Table 2.1 demonstrates that the 10 percent gap in support for Donald Trump is only slightly above the average for this period and two points lower compared with the previous election. As was the case in 2016, when Hillary Clinton was the Democratic Party's nominee, the presence of a woman candidate at the top of the Democratic ticket did not result in a dramatic shift in women's voting behavior.

While there is evidence that some women want to be represented by women leaders, a phenomenon referred to as *demand for descriptive representation*, there is little data to support the idea that the mere presence of women candidates on the ballot fundamentally shifts women's electoral choices.[6] Instead, women often seek to be descriptively represented by a woman who also shares their partisanship.[7] And, as the political parties become increasingly polarized, the likelihood of a gender affinity effect grows even smaller, because a candidate from the opposing party becomes more ideologically distant.[8] The electorate grows more calcified and there is less crossover voting for any reason, regardless of candidate characteristics.[9] In other words, partisanship generally proves to

---

[5] Kathleen Dolan, Is There a "Gender Affinity Effect" in American Politics? Information, Affect, and Candidate Sex in U.S. House Elections, *Political Research Quarterly* 61(1) (2008): 79–89.

[6] Peter Allen and David Cutts, Exploring Sex Differences in Attitudes towards the Descriptive and Substantive Representation of Women, *The British Journal of Politics and International Relations* 18(4) (2016): 912–29.

[7] Beth Reingold and Jessica Harrell, The Impact of Descriptive Representation on Women's Political Engagement: Does Party Matter?, *Political Research Quarterly* 63(2) (2010): 280–94.

[8] Danielle M. Thomsen, Why So Few (Republican) Women? Explaining the Partisan Imbalance of Women in the US Congress, *Legislative Studies Quarterly* 40(2) (2015): 295–323.

[9] John Sides, Lynn Vavreck, and Chris Tausanovitch, *The Bitter End: The 2020 Presidential Campaign and the Challenge to American Democracy* (Princeton, NJ: Princeton University Press, 2022).

be much more important to voters than other candidate characteristics, including gender.

Partisanship is a key factor that divides women voters, but there are others to consider as well. In the next section, we look at additional sources of diversity among women that shape their political thinking and behavior. Our analysis of the demographic drivers of the gender gap suggest that it is both more useful and more accurate to think of the electoral impact of gender in terms of *gender gaps* rather than the singular gender gap we have considered thus far.

INTERSECTIONALITY AND VOTING: FROM GENDER GAP TO GENDER GAPS

The typical way of calculating the gender gap compares all women voters with all men voters. This can be a useful starting point for thinking about the political implications of gender. But, by generalizing across these two groups, the many factors that cause divisions among women and among men are glossed over. To gain a more granular understanding of voting behavior and the factors that drive it, it is often necessary to look at a constellation of social and demographic factors that includes gender. To this end, we revisit the concept of intersectionality, which was introduced in Chapter 1 of this volume. Intersectionality is useful for understanding how social identities tied to demographic categories create subsets of voters (or electoral blocs) with distinctive political preferences and behavior.

The gender gaps within various social and demographic categories in the 2020, 2022, and 2024 elections are presented in Table 2.2. These figures highlight that the influence of gender is variable and contingent on other voter characteristics. For instance, the size of the gender gap depends heavily on voters' racial and ethnic identifications. In presidential election years, the gender gap among white voters is unique in that it is considerably smaller than for Black or Hispanic voters. Generally speaking, white Americans are more likely to vote for Republican presidential candidates compared with other racial and ethnic voter groups. Although white men vote for Republican candidates at higher rates than white women, majorities of white women still voted for Republican candidates in all three election years.

This is not a new development but reflects a persistent trend in American elections. In fact, if we look back over the past nineteen presidential elections, there are only two cases in which a majority of white

Table 2.2 Gender gaps across demographic groups and election years, 2020–24

| | 2020 | | | 2022 | | | 2024 | | |
| | % Biden Vote | | | % House Democrat Vote | | | % Trump Vote | | |
	Women	Men	Diff.	Women	Men	Diff.	Women	Men	Diff.
Race or Ethnicity									
White	44	38	6	45	35	10	53	60	−7
Black	90	79	11	88	82	6	7	21	−14
Latinx	69	59	10	66	53	13	39	54	−15
Asian	58	63	−5	62	55	7	43	38	5
Educational Attainment									
College	60	51	9	60	48	12	37	47	−10
<College	55	41	14	49	37	12	52	61	−9
Marital Status									
Married	47	44	3	42	39	3	52	60	−8
Unmarried	63	52	11	68	45	23	38	48	−10
Age									
18–29	67	52	15	72	54	18	38	49	−11
30–44	56	48	8	57	43	14	41	52	−11
45–64	56	42	14	49	39	10	50	59	−9
65+	52	41	11	48	38	10	46	56	−10
Geography									
Urban	64	55	9	64	51	13	33	43	−10
Suburban	56	44	12	52	40	12	47	57	−10
Rural	50	35	15	39	29	10	61	68	−7

Source: Edison Research National Exit Polls, 2020, 2022, 2024.

women voted for a Democratic presidential candidate: 1964 and 1996.[10] At first blush, this might seem at odds with how we have been describing the gender gap thus far – that women, on average, support Democratic

[10] Jane Junn and Natalie Masuoka, The Gender Gap Is a Race Gap: Women Voters in US Presidential Elections, *Perspectives on Politics* 18(4) (2020): 1135–45.

candidates at higher rates than men. But that singular notion of the gender gap belies that race is an important source of diversity among women. White women are more likely to support Democratic candidates than men, which is consistent with the basic premise of the gender gap, but this gap is small and does not reflect overwhelming support for Democratic candidates, as is the case among, for example, Black voters. What these gender–race gaps suggest is that the strong preference for Democratic candidates among women of color is the driving force behind much of the gender gap between all men and all women voters generally, while white women represent an important demographic base for the GOP.

In their recent analysis of race–gender gaps in voting, political scientists Jane Junn and Natalie Masuoka explain that compositional changes in the electorate driven by the Voting Rights Act along with trends in immigration and naturalization increased the proportion of nonwhite women voters and contributed to the modern gender gap.[11] They explain that nonwhite women's greater support for the Democratic Party stems in large part from partisan polarization on racialized policy issues. The parties have staked out very distinctive positions on issues such as civil rights and immigration, and many nonwhite women view the racial policies of the Democratic Party as better aligned with their interests.

To illustrate this point, Junn and Masuoka use public opinion data to show that Black, Latina, and Asian women who feel discrimination based on race and on gender are important social problems are more likely to support the Democratic Party, and those who buck the trend are less likely to do so. By contrast, white women are more divided on racial policy. Some view Democratic racial policies as antithetical to their own interests as white Americans. White women who do not believe that women and racial minorities face structural disadvantages in American society tend to support Republican candidates.[12] Thus, there is more political diversity among white women compared with Black women and Latinas because they are more deeply divided on racial politics relative to these other groups of women.

Though we observe largely similar patterns for Black and Latinx voters in these election years, it is worth mentioning that voters of color are not a political monolith. Looking at the data for Asian voters in Table 2.2, one

---

[11] Jane Junn and Natalie Masuoka, *Women Voters: Race, Gender, and Dynamism in American Elections* (Cambridge: Cambridge University Press, 2024).

[12] Erin C. Cassese and Tiffany D. Barnes, Reconciling Sexism and Women's Support for Republican Candidates: A Look at Gender, Class, and Whiteness in the 2012 and 2016 Presidential Races, *Political Behavior* 41 (2018): 677–700.

can see that majorities of Asian-American women support Democratic candidates, though support is somewhat more modest compared with Latina and especially Black women. However, Asian *men* voted for Democratic candidates at higher rates than Asian women in 2020 and 2024, such that the gender gap is opposite the expected direction in these years.

This discrepant finding can likely be attributed to quality issues with exit polling. Asian Americans make up only about 6 percent of the US population and are somewhat underrepresented in exit polling.[13] Research drawing on the Collaborative Multiracial Post-Election Survey – a survey that oversamples various racial and ethnic groups, including Asians, to gain more accurate estimates of their attitudes and behaviors – tells a different story. For instance, in 2020, 72 percent of Asian women voted for the Democratic candidate compared with 68 percent of Asian men.[14] This six-point gender gap is more consistent with the gender gaps for other racial groups reported here. Data from Pew Research shows a similar gender difference in voter registration – with 67 percent of Asian women registered with the Democratic Party compared with 56 percent of Asian men.[15] These figures suggest we must exercise caution when evaluating the data for small groups in the exit polls. You will learn more about these race–gender gaps in Chapters 4 and 5, but a key takeaway from this look at the exit poll data is that women voters are diverse, and race is an important and consequential source of diversity among women.

Gender gaps that intersect with other social and demographic categories are a bit more variable across election years. For instance, earning a college degree is generally associated with higher levels of support for Democratic candidates, regardless of a voter's gender identification.[16] But, as Table 2.2 demonstrates, there is some variation across election years. In the 2020 election, there was a bigger gender gap among Americans without a college degree (fourteen percentage points) compared with Americans with a college degree (nine percentage points). Yet gender gaps were comparable across levels of educational attainment in 2022 and 2024.

[13]   Karithick Ramakrishnan, Exercise Caution in Interpreting Asian American Exit Polls, *AAPI Data*, November 2, 2020, https://aapidata.com/blog/exit-polls-caution

[14]   Junn and Masuoka, *Women Voters*.

[15]   Katherine Schaeffer, Asian Voters in the U.S. Tend to Be Democratic, but Vietnamese American Voters Are an Exception, *Pew Research Center Short Reads*, May 25, 2023, https://shorturl.at/xSWmF

[16]   Joshua N. Zingher, Trends: Diploma Divide: Educational Attainment and the Realignment of the American Electorate, *Political Research Quarterly* 75(2) (2022): 263–77.

Marital status also intersects with gender in meaningful ways. In 2020, there was a large gender gap between unmarried men and women (eleven points) and only a very small gap between married men and women (three points). The gap among unmarried men and women was even more pronounced in the 2022 midterms, at twenty-three percentage points – a change some analysts have attributed to the mobilization of this group around reproductive rights. Yet, in 2024, an election where reproductive rights were again expected to be highly salient, the gender gap among unmarried voters reverted back to ten percentage points – essentially the same size as it was in 2020. The gap among married voters nearly tripled in size, however, from three percentage points in 2020 and 2022 to eight percentage points in 2024.

Gender differences across age cohorts and geography are also included in Table 2.2. Again, there is evidence of variability across election years. For instance, the gender gap is smallest in urban areas and largest in rural areas in 2020, but the reverse is true in 2024. Gender differences also vary across age cohorts and election years. In 2024, many journalists argued that the gender gap among Generation Z (Gen Z) voters was growing and poised to play an outsized role in the presidential race. Yet, as we can see from exit polling, the gender gap among this age cohort was actually considerably smaller in 2024 (eleven percentage points) than in 2020 (fifteen percentage points) and 2022 (eighteen percentage points).

Collectively, this data highlights meaningful intersections between gender and other social and demographic categories. Some – such as race and ethnicity – have fairly consistent effects across these elections, whereas others are more fluid and potentially more responsive to campaign context. Of course, we have focused only on the intersection of two categories at a time here, but this approach is useful for thinking of smaller slices of the electorate as well. For instance, a group that received a lot of attention in media coverage of the 2024 campaign was "college educated white women in the suburbs" – a group expected to show strong support for Harris, in spite of white women's historical tendency to support Republican candidates. In a later section of this chapter, we will dig deeper into the ways that representations of women voters in media narratives often diverge from research on women voters. But first, we turn to political identity and issue attitudes.

BEYOND VOTING: POLITICAL IDENTITY AND ISSUE ATTITUDES

Efforts to understand the root causes of the gender gap in presidential voting have often considered how factors such as identity and public opinion underlie vote choice. This work has revealed an evolution in the relationship between gender and party identification over time. From the 1960s to the 1980s, white men shifted to the Republican Party at a more rapid rate than white women.[17] And, in the 1990s, women shifted into the Democratic Party, further widening the gender gap.[18] These changes coincided with heightened partisan polarization on a series of political issues ranging from civil rights to social welfare spending, reproductive rights, and other "culture wars" issues.[19] As the parties and their elected representatives took more distinctive positions on these issues – more liberal positions for Democrats and more conservative positions for Republicans – the American public responded to these cues by sorting into the party that best reflected their views.[20] A similar pattern occurred for ideological identification as well, as partisanship and ideology became more strongly connected in the minds of voters during this same period.[21] These changes help to explain the gender gap in presidential voting because the primary determinant of vote choice in the United States is party identification. For example, in 2024, exit polls indicated that 95 percent of voters who identified as Democrats voted for Vice President Kamala Harris, and 94 percent of self-identified Republicans voted for former President Donald Trump.

Public opinion data also reveals small but persistent gender differences in attitudes toward some policy issues. On average, women tend to be more supportive of the welfare state and government spending on social programs related to poverty, health, childcare, and education – a modest difference of about three to four percentage points.[22] The presence

---

[17] Barbara Norrander, The Evolution of the Gender Gap, *The Public Opinion Quarterly* 63(4) (1999): 566–76.

[18] Karen M. Kaufmann, Culture Wars, Secular Realignment, and the Gender Gap in Party Identification, *Political Behavior* 24(3) (2002): 283–307.

[19] The term "culture wars" is used to denote a set of issues that divide voters on the basis of traditional or progressive values (e.g., abortion rights, school prayer, gay rights). The term was popularized during the 1992 presidential race when Republican political strategist Pat Buchanan delivered a speech at the Republican National Convention defining the election as a "cultural war" "for the soul of America." For more information, see James Davison Hunter, *Culture Wars: The Struggle to Control the Family, Art, Education, Law, and Politics in America* (New York: Avalon Publishing, 1992).

[20] Thomas M. Carsey and Geoffrey C. Layman, Changing Sides or Changing Minds? Party Identification and Policy Preferences in the American Electorate, *American Journal of Political Science* 50(2) (2006): 464–77.

[21] Lilliana Mason, *Uncivil Agreement: How Politics Became Our Identity* (Chicago, IL: University of Chicago Press, 2018).

[22] For a detailed discussion of how these percentages were obtained for the issue areas discussed in this paragraph, please see Leonie Huddy, Erin Cassese, and Mary-Kate Lizotte, Gender, Public Opinion, and Political Reasoning, in *Political Women and American*

of a consistent gender gap on these issues has caused some scholars and journalists to label them "women's issues." A common explanation for these differences of opinion is that they reflect women's greater economic insecurity relative to men as well as women's roles as caregivers. In addition to being characterized as women's issues, they are also sometimes described as "compassion issues." Crime, economic performance, and national defense, by contrast, are often characterized as "men's issues." Men's distinct preferences in these areas are often attributed to greater acceptance of the government's use of force relative to women (on average, a difference of seven to eight percentage points) and also to the male breadwinner model, in which men outearn women and control family finances. As we will discuss further later, this conceptualization of issues maps on to common gender stereotypes tied to traditional gender roles.

In addition, it is important to note that a gender gap in public opinion is not present for all issues that pertain to women's rights. For example, men's and women's average levels of support for reproductive rights have been comparable for decades. However, sometimes gender differences on these kinds of issues are not apparent in terms of the positions men and women take but instead manifest as differences in issue priorities. This point is illustrated in Figure 2.1. Panel A of the figure shows the issue positions selected by men and women on a survey question about abortion from the 2020 American National Election Study. The question asks:

> There has been some discussion about abortion during recent years. Which one of these options best agrees with your view? (1) By law, abortion should never be permitted, (2) The law should permit abortion only in case of rape, incest, or when the woman's life is in danger, (3) The law should permit abortion other than for rape/incest/danger to woman but only after the need is clearly established, (4) By law, a woman should always be able to obtain an abortion as a matter of personal choice.

As the figure shows, men and women choose these options in similar proportions, and the modest differences between categories are not statistically significant. Compare this with responses to a second question that asks: "How important is this issue to you personally? (1) not at all important, (2) not too important, (3) somewhat important, (4) very important, and (5) extremely important." Average responses to this question for men and women are depicted in Panel B of Figure 2.1. Here gender differences

Democracy, eds. Christina Wolbrecht, Karen Beckwith, and Lisa Baldez (Cambridge: Cambridge University Press, 2008), pp. 31–49.

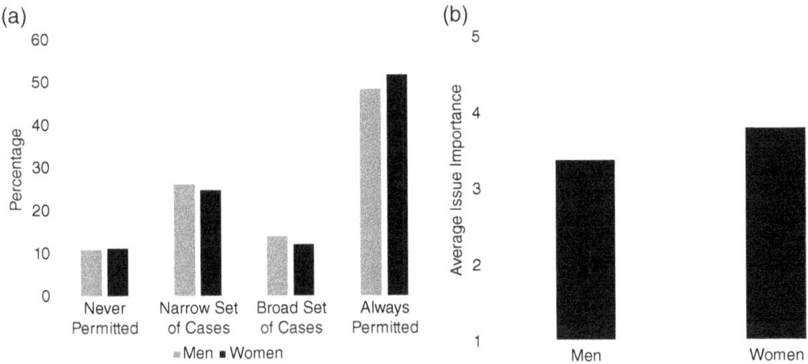

Figure 2.1 Gender differences in abortion attitudes (A) and issue importance (B). *Source:* 2020 American National Election Study (ANES).

are evident, with women clearly rating the issue as more important relative to men. Women's average score is closer to a four on the scale, which corresponds to rating the issue as "very important." The average score for men is closer to a three, indicating the issue is "somewhat important." The difference between these two average scores is statistically significant, which suggests a meaningful difference in the importance men and women attribute to this issue.

The intersection between gender and partisanship provides important context here, too. As was the case for voting, we can learn more about how gender shapes issue attitudes by moving past a singular gender gap to look at the multiple gaps defined by gender and other categories such as party. When comparing all men with all women in the electorate, gender differences in opinion often reflect gender differences in partisanship. But, when you compare men and women *within the same party*, a different story emerges. Often, the preferences of Republican women across policy issues are very similar to those of Republican men. And, they tend to be quite dissimilar from the preferences of Democratic women and men. Although there are a few "compassion" issues where Republican women report slightly more moderate preferences than Republican men, they are still much closer to Republican men than to their Democratic counterparts.

A direct comparison of the preferences of Democratic and Republican women is instructive. In Figure 2.2, we plot answers to a few additional survey questions from the 2020 American National Election Study about government spending in three areas: welfare (commonly considered a "women's issue"), environmental protection, and border security (commonly considered a "men's issue"). Participants in the survey were asked whether spending in each area should be increased, decreased, or

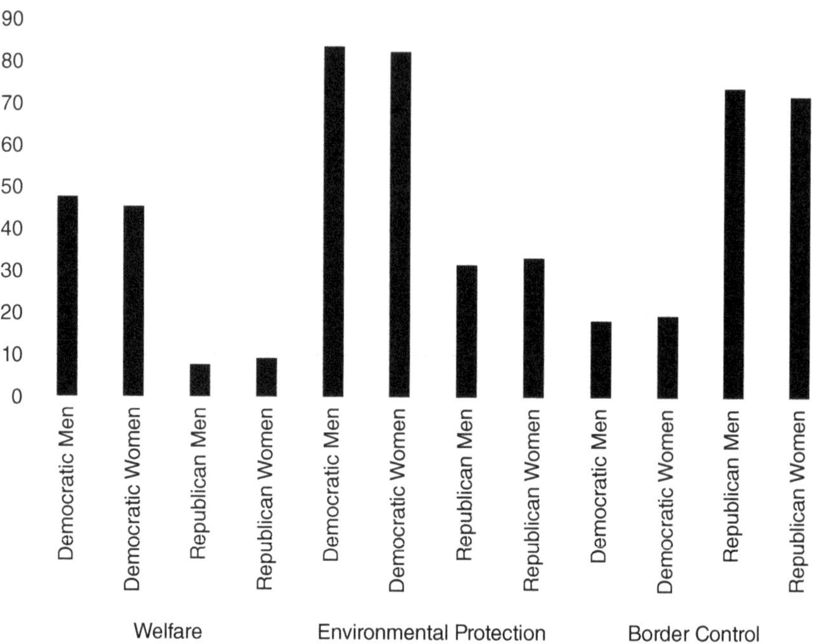

Figure 2.2 Support for increased spending in three policy areas by gender and partisanship.
Source: 2020 American National Election Study (ANES).

kept the same. In the figure, we plotted the percentage of people who wished to see *increased* government spending in each issue area, subset by gender and party identification.

As Figure 2.2 demonstrates, differences in spending preferences between Democratic women and Republican women are quite stark. About 45 percent of Democratic women would like to see spending on welfare programs increased, compared with only 9 percent of Republican women: a thirty-six-point difference. The difference between women based on partisanship is even larger for environmental protection (forty-nine points) and border security (fifty-two points). What is also clear from Figure 2.2 is that across all three issue areas, Democratic women answer these questions in a way that is very similar to Democratic men, and Republican women answer quite similarly to Republican men. Essentially, what divides Americans on these issues is party and not gender, even though one of these issues is often coded as a women's issue (welfare) and one as a men's issue (border security).

Given the primacy of partisanship, candidates and parties looking to appeal to women voters across party lines on "women's issues" are unlikely to be successful because women voters in the other partisan camp actually have very divergent opinions on policy issues, even those characterized as "compassion" or "women's issues." For this reason, some political scientists have argued against thinking of women's interests in a fixed sense and instead recommend conceptualizing them as the outcome of political processes where the parties and their representatives work strategically to define women's interests in particular ways that may appeal to and mobilize targeted groups of women voters.[23] Doing otherwise runs the risk of overinterpreting small differences and searching for explanations that emphasize modest average differences between men and women but ignore important sources of heterogeneity among women.

THEORETICAL PERSPECTIVES ON THE GENDER GAP

Much of the scholarly work on the gender gap has offered explanations for women's political thinking and behavior tied to broader theories of gender difference. These theories are not mutually exclusive – many contain common elements and propose mechanisms that might be mutually reinforcing. At the same time, none of these perspectives fully explain gender differences in political behavior and how they fluctuate over time. As we observed in the previous section, women do not operate as a united front in politics, and *intersectional theories* of gender difference can add important nuance to our understanding of gender and political behavior. To the extent that other theories of gender difference do not incorporate insights from intersectionality research, they can overgeneralize about what women share in common and overlook points of commonality between women and men, producing an oversimplified account of women's political motivations and misrepresenting the political significance of gender.

This is a problem for *essentialist theories* of gender difference. These perspectives emphasize what they consider inherent differences between men and women that are often tied to reproductive biology and factors such as genetics. These viewpoints typically emphasize complementary roles for men (i.e., breadwinners) and women (i.e., caregivers) as an ostensibly natural outcome of these biologically based differences and then tie these distinct roles to men's and women's political preferences. For instance, the idea that men prioritize economic policy due to their breadwinner role and women prioritize policy related to "compassion issues" due to their caregiving role would be consistent with gender essentialism. Many contemporary gender stereotypes map on to this distinction between breadwinners and caregivers.

---

[23] Beth Reingold and Michele Swers, An Endogenous Approach to Women's Interests: When Interests Are Interesting in and of Themselves, *Politics & Gender* 7(3) (2011): 429–35.

Essentialist perspectives tend to emphasize factors dividing men and women.[24] As we noted in a previous section, the gender gap in presidential voting behavior is relatively modest in size (between eight and nine percentage points on average) compared with other group differences (e.g., a gap between Black and white voters typically around 40 percentage points), which suggests men and women are not deeply divided on the basis of gender. Beyond this, the gender gap in presidential voting behavior fluctuates across election years, meaning it is more variable than changes in gender roles or the relative status of men and women in society, which tend to change more slowly over time.

Essentialist theories of gender often lean into the idea that gender differences are inherent or immutable, based on biological foundations. By contrast, other perspectives emphasize the social construction of gender, predicated on the idea that gender arises from social learning processes rather than biology. Interpersonal interactions, cultural norms, media, laws, and institutional practices create a context that influences individuals' gender expression and behavior broadly, including political behavior. *Social role theory*, developed by psychologists Alice Eagly, Wendy Wood, and Amanda Diekman, focuses on the social construction of gender and its relationship to labor.[25] As we noted previously, under the male breadwinner model, men and women occupy "separate spheres," with men engaging in paid labor outside the home and women focusing on unpaid labor in the home. These distinct roles for men and women lead to a specialization in instrumental tasks for men tied to their workplace responsibilities and a specialization in more expressive or communal tasks for women, coinciding with their care work. When men and women occupy distinct roles in a society, like those outlined in the male breadwinner model, they practice and come to embody the traits and values associated with these roles, leading to greater differentiation along stereotypical lines.

---

[24] There is also more variation in household economic arrangements than these perspectives suggest. For example, among adults living in heterosexual couples in the United States, in about 55 percent, the male partner is the sole or primary breadwinner (earning >60 percent of the household income). In the remaining 45 percent of households, men and women contribute similar amounts or women are primary breadwinners, meaning the "male breadwinner" is far from universal. For more information, see Richard Fry, Carolina Aragao, Kiley Hurst, and Kim Parker, In a Growing Share of U.S. Marriages, Husbands and Wives Earn about the Same, *Pew Research*, April 13, 2023, https://shorturl.at/ktbZr

[25] Alice H. Eagly, Wendy Wood, and Amanda B. Diekman, Social Role Theory of Sex Differences and Similarities: A Current Appraisal, in *The Developmental Social Psychology of Gender*, eds. Thomas Eckes and Hanns M. Trautner (New York: Psychology Press, 2000), pp. 92–119.

However, social role theory maintains that these differences are not fixed. Gender roles can evolve over time and differ across contexts, and when they do, so do social expectations about gender and manifestations of gender difference. Research on the gender gap globally helps to illustrate this point. In the 1950s and 1960s, researchers observed a pattern called the "traditional" gender gap, with women more likely to support right-of-center parties and candidates. In the 1970s, this gap narrowed, eventually reversing in the 1980s and 1990s, resulting in the relationship between gender and support for left-of-center parties we observe today – the "modern" gender gap. But not all countries transitioned from a traditional (women are right-leaning) to modern (women are left-leaning) gender gap. This change was limited to many, but not all, advanced Western democracies. The traditional gender gap has persisted in many post-communist countries and developing nations, particularly where religious adherence is high and traditional gender roles are common. And, even in advanced Western democracies where the modern gender gap is present, its size varies considerably in magnitude across countries, suggesting a complex underlying dynamic is at play.

Political scientists Ron Inglehart and Pippa Norris outlined a *developmental theory* of gendered political behavior to account for these trends. This perspective posits that structural factors such as economic development and women's greater educational attainment and workforce participation have significantly impacted gender roles and beliefs about gender. This is particularly true among women, many of whom became proponents of policies that support the integration of women's employment and family responsibilities (i.e., subsidized childcare, public education, etc.). Cultural and attitudinal factors such as postmaterialist and egalitarian values and support for the women's movement have pushed women to the left ideologically, whereas men in these societies have held more stable preferences in these areas. This account of the gender gap complements *social role theory* by showing how gender roles are dynamic rather than static and how gender differences in political behavior are linked to economic and social factors rather than biological factors.

While this work has focused on the big picture or macro-level relationships between economic conditions in a country and the size and direction of the gender gap in voting behavior, some political scientists have also looked at how factors such as *resource inequality and personal autonomy* shape women's political behavior at the individual level and contribute to the gender gap. Historically, more limited educational and economic opportunities for women meant they amassed less personal wealth compared with men. Though educational attainment and workforce participation have increased markedly for women, factors such as occupational segregation in "pink collar" jobs, the "motherhood wage penalty," and persistent divisions in the distribution of household labor mean that many women still lag behind men in terms of their economic resources.[26] Research on the connection between women's economic circumstances and their political preferences has produced competing expectations about resources, autonomy, and women's political preferences.

The *economic vulnerability hypothesis* suggests that economically insecure women may rely more on social welfare programs, or anticipate needing to do so in the future, and thus exhibit more support for a social safety net and empathy for the Americans who need to rely on it in times of need. The *economic autonomy hypothesis* argues that women with greater economic resources have more options for self-determination, and this translates to distinctive preferences linked to protecting the opportunities these women have benefitted from (e.g., affirmative action programs, anti-discrimination laws).[27] These women, who have higher levels of educational attainment and professional status, may wish to see more state support for combining work and family responsibilities through social spending on welfare, childcare, and education. In addition, women are more likely than men to be employed in public sector jobs and interfacing with public programs, which might explain their greater support for Democratic administrations. Research on this area thus far has focused more on women's autonomy compared with vulnerability, though this is an important point of intersection (gender and socioeconomic status) warranting further inquiry.[28]

Additional research into the gender gap has focused on the ways that *gender and feminist consciousness* shapes women's political thinking and behavior. Efforts by the women's movement have helped some women to articulate their political interests in gendered terms – meaning they observe social, political, and economic inequalities tied to gender; perceive these inequalities as systemic and unjust; and favor a collective

---

[26] "Pink collar jobs" are typically careers in the service sector that are predominantly held by women. Women are disproportionately employed in care work sectors, which are more closely aligned with traditional gender roles and commonly characterized by lower wages. The motherhood wage penalty is the difference in wages between women with and without children. Women with children tend to have lower wages, and this in large part contributes to the average gender wage gap.

[27] Carroll, Women's Autonomy.

[28] Huddy, Cassese, and Lizotte, Gender, Public Opinion, and Political Reasoning.

orientation to redressing these inequalities.[29] Women who adopt a feminist identity tend to hold more liberal policy preferences, identify with the Democratic Party, and support its candidates.[30] But there is considerable variation in women's feminist identification. In a survey conducted by Pew Research in 2020 to celebrate the centennial anniversary of women's suffrage, about 19 percent of American women said the term "feminist" described them very well and another 42 percent said the term described them somewhat well.[31] Some women identify with the goals of the feminist movement but do not self-identify as feminists.[32] Others also identify explicitly as anti-feminist – a label that often coincides with a preference for traditional, complementarian gender roles, political conservatism, and religiosity (especially evangelical adherence) among women.[33]

Consider an example. The #MeToo movement – a campaign to raise awareness about sexual harassment and violence – tapped into gender identity to mobilize voters, particularly women voters, around this issue in the 2018 midterm elections. Yet women did not respond to messaging about #MeToo in a uniform fashion. Clear and distinctive position-taking by the parties further polarized voters along party lines, regardless of their gender.[34] And survey data suggested Republican women, like Republican men, were less supportive of the movement, were more likely to attribute claims of sexual harassment to "misunderstandings between women and men," and expressed greater concerns about false accusations of sexual misconduct.[35] Thus, not all women apply the same political lens to their gender identity, nor do all women share a sense of linked fate with other women.

<hr>

29 Patricia Gurin, Women's Gender Consciousness, *Public Opinion Quarterly* 49(2) (1985): 143–63.

30 Pamela Johnston Conover, Feminists and the Gender Gap, *The Journal of Politics* 50(4) (1988): 985–1010.

31 Amanda Barroso, 61% of U.S. Women Say "Feminist" Describes Them Well; Many See Feminism as Empowering and Polarizing, *Pew Research Center: Short Reads*, July 7, 2020, https://shorturl.at/zn3rp

32 Rachel Minkin, Most Americans Support Gender Equality, Even if They Don't Identify as Feminists, *Pew Research Center: Short Reads*, July 14, 2020, https://shorturl.at/0kApZ

33 Erin C. Cassese, Straying from the Flock? A Look at How Americans' Gender and Religious Identities Cross-Pressure Partisanship, *Political Research Quarterly* 73(1) (2020): 169–83.

34 Mirya R. Holman and Nathan P. Kalmoe, Partisanship in the #MeToo Era, *Perspectives on Politics* 22(1) (2024): 44–61.

35 Michael A. Hansen and Kathleen Dolan, Cross-Pressures on Political Attitudes: Gender, Party, and the #MeToo Movement in the United States, *Political Behavior* 45(4) (2023): 1377–400; Melissa Deckman, MeToo and the Midterms, *CAWP (Center for American Women and Politics) Blog*, May 8, 2018, https://cawp.rutgers.edu/blog/metoo-and-midterms

A final consideration is the *institutional factors* affecting the gender gap. As noted earlier in our discussion of global trends in gender and voting, the nature of government institutions can shape the expression of the gender gap. The modern gender gap observed in the United States and other established Western democracies is absent in many developing and post-communist nations. Other institutional factors – such as gender quotas requiring set levels of representation for specific groups and party systems – shape the gender gap as well. In countries without gender quotas, such as the United States, women tend to emerge more frequently in left-leaning parties. In countries with party-level quotas, left-leaning parties tend to adopt quotas at higher rates than right-leaning parties, and thus more women serve in legislative roles on the left side of the ideological spectrum, leading to a similar kind of gender gap.[36] However, in countries with legislative quotas, all political parties must include more women on their list of candidates, meaning women leaders tend to be represented in all parties regardless of ideological orientation. In countries with multiparty systems and legislative quotas, voters have more parties to choose from and women are more visible across party lines. This means that left-leaning parties cannot claim to better represent women purely on the basis of descriptive representation, and gender does not act as a cue to voters in quite the same way as it does in places such as the United States. As a result, the modern gender gap tends to be absent in these types of institutional contexts.[37]

This review of major theoretical perspectives highlights the complexity of the gender gap. Women's characteristics, experiences, and even their beliefs about gender roles are diverse and varied. Placing the American gender gap in a global perspective also highlights that gender differences in political behavior are not universal but vary across systems of government, levels of economic development, religious adherence, and cultural norms. As a result, it is challenging to pin down a simple explanation for the gender gap. Collectively, this research shows that gender is politically significant, but its effects on political behavior are contingent on the characteristics of individual women as well as broader social, economic, and political factors.

<hr>

[36] Diana Z. O'Brien, "Righting" Conventional Wisdom: Women and Right Parties in Established Democracies, *Politics & Gender* 14(1) (2018): 27–55.

[37] Jana Morgan, Gender and the Latin American Voter, in *The Latin American Voter: Pursuing Representation and Accountability in Challenging Contexts*, eds. Ryan E. Carlin, Matthew M. Singer, and Elizabeth J. Zechmeister (Ann Arbor, MI: University of Michigan Press, 2015), pp. 143–68.

In the next section, we consider the strategies employed by political actors when appealing to women voters and discuss the extent to which common approaches track with empirical evidence about the true preferences and motivations of American women.

ELECTORAL APPEALS TO WOMEN VOTERS

Beliefs about the origins of the gender gap often underlie the approaches parties, leaders, and candidates use to appeal to women voters. Often these beliefs reflect stereotypes and misconceptions rather than the realities of women's political interests and behaviors. For instance, political communication can reflect overgeneralizations about women – assuming a shared set of "women's interests" based on women's traditional roles as wives and mothers. But, as we noted previously, the average differences between men and women on these "women's issues" are quite small, typically less than five percentage points, meaning there is more to the gender gap than a traditional gender roles explanation can account for.[38]

The groups of women voters singled out for targeted campaign appeals in a given election often reveal something about how politicians and journalists conceptualize women as political actors. For instance, in the run-up to the 2024 presidential race, many speculated that suburban women were poised to play an outsized role in the election. The social category "suburban women" tends to be defined narrowly in political communication and journalistic accounts of the campaigns as a group of middle-class and middle-aged married white women who earned college degrees and reside in the suburbs with their children. This characterization is sometimes referred to as the "social construction" of suburban women, because it highlights how the group is defined through political discourse, which in turn shapes the ways the public, and politicians, think about this group as a political force.

The focus on suburban women in 2024 largely stemmed from trends in prior races, which suggested Republicans were losing their suburban stronghold. In 2016, Donald Trump had won white voters in the suburbs by sixteen points, and by 2020 that lead had eroded to only four points.[39] A common explanation floated for this change was that some

---

[38] Huddy, Cassese, and Lizotte, Gender, Public Opinion, and Political Reasoning.
[39] Ruth Igielnik, Scott Keeter, and Hannah Hartig, Behind Biden's 2020 Victory, *Pew Research Center: U.S. Politics & Policy*, June 30, 2021, https://pewresearch.org/politics/2021/06/30/behind-bidens-2020-victory/

of these women had shifted left in response to the events of Trump's first presidential administration, and it cost him in 2020.

In 2024, many journalists and campaign strategists expected the heightened salience of abortion rights following the Supreme Court's decision in *Dobbs v. Jackson Women's Health Organization* would lead to a further loss of Republican support in the suburbs, particularly among women. However, the suburbs are increasingly more diverse than the common characterization of suburban women suggests. And, as these areas become increasingly more diverse in terms of factors such as race, ethnicity, and class, the overall political composition of the suburbs may be shifting left, rather than just the specific subgroup of educated white suburban women.[40]

Exit polling suggests a broader suburban shift was likely at work. Harris was the favored candidate for suburban women; she received 52 percent of the vote from this group. However, a majority of suburban white women – 53 percent – cast their votes for former President Trump, as did 62 percent of white suburban men. This tracks with our prior observations about the electoral behavior of white women. White women are more likely to vote for Democratic candidates compared with white men but a majority still supports the Republican candidate. This challenges the notion of white women as swing voters – rather, they are a closely divided group with a narrow GOP advantage.

The focus on suburban women in 2024 was not a new narrative about women voters but instead a continuation of a more persistent way of conceptualizing them as soccer moms, hockey moms, security moms, waitress moms, Walmart moms, and even wine moms. Political scientist Susan Carroll has coined this phenomenon "electoral momification."[41] For example, appeals to "soccer moms" – typically coded as white, suburban, middle-class women with young children – were common in the 1996 presidential election.[42] This image of women voters emphasized how their roles as mothers shaped their issue priorities. Importantly, the supposed priorities of women voters placed them in a position where they favored some policies from the Democratic Party platform and some from the Republican Party platform. For instance, women voters were

---

[40] PRRI, Suburban Women and Abortion Politics Ahead of the 2024 Presidential Election, Public Religion Research Institute (PRRI), October 28, 2024, https://shorturl.at/2KlXY

[41] Susan J. Carroll, Moms Who Swing, or Why the Promise of the Gender Gap Remains Unfulfilled, *Politics & Gender* 2(3) (2006): 362–74, p. 370.

[42] Susan J. Carroll, The Disempowerment of the Gender Gap: Soccer Moms and the 1996 Elections, *PS: Political Science & Politics* 32(1) (1999): 7–11.

described as favoring Democratic health care and public education programs, but also the Republican Party's approach to crime and public safety, all because these various programs promoted a healthy and secure future for their children. Said differently, these women were assumed to be cross-pressured or torn between the two parties and could be persuaded to support either side, potentially swinging an election. In the end, election returns did not support this notion of soccer moms as swing voters. Yet candidates continued to appeal to soccer moms and, soon after, "security moms" with little update to the description of their political preferences other than being worried about the threat of additional terrorist attacks facing their families post-9/11.[43]

Ultimately, campaign communication and media coverage of campaigns that rely on these social constructions of women tend to reinforce stereotypes about women as political actors. This is often to the detriment of the political interests of women. In her work on this topic, Carroll explains that the "electoral momification" of women voters "deflected attention away from the concerns of many other subgroups of women, including feminists, older women, women on welfare, women of color, and professional women. The focus on the soccer mom allowed both the media and the campaigns to appear to be responsive to the concerns of women voters while actually ignoring the vast majority of women."[44] This also accounts for why the supposed electoral influence of women voters in some of these key elections did not translate into actual policy gains for women. "Momification" is less about women's electoral influence and more about aligning certain issues with a palatable subgroup of women whose lives and interests reflect traditional gender roles.

Along these lines, Donald Trump's 2024 appeals to women relied on traditional notions of masculinity. As discussed in Chapter 1 of this volume, Donald Trump described himself as a "protector" of women and children. This offer of protection spanned many issue areas, as the following excerpt from reporting on the campaign highlights:

> I'm going to protect [women] from migrants coming in … I'm going to protect them from foreign countries that want to hit us with missiles and lots of other things." [Trump's] comments echoed those from earlier in the day at a rally in Rocky Mount, North Carolina, when

---

[43] Susan J. Carroll, Security Moms and Presidential Politics: Women Voters in the 2004 Election, in *Voting the Gender Gap*, ed. Lois Duke Whitaker (Urbana: University of Illinois Press, 2008), pp. 75–90.

[44] Carroll, Disempowerment of the Gender Gap, p. 7.

Trump told attendees that millions of people have illegally entered the country, including "savage criminals who assault, rape and murder our women and girls."[45]

It also applied to abortion. At a campaign rally, Trump told his supporters, "As president, I have to be your protector … Women will be happy, healthy, confident and free. You will no longer be thinking about abortion."[46] The Harris campaign issued contrast messaging on this point, arguing that unlike Trump, who viewed women as subordinate to men and dependent on them for protection, Harris aimed to protect women's rights and agency, particularly with respect to reproductive rights.

Much like "electoral momification," Trump's comments reflect traditional beliefs about gender roles, highlighting stereotypically masculine traits like dominance and stereotypically feminine traits like vulnerability. The idea that women depend on the men in their lives for protection and guidance is sometimes referred to as "protective paternalism." This benevolent posture is often criticized for undermining women's authority and agency, particularly by women with more progressive attitudes toward gender roles. And these comments elicited some critical coverage, raising concerns about alienating women voters – for example, the *New York Times* headline "Trump Says He'll Protect Women, 'Like It or Not,' Evoking His History of Misogyny."[47] Yet this messaging likely appealed to women with more traditional views on gender roles, and this was not reflected in such reporting.

Similar themes were evident in discussions about transgender rights. Donald Trump promised to protect women from the supposed threat posed by trans women in public restrooms and to protect girls from competing against trans athletes in school sports. Trump's campaign also promised to extend parental rights over children's gender expression by sanctioning educational professionals for supporting gender transitions in schools (e.g., by using preferred names and pronouns) and medical professionals providing gender-affirming care to minors. This tracked with broader messaging appealing to women's desire for greater autonomy over health

---

[45] Mariel Padilla, Trump Says He Will Protect Women "Whether They Like It or Not," *19th News*, October 31, 2024, https://19thnews.org/2024/10/trump-rally-protector-women/

[46] Kate Sullivan and Eric Bradner, Trump Says Women Won't Be "Thinking about Abortion" if He's Elected, Casting Himself as Their "Protector," *CNN*, September 4, 2024, https://shorturl.at/75GC1

[47] Nicholas Nehamas and Erica L. Green, Trump Says He'll Protect Women, "Like It or Not," Evoking His History of Misogyny, *New York Times*, October 31, 2024, https://nytimes.com/2024/10/31/us/politics/trump-women-like-it-or-not.html

care decisions involving their children, including vaccination. This protective frame was very explicit in one of President Trump's early executive orders on this subject: Executive Order (EO) 14168, which was titled "Defending Women from Gender Ideology Extremism and Restoring Biological Truth to the Federal Government."

Again, the key takeaway here is that women think about the political implications of their own gender in markedly different ways, and thus appeals attracting some groups of women will repel others. As we documented in a previous section using public opinion data from the ANES, women's interests are diverse and strongly related to partisanship. As a result, crafting campaign messaging that appeals broadly to women voters across party lines is challenging. In 2024, Trump's campaign kept Republican women in the fold with appeals oriented toward traditional ideas about gender and the rights of mothers to make decisions for their children. Harris's campaign employed progressive messaging on women's rights and autonomy extending beyond women's roles as mothers but including an emphasis on women's right to decide whether to become mothers (more on this later). And of course, these appeals likely resonated with men based on their beliefs about these issues as well.

APPEALS TO MEN AND MASCULINITY

Characterizations of men as voters are also often reductive. For example, the 1994 election was dubbed the "Year of the Angry White Male" by journalists who attributed the "Republican Revolution" to white men's swing toward the Republican Party.[48] The 2004 election featured "Nascar Dads," a group of white working-class men affected by the economic downturn who might stray from the GOP.[49] This group was reupped in media narratives of the 2016 election, when "white working-class men" were credited with Donald Trump's unexpected victory.

As is the case for women, this way of conceptualizing men tends to rely on stereotypes. A common thread among these characterizations of men as voters is a focus on economic issues, which, as noted earlier, are

---

[48] Not coincidentally, this came on the heels of the 1992 midterm elections, which some journalists hailed as the "Year of the Woman" due to women's unprecedented representational gains in the US Congress.

[49] Jeff MacGregor, The New Electoral Sex Symbol: Nascar Dad, *New York Times*, January 18, 2004, https://nytimes.com/2004/01/18/weekinreview/the-new-electoral-sex-symbol-nascar-dad.html

often dubbed "men's issues" based on the male breadwinner model. In 2016, the idea was that this group of men was losing out on economic opportunities due to globalization and struggling to play the breadwinner role in their families. They were "men's men" who were not turned off by Donald Trump's "locker room talk" or the accusations of sexual assault and harassment made against him. This narrative perhaps contributed to an overreliance on this group to explain Donald Trump's victory in 2016 and overlooked other core bases of support, such as white women voters, who again played a key role in supporting Trump during his 2024 presidential bid.

Ideas about masculinity played an important role in 2024. As discussed in Chapter 1 of this volume, Donald Trump stressed traits associated with traditional notions of masculinity (e.g., strength, aggression, and dominance), leaning into the idea that voters, regardless of gender, support masculine qualities in their leaders. Trump's appeals to masculinity were echoed by the *manosphere* – a shorthand term used to describe general interest content on TikTok, YouTube, Twitch, and podcasting platforms developed for a primarily male audience. For instance, Donald Trump appeared on *The Joe Rogan Experience* podcast, and the three-hour episode had tremendous reach – about forty million views on YouTube prior to Election Day.[50]

According to GOP digital strategist Eric Wilson, the focus on these content creators was a deliberate strategy for reaching young men in particular.[51] The "Gen Z Gender Gap" emerged as an important narrative in coverage of the presidential contest due in part to this unique strategy that eschewed more traditional news outlets in favor of new media focused on men's interests. Polling also played a role. In August of 2024, the *New York Times* reported on a poll conducted in the battleground states of Arizona, Georgia, Michigan, Nevada, Pennsylvania, and Wisconsin,

---

[50] Dominick Mastrangelo, Trump, Rogan Interview Tops 38 Million Views, *The Hill*, October 29, 2024, https://thehill.com/homenews/media/4959974-joe-rogan-trump-interview. Though references to the "manosphere" were common in media coverage of the campaign, there is debate over which content creators fall into this camp, with some arguing that a narrow definition is more appropriate. For instance, Joe Rogan is often equated with the manosphere in public discourse (see footnote 51 for an example), but he does not personally identify as part of the manosphere. For more information on this debate, please see Jessica Aiston, What Is the Manosphere and Why Is It a Concern?, InternetMatters.org, October 4, 2021, www.internetmatters.org/hub/news-blogs/what-is-the-manosphere-and-why-is-it-a-concern/.

[51] Laura Barrón-López, Trump's Success among Young Men Illustrates Influence of Online "Manosphere," *PBS NewsHour*, November 25, 2024, https://shorturl.at/wkoWd

focusing on an unprecedented thirty-nine-point gender gap between men and women ages eighteen to twenty-nine.[52]

This article drew criticism in some circles for inflating the size of the gap between men and women by adding the difference in support between the two candidates for men and women rather than comparing the percentage supporting a single candidate for men and women, as is the convention in the gender gap literature and what we present here. Other pre-election polls found more modest differences. For instance, the Harvard Youth Poll estimated that 51 percent of young women supported Harris compared with 43 percent of young men – a gap of only eight points.[53] The NBC News Stay Tuned Gen Z Poll (conducted by SurveyMonkey) showed 59 percent of young women supporting Harris compared with 42 percent of young men – a seventeen-point gap.[54] It was not only the size of the gender gap that varied across polls, but also the leading candidate. Donald Trump was not leading among young men consistently across these polls, some of which suggested young men favored Harris. The uncertainty around this group likely stemmed from dividing samples into narrow age–gender categories, which increased the uncertainty (i.e., the margins of error) around these estimates considerably.[55]

Yet in spite of this problem, the *New York Times* article generated widespread public interest. A widening gap between young men and women in the United States seemed to track with global trends toward a widening gender gap in the political attitudes of Gen Z men and women.[56] Some analysts attributed young men's conservatism to higher levels of religiosity and growing divisions over gender roles, while others focused on more psychological factors, including mental health issues, such as growing despair.[57] Still others argued that young men felt left behind

[52] Claire C. Miller, Many Gen Z Men Feel Left Behind. Some See Trump as an Answer, *New York Times: The Upshot*, August 24, 2024, https://nytimes.com/2024/08/24/upshot/trump-polls-young-men.html

[53] Harvard Youth Poll, 49th Edition, https://iop.harvard.edu/youth-poll/latest-poll

[54] NBC News Stay Tuned Gen Z Poll Results, October 24, 2024, https://bit.ly/48tKx3m

[55] John Sides, Another Viral Gender Gap Graph Doesn't Tell the Whole Story, *Good Authority*, September 17, 2024, https://goodauthority.org/news/gender-gap-2024-us-elections-polls-surveys/

[56] Glocalities, Growing Despair and Polarization between Young Women & Men Impacts Elections, *Glocalities: Reports*, 2024, https://glocalities.com/reports/trend-report-polarization

[57] Erica Pandey, Young Men and Women Are Moving in Opposite Directions, *Axios*, September 28, 2024, https://axios.com/2024/09/28/young-men-women-divided-politics-religion; Anthony Deutsch, "Despair" Makes Young U.S. Men More Conservative Ahead of U.S. Election, Poll Shows, *Reuters*, April 12, 2024, https://bit.ly/48oCo1E

economically, tapping into the same economic grievance narrative evident in 2016, though with a generational rather than blue-collar spin.[58] Some survey data suggests the real outliers in 2024 were Gen Z women, who showed demonstrably greater support for Harris than women in other age cohorts. Gen Z men, by contrast, were not as distinct from older men voters in terms of their candidate preferences. Additional research on young women attributes their shift leftward to changing issue priorities and growing dissatisfaction with government action on issues such as reproductive rights and climate change.[59] Others point to additional factors including the influence of the #MeToo movement as well as role model effects.[60]

These ideas about gender differences among Gen Z voters shaped campaign strategy. For example, Harris focused a great deal of attention on abortion rights, including holding a reproductive rights-focused rally in Texas just prior to Election Day, working from the expectation that this was an especially important issue to Gen Z women. Trump and Vance doubled down on their manosphere strategy, appearing frequently on podcasts popular with young male audiences and leaning into these media personalities for their lynchpin Madison Square Garden event.[61] Ultimately, an explosive Gen Z gender gap did not emerge. Edison's exit polling indicates that the gender gap among eighteen- to twenty-nine-year-old voters was actually *smaller* in 2024 than in 2020 by four percentage points (see Table 2.2 for details). Gen Z men and women were not significantly more divided compared with other generational cohorts. Instead, the difference is only modestly larger (one to two percentage points). The viral buzz created by the *New York Times* Gen Z gender gap poll shaped the way the media talked about young voters, particularly young men, for the remainder of the campaign, making it an important cautionary tale of how a single poll can drive an inaccurate media narrative about gender and voting behavior.

This section and the one preceding it highlight consistency in the way candidates have appealed to voters on the basis of gender issues over

---

[58] Miller, Many Gen Z Men Feel Left Behind.

[59] Lydia Saad, Sarah Elizabeth Jones, and Sarah Fioroni, Exploring Young Women's Leftward Expansion, *Gallup News*, September 12, 2024, https://shorturl.at/EJfu8

[60] Melissa Deckman, *The Politics of Gen Z: How the Youngest Voters Will Shape Our Democracy* (New York: Columbia University Press, 2024); Jennie Sweet-Cushman, *Inspired Citizens: How Our Political Role Models Shape American Politics* (Philadelphia, PA: Temple University Press, 2023).

[61] Danielle Kurtzleben, How Trump and Vance's Tour of "Dude Influencers" Might Help Them Win, *NPR*, September 24, 2024, https://shorturl.at/ZCHJw

time. It is clear that common representations of men and women and their political interests – whether accurate or not – can shape how campaigns structure their political communication and appeals, reinforcing the power of gender stereotypes in American politics. The 2024 presidential race was no exception: as the previous examples illustrate, ideas about gender played a significant role in structuring candidate outreach. In the next section, we dig deeper into a final issue that played a distinctive role in the 2024 presidential election: reproductive rights.

WOMEN VOTERS POST-*ROE*

A major development between the 2020 and 2024 elections was the Supreme Court's decision in *Dobbs v. Jackson Women's Health Organization*, which overturned the constitutional right to an abortion established in the 1973 *Roe v. Wade* ruling. Many politicians, journalists, and analysts expected this would have a major impact on the 2024 election cycle, in part because it seemed to play a significant role in the 2022 midterm elections. In this section, we outline key developments regarding reproductive rights and analyze the role this issue has played in voter mobilization.

The Supreme Court's ruling in *Dobbs* was rendered less than six months before the 2022 midterm election. The *Dobbs* decision remanded policy-making to the states, many of which already had "trigger laws" in place that severely restricted or outright banned abortion, meaning the policy landscape for reproductive rights in the United States shifted radically and immediately in the wake of *Dobbs*. Frequent media coverage and campaign ads focused on reproductive rights kept abortion at the forefront of voters' minds.[62] Survey data suggested abortion was a critical issue priority for voters, especially Democrats.[63] Rates of new voter registrations outpaced those in past elections, particularly among women in states with direct ballot measures related to abortion rights.[64] In 2022, voters in six states weighed in on direct ballot measures addressing abortion rights,

---

[62] Erin C. Cassese, Heather L. Ondercin, and Jordan Randall, *Abortion Attitudes and Polarization in the American Electorate* (Cambridge: Cambridge University Press, 2025).

[63] Pew Research Center, Abortion Rises in Importance as a Voting Issue, Driven by Democrats, *Pew Research Center: U.S. Politics & Policy*, August 23, 2022, https://shorturl.at/iWR8w

[64] Francesca Paris and Nate Cohn, After Roe's End, Women Surged in Signing Up to Vote in Some States, *New York Times*, August 25, 2022, https://nytimes.com/interactive/2022/08/25/upshot/female-voters-dobbs.html

the most on record. In each case, a majority of voters cast their votes to protect reproductive rights.

The role abortion played in the midterms led many observers of American politics to expect the issue would be a major focus of campaigning in 2024 as well. State-level abortion bans were increasingly referred to as "Trump abortion bans" to remind voters of the role the former president played in selecting the Supreme Court nominees that produced this outcome. Developments at the state level played a role as well, with more state residents set to vote on ballot measures in 2024 than in 2022. Initiatives related to reproductive rights were on the ballot in ten states (New York, Maryland, Florida, Missouri, Nebraska, South Dakota, Montana, Colorado, Arizona, and New Mexico). In most of these states, voters weighed in on amendments that would extend protections for abortion rights, but Nebraskans voted on competing measures – one to protect and one to restrict abortion rights.[65] The presence of these initiatives on the ballot, coupled with polling suggesting abortion was an important issue for women voters and Democrats, contributed to expectations that the issue would again be decisive in 2024.

Concerns about abortion rights were also linked to Project 2025, a playbook for a second Trump administration created by a conservative think tank called the Heritage Foundation. Project 2025 proposed curtailing access to mifepristone (colloquially known as the abortion pill), which accounted for about two-thirds of all abortion procedures at the time.[66] It also recommended further restrictions on the use of federal funds for abortion, as well as changes to programs such as Title X and the Affordable Care Act that might limit women's access to contraception.[67] Project 2025 outlined a plan to dismantle abortion provisions in the Emergency Medical Treatment and Labor Act (EMTALA), which required hospitals receiving Medicare funds to provide emergency care to stabilize a person's condition regardless of their ability to pay.

Following the *Dobbs* decision, hospitals in states with restrictive abortion policies sometimes interpreted these policies as conflicting with EMTALA,

---

[65] KFF, Ballot Tracker: Outcome of Abortion-Related State Constitutional Amendment Measures in the 2024 Election, *KFF: Women's Health Policy*, November 6, 2024, https://shorturl.at/5R0ic

[66] Rachel K. Jones and Amy Friedrich-Karnik, Medication Abortion Accounted for 63% of All U.S. Abortions in 2023, an Increase from 53% in 2020, *Guttmacher Institute*, March 19, 2024, https://shorturl.at/2FJZZ

[67] Anna Bernstein, Amy Friedrich-Karnik, and Samira Damavandi, How Project 2025 Seeks to Obliterate Sexual and Reproductive Health and Rights, *Guttmacher Institute*, October 2024, https://shorturl.at/P1NZg

and pregnant women seeking emergency care were turned away as a result, often with dire consequences.[68] The Department of Health and Human Services attempted to issue a clarification indicating that EMTALA supersedes state-level abortion bans that do not include an exemption for the health of the mother. Two cases about the conflict between state and federal law made their way to the Supreme Court in the fall of 2024, and the Court declined to clarify the relationship between these laws. This reinforced messaging on the Democratic side emphasizing the ongoing health threat facing women in states with "Trump abortion bans."

Campaign rhetoric about abortion shifted over the course of the race. Former President Trump's messaging was mixed. He took credit for the Supreme Court appointments that delivered the *Dobbs* decision and reverted abortion policy back to the states. At the same time, he distanced himself from a proposed national abortion ban and some state-level bans proposing to limit or outlaw IVF and other assisted reproductive technologies, likely as a concession to Republicans and Independents with more moderate views on abortion. Democratic messaging on abortion underwent a major shift when Harris replaced Biden on the ticket. President Biden, a devout Catholic, had a mixed voting record on reproductive rights. For example, he supported the Hyde Amendment, a policy that banned the use of federal funds for abortion, up until 2019 when he became the Democratic Party's presidential nominee.

Critics noted Biden avoided using the word "abortion" almost entirely in his 2024 State of the Union address, which raised concerns that he would not be an effective messenger on abortion at a time when it was highly salient to voters.[69] When Harris became the nominee, the campaign's messaging on abortion sharpened and Harris offered full-throated support for abortion rights. She argued in favor of eliminating the Senate filibuster rule to facilitate the passage of legislation that would reinstate *Roe*.[70] Women and their husbands sharing their own personal experiences in states with restrictive abortion laws became a cornerstone of Democratic messaging. These stories were featured in powerful, emotionally evocative

[68] Laurie Sobel, Alina Salganicoff, and Mabel Felix, Abortion Back at SCOTUS: Can States Ban Emergency Abortion Care for Pregnant Patients?, *KFF: Women's Health Policy*, April 22, 2024, https://shorturl.at/wxJYV

[69] Christine Fernando, Biden's Big Speech Showed His Uneasy Approach to Abortion, an Issue Bound to Be Key in the Campaign, *AP News*, March 10, 2024, https://shorturl.at/BBBii

[70] Jason Breslow, Harris Says She Would Support Ending the Filibuster to Bring Back *Roe v. Wade*, *NPR*, September 24, 2024, https://shorturl.at/MZuSG

ads, delivered by speakers at the Democratic National Convention and reiterated by Harris in her stump speeches on the campaign trail.[71] This intense focus on a "women's issue" raised questions about gender and mobilization in 2024 – namely whether the election would reflect a historic gender gap among voters. Again, this gap did not materialize, upending expectations about the mobilizing effects of abortion rights. According to Edison's exit poll data, only 19 percent of women voters cited abortion as the most important issue shaping their vote choice. Higher proportions chose the economy (29 percent) and democracy (33 percent).

Ultimately, the combination of explicitly gendered campaign rhetoric, the salience of a policy area with high personal relevance for women, and the presence of a woman candidate in 2024 did not translate into a seismic shift in the electoral landscape for women voters. Forty-four years earlier, when the modern gender gap was initially recognized, the parties had just begun to take very distinct positions on gender issues and stake out distinct gender ideologies; for example, the Republican Party removed support for the Equal Rights Amendment from its platform that year. Voters responded to this change in messaging. Over time, these party positions consolidated, and Americans know what to expect from the parties when it comes to these issues. Thus messaging focused on women's traditional roles from the Republican ticket was largely consistent with the GOP's brand – unsurprising to many Republican women and unlikely to push them from the fold. Rather, it was what attracted them to the party in the first place.

CONCLUSIONS

The primary takeaways from this body of research on the gender gap is that American women are a politically diverse social group. Though more liberal and more supportive of Democratic candidates, on average, than their male counterparts, women vary considerably in their political identification, attitudes, and behaviors, and this variation is systematically related to factors such as race, ethnicity, religiosity, and socioeconomic status, among others. Beyond this, evidence of variability in the size of the gender gap across elections and national contexts further speaks to the critical need to avoid reductive and essentialist explanations of political gender difference.

---

[71] Rosemary Westwood, Women Sharing Personal Stories about Abortion Bans Have Become a Political Force, *NPR*, November 2, 2024, https://shorturl.at/BHiPK

Yet journalists, campaign professionals, and candidates have often overlooked women's diversity and instead relied on gender stereotypes, particularly those tied to motherhood, in ways that may undermine women's electoral influence. People working in these fields should take care to avoid overgeneralizations and instead think intersectionally about the political implications of gender. And, as consumers of media and campaign communications, we should keep these same pitfalls in mind. In their recent book *Women Voters: Race, Gender, and Dynamism in American Elections*, political scientists Jane June and Natalie Masuoka put it this way: "Ignoring dynamism and continuing to rely on outdated concepts and assumptions – that men are the modal voter or that women across the board favor Democrats, for example – come with the price of blindness to both seeing relevant systematic variation among voters and being unable to anticipate and explain change in electoral politics in the United States."[72] In the case of 2024, these assumptions also left many citizens and political analysts unable to anticipate *continuities* in American gender politics that contributed to the reelection of Donald Trump.

These are important lessons to carry forward into 2028. President Trump will not be eligible for another term in office, meaning we can expect large and diverse fields of primary candidates for both parties. To stand out in these crowded fields, candidates must think beyond "soccer moms" and "angry white men."

---

[72] Junn and Masuoka, *Women Voters*.

3 Gendered Mobilization and Elections

The Intersectional Politics of Protest

On January 20, 2025, Donald J. Trump was sworn into office for the second time. The ceremony was held indoors, after an arctic blast dropped temperatures well below freezing. The day seemed almost anticlimactic after the tumult surrounding the previous two inaugurations. In 2017, the day after Trump was inaugurated for the first time, the world witnessed one of the largest single-day protests in US history. The 2017 Women's March spread not only across the United States but also worldwide. Four years later, on January 6, 2021 – the day that Joe Biden was scheduled to become the certified winner of the 2020 presidential election after beating the incumbent Trump – another type of protest took shape. What started as a rally for Trump turned into a violent insurrection at the Capitol; Congress was forced to adjourn and take shelter.

There are many important comparisons and contrasts to be made between these two mobilizations. While both events were planned by women and prompted by the outcome of a recent presidential election, they are a part of two very different and oppositional social movement trajectories that have long shaped US politics, one focused on challenging gendered and racial power structures and the other seeking to uphold them. While the election of 2024 has yet to produce mobilization that matches the optics of either of these events – at least at the time this chapter is being drafted – that may soon change. As Trump advances the Make America Great Again (MAGA) movement's reactionary agenda in an unprecedented manner, the progressive countermovement appears to be revitalizing, with protests and boycotts growing in size and scope. The two oppositional movements that prompted the events of 2017 and 2021 are still present and deeply intertwined in US electoral and partisan politics, with profound implications for the future of democracy.

This chapter explores the relationship between social movements and elections, with an emphasis on the role that both gender and race play. An intersectional analysis provides important insights into why and how some groups have mobilized and to what effect, as well as what we might expect in the years to come. This chapter is organized as follows. First, I provide an intersectional framework for the study of race-gendered social movements, as well as their relationship with elections. Next, I provide a historical overview of oppositional mobilizations and their interaction with US elections, including the role they have played in expanding or contracting voting rights and the impact they have had on parties and their electoral coalitions. I focus on the intersectional dynamics of progressive movements and their conservative backlashes in three time periods: (1) the abolition and women's suffrage movements in the late 1800s and early 1900s; (2) the civil rights movement(s) and women's liberation movements of the 1960s, 1970s, and 1980s; and (3) the contemporary mobilizations in the first two decades of the new millennium (including the 2017 Women's March and the 2021 insurrection). Finally, I focus on the mobilizations surrounding the 2024 election, demonstrating how they continue the historical pattern, while also highlighting some of the shifting developments.

GENDERED MOBILIZATION

Within the gender and politics literature, much attention is given to feminist mobilizations. This is with good reason. Feminist movements have been a key means of increasing women's representation both descriptively (securing women's right to vote and legitimizing women's political participation and leadership) and substantively (getting important gendered issues on the political agenda). Feminist movements, however, are only one specific type of gendered mobilization. Scholars have made important distinctions between "women's movements," "feminist movements," and "women in movement."[1] As Figure 3.1 visualizes, each is an important component of gendered mobilization, but with markedly different focus and impact. Women's movements are a subset of movements that are "characterized by the primacy of women's gendered experiences, women's issues, and women's leadership and decision making."[2] Here, how

---

[1] Karen Beckwith, The Comparative Study of Women's Movements, in *The Oxford Handbook of Gender and Politics*, eds. Georgina Waylen, Karen Celis, Johanna Kantola, and S. Laurel Weldon (New York: Oxford University Press, 2013), pp. 411–36.

[2] Ibid.

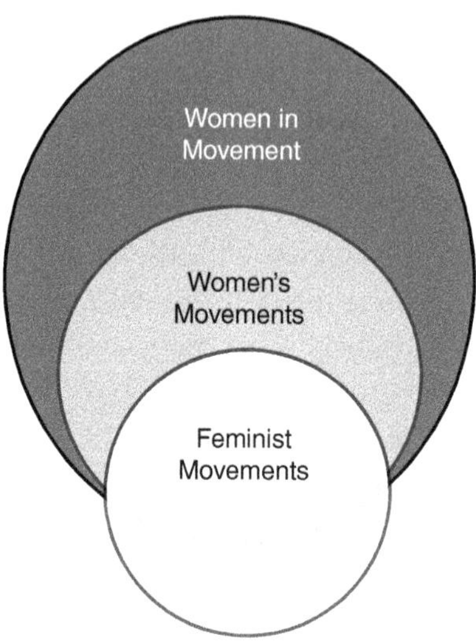

Figure 3.1 Women in movement, women's movements, and feminist movements.
Source: Author's own elaboration.

a movement defines itself and articulates issues are specific to women, developed and organized by them with reference to their gender identity. Women's movements might encompass some feminist movements, but they might also encompass other movements where women are mobilizing as women and using that gender identity in various ways that are not directed at women's rights. This includes conservative women's movements. A third and overlapping form of gendered mobilization is "women in movement," which focuses on women's participation that extends to movements not organized around gender in any explicit manner and/or where men may even dominate leadership and decision-making roles. Women have been a part of other movements that do not emphasize gender but nevertheless may have an important (and gendered) impact on their lives. Figure 3.1 shows the relationship between these three forms of mobilization in terms of potential overlap, but also in regard to extension beyond.

These categories provide a useful but partial typology of gendered mobilization. They do not include every possible type of gendered mobilization and rigid adherence may even obscure important forms. A more expansive understanding of gendered mobilization would include movements in which other gender identities are central to mobilization, such as the men's movements or transgender movements (the latter of which may also fit within or overlap with the various categories discussed earlier). You might also apply a gendered analysis to any movement. Are there any gendered patterns in who is participating, in the leadership structures, in the way that issues are prioritized, addressed, or framed?

It is also important to recognize that gender may not be the only relevant characteristic of a mobilization. An intersectional analysis – one that examines how gender intersects with race, class, sexuality, and other axes of identity – provides a more thorough analysis of gendered mobilization. It is a better means of highlighting the experiences of those at the intersection of multiple marginalities, such as women of color, working-class women, queer or trans women, disabled women, and so on. Such groups have often mobilized between or across movements, engaging in multi-issue organizing or working on several political fronts that may or may not put gender at the center, but that have a gendered impact nonetheless.[3]

Intersectional analysis can also show how a particular group might experience oppression along one dimension and privilege along another. An intersectional approach helps to uncover the challenges of working across difference in a single movement. It also helps to explain how women might end up in diametrically opposed movements.

SOCIAL MOVEMENTS AND ELECTIONS

Social movements are often framed as separate from electoral politics. Whereas an institutional mechanism for change is offered by electoral politics, social movements are often seen as extra-institutional, a means of creating change when institutions fail to provide adequate representation. There is, however, a "fuzzy and permeable boundary" that exists between institutionalized and noninstitutionalized politics, with social movements serving less as an alternative to electoral politics, and more as a complementary and intertwined mode of political action.[4] The ebb and flow of movements can shift electoral politics, and electoral politics can shift the ebb and flow of movements.

---

[3] Maylei Blackwell, *Chicana Power! Contested Histories of Feminism in the Chicano Movement* (Austin, TX: University of Texas Press, 2011); Celeste Montoya and Mariana Galvez Seminario, Guerreras y Puentes: The Theory and Praxis of Latina(x) Activism, *Politics, Groups, and Identities* 10(2) (2020): 171–88.

[4] Jack A. Goldstone, More Social Movements or Fewer? Beyond Political Opportunity Structures to Relational Fields, *Theory and Society* 33(3–4) (2004): 333–65; Doug McAdam and Sidney Tarrow, Social Movements and Elections: Toward a Broader Understanding of the Political Context of Contention, in *Future of Social Movement Research: Dynamics, Mechanisms, and Processes*, eds. Jacqueline van Stekenlenburg, Conny Roggeband, and Bert Klandermans (Minneapolis, MN: University of Minnesota Press, 2013), pp. 325–46.

Political scientists have found several prominent linkages between social movements and elections.[5] First, social movements play a pivotal role in the creation, expansion, and maintenance of democracies, including the United States. Under the original Constitution, only white men aged twenty-one and older who owned land could vote. The abolition movement to end slavery, the women's suffrage movement, and various civil rights movements have worked toward expanding US democracy to include people of all gender, ethno-racial, and socioeconomic groups. This includes the expansion of voting rights as well as the subsequent mobilization of new electorates. Social movements can even produce new leaders in the electoral arena, as activists from marginalized groups seek institutional modes of change by running for office. Not all social movements, however, are oriented toward expanding democracies. Many of the "progressive" movements aimed at expanding the rights of previously excluded groups have been met with backlash or countermobilizations by "regressive" or "conservative" groups that seek to return to the previous status quo.

Another important link is between social movements and political parties. Parties and social movements have an important but uneasy symbiotic relationship. Parties are important targets for social movements because they can get issues on the political agenda and are key to translating movement demands into policy changes. Social movements are important to parties because they can mobilize the electorate, providing a competitive advantage to political parties when they mobilize new or key constituencies.[6] At the same time, there is the possibility of hostility between the two as they compete for resources and over the priority and framing of issues. Social movement actors are often critical of parties for their perceived role in upholding the status quo. Parties can be critical of social movements, particularly when they see them as disrupting their policy agenda and potentially destabilizing the electoral coalitions necessary to keep them in power.

During cycles of protest – a time period in which social movement activity is expansive in its geographic scale; the number, size, and diversity of social groups participating; and the prevalence of disruptive and

[5] Michael Heaney, Elections and Social Movements, in the Wiley-Blackwell *Encyclopedia of Social and Political Movements*, online edn., 2013; Doug McAdam and Sidney Tarrow, Ballots and Barricades: On the Reciprocal Relationship between Elections and Social Movements, *Perspective on Politics* 8(2) (2010): 529–42.

[6] Mildred A. Schwartz, Interactions between Social Movements and US Political Parties, *Party Politics* 16(5) (2010): 587–607.

confrontational activity – social movements can substantially change the electoral landscape. In the United States, the success or failure of the two major parties depends on their ability to appeal to a wide swath of voters and mobilize an electoral coalition large enough to secure a plurality, if not a majority, of votes. Mass movements can destabilize these coalitions. They put on the agenda new issues that challenge party platforms and mobilize different constituencies. This can polarize parties internally or from each other and can even trigger significant party realignments. They can direct voters to vote for third parties or even to stay at home, particularly if both traditional parties are seen as upholding troublesome status quos and/or acting in opposition to the movement and movement objectives.

Shifts in electoral regimes can also have significant and long-term impacts on the prospects for social movements, which is why groups may mobilize proactively for or against candidates that they see as helping or hurting their interests.[7] Social movements might also mobilize reactively, after the election. When the outcome of an election is seen as threatening the interests of the group, this may prompt mobilization as resistance. A favorable outcome might also serve to mobilize. If groups perceive a new administration as opening up political opportunities, they may see this as precisely the time to mobilize. A more favorable election outcome might also serve to demobilize movements. It may diminish the sense of urgency for some participants or coalition members.

An administration can also shape the mobilizing prospects of a group by easing or increasing restrictions or in the authorization of force. For example, many people noted the difference in the relative lack of police or national guard presence on January 6, when a primarily white group of protesters was expected, in comparison with other mobilizations by and for people of color, where law enforcement has responded in greater numbers and with greater use of force. Although the First Amendment protects freedom of speech and assembly, government officials have been given a large degree of latitude in regulating and policing protest.

The interactions between race-gendered social movements and elections are a key component of US political history. The next two sections provide an overview of this history, setting the necessary context for understanding contemporary politics.

---

[7] Kathleen M. Blee and Ashley Currier, How Local Social Movement Groups Handle a Presidential Election, *Qualitative Sociology* 29(3) (2006): 261–80.

RACE-GENDERED MOBILIZATION IN US HISTORY

Race-gendered mobilization has played an important role in expanding US democracy, not only via the more recognized forms of women's and feminist movements but also by women who have fought for full citizenship rights through a diverse array of racial justice movements. Race-gendered mobilization has also been part of the powerful backlash and countermobilizations aimed at restricting access and maintaining inequality. This section focuses on the oppositional race-gendered mobilizations that have occurred in three different time periods of US history and the ways in which they have been shaped by and shaped elections.

Race-Gendered Mobilization and Elections in the Late 1800s and Early 1900s

Two of the most significant expansions of US democracy occurred with the ratification, in 1870, of the Fifteenth Amendment – granting the right to vote to male citizens "regardless of race, color, or previous condition of servitude," and in 1920, of the Nineteenth Amendment – establishing the right of women to vote. Race-gendered mobilization played an important role in establishing these rights as well as in the backlash that followed. In this section, I focus on the period between the two amendments, focusing on the racial tension within the suffrage movement and beyond, as well as highlighting the work that women of color were doing within and across the suffrage movement as well as ethno-racial justice movements. I also focus on the role that race and gender played in the electoral and partisan politics of the time.

Racial Tensions in the Suffrage Movement

While there were significant overlaps between the abolition movement seeking to end slavery and the early women's rights movements – with many supporting universal voting rights – there was also tension between them. Not all supporters of abolition supported or prioritized women's suffrage. Not all women's suffragists supported or prioritized the voting rights of Black or other racialized groups. This tension came to a head when the Fifteenth Amendment was ratified without the inclusion of women, leading to a disbanding of the American Equal Rights Association as well as the emergence of two rival suffrage organizations, one supporting the Fifteenth Amendment, seeing it as a step in the right direction, and one vehemently opposed for its exclusion of women.

This split marked a shift by some from an antebellum suffrage ideology that "emphasized a common victimhood" between women and those adopting a postbellum suffrage ideology that "stressed white women's racial-cultural superiority to newly enfranchised male constituencies – not just black men, but also naturalized immigrant men."[8] When the two organizations merged in 1890, a relentless focus on the Nineteenth Amendment yielded exclusionary strategies to maintain an alliance with women's suffragist organizations in the South, many of whom did not allow Black members. This included leveraging racist rhetoric, such as justifying votes for white women as a means of maintaining white electoral power, as well as a reluctance to allow Black women to participate in public events.

The gendered racial tension within the suffrage movement occurred alongside and in tandem with the wave of nationalistic white supremacist organizing that swept the rural South after the Civil War. For a short while after the Civil War amendments were passed, newly enfranchised Black men gained a voice in government for the first time in US history, not only by voting but also by running for office. Black political (and economic) power expanded dramatically, with more than 1,500 Black men holding public office in the South. As the federal government withdrew troops, however, a white backlash was mobilized to usher in the Jim Crow era of racial violence and oppression. An even bigger wave of white supremacist organizing emerged in the 1920s influenced by the spread of anti-Black racism following the postwar migration of Blacks from the South to the North and an increase in nationalistic anti-immigration sentiment fueled by World War I propaganda and a rise in religious and political fundamentalism.[9]

White women were a vital part of white supremacist movements, often developing distinct race-gendered ideologies. For example, with the Women of the KKK (Ku Klux Klan) some Klanswomen sought to uphold both gender and racial hierarchies, while others developed a complex ideology that carried gender equality into their struggle against Blacks, Jews, Catholics, labor radicals, socialists, Mormons, and immigrants.[10] While

[8] Louise Michele Newman, *White Women's Rights: The Racial Origins of Feminism in the United States* (New York: Oxford University Press, 1999).

[9] Kathleen M. Blee, *Understanding Racist Activism: Theory, Methods and Research* (New York: Routledge, 2017).

[10] Kathleen M. Blee, Women in the 1920s' Ku Klux Klan Movement, in *US Women in Struggle: A Feminist Studies Anthology*, eds. Claire Goldberg Moses and Heidi I. Hartmann (Urbana, IL: University of Illinois Press, 1995), pp. 89–109.

women were rarely involved in the violence or vigilantism perpetrated by the men, they helped in legitimizing organizations, planning events to mobilize the political base, and leading political assaults (often via boycotts and whispering campaigns) against businesses owned by people of color, political officials of color, and those who supported racial equality.

Mobilized white backlash successfully impeded the ability of people of color to participate in elections in many parts of the country. Poll taxes, literacy tests, grandfather clauses, and voter intimidation and violence were used against Blacks, Mexicans, Asians, and Native Americans in the South and the West. In the northern cities, poll watchers targeted immigrants (often relying on racial and ethnic cues), demanding proof of citizenship. Gendered violence was a part of the intimidation; sexual assault was used against women of color and accusations of rape (of white women) were used to justify violence against men of color. It was not until the rise of the civil rights movement of the mid-twentieth century that groups were able to effectively push for federal protections.

Women of Color Mobilizing on Multiple Fronts

Despite the discrimination they faced within the women's suffrage movement, women of color continued to fight for women's right to vote. They were also mobilizing on other political fronts aimed at establishing political rights and justice for their communities. Black women were strong supporters of women's suffrage, something they pursued alongside other issues important to their own organizations. The National Association of Colored Women, which was formed in 1896, included among its membership prominent suffragists such as Harriet Tubman, Mary Church Terrell, and Ida B. Wells. It was a part of the outgrowth of the Black women's club movement, which addressed issues similar to those addressed in white women's clubs (suffrage, education, health, etc.), but also racial uplift and efforts to combat racism, including lynching.

Native, Mexican, and Asian American women were also engaged in the struggle for suffrage, often alongside broader struggles for citizenship rights and protections that were less focused on gender. The 1848 Treaty of Guadalupe-Hidalgo – ending the Mexican–American War and redrawing the borders of the Southwest – promised but did not deliver full citizenship rights to the new Mexican Americans on the US side of the border. The 1882 Chinese Exclusion Act halted Chinese immigration and prohibited those already living in the United States from becoming citizens. Native American tribes were subjected to different treaties, some of which granted some voting rights, but for the most part Native Americans were involuntarily treated as wards and excluded from democratic partic-ipation, granted neither sovereignty nor full citizenship rights. Like Black women, these women fought for women's suffrage alongside ethno-racial citizenship rights. This included women such as Jovár Idar, who spoke out against the lynchings used to terrorize the Mexican American community in Texas while also supporting women's suffrage and encouraging women to vote, founding and becoming the first president of La Liga Femenil Mexicanista (The League of Mexican Women) in 1911. Mabel Ping-Hua Lee, a Chinese immigrant from Guangzhou, wrote essays on feminism and women's right to vote. Marie Louise Bottineau Baldwin, a North Dakota Turtle Mountain Chippewa, participated in suffrage events (including the 1913 parade, and as part of the delegation to speak to Woodrow Wilson in 1914) as a part of her lifelong fight for Native American rights.

Race, Gender, and the Political Parties

Electorally, race-gender patterns in party support were still somewhat mixed. The racial alignment of the Democratic and Republican par-ties at the start of the twentieth century was shaped in the post-Civil War era. Whereas (northern) Republicans played a vital role in estab-lishing the formal constitutional rights to racial equality, white elites transformed the South into a one-party racial autocracy and the "Solid South" became the electoral cornerstone of the national Democratic Party. When and where Black men could register to vote, most iden-tified with the Republican Party. In southern states such as Louisiana, Black registration rates went from almost 100 percent right after the Civil War to the single digits, where they would remain until the civil rights movement began.[11]

After the Nineteenth Amendment was passed, women were slow to enter the electorate and did not constitute a distinct or influential voting bloc. While some women continued to work for women's rights and in other movements, the mass movement dissipated. Both parties worked to incorporate (primarily white) women voters, but gender was not a particularly salient dimension of party platforms or identification. There is some evidence to suggest that early women voters favored the Republican Party, but geography also played a role.[12] Women (primarily

---

[11] Luke Keele, William Cubbison, and Ismail White, Suppressing Black Votes: A Historical Case Study of Voting Restrictions in Louisiana, *American Political Science Review* 115(2) (2021): 694–700.

[12] Christina Wolbrecht and Kevin J. Corder, *A Century of Votes for Women* (New York: Cambridge University Press, 2020).

white) were more likely to support Democrats in Democratic-leaning states (the Solid South) and Republicans in Republican-leaning states (the North and West).

The first racial partisan shift occurred in the New Deal Era of the 1930s. The Great Depression and the labor movement made class a particularly salient dimension of partisan politics. Democratic President Franklin D. Roosevelt's economic policies helped create a northern, liberal, labor wing of the Democratic Party. African Americans in the North, many of whom were a part of the working class, started to move to the Democratic Party. Roosevelt's economic policies were also well liked in the poverty-stricken South. While Roosevelt had expressed pro-civil rights ideas, he retained southern support by mostly staying silent on issues of race.

The party positions on gender reflected some of the socioeconomic and ideological divisions that were emerging in feminism. Democrats adopted the positions of working-class socialist feminists, which included women of color, in the labor movement. They advocated for protectionist labor policies aimed at improving the working conditions for women and children employed in factories. These protectionist policies were at odds with the liberal feminist anti-discrimination approach to equal employment rights, a position supported by the Republicans, who were the first to add the Equal Rights Amendment (ERA) to their party platform in 1940. The amendment stated, "Equality of rights under the law shall not be denied or abridged by the United States or by any state on account of sex." The Democrats added this to their platform in 1944. In 1950 and 1953 the ERA was passed – with greater support by Republicans – in the US Senate, with a provision that allowed special protections for women. It was blocked, however, in the US House by (southern) Democrats.

Race-Gendered Mobilizations in the 1960s, 1970s, and 1980s
Race-gendered mobilization in second half of the 1900s would play a pivotal role not only in securing voting rights but also in shaping the modern political parties. While the first major racial partisan shifts began with the New Deal, significant race and gender realignment would occur after the progressive cycle of protest that included the civil rights movement, women's liberation, and gay liberation, as well as the backlash of the Stop the ERA movement and the rise of the religious right.

The Civil Rights Movement and Racial Realignment

After decades of discrimination and oppression, the Black civil rights movement began to mobilize in the 1940s and 1950s, hitting its peak in the 1960s. It addressed a range of issues related to racial injustice, including the ongoing challenges to voting rights. Although rarely in the spotlight, Black women's organizations and women in Black churches were an important part of this mobilizing effort. They helped organize and run voter drives. Later, other women of color would play a similarly vital role in mobilizing their communities in the Chicano, Asian American, and American Indian movements.

Initially, Republicans were the more receptive, albeit sometimes reluctant, supporters of civil rights. President Harry Truman initiated the civil rights agenda in 1948 with an executive order to end discrimination in the military. The Eisenhower administration worked to desegregate the armed forces, the federal bureaucracy, and the schools. They initiated and helped pass the Civil Rights Act of 1957, which included a number of important provisions protecting voting rights, and established the Civil Rights Division of the Justice Department. But the movement was also gaining support from Democrats who now faced a fracturing electoral coalition. Democratic President John F. Kennedy won the presidency with the New Deal/labor coalition of Black and southern white voters. Like Roosevelt, Kennedy initially tried to balance the demands of both but started to develop a proactive civil rights agenda before his death. Even knowing the partisan consequences, his successor Lyndon B. Johnson (a Texan) continued this agenda. It was in his reelection in 1964 that some white southerners cast their first votes for the Republican Party.

The 1960s were turbulent. The civil rights movement had gained momentum, but it faced violent backlash in the South. During the Freedom Summer of 1964, Black women marched alongside men and were not spared the violence. Police often used tear gas and billy clubs on the participants of peaceful marches. One of the most powerful testimonies in Congress for the Voting Rights Act of 1965 came from Fannie Lou Hamer, a key organizer in the Mississippi Freedom Summer. In her testimony, she spoke of the beatings and sexualized abuse she experienced at the hands of Winona police after she was arrested for attending a voter registration workshop.

As the Democratic Party was moving to take more progressive stances on racial equality, the Republican Party started moving in the opposite direction, influenced by a different movement. A white southern segregationist movement seeking to uphold racial hierarchy once again inspired a national backlash. This included white women, who mobilized as mothers against the desegregation of the schools.[13] George Wallace, governor of Alabama and a staunch segregationist, ran against Johnson in the 1964 Democratic primary, with some success not only in the South but also among the white working class in the industrial North. He left the Democratic Party, running as a third-party candidate in the 1968 presidential election. The Republican Party, fearing that Wallace might split the conservative vote and seeing an opportunity in the destabilization of the Democratic electoral coalition, began to pursue a "Southern Strategy" that reversed previous positions supporting racial equality and instead relied on "targeting white southerners who felt alienated from, angry at, and resentful of the policies that granted equality."[14] This included courting both those who held explicitly racist positions and the white southern moderates who might have accepted an abstract notion of equality but objected to federal efforts to achieve it. The party accomplished this through subtle racial coding or "dog whistle" politics. This strategy helped secure a presidential victory for Republican Richard Nixon – once a supporter of civil rights – and charted a new course for the party.

Overlapping but distinct from the Black civil rights movements was the Chicano movement. Inspired by the political activism of African Americans, Mexican Americans began to mobilize to address racial discrimination, voting disenfranchisement, education segregation, and exploitative labor practices. Many of the figureheads of this movement were men, but women played a critical role both behind the scenes and at the forefront, with Dolores Huerta perhaps being the most well-known.

Prior to the Chicano movement, neither party gave much attention to Mexican Americans. Mexican Americans faced voter suppression practices in the Southwest that were similar to those experienced by African Americans in the South. John F. Kennedy was one of the first Democrats to form an outreach program. Carlos McCormick, a campaign worker who was part Irish and part Mexican, encouraged the formation of what would become "Viva Kennedy." The campaign translated press clippings, worked with existing and newly formed advocacy organizations, and started local clubs, including on college campuses.

---

[13] Elizabeth Gillespie McRae, *Mothers of Massive Resistance: White Women and the Politics of White Supremacy* (New York: Oxford University Press, 2018).

[14] Angie Maxwell and Todd Shields, *The Long Southern Strategy: How Chasing White Votes in the South Changed American Politics* (New York: Oxford University Press, 2021).

Many important leaders of the Chicano movement initially started some of their mobilizing work in this campaign. As the movement grew, however, there was a split between those who wanted to continue to work with the Democratic Party and those who had grown disillusioned with it and formed their own party, La Raza Unidas. Chicanas participated in both, and it was during the 1970s and 1980s that some of them started running for office.

The issue of gender equality was a contentious one, and when the feminist movement began mobilizing there was a split between Chicana feminists and the "loyalist" women in the movement. Like other women of color, Chicana feminists often moved between the two movements; however, they experienced discrimination in both spaces. For this reason, they created their own spaces, sometimes in coalition with other women of color.

Feminism and Women's Liberation

Also overlapping, but distinct from a number of progressive movements (i.e., civil rights, labor, and anti-war), was the women's rights movement. It was politically diverse, with multiple wings representing very different understandings and approaches to gender equality. There was a liberal wing, focused on anti-discrimination laws and working within the institutions, and there was the more radical women's liberation wing, focused on a larger societal transformation. Front and center on the liberal policy front were employment discrimination and the ERA. The more radical wing took on abortion and gender violence.

Women at the intersection of multiple marginalities (e.g., gender, race, class, sexuality) mobilized within the feminist movement, but their experiences and needs were not always recognized there, or in the other movements in which they might participate. They often engaged in intersectional organizing that took different forms. This included making intersectional interventions within a given movement: addressing racism within feminist and queer movements, addressing sexism within queer and racial justice movements, and addressing homophobia within feminist and racial justice movements. It also included transversal organizing – moving between movements – as well as creating their own spaces.

Electorally, the shifting coalitions caused by the racial realignment had important implications for women's rights. The movement of white southerners, many of whom held traditional and socially conservative policy preferences, into the Republican Party and the movement of moderate northerners into the Democratic Party started to influence party positions on gender. Women's rights became linked to race in various ways, as feminists sought to add sex to civil rights legislation that Democrats increasingly backed. The Republicans, however, continued to support women's rights until a growing movement of conservative (mostly white) women gave them reason not to.

As with the civil rights movement, the feminist movement inspired a powerful backlash. The STOP ERA ("Stop Taking Our Privileges") campaign was the start of an influential movement of socially conservative women, led by Phyllis Schlafly, that helped justify a change in course for Republicans who had previously been supportive of the amendment. Schlafly argued that the ERA would take away women's gender privileges such as "dependent wife" benefits and alimony, end separate bathrooms, and subject women to the draft. The movement – made up of mostly white, Evangelical women from the middle and upper classes – gained grassroots support and momentum, spreading in the suburbs and rural areas through church organizations and Bible study groups. They drew heavily from conceptualizations of traditional (white) motherhood, casting aspersions on those not falling within its parameters (the unmarried, single moms, gay women, and women of color), whom they conflated with feminists and feminism. Anti-feminism, like (and intertwined with) white backlash, was aimed at preserving a particular way of life, one imbued with intersecting social hierarchies.

Phyllis Schlafly's approach became part of a "Long Southern Strategy," with the GOP adopting the demonization of feminism and working to court (white) women voters on the basis of religion and family values.[15] It was institutionalized into party platforms in the 1980s, as the social conservative wing of the Republican Party grew in strength.[16] After forty years of support, the Republican Party removed the ERA from its platform and started adopting socially conservative platforms that were increasingly hostile to women's rights (and LGBTQ+ rights) and more supportive of traditional gender hierarchies. Although not all Republican women were explicitly antagonistic toward women's rights, they were not supportive of them either.[17] The agnostic laissez-faire approach of those who were both economic conservatives and social moderates posed little opposition to those hostile to feminism.

[15] Ibid.
[16] Christina Wolbrecht, *The Politics of Women's Rights: Parties, Positions, and Change* (Princeton, NJ: Princeton University Press, 2000).
[17] Ronnee Schreiber, *Righting Women: Conservative Women and American Politics* (New York: Oxford University Press, 2008).

Race-Gendered Mobilizations and Contemporary Elections

In the new millennium, the oppositional trajectories of race-gendered mobilization and their impact on electoral and partisan politics has continued. This section looks at the patterns of race-gendered mobilization on the left and on the right, as well as their connection to elections.

Race-Gendered Mobilization on the Left

The largest and most visible (race)gendered mobilization on the left was the 2017 Women's March, held the day after Donald J. Trump was inaugurated for the first time. It broke records as the largest single-day protest in US history.[18] The 2017 Women's March spread not only across the United States but also worldwide. From major metropolitan areas to small rural towns, the streets filled, accented by pink knitted hats, and with signs reflecting messages from an array of social justice movements (e.g., feminist, racial justice, LGBTQ+, immigration, environmental, and labor). What started as a call for a women's march on social media – initially drawing on a mostly white, elite liberal feminist movement – transformed into a broader-based, intersectional march. More than just a women's march, the massive scale of this event was achieved by drawing on an array of existing activist networks as well as mobilizing people (of all ages) to participate in protest activity for the first time.

Part of the success of this mobilization should be attributed to the multiracial team of women community activists who chaired the Washington, DC, march. They were recruited in response to the criticism levied against the initial framing of the event in the viral Facebook invite for the "Million Woman March." Activists from communities of color questioned whether white women had the authority to lead such a movement, given that 53 percent of white women had voted for Trump in 2016. Furthermore, groups questioned the framing of a march around women specifically, given that the Trump administration represented a threat to so many other groups, including queer communities and communities of color.

The new leadership worked to reframe the march in more intersectional terms. Its "unity principles," created with the input of more than twenty leaders from various movements, included traditional feminist commitments such as reproductive rights and gender violence, but

---

[18] Marie Berry and Erica Chenoweth, Who Made the Women's March, in *The Resistance: The Dawn of the Anti-Trump Opposition Movement*, eds. David S. Meyer and Sidney Tarrow (New York: Oxford University Press, 2018), pp. 75–89.

it also included LGBTQ+ rights, workers' rights, civil rights, disability rights, immigrant rights, and environmental justice. The outreach was also intentionally intersectional. It drew on two streams of social justice activism: a more institutional stream that included the larger and more established progressive and feminist organizations, for example NOW, Planned Parenthood, CODEPINK, ACLU, AFL-CIO, and the National Union of Healthcare Workers; and a younger grassroots stream of activism, including online groups and networks, such as Occupy, Black Lives Matter (BLM), immigrant justice, Indigenous rights, and climate action.

This younger grassroots stream is notable for a number of reasons. First, it represents a new and diverse generation of activists, one that reflects the growing racial (and gender/sexual) diversity of the population. These activists bring with them a different model of activism, one that is more decentralized and democratized. This "leaderful" approach allowed for better representation of women, people of color, and LGBTQ+ activists than had previous generations of leftist organizing. Second, it is a group frustrated with party politics. This includes animus toward what is perceived as the moderate tendencies of the Democratic Party. Many of these movements mobilized under the Obama administration, a period of ostensibly more open political opportunities for progressive mobilizing but also one of policy disappointment. The youth-led Dreamers' movement grew out of the 2006 immigration rights protests under George W. Bush but continued mobilization throughout the Obama administration, both to push for the promised policy reform and to protest the increased level of mass deportations. The Occupy Wall Street movement began in 2011 and addressed growing economic inequality and corporate influence in politics. The movement criticized the government strategy of prioritizing the bailout of banks and corporations rather than the distribution of public resources. BLM, addressing police brutality and racially motivated violence against Black people, began on social media in 2013 after the acquittal of George Zimmerman in the shooting death of Black teenager Trayvon Martin. The protests against the Dakota Access Pipeline, and its threat to water sources on and near the Standing Rock Indian Reservation, started in the spring of 2016, raising the intersecting issues of Indigenous and environmental rights. These movements were all critical of Barack Obama and Hillary Clinton, but their participants also understood the increased threat of a Trump administration.

The Women's March tipped off a renewed cycle of protest and provided a coalitional focal point for "The Resistance." The Women's March organization continued to work after January 2017, holding subsequent marches in 2018 and in 2019. Beyond that, much of their work was aimed at participating in and endorsing events organized by the broad array of partners they had amassed in the original march. Many of the movements that predated the Trump administration continued their work, albeit with a renewed sense of urgency and sometimes with a broader array of support as they tapped into the expanding networks of oppositional activists. New mobilizations emerged as well, such as the #MeToo movement addressing sexual violence and harassment and the youth-led March for Our Lives, working for gun reform after a mass school shooting in Florida.

The energy of these mobilizations carried into the 2018 midterm elections, which were unprecedented in a number of ways. Fifty-three percent of eligible voting-age citizens voted, up almost twelve percentage points from 2014 and the highest midterm turnout in four decades.[19] This included increases in turnout among youth (+16%), Asian Americans (+13%), Hispanics (+13%), and African Americans (+11%) and contributed to a record-breaking number of women (127), people of color (116), and LGBTQ+ (ten) members of Congress. Thirteen of the thirty-six non-incumbent women elected to the US House were women of color – all Democrats. Some of the candidates came – if not directly then indirectly – from the contemporary movements. Most notable, perhaps, was the election to the House of "the Squad": Alexandria Ocasio-Cortez, Ayanna Pressley, Rashida Tlaib, and Ilhan Omar. The four Democratic women of color are young, unapologetic progressives who were quick to chastise not only the Trump administration and Republicans but also Democratic leadership. They ran grassroots campaigns and maintained their activist approach while in office, participating in direct action and utilizing social media repertoires of action.

Progressive race-gendered mobilization ramped up in 2020. The United States, like the rest of the world, was dealing with the ravages of the COVID-19 pandemic. The Trump administration was slow and limited in its response, and the health and economic costs were disproportionately felt by communities of color. Most notable, however, were the BLM protests in the summer before the election. The recorded killing of George Floyd by a Minneapolis police officer on May 25, 2020, two months after the death of Breonna Taylor, who was fatally shot in her apartment by Louisville police, inspired another record-breaking mobilization that peaked on June 6, 2020, when nearly half a million people turned out in

---

[19] US Census Bureau, Current Population Survey, Voting and Registration Supplement, www.census.gov/programs-surveys/cps.html

nearly 550 locations across the United States.[20] In the months of protests, it is estimated that anywhere from fifteen to twenty-six million people participated, potentially making this the largest movement in US history. The scale demonstrated a significant shift in the movement and in public perception, which was more favorable to it than in the past.

Voter turnout in 2020 was also record-breaking. Two-thirds of eligible US voters cast ballots. This included increased turnout by Black, Latinx, Asian, and Native American voters in places with long histories of voter suppression. Most notable were Arizona and Georgia, two states that ultimately flipped from red to blue in presidential vote choice. The extraordinary mobilization effort can be attributed to a vast multiracial coalition of local and national organizations, many of whom started their efforts almost a decade earlier. Gendered mobilization, in its expansive and intersectional understanding, was an important component of this. Women of color played a vital role in leading the initiative.

Race-Gendered Mobilization on the (Far) Right

While the Trump administration was perceived as a threat by some, to others it was received as an opening for political opportunities. The mobilization on January 6, 2021, to reject Trump's defeat also had deeper roots. It connected various streams of right and far-right movements, some of which had arisen in resistance to the Obama administration and were legitimized and emboldened under Trump. Like the Women's March, the Save America rally was, in part, initiated by a group of white women, albeit a group with very different politics and coalition partners. Kylie Jane Kremer, the executive director of Women for America First, filed the permit for the event. Her organization was joined by two other right-wing women's organizations, Phyllis Schlafly Eagles and Moms for America. Also a part of the event were two influential right-wing organizations, the Tea Party Patriots (cofounded by Tea Party movement activists Jenny Beth Martin, Amy Kremer, and Mark Meckler) and Turning Point Action (a student-oriented organization led by Charlie Kirk).

One of the most important movements shaping Trump support in 2016 and again in 2020 was the Tea Party. It first mobilized in 2009, after the inauguration of Barack Obama, the first Black US president, who had been elected by a multiracial coalition (with record levels of Black

---

[20]　Larry Buchanan, Quoctrumg Buid, and Jugal K. Patel, Black Lives Matter May Be the Largest Movement in US History, *New York Times*, July 3, 2020, www.nytimes.com/interactive/2020/07/03/us/george-floyd-protests-crowd-size.html

turnout). While the Obama administration was an important target of the Tea Party, so was the Republican Party. They criticized it for its moderation, with frustration aimed at the "compassionate conservativism" espoused by former Republican President George W. Bush. The Tea Party was disproportionately white and often focused on the racially coded framing of issues that had been used in the past. Central among these was a staunch anti-immigration stance with an emphasis on national security. These issues would become the focus of the Freedom Caucus – a group formed by Republicans in Congress in 2015, many of whom were ideologically aligned with the Tea Party movement and were elected in 2012 after successfully challenging moderate Republican incumbents.

Women played an important part in the Tea Party. Whereas the party's rhetoric often served to reify racial and class inequalities, their approach to gender was more complicated. As with earlier iterations of the conservative movement, Tea Party women drew on motherhood and pro-family frames in their activism, arguing big government was harmful to American families and promoted women's dependence on government rather than empowerment.[21] Participation in the movement itself became a form of political empowerment for these women, some of whom took on important leadership roles and even entered the electoral realm as political candidates.[22] Tea Party activists used pro-women and even pro-feminist rhetoric to support their conservative positions, including that of gun rights and restrictive immigration policies. The resonance and power of this type of gendered activism, and the growing importance of the Tea Party, were perhaps best foretold by the nomination of "Mama Grizzly" Sarah Palin as the vice presidential candidate in 2008. Her nomination was seen as a strategic move by Republican presidential nominee John McCain (who had traditionally been considered more of a moderate) to appeal to the far-right contingent, but also as a possible appeal to moderate white women, who had supported Hillary Clinton but were disillusioned by her loss to Obama.

Although Obama ultimately won the election, so did many Tea Party candidates at national and state levels. The Tea Party movement would become the growing right wing of the party and its members – voters and officeholders – the key supporters of the Trump campaign, where the

---

21 Melissa M. Deckman, *Tea Party Women: Mama Grizzlies, Grassroots Leaders, and the Changing Face of America* (New York: New York University Press, 2016).

22 Meghan A. Burke, *Race, Gender, and Class in the Tea Party: What the Movement Reflects about Mainstream Ideologies* (London: Lexington Books, 2015).

racialization became less coded and more blatant. The Trump campaign in 2016 drew heavily from this wing of the party. Throughout his campaign, Trump praised the Tea Party and spoke directly and explicitly to their concerns, particularly in regard to immigration and national security. In the speech announcing his candidacy, he promised to suspend immigration from certain parts of the world. Using right-wing race-gendered strategies, he stated that "Radical Islam is anti-woman, anti-gay and anti-American" and that Mexicans were "bringing drugs, they're bringing crime. They're rapists ..."[23]

The Trump presidency reenergized the various elements of the Tea Party movement, who embraced "Trumpism," mobilizing on the president's behalf and in his defense against the protests of "The Resistance." Furthermore, the president emboldened far-right extremist groups. Throughout his campaign and presidency, Trump signaled his support, circulating their ideas and materials, refusing to disavow them, and even going so far as to remove government resources designated for investing and combating right-wing extremism. A series of well-publicized rallies were held, bringing together self-identified members of white nationalist groups and militias. The first was a night-time rally held in Charlottesville, Virginia, on August 11, 2017, to protest the city's plans to remove a statue of Confederate General Robert E. Lee. The spectacle included protesters, many of them young white men, carrying torches and chanting "Jews will not replace us!" The Unite the Right Rally was held the next day. Participants carried flags and wore clothing with the symbols of the Tea Party, the Confederacy, neo-Nazis, and the KKK. That day, a rally participant deliberately drove his car into a crowd of counterprotesters, killing a young woman and injuring nineteen others. Trump responded initially with statements commenting on the "violence on many sides" and later that there were "very fine people on both sides."[24] It would be one of the many times he signaled his favoring of white supremacist groups. This event, and Trump's response to it, also had electoral implications. Joe Biden pointed to this as the moment he decided to run for president, and racial justice movement advocates sought to hold him accountable to promises that he would "restore the soul of the nation" by addressing the scourge of white supremacy.

[23] Full Text: Donald Trump Announces a Presidential Bid, *Washington Post*, June 16, 2015, https://shorturl.at/d68Es

[24] Ayesha Rascoe, A Year after Charlottesville, Not Much Has Changed for Trump, *NPR*, August 11, 2018, https://bit.ly/4pR7MLZ

As the progressive movements ramped up their protest efforts during the Trump administration, so did the far right, often in the form of emboldened counterprotest. From Georgia to Oregon, violent clashes broke out between BLM protesters and far-right groups, such as the Proud Boys. These protests made it onto the presidential debate stage. When Trump was asked by Fox News correspondent Chris Wallace if he was ready to denounce the violence of the white supremacist and militia groups at these protests, he notably responded, "Proud Boys, stand back and stand by." Right-wing protest was also a major part of the anti-lockdown protests during the pandemic, which included mainstream Republicans, far-right groups, and armed militia members. The FBI arrested thirteen men linked to a militia group for plotting to kidnap Gretchen Whitmer, the governor of Michigan.

SOCIAL MOVEMENTS AND THE 2024 ELECTION

The 2024 election and its aftermath are strong evidence that race-gender mobilization is still a major component of US electoral and partisan politics. The election of Donald J. Trump for a second term was facilitated not only by the race-gendered mobilization of the far-right MAGA movement, but also perhaps by the failure of the Democrats to fully engage race-gendered progressive movements. In the aftermath, the Trump administration has moved quickly to implement an agenda that looks to destroy many of the institutions establishing gender, race, and even class equality. This has prompted a renewed wave of progressive and intersectional mobilizations, seeking to preserve and protect the hard-fought gains established by their predecessors.

In this section, I first discuss the race-gendered dynamics of Donald J. Trump and his MAGA movement. I then discuss the various progressive movements mobilized both before and after the election, highlighting both their race-gendered dynamics and their (sometimes contentious) interactions with the Democratic Party.

Mobilizing MAGA

Race and gender played a prominent role in mobilizing Trump voters in 2016, but they arguably played an even bigger role in 2024. In 2016, Trump capitalized on growing populist discontent in his first election to launch his own brand in the form of MAGA. While progressive organizing helped swing support in the other direction in 2020, the MAGA movement was still growing, gaining political power at the local and state levels. MAGA has been described as an umbrella movement with "continuity, shared identity, diverse claims, networked by an array of groups and organizations" and with "mobilizing structures that stand mostly apart from the Republican Party."[25] Ideologically, the movement includes elements of conservativism, populism, majoritarian nationalism, and authoritarianism and might by groupings. The first and largest is an eclectic grouping that includes churches, gun clubs, local party groups, parental rights groups, antiabortion groups, antivaxxers, homeschool networks, fishing/hunting clubs, and others. The next includes the far-right militias, alt-right organizations, white supremacists, KKK, Christian nationalists, neo-Nazis, and others. The third includes online conspiracy extremist groups, such as QAnon.

The Panel Study of the MAGA Movement, conducted in 2020 and 2021, found it to be "overwhelmingly white, male, Christian, retired, and over sixty-five years of age."[26] Women, however, have played a visible role in the movement, both in office (e.g., Marjorie Taylor Greene and Lauren Boebert) and at the grassroots level. Furthermore, there has been increased outreach to young voters on college campuses and via social media (e.g., TikTok) by groups such as Turning Point USA. Data from the American Electorate Voter Poll, a poll that is designed to capture the intra-group diversity of ethno-groups – with samples large enough to more reliably allow for intersectional analysis – shows that Trump had the most support from younger men across the race-gender groupings of white, Latino, and Black voters (Table 3.1).[27]

While the Republican Party was able to capitalize on the growing strength of MAGA in the 2024 election, MAGA should be understood as distinct from the party. That distinction, however, is becoming harder to make as the movement gains strength within the party, particularly in parts of the country where the electoral risks for opposing Trump have begun to outweigh the advantages. Critics have stated that while not all Republicans (officials or voters) agree with MAGA, there seem to be many who are either willing to tolerate it or unwilling to challenge it.

[25] Hank Johnston, The MAGA Movement's Big Umbrella, *Mobilization: An International Quarterly* 28(4) (2024): 409–33.

[26] Rachel M. Blum and Christopher S. Parker, Panel Study of the MAGA Movement, *University of Washington MAGA Study*, accessed April 2, 2025, https://sites.uw.edu/magastudy/

[27] 2024 American Electorate Voter Poll, African American Research Collaborative and BSP Research, n.d., https://2024electionpoll.us/

Table 3.1 Voter support for Donald Trump in election 2024

Ages	White		Latino		Black	
	Men	**Women**	**Men**	**Women**	**Men**	**Women**
18–39	**63**	45	**48**	32	**28**	11
40–59	63	57	40	30	16	8
60+	57	57	37	38	7	5

Source: Data from the 2024 American Electorate Voter Poll (African American Research Collaborative and BSP Research), November 2024. Cells represent the percent of respondents in each group that reported voting for Donald Trump in the 2024 election.

Prominent in MAGA's discourse has been an increasingly blatant hostility toward racial and gender diversity, often with attacks against "wokeness" or, more recently, "DEI" – diversity, equity, and inclusion. While the nativist sentiments of 2016 reappeared in the 2024 election, with racialized attacks on immigrants and promises of mass deportation, also prominent on the agenda were broad attacks on transgender rights and on DEI in education (in terms of both curriculum and civil rights protection based on gender, race, disability, etc.). In this section, I focus on these two mobilizing issues within the MAGA movement.

Restricting Transgender Rights

Despite prior attempts to restrict transgender rights, some of the first efforts to bear fruit coincided with Trump's first successful run for office. In 2016, both North Carolina and Mississippi passed legislation regulating gender access in public bathrooms. While different laws were passed and were challenged over the next few years, anti-trans legislation began to gain momentum in 2021, when Arkansas passed the "Arkansas Save Adolescents from Experimentation (SAFE) Act," becoming the first state to prohibit gender-affirming care. Although it was later deemed unconstitutional by a federal judge, it helped kick-start a wave of similar legislation.[28] Over the past several years, the amount of anti-trans legislation being proposed has increased exponentially.[29] In 2021, 143 bills were proposed and eighteen passed. In 2024, 674 bills were proposed and fifty passed. The legislation that passed included restrictions on

[28] CQ Quinn, From Criminalization to Erasure: Project 2025 and Anti-trans Legislation in the US, *Crime Media Culture: An International Journal* 21(4) (2025): 529–47.

[29] 2025 Anti-Trans Bill Tracker, Trans Legislation Tracker, n.d., https://translegislation.com

gender-affirming medical care, restroom access, and sports participation for transgender people, as well as restrictions on teaching gender identity in school.

As referenced in Chapter 2, a lot of the mobilization against trans inclusion uses patriarchal framing, including the need to protect women and children, with much of it focused at the local level and/or at school districts. Campaigns regulating gender access in public bathrooms juxtaposed portrayals of transgender people as "sexually predacious, mentally ill, deceitful, and socially disruptive against that of White female fragility."[30] The legislation prohibiting gender-affirming care or teaching about gender identity in the curriculum has focused on protecting children and parents' rights. Anti-trans mobilizations in sports also use this protection framing (the need to protect (cis)girls and women from physical harm). They are combined, however, with co-opted feminist messages on gender equality, emphasizing the "unfair advantages" that trans athletes might have, especially in girls' and women's sports, and the ways in which this might take away opportunities meant for (cis)women and girls.[31] Some (mostly white) female athletes and coaches have joined the mobilizations against trans inclusion. Riley Gaines, a swimmer who competed against Lia Thomas, a transgender swimmer, has been a vocal advocate for restrictions of trans athletes in sports.

While the anti-trans legislation aligns with partisan divides in the legislatures (it is proposed primarily by Republican legislators and has passed primarily in Republican-governed states), public attitudes on transgender rights are more complex.[32] A 2025 Pew Research Center Survey found that while there is still a large partisan gap, public opinion in general has become less supportive of transgender rights and more supportive of restriction (see Table 3.2).[33] A majority of respondents still expressed support for policies aimed at protecting trans people from discrimination in jobs, housing, and public space. A plurality, however, supported requiring trans people to use public bathrooms that match their sex assigned at birth and banning public school districts from teaching about gender identity in elementary school. A majority of respondents

---

[30] Susan Gluck Mezey, Transgender Policymaking: The View from the States, *Publius: The Journal of Federalism* 50(3) (2020): 494–517.

[31] Quinn, From Criminalization to Erasure.

[32] Gary M. Reich and Kristopher J. Long, Could Opposition to Gender-Neutral Language Become a Wedge Issue?, *PS: Political Science & Politics* 58(1) (2025): 37–43.

[33] Americans Have Grown More Supportive of Restrictions for Trans People in Recent Years, *Pew Research Center*, February 26, 2025, https://shorturl.at/4W3ZK

Table 3.2 Public perceptions on transgender rights

	Survey Year	Favor	Oppose	Neither
Protect transgender people	2022	64	**10**	25
from discrimination in job, housing,	2025	56	**16**	27
and public space				
Make it illegal for public school districts	2022	**41**	38	21
to teach about gender identity	2025	**47**	34	19
in elementary schools				
Require trans people to use public	2022	**41**	31	28
bathrooms that match the sex they were	2025	**49**	26	25
assigned at birth				
Make it illegal for health care professionals	2022	**46**	31	22
to provide minors with medical care	2025	**56**	26	17
for gender transition				
Require health insurance companies to	2022	27	**44**	28
cover medical care for gender transitions	2025	22	**53**	25
Require trans athletes to compete on	2022	**58**	17	24
teams that match the sex they were				
assigned at birth	2025	**66**	15	19

Source: Data from Pew Research Center, February 2025. Cells represent the percent of respondents in each group.

supported banning health care professionals from providing gender affirming care for minors and requiring trans athletes to compete on teams that match their sex assigned at birth.

Restricting transgender rights has been a successful mobilizing issue for Republicans in some parts of the country, not only because this appeals to the conservative gender ideologies of right-leaning movements, but also because it is one that some Democrats and left-leaning movements have been more reluctant to defend. As detailed in Chapter 2, this new mobilization strategy was one fully taken up by Trump, who emphasized anti-trans rhetoric across his campaign in speeches, ads, and written platforms. Republicans spent nearly $215 million on anti-trans ads during the 2024 election,[34] with slogans such as "Kamala is for they/them, Trump is for you." In his "Agenda 47," he included as #17 "Keep men out of women's sports."

[34] Rebecca Schneid, What Trump's Win Means for LGBTQ+ Rights, *Time*, November 12, 2024, https://time.com/7174687/what-donald-trump-win-means-for-lgbtq-rights/

Mobilizing against Critical Race Theory, Gender Studies, and DEI

Overlapping but distinct from the focus on restricting transgender rights has been the mobilization against critical race theory, gender ideology, and DEI in education and the workplace. While efforts to challenge anti-discrimination and affirmative action policies have long been on the conservative agenda, the issues have often been taken up by conservative think tanks and lawyers and framed as government overreach or "reverse discrimination." They have slowly chipped away at these civil rights-era policies (and many others) through persistent legal challenges that have become increasingly successful alongside the conservative campaign to transform the judiciary. Trump and MAGA, however, have revitalized more active mobilization that mimics that of early anti-civil rights and anti-women's rights movements, including the grassroots activism of white mothers aimed at school boards. A tipping point may have been Trump's 2020 Executive Order on Combating Race and Sex Stereotyping, in which he calls out ideologies "rooted in the pernicious and false belief that America is an irredeemably racist and sexist country; that some people simply on account of their race or sex, are oppressors; and that racial and sexual identities are more important than our common status as human beings and Americans." It prohibited the use of "divisive concepts" and "scapegoating" related to race and gender. Although Biden repealed the ban, it started a wave of local efforts and activism aimed at school boards to ban the teaching of "critical race theory" and "gender ideologies" in K-12 and in higher education. CRT Forward, an initiative of the Critical Race Program at UCLA Law School, has tracked attempts to ban critical race theory through December 31, 2024, mapping 861 efforts introduced at the local, state, and federal levels. Anti-CRT measures were passed in twenty-nine states.

Since taking office in 2025, Trump has expanded the scope of his attack to more broadly address all DEI efforts in public and private domains. It has become the coded language for going after all policies or practices that have been established to protect any marginalized group.

Progressive Protests and the Polls

While MAGA has come to play a more dominant role with the Republican electoral coalition, and a huge component of MAGA mobilization is the cult of personality about its presidential candidate (among others), the Democrats have a mixed and sometimes more contentious relationship with progressive movements. Some of this tension was evident in the

2024 election. The lack of enthusiasm around incumbent Joe Biden, as well as concerns about his mental fitness after the first presidential debate, led to his withdrawal from the 2024 presidential election. He endorsed Vice President Kamala Harris as his replacement. Her candidacy sparked enthusiasm and mobilization, particularly among some mobilizing networks, but not all progressive movements responded the same. In this section, I look at how Harris's candidacy resonated with different gendered and race-gendered progressive movements.

Win with Black Women and the Intersectional Coalition of Supporters

The night that Harris's presidential candidacy was announced, a number of Black women went to work. In an interview with MSNBC, US Representative Joyce Beatty casually mentioned that she would be getting on a call with 20,000–30,000 Black women.[35] She was referencing the group Win With Black Women, a collective that started in 2020 over frustration with how Black women who were being considered as running mates for Biden were treated. That night, at least 44,000 women joined the meeting. Within three hours, they had raised $1.6 million.

Black women have been among the most consistent mobilizers, both in progressive social justice movements and for the Democratic Party. In 2020, women of color were prominent leaders in mobilizing the Democratic vote in swing states amid significant voter suppression. This included organizations started by Stacey Abrams, Fair Fight (led by Lauren Groh Wargo), and New Georgia Project (led by Nsé Ufot), alongside many others led by Black women, and a few by Latinas (such as the Georgia Latino Alliance for Human Rights, led by Adelina Nichols). This coalition of organizations did what many thought was impossible. Many of these networks were reactivated in 2024, and Harris's candidacy helped reenergize them. They were joined by other networks, such as Win With Black Women, but also Alpha Kappa Alpha – one of the country's oldest Black sororities – of which Vice President Harris was a member. It is 116 years old and has more than 360,000 members across 1,074 chapters.

After the Win With Black Women call, other groups began to follow suit. There were Zoom calls for Black men, Asian-Americans (Harris's

---

[35] Errin Haines and Jennifer Gerson, Four Hours, 44,000 Black Women and One Zoom Call, *19thnews*, July 23, 2024, https://19thnews.org/2024/07/win-with-black-women-zoom-call-harris-organizers/

mother is Indian), Latinas, and even white women. While Kamala Harris's identity opened her up to intersecting forms of discrimination, it also demonstrated the intersectional coalition formation it might inspire. Harris was endorsed by a range Black, Asian American, women's, and immigrant groups.

Reproductive Rights

An important issue mobilizing women for the 2024 election was that of reproductive rights. In June 2022, the US Supreme Court overturned *Roe v. Wade* with its decision in *Dobbs v. Jackson Women's Health Organization*, ending the federal right to abortion. Almost immediately, this impacted women's ability to access reproductive health care. Within a year, abortion was banned in thirteen states. Even before the decision was officially made, but after a draft had been leaked, women took to the streets. On May 14, 2022, tens of thousands of demonstrators participated in hundreds of protests across the country.[36] Protests continued in June, when the decision came out.

The shift from Biden to Harris was a good one for connecting with the reproductive rights movement. Biden, a practicing Catholic, often took a more moderate position on the issue of abortion, although he became more vocal when *Roe v. Wade* was overturned. Vice President Harris has been a more outspoken advocate for abortion rights, going further than Biden in not only critiquing the Supreme Court's overturning of *Roe v. Wade*, but also becoming the first vice president to visit a clinic run by Planned Parenthood.[37] Reproductive rights were a strong theme in Harris's campaign.

Beyond the candidates, however, the 2024 election was an important one for the reproductive rights movement in that abortion showed up on state ballots. Ten states voted on proposed constitutional amendments to protect abortion access. These initiatives passed in Arizona, Colorado, Maryland, Missouri, Montana, Nevada, and New York. They failed in Florida, Nebraska, and South Dakota. Perhaps most notable in this group were the victories in Arizona, Missouri, and Montana, all of which are red states in which Trump won. They joined Ohio, also a red Trump state, which passed a similar ballot measure in 2023.

---

[36] Nicole Acevedo, Nationwide Protests Draw Thousands in Support of Abortion Rights, *NBC News*, May 14, 2022, https://shorturl.at/jRMW4

[37] Mary Kekatos, As Kamala Harris Campaigns for Presidency, Where She Stands on Health Care Issues, *ABC News*, July 22, 2024, https://shorturl.at/P4ger

An important intersectional consideration to make is between the reproductive rights movement and the reproductive justice movement. While the reproductive rights movement in the United States has been more narrowly focused on abortion rights, the reproductive justice movement – founded by women of color – has been more expansive. Its tenets include the right not to have a child; the right to have a child; and the right to parent children in safe and healthy environments. Thus, while voters taking a reproductive rights approach might be more narrowly focused on abortion rights, those in the reproductive justice movement look more broadly to a wide range of intersectional human rights issues, environmental issues, living wages, police and immigration reform, and so forth. It is along some of these issues that Harris received more mixed support.

Racial Justice

Vice President Kamala Harris's identity as a Black woman and a second-generation Indian immigrant provided powerful avenues of connection with many communities of color. This was not, however, enough to garner the loyalty of racial justice movements, where there was mixed support. There, her experience as a former prosecutor and attorney general for California, and her connection with the Biden administration, complicated the picture.

While some Black women went to work campaigning for Harris almost immediately, others were more reluctant. On July 23, 2024, the Black Lives Matter organization (an abolition organization founded by three black women in response to the acquittal of George Zimmerman after he killed Trayvon Martin) called on the Democratic National Committee to host an informal primary prior to the convention, calling into question the democratic process for choosing a replacement for Biden.[38] They later declined to endorse her.

In her campaign, Harris placed strong emphasis on her immigrant roots. Her support of Dreamers and a path to citizenship put her in sharp contrast with Trump's immigrant hardliner approach. United We Dream, the largest youth immigrant rights network, went "all in" to support Kamala with a "Here to Stay" campaign to stop a Trump takeover.[39] In a press release, they framed the endorsement as a strategic decision, a choice to make Kamala their mobilizing target for the next four years.

---

[38] Black Lives Matter Statement on Kamala Harris Securing Enough Delegates to Become Democratic Nominee, *Blacklivesmatter.com*, July 23, 2024, https://shorturl.at/ISWzN

[39] United We Dream Action Is Going All In to Push Kamala Harris to Deliver for Our Generation, *United We Dream Action*, September 9, 2024, https://bit.ly/4phIJ4R

Palestinian American women, and Arab American women more broadly, were also skeptical of Harris. On October 7, 2023, Hamas led an attack on Israel from the Gaza Strip that killed over one thousand people. Israel retaliated quickly. As of January 2025, it is estimated that over 46,000 Palestinians have been killed, 109,000 injured, and close to 1.9 million (90 percent) displaced.[40] The escalated conflict generated a dynamic wave of protest in the United States and beyond. Between October 7, 2023, and June 7, 2024, there were over 12,000 events held in the United States with at least 1.5 million participants.[41] While there was mobilization in different directions, including pro-Israel, the anti-war and/or Palestine solidarity protests were more numerous, serving as an extra-institutional mode of mobilization criticizing the US government's ongoing support of Israel. The protests were particularly prevalent on college campuses, with intersectional coalitions that included anti-racist, queer, and feminist campus groups. Abolition groups, in particular, spoke up in support of Palestine, echoing a long history of solidarity that traces back to the Black Panthers.

While Harris articulated a more compassionate and nuanced position than Trump, she was still perceived as supporting the status quo of providing military support to Israel. The "Uncommitted Movement" encouraged voters to not vote for Harris or Trump. After meeting with Kamala Harris, the co-chair of the "Uncommitted Movement," Layla Elabed, remarked, "I did feel like her sympathy and empathy towards me was very genuine, but Palestinian children cannot eat words. We need action."[42] While some "Uncommitted" voters chose to direct their support to third-party progressive candidates, many of these voters just withheld their support from either candidate. This likely made a difference in key states, such as Michigan and Wisconsin, as well as in the popular vote.[43] For example, in the city of Dearborn, Michigan, Trump won with 42.5 percent of the vote, over Harris's 36 percent. Jill Stein won 18 percent of the vote. In 2020, nearly 70 percent of Dearborn Muslim Americans voted for Biden, while only 36 percent voted for Harris in 2024. While much attention

---

[40] The Israel-Hamas War's Devastating Toll, by the Numbers, *AP News*, January 15, 2025, https://bit.ly/3XGvLBz

[41] Erica Chenoweth, Soha Hammam, Jeremey Pressman, and Jay Ulfelder, Protests in the United States on Palestine and Israel, *Social Movement Studies* (2024): 1–14.

[42] "Uncommitted" Co-Chair Layla Elabed on meeting with Kamala Harris, Pressing VP for Arms Embargo on Israel, Democracy Now, August 9, 2024.

[43] Nura Ahmed Sediqe, "Uncommitted": The Limitations of Election Forecasting on Minorities and the Case of American Muslim Voters, *PS: Political Science & Politics* 58(2) (2025): 280–85.

was focused on the gender gap between Harris and Trump voters, there was also a modest gender gap for Stein voters, who skewed more female than male.

Progressive Organizing after Trump's Inauguration

At the time this chapter is being written, Trump has been in office for almost two months. During that time, he has made a flood of decisions related to the issues discussed in the chapter, and beyond. In addition to oppressive executive orders dismantling transgender rights and civil rights-era protections and ramping up anti-immigration policies and infrastructures, his administration has exceeded its constitutional authority and begun shutting down governmental programs and agencies. Trump has implemented tariffs against and threatened US allies, including Canada. Protests and boycotts have been planned and are growing in size and scope, with a wider array of participants. At the same time, however, Trump has threatened the use of state violence against mobilization he deems "illegal." His administration has begun threatening college campuses where protests have been held and revoking the green cards of movement participants. This may have a chilling effect on progressive organizing. Those in the institutions that provide crucial checks and balances have been slow to react, and in the few cases where they have (particularly in the judiciary), it is not yet apparent if he will comply.

Throughout history, race-gendered mobilization has influenced and been influenced by electoral politics. It has been key to expanding democracy, but it has also challenged it. This will undoubtedly continue in the near future. How and to what extent, however, is an open question. Currently, there are no clear indications of a realignment or the direction that might take. There is, however, much at stake. The future of American democracy – what it might look like, who is allowed to participate, who is granted rights and protections, or if it even exists – hangs in the balance.

4 Black Women and Electoral Politics

Examining Trends and Putting Black Women's Behavior in Context

On election night 2024, a crowd of Vice President Kamala Harris supporters amassed at Harris's election watch party on the grounds of Howard University, her alma mater. Just a few months earlier, amid a presidential candidacy shake-up, incumbent President Joe Biden dropped his reelection bid, and the Democratic Party rallied around Harris to be the party's nominee for president of the United States. Following in the footsteps of Shirley Chisholm, the first Black woman to run for the office from a major political party, Harris made history as the first Black and South Asian woman to receive a major-party nomination.[1] As election night progressed and election returns rolled in, the excited crowd became increasingly anxious as the election returns suggested close race outcomes in battleground states. By the end of the night, that anxiety became disappointment as news outlets called the election in favor of former President Donald Trump. Kamala Harris, the Black and South Asian woman who had risen through the ranks of politics as San Francisco district attorney, California attorney general, US senator, and US vice president, had lost. In her concession speech the next day, Harris is credited with saying, "Sometimes the fight takes a while ... that doesn't mean we won't win."

---

[1] It should be noted that Shirley Chisholm and Kamala Harris are two of the nine Black women who have had ambitions for presidential office. These women include Carol Moseley Braun, who sought the Democratic Party nomination for president in 2004, and others who have run for presidential office as third-party nominees such as Charlene Mitchell (1968), Lenora Fulani (1988 and 1992), Margaret Wright (1976), Isabel Masters, (1992 and 1996), Monica Moorehead (1996 and 2000), and Cynthia McKinney (2008).

Harris's quote aptly describes not only her presidential candidacy story but also the push and pull of progress that has characterized Black women's electoral politics journey more broadly. Elections have traditionally served as a space for race-gendered contention, and this continues today. Despite the promise of the Fifteenth Amendment extending the right to vote to Black people, in reality the franchise was only extended to Black men.[2] This lack of inclusion under the law led Black women to seek coalition with other women to advocate for women's suffrage, but Black women faced marginalization and discrimination within the movement.[3] Even with enfranchisement under the Nineteenth Amendment, Black women still faced a great deal of difficulty in accessing the right to vote because of intimidation and unfair requirements for voter registration, such as poll taxes, grandfather clauses, and literacy tests imposed on all Black people.[4] It was not until the passage of the 1965 Voting Rights Act that Black women were able to fully exercise the right to vote, a product of protest and forms of civil disobedience, during the civil rights movement.[5]

Today, we can see Black women's electoral gains – from access to the vote to now being key decision-makers in some electoral races – but these gains still are accompanied by challenges. Black women have continuously been strong supporters of the Democratic Party,[6] but it was not until more recently that Black women received recognition from party leaders for their electoral support.[7] Further, recognition as a voter does not necessarily translate into support as a candidate. Some Black women candidates have described not feeling supported by the Democratic Party in their attempts to seek office, which may have implications for who is able to make it to the general election stage.[8] While we know the names of

[2] Alexander Keyssar, *The Right to Vote: The Contested History of Democracy in the United States* (New York: Basic Books, 2009).

[3] Cathleen D. Cahill, *Recasting the Vote: How Women of Color Transformed the Suffrage Movement* (Chapel Hill: University of North Carolina Press, 2020).

[4] Manning Marable, *Race, Reform, and Rebellion: The Second Reconstruction and beyond in Black America, 1945–2006* (Jackson: University Press of Mississippi, 2009).

[5] Daniel Q. Gillion, Protest and Congressional Behavior: Assessing Racial and Ethnic Minority Protests in the District, *The Journal of Politics* 74(4) (2012): 950–62.

[6] Christine Slaughter, Chaya Crowder, and Christine Greer, Black Women: Keepers of Democracy, the Democratic Process, and the Democratic Party, *Politics & Gender* 20(1) (2024): 162–81.

[7] Wendy Smooth, Obama, African American Women, and the Limitations of Recognition, in *After Obama: African American Politics in a Post-Obama Era*, eds. Todd Shaw, Joseph McCormick, and Robert Brown (New York: New York University Press, 2020), pp. 149–69; Andra Gillespie and Nadia E. Brown, #BlackGirlMagic Demystified, *Phylon (1960–)* 56(2) (2019): 37–58.

[8] Nadia E. Brown and Danielle C. Lemi, "Life for Me Ain't Been No Crystal Stair": Black Women Candidates and the Democratic Party, *Boston University Law Review* 100 (2020): 1613.

Black women such as Shirley Chisholm and Crystal Bird Fauset, there are many others we do not know because they were not successful in their attempt to attain electoral office, or their contribution to electoral politics was more local and less visible.[9]

In this chapter, I examine the 2024 election cycle with a focus on Black women's political contributions – both as voters and as political actors. I place the 2024 electoral outcomes in the context of the historic moments of progress for Black women, marking both wins and setbacks that suggest Black women's political fight continues. Black women continue to break barriers in electoral office. Kamala Harris represents a historic first among presidential nominees. And Angela Alsobrooks and Lisa Blunt Rochester both became the first Black women to serve as senators for their states as a result of the 2024 election. But there is still more progress to make in Black women's electoral success at the state, local, and national levels. I consider how the location and level of office for which Black women run may have implications for their electoral success.

While the 2024 election cycle revealed that Black women maintained their electoral loyalty to the Democratic Party, with 92 percent of Black women turning out to support Kamala Harris, there is a growing generational divide between older and younger generations of Black women in their perceptions of the importance of showing up on Election Day. Thinking through how Black women, across generations, see themselves in relation to the Democratic Party is especially important given the long-standing support that Black women have shown as reliably Democratic voters. Further, while 92 percent of Black women voters supported Kamala Harris, it is worth considering how the remaining 8 percent voted, especially in the face of a growing number of Black women Republicans running for and serving in electoral positions.

Regardless of whom Black women support in the voting booth, we cannot ignore the economic realities that shape Black women's everyday lives and, by extension, their political outlook. Recent survey evidence suggests that about 50 percent of Black women believe who is in office makes no difference to their financial situation, and affording essential household items was a major concern.[10] Indeed, a growing number of Black women are attaining higher education, but we cannot expect that Black women's educational attainment will

---

[9] Crystal Bird Fauset was the first Black woman to hold state legislative office.

[10] Audrey Kearney, Isabelle Valdes, Ashley Kirzinger, and Liz Hamel, Polling Insight: 4 Takeaways about Black Women Voters in the 2024 Election, *Kaiser Family Foundation*, October 11, 2024, https://shorturl.at/GugdM

predict their earning power.[11] Previous research has long pointed out that the usual indicators associated with political participation – education and income – are not strong predictors for Black women's political participation.[12] Black women continue to be materially disadvantaged, yet they persist and continue to engage in electoral politics. I question whether this will always be the case, especially given Black women's concerns about the state of democracy after the 2024 election.[13]

Altogether, this chapter seeks to bring into perspective what we know about Black women's engagement with electoral politics from the extant literature and how it matters for Black women's electoral outcomes in 2024. What becomes clear from the evidence presented in this chapter is that Black women's fight today for political rights, recognition, and access to political power is part and parcel of a more prolonged struggle for Black women in the American political system. While times have changed, some of the same questions remain about Black women's relationship to the political party structure and if being one of the few, or the first, Black women in electoral office is progress enough to make change. What is new is the question of whether some of the more recent challenges to democracy will inspire Black women to stand on the front lines or cause them to stay at home.

BLACK WOMEN'S REPRESENTATION STORY

Representational Change from 2000 to 2024

Over the last twenty-four years, the number of Black women elected to legislative office has more than doubled. As noted in Figure 4.1, between 2000 and 2024, Black women went from representing just over 2 percent of officeholders in Congress and state legislatures, respectively, to now representing over 5 percent of legislative officials at the state and federal levels. The fact that Black women's numbers in political office are increasing is meaningful because of the psychological benefits that descriptive representation can have for constituents and because of the work that

---

[11] Jessica Lynn Stewart and Jamil S. Scott, Are We All Alright? The Influence of Socioeconomic Status on Black Women's Political Beliefs and Policy Preferences by Region, *Journal of Race, Ethnicity, and Politics* 9(3) (2024): 571–99.

[12] Emily M. Farris and Mirya R. Holman, Social Capital and Solving the Puzzle of Black Women's Political Participation, *Politics, Groups, and Identities* 2(3) (2014): 331–49; Sandra Baxter and Marjorie Lansing, *Women and Politics: The Invisible Majority* (Ann Arbor: University of Michigan Press, 1980).

[13] Black Women's Roundtable and Essence, Power of the Sister Vote 2024 (National Coalition on Black Civic Participation, February 2024).

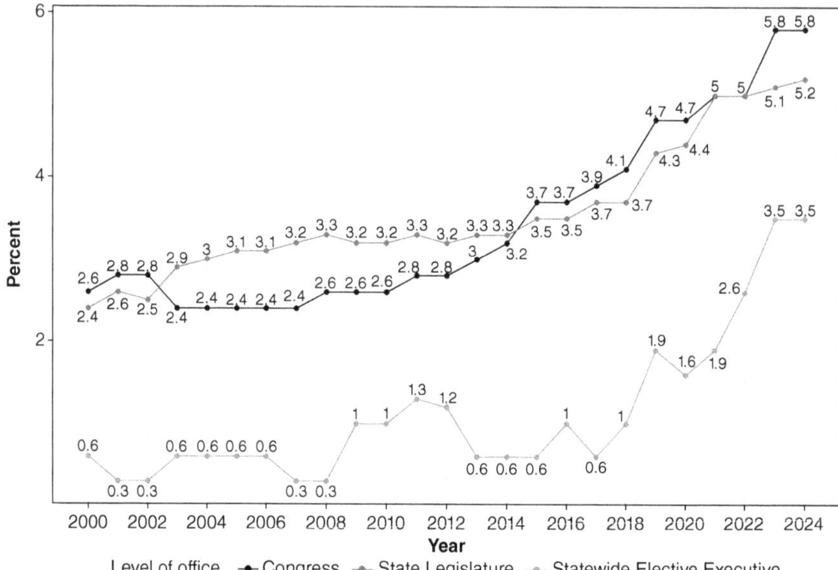

Figure 4.1 Black women's presence in elected office, 2000–24.
Note: This line graph captures the percent of Black women officeholders of all officeholders from 2000 to 2024. The count of members of Congress includes delegates, such as long-standing District of Columbia delegate Eleanor Holmes Norton.
Source: Center for American Women and Politics Women Elected Officials Database.

Black women do when they serve in office.[14] In particular, Black women are more likely to sponsor bills that speak to the interests of women and people of color across levels of office.[15] Regardless of the challenges they may face in legislative institutions, Black women officeholders are mission-driven to make policy changes. This is reflected in their reasonings for seeking political office as well. Scholars have shown how Black women's motivation for running comes from a desire to serve their communities.[16]

[14] Lawrence Bobo and Franklin D. Gilliam Jr., Race, Sociopolitical Participation, and Black Empowerment, *American Political Science Review* 84(2) (1990): 377–93.

[15] Michael D. Minta and Nadia E. Brown, Intersecting Interests: Gender, Race, and Congressional Attention to Women's Issues, *Du Bois Review: Social Science Research on Race* 11(2) (2014): 253–72; Beth Reingold, Kerry L. Haynie, and Kirsten Widner, *Race, Gender, and Political Representation: Toward a More Intersectional Approach* (New York: Oxford University Press, 2020).

[16] Pearl K. Ford Dowe, *The Radical Imagination of Black Women: Ambition, Politics, and Power* (New York: Oxford University Press, 2023); Mirya R. Holman and Monica C. Schneider, Gender, Race, and Political Ambition: How Intersectionality and Frames Influence Interest in Political Office, *Politics, Groups, and Identities* 6(2) (2018): 264–80.

The year 2000 marks sixty-one years since the first Black woman, Crystal Bird Fauset, was elected to state legislative office in Pennsylvania in 1939. By the end of 2000, 179 Black women were serving in state legislatures (2.4% of all officeholders). By 2024, the number of Black women in political office had more than doubled to 386 (5.2% of all officeholders). Thirty years after the election of the first Black woman to a state legislative seat, Shirley Chisholm became the first Black woman in Congress. She represented New York in the US House of Representatives. It was not until 1993 that the first Black woman – Carol Moseley Braun – was sworn into the US Senate. In Congress, just as with state legislative officeholders, the number of Black women officeholders more than doubled from fourteen in 2000 (2.6% of all members of Congress) to thirty-one in 2024 (5.8% of all members of Congress). The vast majority of these women have identified as Democrats. That many Black women elected officials identify as Democrats is not surprising given Black women's long-standing ties to the Democratic Party. In fact, Mia Love was the first and only Black woman Republican to serve in Congress, from 2015 to 2019.

While our first Black women officeholders in state and congressional office were elected from cities in the northeast, many Black women officeholders have hailed from southern states. For instance, scholars studying Black women officeholders have selected states such as Georgia, Mississippi, and Maryland as sites for investigation because of the number of Black women elected officials – particularly at the state level – in those states.[17] Arguably, the success of the Voting Rights Act of 1965 is not just in allowing Black voters access to the franchise, but also in allowing Black voters to select their preferred representatives. Under the Voting Rights Act, states, many in the south, were monitored and/or subject to pre-clearance requirements to ensure legislative districts were structured in such a way that would still protect minority voter rights.[18] One of the outcomes of this effort to protect minority voter rights is the

17 Nadia E. Brown, *Sisters in the Statehouse: Black Women and Legislative Decision Making* (New York: Oxford University Press, 2014); Byron D'Andrá Orey, Wendy Smooth, Kimberly S. Adams, and Kisha Harris-Clark, Race and Gender Matter: Refining Models of Legislative Policy Making in State Legislatures, *Journal of Women, Politics, & Policy* 28(3–4) (2013): 97–119.

18 Pei-te Lien, Dianne M. Pinderhughes, Carol Hardy-Fanta, and Christine M. Sierra, The Voting Rights Act and the Election of Nonwhite Officials, *PS: Political Science & Politics* 40(3) (2007): 489–94.

legal recognition of majority-minority districts. Scholars point to the creation of majority-minority districts as a major factor in the election of Black representatives.[19] Black voters, particularly Black women voters, tend to support Black women candidates when they run for office.[20] In 2024, for example, LaMonica McIver won a US House contest in a majority-minority district to become the second Black woman elected to Congress from New Jersey.

That Black women tend to be elected in majority-minority districts is in part due to the support that voters offer and the strategic choice that many of these candidates make to run in these districts.[21] One reason that Black women might make this strategic choice is the history of negative stereotypes applied to Black women – both in society at large and in politics.[22] One of the most negative stereotypes about Black women in American politics is the welfare queen, a Black mother who takes advantage of government resources. This stereotype is both a source of shame for Black women and a stereotype continually used against the group.[23] Though voters perceive Black women elites as distinct from Black women without elite status,[24] they can still be disadvantaged when running for office depending on their opponent. Black women elites are perceived as more liberal than their male counterparts, even Black men, which may deter more conservative votes.[25] Further, some Black women, particularly darker-skinned Black women, are perceived as unlikely to be electorally successful, especially in comparison with white opponents.[26] This may be why some Black women candidates consider their best electoral chance to be in majority-minority districts.

---

[19] Charles Cameron, David Epstein, and Sharyn O'Halloran, Do Majority-Minority Districts Maximize Substantive Black Representation in Congress?, *American Political Science Review* 90(4) (1996): 794–812.

[20] Tasha S. Philpot and Hanes Walton Jr., One of Our Own: Black Female Candidates and the Voters Who Support Them, *American Journal of Political Science* 51(1) (2007): 49–62.

[21] Paru Shah, It Takes a Black Candidate: A Supply-Side Theory of Minority Representation, *Political Research Quarterly* 67(2) (2014): 266–79.

[22] Julia S. Jordan-Zachery, *Black Women, Cultural Images and Social Policy* (New York: Routledge, 2009).

[23] Melissa V. Harris-Perry, *Sister Citizen: Shame, Stereotypes, and Black Women in America* (New Haven, CT: Yale University Press, 2011).

[24] Monica C. Schneider and Angela L. Bos, An Exploration of the Content of Stereotypes of Black Politicians, *Political Psychology* 32(2) (2011): 205–33.

[25] Jessica Carew, How Do You See Me? Stereotyping of Black Women and How It Affects Them in an Electoral Context, in *Distinct Identities: Minority Women in US Politics*, eds. Nadia E. Brown and Sarah Allen Gershon (New York: Routledge, 2016).

[26] Ibid.

However, Black representatives can be electorally successful in non-majority-minority districts as well.[27] The first Black woman elected to Congress from New Jersey – Bonnie Watson Coleman – was elected in a majority-white district in 2014. In fact, the number of Black women in the US House from majority-white districts has increased over time. In 2025, ten of twenty-seven Black women voting members of the House represent majority-white districts, and seventeen represent majority-minority districts.[28]

Though it remains the case that no Black woman has ever been elected governor, the percentage of Black women in the ranks of statewide elective executives has increased as well. Just two Black women served in statewide elective executive offices at the end of 2000, and by 2024, Black women accounted for eleven of 100 (11%) of all women statewide elective executives. As of 2025 twenty-five Black women have served in statewide elective offices, with eight serving as lieutenant governor (32%) and five serving as attorney general (20%). Interestingly, these two positions fall outside the traditionally feminine state executive positions in which women are thought to have an advantage.[29] Some scholars point to the selection of a diverse candidate for the lieutenant governor position as a strategic choice to appeal to voters for both Democrats and Republicans.[30] Indeed, the partisan identification of Black women state executives has been more diverse (20% have been Republican) than in legislative offices, and some of these Black Republican women – such as Lieutenant Governor Jennifer Carroll of Florida and Lieutenant Governor Winsome Sears of Virginia – have been the first Black women of either party to hold their positions.

Notably, Kamala Harris became the first Black and South Asian woman to serve as US vice president in 2021. While Joe Biden, the 2020 Democratic presidential nominee, had already committed to selecting a woman as a vice presidential running mate,[31] Harris's selection as vice

---

[27]   Christian R. Grose, *Congress in Black and White: Race and Representation in Washington and at Home* (New York: Cambridge University Press, 2011).

[28]   I note that this number of officeholders does not include delegates to the House of Representatives.

[29]   Richard L. Fox and Zoe M. Oxley, Gender Stereotyping in State Executive Elections: Candidate Selection and Success, *The Journal of Politics* 65(3) (2003): 833–50.

[30]   Richard L. Fox and Zoe M. Oxley, Does Running with a Woman Help? Evidence from US Gubernatorial Elections, *Politics & Gender* 1(4) (2005): 525–46.

[31]   Kate Sullivan, Biden Says He Will Pick Woman to Be His Vice President, *CNN*, March 15, 2020, https://cnn.com/2020/03/15/politics/joe-biden-woman-vice-president/index.html

president was largely due to the advocacy of Black women leaders and activists.[32] Those leaders and activists emphasized the importance of Black women as a voting bloc in the Democratic Party and pressured Joe Biden to select a Black woman running mate. Despite Biden and Harris being rivals in the Democratic primary, Biden publicly named Harris his running mate in August 2020. Arguably, Harris's vice presidency paved the way for her successful nomination as the Democratic Party's presidential nominee in 2024.

2024 Elections

Black women marked many electoral milestones in 2024, some of which resulted in new firsts for Black women in various elective offices. That Vice President Kamala Harris secured the Democratic Party nomination for president was a historic moment that followed in the path of Black women who came before her, such as Carol Moseley Braun and Shirley Chisholm, who both sought the Democratic Party's nomination but were unsuccessful. As the first Black and South Asian woman to receive the Democratic Party nomination for president, Harris could have been the first woman and the first woman of color to be president. Despite receiving majority electoral support from communities of color, Vice President Harris lost both the popular vote and the Electoral College vote. Just as in 2020, the majority of white voters supported former President Trump's election bid. As Kelly Dittmar notes in Chapter 1 of this volume, the presidency remains a gendered and raced institution that privileges whiteness and masculinity – the axis of race and gender that Kamala Harris is not part of – which disadvantaged Harris as a candidate.

While Vice President Kamala Harris's election bid was not successful, there were notable victories for Black women at the national level. Namely, Angela Alsobrooks (D-MD) and Lisa Blunt Rochester (D-DE) became the first Black women elected to the US Senate in their respective states; Rochester is also the first woman senator from Delaware. Their victory also means that two Black women serve in the US Senate simultaneously for the first time in history; before them, just three Black women served in the Senate and none simultaneously. With Janelle Bynum's victory against the incumbent in Oregon's 5th Congressional District in 2024, she became the first Black woman to be elected to Congress from Oregon. Bynum joins the list of Black women who have upended the

---

[32] Asma Khalid, Pressure Grows on Joe Biden to Pick a Black Woman as His Running Mate, *NPR*, June 12, 2020, https://shorturl.at/coSm5

norm of the incumbency advantage to go on to serve in congressional office in earlier elections, such as Ayanna Pressley of Massachusetts and Cori Bush of Missouri.[33] Further, the list of reelected Black women incumbents includes the likes of Nikema Williams (GA-5), Lauren Underwood (IL-14), Ayanna Pressley (MA-7), Summer Lee (PA-12), and Jasmine Crockett (TX-30), all Black women members of Congress making a name for themselves in the Democratic Party.

These wins for Black women in Congress, however, were paired with departures of Black women incumbents due to retirement, running for other offices, or electoral defeat to yield overall stasis in Black women's congressional representation from 2024 to 2025. While the number of Black women in the Senate doubled from 2024 to 2025, the number of Black women in the US House dropped by one from Election Day to the start of the 119th Congress (2025–27). In addition to Lisa Blunt Rochester's move from the House to the Senate, incumbent Representative Cori Bush (D-MO) was defeated in a competitive Democratic primary, and longtime Representative Barbara Lee (D-CA) was defeated in her bid for the US Senate in California.

When it comes to statewide elected executive positions, there were fewer elections for these positions in 2024, but these elections did lead to some notable changes for Black women elites. Namely, the number of Black women in statewide elective executive positions decreased by one (from eleven to ten) from 2024 to 2025 due to the defeat of incumbent Auditor Jessica Holmes (D-NC). Further, none of the nonincumbent Black women who ran for statewide elective executive positions were successful. An important exception to the story of statewide election losses for Black women is Black women's gains in elected state judicial positions.[34] While the representation of Black women in judicial office has not been tracked in the same ways as legislative and executive offices, these positions represent another important site for political power.

---

[33] The incumbency advantage is described as the name recognition with voters and greater ability to fundraise for elections that current officeholders have when seeking reelection.

[34] It should be noted that not all states have elected judicial positions. The states that do not have judicial elections include Delaware, Hawaii, Massachusetts, New Hampshire, New Jersey, Rhode Island, and Virginia. For states that do have judicial elections, there is variation in how judges are elected. In particular, there are three main election methods: partisan elections (judicial candidates are listed on the ballot with their party affiliation), nonpartisan elections (judicial candidates are listed on the ballot without their party affiliation), and retention elections (judicial candidates run without opposition and the public votes on whether a judge remains on the court).

One example of these state-level elected judicial gains is Pamela Goodwin. Pamela Goodwin became the first Black woman to be elected to Kentucky's state supreme court. She holds the record as the fifth person to have served at every level of the judiciary in the state and the record for being the first Black woman to serve in each position. Goodwin's victory is notable because existing work on Black women in judicial office notes the challenges Black women face in reaching the bench,[35] and how their authority is challenged in their positions.[36] Further, her victory is reminiscent of the growing trend of Black women running for and serving in judicial and prosecutorial offices. Of the states with state supreme court elections, about 42 percent have Black women represented on the state supreme court.[37] Like Pamela Goodwin, 33 percent of these Black women on state supreme courts are the first to hold their elected position.[38]

A story of electoral gains and losses for Black women is also evident in state and local elections. From 2024 to 2025, the number of Black women in state legislative office increased from 386 to 399. These gains are in part due to the 13.8 percent of Black women officeholders who are newly elected – in both lower and upper chambers of state legislatures. Further, about 2 percent of Black women officeholders moved from the lower chamber to the upper chamber – an example of progressive ambition (officeholders seeking higher office).[39] However, the gains in state legislatures were not reflected in local-level offices, at least in the 100 most populated cities. After the 2024 election cycle, eight of the thirty-six women mayors in the 100 most populated cities were Black women. This number represents a decrease from the nine in office before the election. London Breed, the former mayor of San Francisco, lost her mayoral reelection bid.

Altogether, 2024 was marked by Black women achieving historic milestones – the first or the few to be in their positions. Indeed, Black women's representation in office continues to grow, as demonstrated in Figure 4.1. However, the story of electoral wins is also accompanied by

---

[35] Taneisha N. Means et al., The Phenomenon of Autocannibalism and Black Women Judges' On-the-Bench Experiences, in *Distinct Identities*, eds. Nadia E. Brown and Sarah Allen Gershon (New York: Routledge, 2023), pp. 244–63.

[36] Taneisha N. Means, Her Honor: Black Women Judges' Experiences with Disrespect and Recusal Requests in the American Judiciary, *Journal of Women, Politics & Policy* 43(3) (2022): 310–27

[37] Alliance for Justice, The Faces of Justice Report series, https://afj.org/the-faces-of-justice-report/

[38] Ibid.

[39] Karen Shafer, *Political Ambition*, Oxford Bibliographies (New York: Oxford University Press, 2018).

electoral losses and some retirements. As of April 2025, Black women hold about 5.8 percent of all congressional seats (including nonvoting members), 3.2 percent of all statewide elected offices, 5.4 percent of all state legislative seats, and 7 percent of major-city mayoral offices. While the percentage of Black women in state legislative office represents a steady growth in the number of Black women holding these seats, the percentage of Black women as members of Congress remains unchanged from the previous year. This suggests that Black women's electoral wins in state legislative and congressional offices have served to maintain the status quo. Further, Black women comprise 7.8 percent of the US population, which suggests that Black women's representation has not reached parity with their presence in the population, but the group is getting closer.

BLACK WOMEN VOTERS AND HISTORICAL TRENDS

Black women have an important presence in elected office, and their presence as a voting bloc is no less meaningful. As seen in Figure 4.2, over 80 percent of Black women have supported Democratic presidential nominees since 1992.[40] However, Black women's support, and Black people's support for Democratic Party candidates more generally, was not always so strong. In the early 1900s, the group was considering the utility of aligning with the Democratic Party.

After the Civil War and the passage of the Fifteenth Amendment in 1870, which prohibited the denial of voting rights based on race or previous enslavement, Black people primarily identified with the Republican Party. This was mainly because the Republican Party was most sympathetic to the issues important to Black people from Reconstruction into the late 1920s.[41] However, in the 1930s, Black women involved in community groups and national organizations in northern cities started to consider the Democratic Party as a political option because the Republican Party was unwilling to attend to the group's economic concerns and policy demands for civil rights and anti-lynching legislation.[42]

---

[40] Center for American Women and Politics (CAWP), Gender Gap: Voting Choices in Presidential Elections, Eagleton Institute of Politics, Rutgers University, 2025, https://cawp.rutgers.edu/data/voters/gender-gaps-vote-choice-and-party-identification

[41] Nancy Joan Weiss, *Farewell to the Party of Lincoln: Black Politics in the Age of FDR* (Princeton, NJ: Princeton University Press, 1983).

[42] Lisa G. Materson, *For the Freedom of Her Race: Black Women and Electoral Politics in Illinois, 1877–1932* (Chapel Hill: University of North Carolina Press, 2009); Deborah Gray White, *Too Heavy a Load: Black Women in Defense of Themselves 1894–1994* (New York: W. W. Norton & Company, 1999).

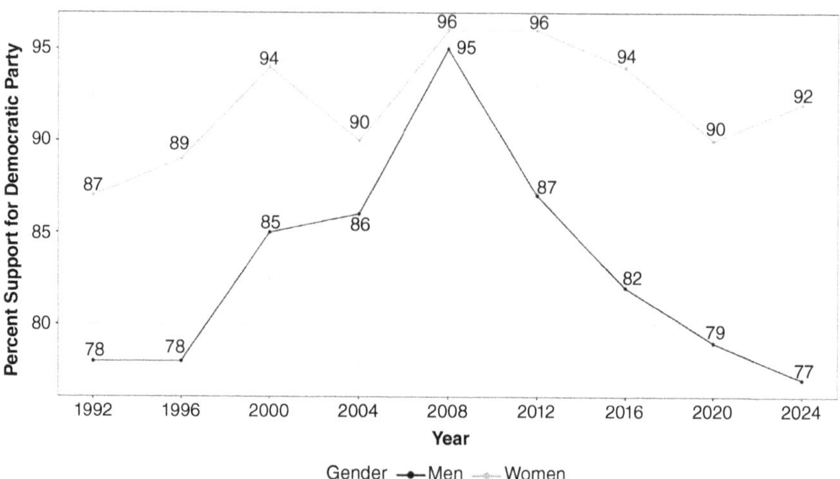

Figure 4.2 Gender gap in Democratic Party support among Black voters.
Note: This line graph captures the percent of support for a Democratic Party presidential nominee among Black men and Black women respectively from 1992 to 2024.
Sources: Voter News Service, 1992, 1996, 2000; Edison Media Research and Mitofsky International, 2004, 2008; Edison Research 2012, 2016, 2020, and 2024.

Despite their dissatisfaction, Black women had room to consider which party might best serve their interests. The promises of economic benefit from Franklin D. Roosevelt's (FDR) New Deal plan and his attempts to incorporate Black thought leaders as unofficial advisors led Black voters to show national electoral support for the Democratic Party, with FDR as the presidential nominee in 1936, 1940, and 1944.[43] However, this did not mean that Black women, and Black people more generally, considered themselves Democrats. It was not until 1948, when Harry Truman was the Democratic Party's nominee and garnered 77 percent of the Black vote, that a majority of Black people would consider themselves Democrats.[44] Still, Black voters did support Republican Party nominees until the 1964 election.[45]

The years 1963 and 1964 were important ones for the civil rights movement as the protests and demonstrations organized by the likes of

---

[43] Roosevelt called his unofficial advisory committee of Black thought leaders the "Black Cabinet." The Black cabinet included notable community leaders, scholars, and activists. Mary McCleod Bethune was one of the most well-known and the only woman included on the committee.

[44] David A. Bositis, *Blacks and the 2004 Democratic National Convention* (Washington, DC: Joint Center for Political and Economic Studies, 2004).

[45] Ibid.

the Southern Christian Leadership Council, the National Association of Colored People, and the Student Nonviolent Coordinating Committee had an impact on John F. Kennedy and led him to propose that Congress consider a comprehensive Civil Rights Bill. Though often not recognized, Black women such as Ella Baker were important behind-the-scenes organizers of the protests and demonstrations that caught Kennedy's attention.[46] Despite Kennedy's assassination, Lyndon Johnson took up the mantle of advocating for the bill and ultimately signed the bill into law in July 1964 after Congress passed it.

In the 1964 election cycle, the Republican Party took a stance against civil rights by nominating Barry Goldwater as the Republican nominee. Goldwater was against civil rights reform and social welfare programs.[47] In fact, the fourteen Black delegates present at the 1964 Republican convention planned a walkout to oppose Goldwater's nomination but received little attention.[48] While the Republican Party nominated Goldwater, the Democratic Party nominated Lyndon Johnson, the same man who supported the Civil Rights Act of 1964 and signed it into law. In the general election, Johnson got 94 percent of Black voters' electoral support, signaling the importance of the Democratic Party's recognition of civil rights for Black voters.[49]

Since the 1968 election, Black people have been consistent supporters of the Democratic Party, but over time, Black women have shown more support than their Black male counterparts.[50] In fact, the gender gap between Black men and Black women has persisted for over thirty years.[51] This is evidenced in Figure 4.2, in which there is a gap of up to five (or more) points between Black men and Black women in their support for Democratic Party presidential nominees. The only year in which this gap was substantially diminished was 2008, the year that Barack Obama was nominated as the first Black Democratic presidential nominee. Notably, the gender gap in support was most pronounced in 2024, when Kamala Harris was nominated as the first Black and South Asian woman nominee.

---

[46] Bettye Collier-Thomas and V. P. Franklin, *Sisters in the Struggle: African American Women in the Civil Rights-Black Power Movement* (New York: NYU Press, 2001).

[47] Edward G. Carmines and James A. Stimson, *Issue Evolution: Race and the Transformation of American Politics* (Princeton, NJ: Princeton University Press, 1989).

[48] Hanes Walton Jr. and C. Vernon Gray, Black Politics at the National Republican and Democratic Conventions, 1868–1972, *Phylon (1960–)*, 36(3) (1975): 269–78.

[49] Bositis, *Blacks and the 2004 Democratic National Convention*.

[50] Carmines and Stimson, *Issue Evolution*.

[51] Ruth Igielnik, Men and Women in the US Continue to Differ in Voter Turnout Rate, Party Identification, *Pew Research Center*, August 18, 2020, https://shorturl.at/vhdFe

Shared race, gender, and a combination of the two are essential indicators for Black women in their beliefs about and support for political candidates.[52] In the case of Barack Obama and Kamala Harris, respectively, shared identity provided important cues for Black women about what they might expect from these officeholders and guided their vote choice. Interestingly, the same story does not hold for Black men. Black men showed strong support for Barack Obama in 2008, but their support was not as strong in 2012 and was even lower in 2024 for Kamala Harris.

This difference in gendered support for Kamala Harris does not mean that all women were supporters of Kamala Harris or of the Democratic Party more generally during the 2024 election cycle. While the gender gap might be aptly described as both Black and Brown, as Latinas tend to show stronger support for Democratic Party nominees than their Latino counterparts (see Chapter 5 in this volume), there is a long-running trend of white women lending majority support to Republican Party presidential nominees.[53] Still, it should be noted that Black women were the most reliable base for the Democratic Party – showing greater electoral support than any other group of women as well as their Black male counterparts in 2024. Specifically, 92 percent of Black women supported Kamala Harris's electoral bid for president compared with 58 percent of Latinas, 46 percent of white women, and 77 percent of Black men, according to the Edison Research exit poll. That Black women showed such strong support for Harris is just more evidence that Black women tend to support their own when Black women run for office.[54] Whereas the Republican Party made gains among Black and Latino men voters, the same cannot be said for Black women.

In recognition of how Black women have shown up for the party, former Democratic National Committee Chairman Tom Perez once called Black women the "backbone" of the Democratic Party and noted that "we can't take that for granted. Period."[55] Indeed, across a range of issues, Black women rate the Democratic Party as being able to better deal with the issues they care about than the Republican Party. Indeed, as Paul

[52] Christina Bejarano, Nadia E. Brown, Sarah Allen Gershon, and Celeste Montoya, Shared Identities: Intersectionality, Linked Fate, and Perceptions of Political Candidates, *Political Research Quarterly* 74(4) (2021): 970–85.

[53] Jane Junn and Natalie Masuoka, The Gender Gap Is a Race Gap: Women Voters in US Presidential Elections, *Perspectives on Politics* 18(4) (2020): 1135–45.

[54] Philpot and Walton, One of Our Own.

[55] Rebecca Savransky, DNC Chair: Black Women are the "Backbone" of the Democratic Party, *The Hill*, December 13, 2017, https://shorturl.at/mgqer

Frymer explains, Black women are a captured group.[56] Here, Frymer is referring to the idea that most Black women do not see themselves as being able to switch their party allegiance from the Democratic Party to the Republican Party. Unlike Black women in the 1930s and up through the 1960s, who felt they could consider political candidates who were Republicans or Democrats, this is not the case today. There are much greater differences between Democrats and Republicans in their political beliefs and their ability to get along today,[57] and some of these differences come down to issues of civil rights and social welfare spending – issues on which Black women voters, in particular, tend to favor the Democratic Party's stance.

At this moment in time, it is difficult for anyone who identifies with either the Democratic or the Republican Party to see the opposing party as a viable voting option. However, for Black women, this issue is more prominent because there can often be influence from Black women and men in their community to support Democratic candidates and issue positions.[58] To be clear, one's family and friends can be important influences on political beliefs and attitudes regardless of race-gender identity.[59] However, because the majority of Black women do identify as Democrats, for the minority of Black women who do not, it can be uncomfortable to exist in Black social spaces such as churches and social organizations where Democratic Party issue positions might be assumed.

Yet there are some Black women who do support the Republican Party. Though the percentage of Black women voting for Donald Trump decreased from 9 percent in 2020 to 7 percent in 2024, about 10 percent of Black women identify as Republicans today.[60] Scholars point to factors such as socialization and occupation to account for this, since Black women with immigrant backgrounds and/or military service are more likely to vote Republican.[61] Notable examples in the public sphere are Winsome Sears, the lieutenant governor of Virginia, who identifies as

---

[56] Paul Frymer, *Uneasy Alliances: Race and Party Competition in America* (Princeton, NJ: Princeton University Press, 2011).

[57] Lilliana Mason, Julie Wronski, and John V. Kane, Activating Animus: The Uniquely Social Roots of Trump Support, *American Political Science Review* 115(4) (2021): 1508–16.

[58] Ismail K. White and Chryl N. Laird, *Steadfast Democrats: How Social Forces Shape Black Political Behavior* (Princeton, NJ: Princeton University Press, 2020).

[59] Betsy Sinclair, *The Social Citizen: Peer Networks and Political Behavior* (Chicago, IL and London: University of Chicago Press, 2012).

[60] Carroll Doherty, Jocelyn Kiley, and Nida Asheer, Changing Partisan Coalitions in a Politically Divided Nation, *Pew Research Center*, April 2024, https://shorturl.at/X5VwH

[61] Tasha S. Philpot, *Conservative but Not Republican: The Paradox of Party Identification and Ideology Among African Americans* (New York: Cambridge University Press, 2017).

Caribbean American, and the former lieutenant governor of Kentucky, Jenean Hampton, who served in the military.

For Trump support in particular, survey data suggests that Black women Trump supporters tend to skew younger and cite immigration as one of the most important issues to them.[62] This level of focus on immigration could reflect a concern that immigrants will challenge or limit access to resources and opportunities for people born in the United States.[63] The majority of Black people in the United States do not hold negative immigration attitudes. However, Black people are aware of how immigrants are placed in a position to be in economic competition with the group because of the American racial hierarchy and the continuing impact of white supremacy.[64] Indeed, President Trump used the narrative of Black people being left behind or left out because of immigration during his 2024 presidential campaign. This may have appealed to the Black women who voted for him.

Growing Generational Divides

The conversation about age is a critical part of the 2024 electoral landscape. The media primarily discussed the age of candidates, such as the fact that President Trump would be the oldest president elected to office (in relation to Vice President Kamala Harris) or concerns about former President Biden's health and his ability to serve another term (before he left the race). For scholars, the age conversation has been about the implications for who controls politics and the generational divides in attitudes about political issues. For instance, scholar Kevin Munger makes the case that older people are better represented in elected office than younger people, and older voters are more likely to vote than their younger counterparts.[65] While Black women largely supported Kamala Harris's candidacy, there were generational differences in both Black women's intention to vote in 2024 and what issues were most important to them. These are differences worthy of conversation because they show the variation that exists among Black women.

---

[62] Tariro Mzezewa, Why Are Fewer Black Women Planning to Vote, *The Cut*, October 29, 2024, https://shorturl.at/rIZDm

[63] Niambi M. Carter and Tyson D. King-Meadows, Perceptual Knots and Black Identity Politics: Linked Fate, American Heritage, and Support for Trump Era Immigration Policy, *Societies* 9(1) (2019): 11.

[64] Niambi M. Carter, *American While Black: African Americans, Immigration, and the Limits of Citizenship* (New York: Oxford University Press, 2019).

[65] Kevin Munger, *Generation Gap: Why the Baby Boomers Still Dominate American Politics and Culture* (New York: Columbia University Press, 2022).

According to the "Power of the Sister Vote" poll conducted in February 2024, 56 percent of Black women noted that they would definitely vote in the 2024 election cycle.[66] On its face, a majority of Black women definitively noting their decision to vote eight months before the election is a good sign. This is particularly true given Black women's pattern of turnout in past elections. For reference, 66.3 percent of eligible Black women reported voting in 2020, and 63.7 percent of eligible Black women reported voting in 2016.[67] However, when we consider differences by age group (Black women aged fifty and above versus Black women below fifty years old), some critical differences emerge. Namely, while only half of Black women under fifty years old reported they were definitely planning to vote, 64 percent of Black women aged fifty-plus confirmed their intention to vote in the 2024 election.

Indeed, support for Harris on Election Day was higher among older Black women voters than younger ones. As noted in Figure 4.3, according to Edison Research exit polls, Black women aged sixty-five or older reported the highest support for Kamala Harris at 97 percent, followed closely by women aged thirty to forty-four and forty-five to sixty-four, respectively at 92 percent and 91 percent. Black women in the age range of eighteen to twenty-nine showed the lowest support at 86 percent. Altogether, the largest difference between the youngest and oldest group of Black women voters was about eleven percentage points.[68] Despite generational differences among Black women, it still cannot be ignored that Black women, across generations, showed higher support for Harris than any other group of women.

A generational difference was not just apparent in voting intentions and exit poll data, though. Older and younger Black women also differed in what they perceived as the most important issues in the country. For instance, concern about the Israel–Palestine conflict was greater among younger Black women than older Black women.[69] Notably, this is an issue for which young people across race and gender engaged in protests on college campuses across the country. Further, younger Black women

---

[66] Power of the Sister Vote 2024.

[67] CAWP, Gender Differences in Voter Turnout, Eagleton Institute of Politics, Rutgers University, https://cawp.rutgers.edu/data/voters/gender-differences-voter-registration-and-turnout

[68] Election 2024: Exit Polls, *CNN*, 2024, https://cnn.com/election/2024/exit-polls/national-results/general/president/0. Note this data was collected by Edison Research for the National Election Pool on behalf of CNN, ABC, CBS, and NBC. These exit polls account for responses from 22,966 respondents and were collected in person.

[69] Power of the Sister Vote 2024.

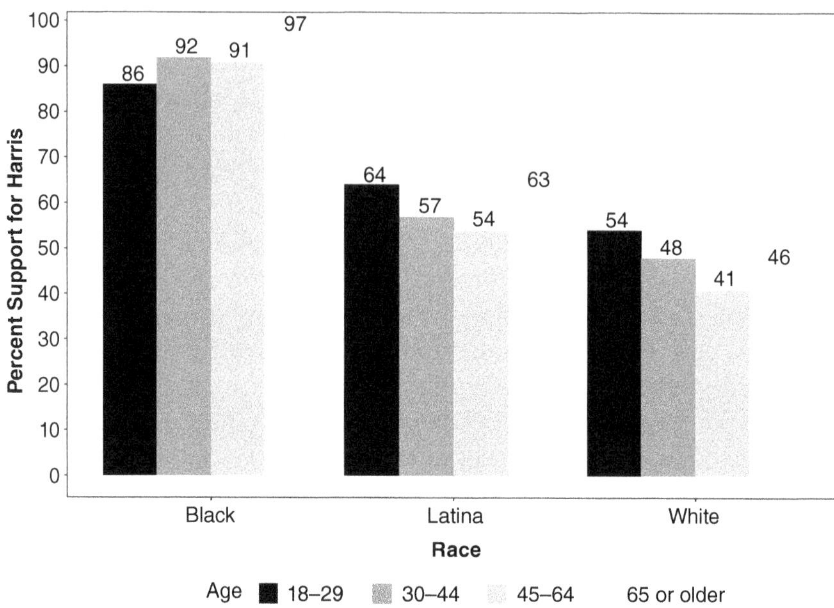

Figure 4.3 Support for Harris among women by age and race.
Note: This bar graph reports exit poll data among women, by race and age, on their reported support for the Democratic Party nominee for president, Kamala Harris.
Source: Edison Research 2024.

thought that addressing rising costs and inflation was most critical, while improving the economy and increasing wages was perceived as the most important issue for the country among older Black women.[70] This tracks with the fact that the majority of younger Black women noted that they were falling behind economically and unable to keep up with rising costs.

These generational divides among Black women speak to the importance of not flattening the group. Yes, many Black women were enthusiastic about the presidential prospects of Vice President Kamala Harris, as evidenced by whom Black women supported in the election and the mobilization efforts that Black women engaged in before the election on behalf of Harris, such as those via Zoom and other venues.[71] But critical to our understanding of the electoral outcomes is the fact that voter turnout among all voters decreased since the last presidential election (63.7% in 2024 versus 66.6% in 2020).[72] In a survey conducted by *The Cut* in

[70] Ibid.
[71] Holly Ramer, "We Were Built for This Moment": Black Women Rally Around Kamala Harris, *AP News*, July 23, 2024, https://shorturl.at/2Mv6j
[72] Ballotpedia, Election Results, 2024: Analysis of Voter Turnout in the 2024 General Election, https://shorturl.at/81XMB

October 2024, about 18 percent of Black women reported no intention to vote, and about 20 percent of these respondents expressed the belief that they had no obligation to vote. These nonvoters were dissatisfied with Harris's job performance and expressed little confidence in political institutions.[73] This suggests that not all Black women see electoral politics as a pathway for meaningful change or outcomes for them.

BLACK WOMEN'S ACTIVISM AND THE FIGHT FOR DEMOCRACY

Electoral politics is not the only venue through which Black women have had a political impact. Throughout the history of the United States, Black women have been present and vocal actors in seeking to improve life outcomes for Black women and Black people more generally. This work – also outlined in Chapter 3 in this volume – has been done to ensure that the group has access to the promises of citizenship and the democratic freedoms espoused in the Constitution. During the abolitionist movement,[74] Black women such as Sojourner Truth and Harriet Tubman were active participants in seeking to end the slave trade – Harriet Tubman through her involvement in the Underground Railroad (an effort to transport enslaved Black people from states practicing slavery to those that were not) and Sojourner Truth through speeches and public appearances to emphasize the cruelty of slavery and the importance of equal rights for Black people in the United States.[75]

We can also trace Black women's activism beyond the abolitionist movement to the current day. From the Reconstruction era to the 1950s, women such as Anna Julia Cooper, Mary Church Terrell, Mary McLeod Bethune, Ida B. Wells, and countless other Black women in local clubs and organizations continued the public fight for Black people's equal treatment under the law in fighting for anti-lynching protections, economic opportunities for the group, and women's rights and protections through speeches, marches, letter writing campaigns, and the development of mutual aid societies.[76] Black women's advocacy continued into the civil rights era for Black people's rights and liberties, and even further

---

[73] Mzezewa, Why Are Fewer Black Women Planning to Vote.

[74] The abolitionist movement is the period between 1783 and 1888 in which activists engaged in a social and political movement to end the practice of slavery and the slave trade.

[75] Darlene Clark Hine and Kathleen Thompson, *A Shining Thread of Hope: The History of Black Women in America* (New York: Broadway Books, 1998).

[76] Ibid.

into the women's rights movement to address the systematic inequalities that women, but especially women of color, faced.[77] Today, we can also credit Black women for being central to the Black Lives Matter movement and the #MeToo movement. The Black Lives Matter movement was started by three Black women: Patrisse Cullors, Alicia Garza, and Opal Tometi. The phrase #MeToo was first introduced by Tarana Burke, a Black woman sexual assault survivor and activist who advocates for marginalized victims.

Black women were part of and participated in the national organizations that we often associate with the suffrage movement (e.g., National American Women's Suffrage Association), civil rights movement (e.g., National Association for the Advancement of Colored People), and even the women's movement (e.g., National Organization for Women), but they also created their own spaces. It was essential for Black women to center their own spaces for organizing to advance the political agenda of survival and civil rights with an emphasis on the implications for Black women.[78] From Black women's social and political organizing came organizations such as the National Association of Colored Women, the National Black Feminist Organization, the Combahee River Collective, countless clubs and mutual aid societies, as well as historically Black sororities.[79]

CONCLUSION

Despite the representational gains that Black women have made in the past twenty-five years, Black women officeholders are still the first or among the few to hold many elective offices in the US. This is not to diminish the work or accomplishments of these Black women but to note that Black women remain in an ongoing struggle for representation in American politics. This is both the case in who is able to run and win and in how the party system responds to Black women's policy interests and demands. While the Democratic Party has traditionally been the home of Black women voters, there are indeed generational differences in how Black women think about the importance of voting. Black women's

---

[77] Paula J. Giddings, *When and Where I Enter* (New York: Bantam Doubleday Dell Publishing Group, 1984).

[78] Ibid.

[79] Historically Black sororities include organizations such as Alpha Kappa Alpha Sorority, Inc., Delta Sigma Theta Sorority, Inc., Zeta Phi Beta Sorority, Inc., and Sigma Gamma Rho Sorority, Inc.

pattern of voting suggests that it is likely not the case that Black women will defect to the Republican Party but that younger generations may continue making the decision to stay home – at least more than their older counterparts.

After the 2024 election results revealed that President Trump had won the presidential race, many Black women were left to consider what happens next. For many Black women, the most important goal of the election was to protect democracy, and by their vote choice it is clear that Black women perceived Harris as the best candidate to do this.[80] While the majority of Latinas supported Harris, white women voted similarly to past presidential elections – mainly in favor of the Republican candidate. Many Black women expressed feelings of betrayal about the election results. These Black women assumed that white women and other women of color would have supported Harris more, especially after the mass women's organizing efforts that took place in the aftermath of Trump's first presidency.[81] Instead of heeding calls to action, Black women have been heeding calls to rest since Election Day 2024.[82] As Tricia Hershey reminds us, rest is a form of resistance and a form of resistance that might be more necessary than ever to deal with the current political landscape.[83]

While Black women are using this moment to emphasize rest, this does not mean that the group has given up on democracy. As noted in the October 2024 survey commissioned by *The Cut*, 80 percent of Black women see voting as an obligation, and this indicates that Black women's continued participation in electoral politics is not likely to change, at least in the near future.[84] Not showing up will require Black women to be okay with the consequences of not trying, and for Black women those consequences will likely come at a more significant cost than for their same-gender counterparts.

The notion of rest that Black women are taking up at this moment is an indicator that Black women know that the next four years will challenge the norms of democracy in the United States. Whether Black women join other same-gender groups in organizing or advance organizing efforts on

---

80   Candaie Norwood, Black Women Voters Strongly Back Harris in an Election They View as Crucial for Democracy, *The 19th*, August 21, 2024, https://19thnews.org/2024/08/black-women-voters-harris-election-democracy/

81   Kenya Hunter, Feeling Betrayed by Increased Minority Support for Trump, Black Women Say They're Stepping Back, *AP News*, November 24, 2024, https://shorturl.at/5k16K

82   Dominique Fluker, Here's How Black Women Are Choosing to Rest Defiantly, *Essence*, December 3, 2024, https://essence.com/lifestyle/national-day-of-rest-for-black-women/

83   Tricia Hersey, *Rest Is Resistance: A Manifesto* (London: Hachette UK, 2022).

84   Mzezewa, Why Are Fewer Black Women Planning to Vote.

their own, the fight will continue. As former Vice President Kamala Harris alluded to in her concession speech, a long-standing struggle does not mean that a victory will not eventually come. While the country may not have been ready for a woman to be president, Black women were ready to elect a woman both in 2016 when Hillary Clinton ran and in 2024 when Kamala Harris was poised to become the first Black and South Asian woman president of the United States.

5 Fracturing Latinidad

Examining Racialized and Gendered Divisions in Voting, Mobilization, Messaging, and Outcomes among the Latiné/x Electorate

The day after the 2024 election generated a mix of emotions within the Latiné/x electorate.[1] Among the preponderance of Latina voters who had supported Democrat Kamala Harris for president, the day after the election felt eerily familiar. Much like the 2016 race where Republican presidential candidate Donald Trump defeated Democratic nominee Hillary Clinton, the 2024 election season was replete with dehumanizing, anti-immigrant narratives, as well as openly racist and sexist discourse invoked by Donald Trump and his surrogates to fuel racial resentment frequently targeted against Latiné/x communities. The outcome of the election in which Trump defeated Harris and promised the "largest deportation program in modern history" left many fearful and anxious for their futures and that of their families.

---

[1] The debates around identity and terminology for the population of persons whose ancestry stems from Latin America but are living in the United States are ongoing and everchanging. While no single term perfectly encompasses the complex, mobile, and intersecting identities of the population, for the purposes of this chapter I opt to use the gender-neutral term Latiné/x when referring to the population at large. This terminology encompasses expansive language common to gender-inclusive movements of both Latin America and the United States as opposed to the default masculine Latino or gender-binary Latina/o. Moreover, I use the term Latina when describing persons with ancestral, genealogical, or cultural origins in Latin America currently residing primarily in the United States who identify as women, and Latino for those who identify as men. On occasions where the data is reported using the label "Hispanic" or specific national origin identifiers, I duplicate the same terms here for consistency. For additional information about these terms, including their origins, and debates around usage, see Laura Gómez, *Inventing Latinos: A New Story of American Racism* (New York: The New Press, 2020); Paola Ramos, *Finding Latinx: In Search of the Voices Redefining Latino Identities* (New York: Vintage Press, 2020); Ed Morales, *Latinx: The New Force in American Politics and Culture* (New York: Verso, 2018).

At the same time, among a growing group of Republican, independent, and conservative-leaning Latiné/x voters, the day after the election was met with aspiration. For the portion of the Latiné/x electorate who voted for Trump and were motivated by economic concerns including worries about jobs and the rising costs of housing and health care, Trump's reelection reflected hope for a brighter economic future. While many pundits and practitioners were surprised by the number of Trump supporters among the Latiné/x electorate, the presence of Republican voters was not new and had steadily expanded over the previous decade. In the 2024 election, gains made by the Republican Party were concentrated among long-standing conservative districts and cohorts such as older Cuban voters and Republican-identified strongholds in Florida, Arizona, and the Lower Rio Grande Valley in Texas. However, a new constituency was also emerging among Latiné/x voters in traditionally Democratic strongholds such as California, New York, New Jersey, and Pennsylvania.

In addition, the Latiné/x electorate embodied unique gender divisions in 2024 marked by a widening gender gap in voting and issue preferences due in part to a distinct mobilization of aggressive masculinity throughout the election. Racialized and gendered campaign messaging centered on expanding immigration restrictions and emphasizing strength and even violence landed differently with Latino men and expanded gender divisions in voting behavior between Latina and Latino voters.

For Latina candidates, the 2024 election season also disrupted previous inroads made into national politics. Since 2018, a growing number of Latina candidates had entered races for congressional office as candidates from major political parties and won. In particular, in each general and midterm election since 2018, a record number of Latinas emerged from states with a high concentration of Latiné/x voters (California, Texas, Florida) as well as emerging communities (Oregon, Colorado, Georgia). Between 2017 and 2023, the number of Latina candidates for Congress had grown by more than 50 percent and the number of Latinas elected to Congress as voting members nearly doubled from ten (2018) to nineteen (2023).[2] However, this pattern was disrupted in 2024 as fewer women of color ran for national office. Despite the public attention to the historic campaign of Kamala Harris as the Democratic presidential nominee, fewer Asian American/Pacific Islander, Black, Latina, and Native women

---

[2] Anna Sampaio, *Mujeres y Movidas: Latina Congressional Candidate Emergence and Experiences in California and Texas*, Center for American Women and Politics (CAWP), 2023, https://shorturl.at/W9bkc

ran for national office in 2024 than in 2022 and fewer Latinas were ultimately successful in winning election or reelection to Congress.[3]

How we interpret these changes and what they mean for the future of Latiné/x politics, and specifically Latinas, remains unclear. Simply measuring the changes in Latiné/x voting behavior remains a heated subject, and the historic absence of consistent comprehensive national data on the Latiné/x electorate and gendered divisions among Latina and Latino participation and preferences has prevented a clear picture from being drawn.

Using an intersectional lens attentive to the raced and gendered context of contemporary politics, this chapter examines the changes in Latiné/x voting behavior in the 2024 election with particular attention to disparities in polling, a widening gender gap, as well as campaign communication including a weaponization of gender and racialized messaging that aggravated gender differences among Latiné/x voters. The chapter also examines the experiences of Latina candidates for national office focusing particular attention on their peak in the 2022 midterm elections and the changes that occurred in the 2024 election cycle. The chapter concludes with an eye to obstacles and opportunities in the future of Latina politics and racial and gendered justice in the United States.

GENDER DIFFERENCES IN LATINÉ/X VOTE CHOICE

Latiné/x Vote Choice from 2008 to 2024

Understanding how Latinas and Latinos voted in the 2024 election is particularly important given the size, strength, and dynamic impact of the population. As of 2020, more than one in ten voters in 2024 were Latiné/x and they represented the largest collection of nonwhite voters in the country. Moreover, both the Latiné/x population and the Latiné/x electorate continue to grow, with more than sixteen million Latinés/xs voting in 2024 – 6 percent more than in 2020 and almost 40 percent more than in 2016. And while Latiné/x voters have historically favored Democratic candidates, their support for the Democratic presidential candidate hit a record low in 2024.[4]

---

[3] Kelly Dittmar, Post-Primary Analysis: Women in 2024 Congressional Elections, CAWP, 2024, https://shorturl.at/G3siQ

[4] Gladys Gerbaud, Chase Harrison, and Khalea Robertson, How Latinos Voted in the 2024 US Presidential Election, *AS/COA*, 2024, www.as-coa.org/articles/how-latinos-voted-2024-us-presidential-election

The diversification of the Latiné/x electorate, including declining support for the Democratic Party, should be understood in the context of fluctuating campaigns and outreach among both major political parties. While Latiné/x voters have historically been more supportive of the Democratic Party – due largely to their disproportionate investment in outreach and mobilization as well as their support for issues such as immigration, jobs, education, and health care – there has also been a steady bloc of Latiné/x Republican voters (fluctuating between 20 and 30 percent of the electorate) concentrated among Cuban Americans and other conservative-leaning Hispanic groups. Republicans expanded their base of Latiné/x support in the early 2000s with George W. Bush's 2001 presidential campaign, and especially his reelection in 2004, which drew support from more than 40 percent of Latiné/x voters. Once considered a marginal voting bloc, by 2008 Latiné/x voters were a decisive factor in the election of Barack Obama to the presidency and were equally paramount to his reelection in 2012.[5]

In 2016 the racialized and gendered dynamics of the presidential campaigns shifted and Latiné/x voters were confronted with a highly polarized election environment that reconfigured their voting behavior. Democratic presidential candidate Hillary Clinton invested heavily in Latiné/x mobilization and incorporation and established a well-heeled Latiné/x outreach effort, replete with multiple Spanish-speaking staff and volunteers as well as field offices in battleground states, early on in her campaign. On the heels of major Democratic Party investments, privately funded Latiné/x outreach campaigns that were critical to the success of Latiné/x mobilization in the 2012 presidential election were expanded and redeployed in 2016.

By contrast, Latiné/x communities and voters were racially targeted, demonized, vilified, and harassed in unprecedented fashion by both Republican presidential and congressional candidates. Beginning with his depiction of Mexican immigrants as "criminals" and "rapists" at the announcement of his presidential bid in June 2015, Trump made strategic racism, white nationalism, and masculinist rhetoric aimed directly against Latinés/xs defining pillars of his campaign. This included his calls to revive the military-style roundups of "illegal immigrants" in the

---

[5] Anna Sampaio, Latinas and Electoral Politics: Expanding Participation and Power in State and National Elections, in *Gender and Elections: Shaping the Future of American Politics*, 3rd edn., eds. Sue Carroll and Richard Fox (New York: Cambridge University Press, 2013), pp. 146–67, p. 146

manner of the 1950s, infamously named "Operation Wetback," to undertake mass deportation of undocumented children, to strip citizenship from American children born to undocumented mothers, and to expand border enforcement through additional personnel and the infamous construction of a 1,000-mile fortified wall between the United States and Mexico, dubbed by some the "Great Wall of Trump."[6] Republican senate candidates Ted Cruz and Marco Rubio replicated these messages with pledges to reverse gains made by the popular immigration policy of DACA (Deferred Action for Childhood Arrivals); to further limit Mexican immigration; to enhance additional scrutiny, detention, and deportation of immigrants; and to punish states and localities that attempted to protect immigrants' rights. Other Republican primary contenders such as Wisconsin Governor Scott Walker extended Trump's gendered demonization of undocumented mothers and calls to strip citizenship from their American-born children, while Governor Bobby Jindal of Louisiana suggested that mayors of so-called sanctuary cities should be held criminally responsible for the action of undocumented immigrants who are released in their jurisdiction.[7]

The results of the 2016 campaign were evident in the increased turnout of Latiné/x voters in the Democratic primaries, expansions of Latiné/x turnout in key states, and the increased distance between Latiné/x voters (and especially Latinas) and the entire Republican Party. In particular, Latiné/x voting as a share of the national electorate increased by approximately 1.5 million voters from 2012 to 2016, with substantial expansions of the Latiné/x electorate in California, Colorado, Florida, Illinois, Nevada, New York, and North Carolina. Overall, Latiné/x voting reached a record high of 12.7 million voters, with 79 percent of Latinés/xs supporting Hillary Clinton, as opposed to only 18 percent voting for Donald Trump.[8] By 2016, the barrage of attacks delivered by Trump and many of the Republican national candidates had effectively deepened the chasm

<hr>

[6] Alexander Burns, Choice Words from Donald Trump, Presidential Candidate, *New York Times*, June 16, 2015, https://shorturl.at/CHir9; Julia Preston, Alan Rappeport, and Matt Richtel, What Would It Take for Donald Trump to Deport 11 Million and Build a Wall?, *New York Times*, May 19, 2016, www.nytimes.com/2016/05/20/us/politics/donald-trump-immigration.html

[7] Trip Gabriel and Julia Preston, Donald Trump Paints Republicans into Corner with Hispanics, *New York Times*, August 18, 2015, https://shorturl.at/qOEU5

[8] National Association of Latino Elected and Appointed Officials, Voting, Victories and Viewpoints: A Look at the Top Races and Issues for Latinos in Election 2016, *NALEO Educational Fund*, 2016, https://shorturl.at/eerJW; Latino Decisions, 2016 Election Eve Poll: National and State by State Toplines, 2016, https://shorturl.at/wsr9n

between Latiné/x voters, and particularly Latina voters, and the entire Republican Party.

During the 2020 elections, the Latiné/x electorate continued to expand, with over 16.6 million Latiné/x voters casting a ballot in the 2020 presidential election – an increase of more than 30 percent over Latiné/x ballots cast in the 2016 election.[9] Much as they had done in the last three presidential elections, during the 2020 election cycle Latiné/x voters overwhelmingly supported the Democratic presidential candidate, Joe Biden, even as Republicans made gains among Latiné/x voters in targeted sites such as Miami-Dade County in Florida and the Lower Rio Grande Valley in Texas. Similarly, Latiné/x voters strongly favored Democratic candidates over Republican candidates in US House and Senate races and proved significant to Democratic victories in key congressional contests in Arizona, California, Colorado, Georgia, Illinois, Nevada, New Mexico, New York, Pennsylvania, Washington, and Wisconsin. They also were critical to Republican state wins in Florida and Texas as well as key House and Senate victories in both states.[10]

By 2024, the Latino electorate remained a critical swing vote in key battleground states such as Arizona, Georgia, Nevada, and Pennsylvania, with both parties vying for their support, particularly in the context of issues such as the economy, health care, and immigration. However, what appeared to be early enthusiasm for Democrat Kamala Harris ultimately faded and fractured as the Democratic Party struggled to retain its base of Latiné/x support. In the weeks after Kamala Harris was announced as the Democratic nominee, polling indicated a groundswell of interest that reversed a growing sense of apathy and dissatisfaction among key Democratic constituencies including Latiné/x voters.[11] Joe Biden stepping down as the Democratic Party's presidential nominee and the subsequent ascension of Kamala Harris appeared to reverse many of these negative impacts. Polling from both Quinnipiac University and Televisa

---

[9] Rodrigo Domínguez-Villegas, Nick Gonzalez, Angela Gutierrez, Kassandra Hernández, Michael Herndon, Ana Oaxaca, Michael Rios, Marcel Roman, Tye Rush, Daisy Vera, et al., Vote Choice of Latino Voters in the 2020 Presidential Election, UCLA Latino Policy & Politics Initiative, 2021, https://latino.ucla.edu/research/latino-voters-in-2020-election/

[10] Ibid.

[11] Polling from the Berkeley Institute for Government Studies released in June 2024 indicated that Black, Latiné/x, Asian, and young voters were dissatisfied with the presidential candidate choices from the major parties, making it less likely these key groups would vote in the general election than both white and older voters. Mark DiCamillo, Release #2024–08: Turnout in the State's General Election Likely to Be High, but Wide Racial and Age Gaps Persist Between Those Most Likely to Vote and Those Less Certain, Institute of Governmental Studies, 2024, https://escholarship.org/uc/item/8rx3d6gj

Univision indicated a notable increase in support and enthusiasm for the Harris–Walz ticket in Pennsylvania among women and nonwhite voters.[12] In addition, polling from Somos PAC (political action committee) and BSP Research among Latiné/x registered voters across seven key battleground states – Arizona, Georgia, Michigan, Nevada, North Carolina, Pennsylvania, and Wisconsin – found a sizable increase in support for Harris as the Democratic nominee as well as increasing enthusiasm to vote in November, especially among Latinas and younger voters.[13]

Although a majority of Latiné/x voters favored Democrat Kamala Harris over Republican Donald Trump, Republicans ultimately gained votes among both Latinos and Latinas and achieved their biggest gains among young Latino men. These gains came through targeted outreach and messaging on economic issues that were of central concern to the population but equally through masculinized appeals to strength, power, and domination, particularly on issues of national security and immigration. Campaign messaging, which often employed racist and sexist stereotypes as well as hypermasculine tropes, were particularly common in Trump's strategic appearances on podcasts, livestream programs, and online shows popular with young men. For example, Trump appeared on *The Joe Rogan Experience* for three hours amplifying racialized and gendered conspiracy theories about the election and immigration and reaching a broad audience of mostly male listeners. He also appeared on male-centered podcasts such as *Six Feet Under* hosted by wrestler Mark Calaway, *Flagrant* with comedian Andrew Schulz, and *Bussin with the Boys* hosted by former NFL football players Will Compton and Taylor Lewan, as well as YouTube programs with figures such as Logan Paul.[14] In one especially notable livestream interview with Adin Ross, an influencer who had previously welcomed guests such as Andrew Tate (a former kickboxer indicted on rape and human trafficking charges in Romania) and Nick Fuentes (an avowed white supremacist), Ross gifted Trump with a gold Rolex watch and a customized Tesla Cybertruck while Trump

---

[12] Pennsylvania 2024: Harris Has Slight Edge Over Trump in Tight Race, Gets Boost from Women, Quinnipiac University Pennsylvania Poll Finds; Senate Race: Casey Up 8 Points Over McCormick, Quinnipiac University Poll, 2024, https://poll.qu.edu/poll-release?releaseid=3902

[13] Somos PAC and BSP Research, Post-RNC Latino Battleground Survey Memo, BSP Research, 2024, https://drive.google.com/file/d/1g7vgYvg2opqdIRqPfuEBi4SubrjxGhvL/view

[14] Ken Bensinger, Adin Ross Gives Trump a Cybertruck, a Rolex and Access to a Heavily Male Audience, *New York Times*, August 9, 2024, www.nytimes.com/2024/08/05/us/politics/trump-adin-ross-livestream-gifts.html

spoke for ninety minutes to his base of mostly male and conservative-leaning viewers.[15]

These appearances served to normalize Trump's otherwise egregious and offensive behavior but even more importantly they created a form of masculine intimacy – an induction and expansion into bro culture – for Trump that made him more likable and accessible to men of all races, including young men of color who had weak or nonexistent relationships with the major political parties. This form of messaging and outreach helped to chip away at the Democratic Party margins among Latiné/x voters, with Trump eventually polling ahead of Harris on key issues surrounding the economy, inflation, and securing the border.[16]

Measuring Latiné/x Vote Choice and Trends

Beyond these initial observations, consensus on how Latiné/x voters behaved and what to make of those changes is exceedingly challenging because of conflicting approaches to measuring the Latiné/x vote and disagreements on how to interpret the data. To be clear, these disagreements are not new to the 2024 election cycle and represent a common feature of robust research. However, such differences in method and data extend beyond merely esoteric or academic concerns. The outcome of the different approaches has yielded a substantially different outlook on outreach and mobilization that has direct implications for how political parties, candidates, campaigns, and practitioners engage issues of race and gender in the future and engage Latiné/x voters in particular.

One of the most contentious claims about Latiné/x voting in the 2024 election centers on a growing gender gap in the Latiné/x electorate and the extent to which Latino men embraced the Trump campaign. In particular, exit polling data reported by several of the major media outlets indicated that for the first time in history a *majority* of Latino men voted for the Republican presidential candidate, leading to Republican gains both across swing states and in Republican-dominant districts that presumably delivered the election to Donald Trump. Headlines such as "Latino Male Voters Switch Toward Trump in the 2024 Election," "Here's Why Growing Numbers of US Hispanics Voted for Trump, and Helped Him Win," and "Latino Men Wanted Trump. Why?" all revolve around the

---

[15] Stephen Pastis, Here Are the Biggest Moments from Trump's "Bro" Podcast Tour, *Forbes*, October 29, 2024, https://shorturl.at/GtKQH

[16] Didi Martinez, Trump Has Made Gains with Latino Men – Why They're Voting Red and How Harris Is Addressing It, *NBC News*, October 25, 2024, https://shorturl.at/nY7Zs

same national exit polling data claiming that 54 percent of Latino men voted for Trump – a radical departure from the 59 percent who supported Biden in 2020, the 66 percent who voted for Clinton in 2020, or the 71 percent who voted for Obama in 2012.[17]

Equally contentious are debates regarding the size of Republicans' gains among the Latiné/x electorate and the degree to which this represents a realignment of Latiné/x voters or a more short-lived pattern. Most notable are reports that the Latiné/x vote swung dramatically toward Donald Trump between the 2020 and 2024 elections, leading to the largest gender gap (fifteen points) ever recorded between Latino and Latina voters. This observation, if accurate, again fundamentally departs from the history of Latiné/x voting in presidential elections and alters the gendered pattern of voting in which both Latinas and Latinos have overwhelmingly favored Democrats.

While the reports of large increases of Latiné/x supporters for Trump – particularly among Latino men – circulated widely both before and after the election, the evidence relied largely on exit polling data drawn from a national sample of voters available to the National Election Pool (NEP) and produced by Edison Research. Edison Research has long been the standard bearer for exit polling data and the source of information for a majority of national news organizations such as CNN, ABC, NBC, and CBS news for their election night coverage.[18] However, the veracity and accuracy of data produced by Edison Research in accounting for the preferences of minority voters has also been a subject of debate in racial and ethnic politics. Questions about the accuracy and generalizability of these exit polls to account for the Latiné/x electorate in particular have centered on the relatively small sample size, the overrepresentation of specific subgroups, the limited sampling in Spanish, and the ability of the

---

17 Edison Research, Latino Male Voters Shift Toward Trump in 2024 Election, 2024, www .edisonresearch.com/latino-male-voters-shift-toward-trump-in-2024-election/; Andres Oppenheimer, Here's Why Growing Numbers of US Hispanics Voted for Trump, and Helped Him Win, *Miami Herald*, November 11, 2024, https://shorturl.at/fTSj9; Audie Cornish, Latino Men Wanted Trump. Why?, The Assignment with Audie Cornish, CNN Audio, November 6, 2024, https://shorturl.at/Z0CNa

18 Edison Research (along with previous iterations of the firm including the partnership of Edison Media Research and Mitofsky International) have produced exit polling data for the National Pool – a consortium of media organizations that buy into the survey including ABC News, CBS News, CNN, Fox News, and NBC News as well as the Pew Research Center. While the aggregate voting data produced through a national exit poll provides a helpful and often reliable snapshot of the general electorate, data from this poll has proven far less reliable in tracking Latiné/x voting behavior in the nearly two decades it has been in effect.

data collected to reflect the diversity of Latiné/x voting behavior across regional differences.[19]

For example, during the 2016 election, initial NEP exit polling data claimed that 29 percent of Latinés/xs supported Trump for president and only 65 percent voted for Clinton – a surprising finding given Trump's vitriolic anti-immigrant and anti-Latiné/x campaign and the inconsistency of such an outcome with numerous pre-election polls. The accuracy of this initial data was quickly challenged as a more sophisticated picture of Latiné/x voting emerged. Specifically, the polling and research firm Latino Decisions released data from a nationwide election eve poll of 5,600 Latiné/x voters indicating that Trump received only 18 percent of their vote, as compared with 79 percent for Hillary Clinton. This outcome was consistent with the pre-election polling by Univision/Washington Post, NBC/Telemundo, NALEO (National Association of Latino Elected and Appointed Officials), and Florida International University/New Latino Voice, whose research repeatedly registered Trump's support among Latiné/x below 20 percent. Moreover, this outcome was supported in additional state-level research on Latiné/x voters in Arizona and Texas.[20]

Similar questions about the accuracy and reliability of Edison Research exit polling for capturing Latiné/x voting arose in the aftermath of the 2024 election. In their 2024 national exit polling, which surveyed 2,750 Latiné/x voters nationally, Edison Research reported that 51 percent of the Latiné/x electorate voted for Harris and 46 percent voted for Trump. This represented a fourteen-point decline in Latiné/x support for the Democratic presidential candidate from the 2020 election (where 65% of Latinés/xs supported Joe Biden) and a fourteen-point gain in votes

---

[19] When asked about these concerns, representatives have previously acknowledged the limitations, noting: "[The National Election Pool] is not designed to yield very reliable estimates of the characteristics of small, geographically clustered demographic groups. These groups have much larger design effects and thus larger sampling errors … If we want to improve the National Exit Pool estimate for Hispanic vote, we would either need to drastically increase the number of precincts in the National Sample or oversample the number of Hispanic precincts." Evaluation of Edison/Mitofsky Election System 2004 prepared by Edison Media Research and Mitofsky International for the National Election Pool, January 19, 2005, https://shorturl.at/OzDbc

[20] Stephen A. Nuno and Bryan Wilcox-Archuleta, Viewpoints: Why Exit Polls Are Wrong about Latino Voters in Arizona, *Arizona Republic*, November 26, 2016, https://shorturl.at/Ac6NV; Francisco Pedraza and Bryan Wilcox-Archuleta, Donald Trump Did Not Win 34% of Latino Vote in Texas. He Won Much Less, *Washington Post*, December 2, 2016, https://tinyurl.com/mvxwh48k; CNN, 2016 Exit Polls, November 8, 2016, www.cnn.com/election/results/exit-polls/national/president; Latino Decisions, 2016 Latino Election Analysis, November 30, 2016, www.latinodecisions.com/files/6514/7880/5462/PostElection2016.pdf

Table 5.1 Fluctuating gender gap between Latinas and Latinos (Edison)

	2024		2020		2016		2012	
Latiné/x voters as percent of electorate	11% (Edison 6% Latino Men/ 6% Latina Women)		9% (Vote Cast 4% Latino Men/5% Latina Women); 13% (Edison)		10% (Pew)		11.2% (Pew) 10% (Roper)	
	Harris (%)	Trump (%)	Biden (%)	Trump (%)	Clinton (%)	Trump (%)	Obama (%)	Romney s(%)
Latinas	58	39	69	30	69	25	76	23
Latinos	44	54	59	36	63	32	65	33
Total LV	51	46	65	32	66	28	71	27
Gap	14pts	15pts	10	6	6	7	11	10

Source: Edison Research 2012, 2016, 2020, 2024.

for Republican Donald Trump from 2020 to 2024. Moreover, Edison exit polling suggested that while Trump gained support among both Latinos and Latinas, it was support from Latino men that secured his election by jumping eighteen points (from 36% support for Trump in 2020 to 54% in 2024). Latina voting for Trump increased by nine points from 30 percent in 2020 to 39 percent in 2024 in the NEP data (Table 5.1).

Efforts to remedy the weaknesses in Latiné/x-centered polling data have resulted in an expansion of public opinion research particularly among a growing cadre of Latiné/x political scientists. Over the last two decades, these efforts have been led by the research firm Latino Decisions (and more recently by Barreto Segura Partners Research (BSP Research)), whose polling of Latiné/x voters consistently draws on larger, more diverse, and more representative population samples of both Latiné/x and other nonwhite/minority communities to estimate voting behavior.[21]

[21] In addition to drawing on a larger sample of Latiné/x voters, in 2010 Latino Decisions/ BSP Research pioneered the practice of measuring voter preferences among early voters as well as Election Day voters, thus allowing for a statewide randomized representative sample and capturing a broader range of voters. Unlike the NEP, Latino Decisions/ BSP also weights the sample of Latiné/x voters to match population demographics for their specific group within each state, creating a more accurate depiction of regional and subgroup differences with the electorate. BSP Research and African American Research Collaborative, 2024 American Electorate Voter Poll: Methodology, BSP Research, 2024, https://tinyurl.com/ympjfvd8

For example, in 2024 BSP Research, along with partners at the African American Research Collaborative and Harvard University, produced the American Electorate Voter Poll – a large-scale poll targeting over 9,400 Black, Latino, Asian American, Native American, and white voters nationally and in key states to measure their preferences in the presidential and congressional races as well as voter preferences on issues and the major political parties.[22]

According to data published from BSP, Latiné/x support for Donald Trump increased in 2024 by eight points from 2020 (from 27% in 2020 to 35% in 2024) but was still strongly Democratic, with 63 percent of Latiné/x voters supporting Kamala Harris. BSP polling data also documents a steady but far more modest decline in Latiné/x support for Democratic presidential candidates, from a high of 79 percent for Hillary Clinton in 2016 to 70 percent for Joe Biden and 62 percent for Kamala Harris. To underscore the differences between research centers, BSP data points to a sixteen-point decline in Democratic support among Latiné/x voters over an eight-year period and across three presidential elections, compared with Edison polling which suggests Democrats experienced a fourteen-point decline in Latiné/x voting support in just one election cycle.

Latina Gender Gap

Equally significant to the debates on Latiné/x support for the presidential candidates are outcomes of gendered voting patterns between Latinas and Latinos reported by BSP and Edison. BSP polling indicates that even as Democrats lost ground among Latiné/x voters in the 2024 election, both Latinas and Latinos retained a strong preference for Democrat Kamala Harris (66% Latinas and 56% Latinos) over Republican Donald Trump (32% Latinas and 43% Latinos). Moreover, the gender gap between Latinas and Latinos was slightly larger in 2024 than in 2020, with a ten-point gap in support for Harris and an eleven-point gap in support for Trump; however, the gender gap remained comparable to previous elections, with both Latinas and Latinos sustaining an investment in and preference for Democratic presidential candidates. According to BSP/Latino

---

[22] The 2024 poll included an oversample of Puerto Rican voters that included a large sample in the battleground state of Pennsylvania, where Puerto Ricans are 50 percent of all Latino voters and where both parties invested significant time, attention, and money attempting to mobilize this population. The practice of oversampling helps to both increase the accuracy of the data and identify nuances and differences in Latiné/x subgroup behavior.

Table 5.2 Fluctuating gender gap between Latinas and Latinos (Latino Decisions/BSP)

Latiné/x voters as percent of electorate	2024		2020		2016		2012	
	11% (Edison 6% Latino Men/ 6% Latina Women)		9% (Vote Cast 4% Latino Men/5% Latina Women)		10% (Pew)		11.2% (Pew) 10% (Roper)	
	Harris (%)	Trump (%)	Biden (%)	Trump (%)	Clinton (%)	Trump (%)	Obama (%)	Romney (%)
Latinas	66	32	73	23	86	12	77	21
Latinos	56	43	67	31	71	24	73	25
Total LV	62	35	70	27	79	18	75	23
Gap	10pts	11pts	6	8	15	12	4	4

Source: BSP Research and African American Research Collaborative 2024 American Electorate Voter Poll: Latino Voters October 18–November 4, 2024; Latino Decisions 2020 Latino Election Eve Poll; Latino Decisions 2016 Latino Election Eve Poll; Latino Decisions 2016 Latino National Election Eve Poll; ImpreMedia/Latino Decisions 2012 Latino Election Eve Poll.

Decisions data, the largest gender gap happened in 2016, with 86 percent of Latinas supporting Hillary Clinton compared with 71 percent of Latino men (Table 5.2).

By contrast, according to data from Edison Research the gender gap expanded significantly in 2024 to a fourteen-point difference in support for the Democratic candidate and a fifteen-point difference between Latina and Latino support for Trump. In addition, this data suggests that for the first time in history, Latina and Latino voting was divided across party lines, with a majority of Latino males supporting Trump (54%) and a majority of Latina women supporting Harris (58%). This is significant not just for the unprecedented nature of this voting behavior but also because, unlike white women and men, Latina and Latino voters had long been thought to embody a modern gender gap where partisan differences existed but were measured in degrees of support for Democratic candidates and not in a difference that divided the Latinas from Latinos across party lines.[23] If true,

---

[23] Anna Sampaio, Presente! Latinas Mobilizing for Political Change across Candidates, Races, and Voters in 2020, in *Gender and Elections: Shaping the Future of American Politics,* 5th edn., eds. Susan J. Carroll, Richard L. Fox, and Kelly Dittmar (New York: Cambridge University Press, 2021), pp. 169–91, p. 169; Christina E. Bejarano, *The Latino Gender Gap in US Politics* (New York: Routledge, 2014).

Table 5.3 Fluctuating gender gap between Latinas and Latinos (VoteCast)

Latiné/x voters as percent of electorate	2024 11% (Edison 6% Latino Men/ 6% Latina Women)		2020 9% (Vote Cast 4% Latino Men/5% Latina Women)	
	Harris (%)	Trump (%)	Biden (%)	Trump (%)
Latinas	59	39	66	32
Latinos	50	48	59	38
Total LV	55	43	63	35
Gap	9pts	9pts	7	6

Source: AP VoteCast: How America Voted 2020, 2024.

this would represent a more profound partisan and gendered difference in Latiné/x communities than had previously been witnessed.

Additional sources of national voting data exist, including a national survey produced by VoteCast (from NORC at the University of Chicago) that began in 2018 and is used by Fox News and the Associated Press. While lacking in the extensive archives of polling and especially in published data on Latiné/x voters, VoteCast data suggests a slightly different pattern in Latiné/x voting behavior from those reported by Edison and BSP Research. According to VoteCast data, in the 2024 election a majority of Latiné/x voters (55%) supported Democratic Kamala Harris over Republican Donald Trump. This represents an eight-point decline from the 63 percent of Latiné/x voters who supported Biden in 2020. Latiné/x voters also increased their support for Donald Trump from 2020 (35%) to 2024 (43%). In other words, VoteCast data noted the same pattern of Democratic decline among Latiné/x voters in 2024 observable by both other surveys of the electorate; however, this drop was far more consistent with the eight-point decline reported by BSP than the fourteen-point drop reported by Edison (Table 5.3).

In addition, according to VoteCast data, both Latina and Latino voters in 2024 favored Democrat Kamala Harris over Republican Donald Trump, indicating that the Latiné/x electorate retained their long-standing preference for Democratic presidential candidates. VoteCast data also suggests an increase in support for Republican Donald Trump among both Latinos and Latinas, albeit a more modest increase consistent with BSP data.

Why and How Differences in Measurement Matter to Understanding Latiné/x Voting Behavior

These distinctions in Latiné/x voting behavior are important for how they translate into support, outreach, and mobilization in Latiné/x communities among the major political parties and in candidate campaigns. They are also significant for where and how political elites and nonpartisan civic organizations invest in Latina and Latino candidates, especially in early primary races or races where there is likely to be significant mobilization of Latiné/x voters to support a candidate. Finally, they are important for social scientists and students of politics who are trying to decipher what happened in 2024 and how best to understand the complexity within the Latiné/x electorate.

Decisions on campaign spending for outreach and mobilization is tethered closely to polling data, with major campaigns spending tens of thousands of dollars on consultants and data designed to reach the right voting blocs. If the 2024 election produced a radical fourteen-point shift in Latiné/x voting and an eighteen-point shift in young Latino male behavior, then both Democratic and Republican campaigns in competitive districts in states such as Florida, Pennsylvania, and Texas will likely tailor their messaging and even agendas in the hopes of attracting these voters. This will undoubtedly mean that agenda items and messages long supported by Latinas – such as universal health care, expansion of reproductive care, and support for women and children – are shelved or at minimum reduced in significance. Moreover, it could also mean that campaign positions such as the draconian immigration restrictions advanced by Trump and long considered anathema in Latiné/x communities actually have a stronger base of support that could be expanded with additional investments. However, if the data from BSP and VoteCast reflects a different picture of Latiné/x voting behavior and the decline of Democratic support in 2024 was part of a more muted pattern of dissatisfaction with the Democratic Party's messaging, then shifts in agenda-setting, outreach, and mobilization are more likely to occur without the radical departure from Democratic norms.

Which data we use to explain Latiné/x voting behavior and how we interpret the differences remains a debatable topic. However, as noted previously, there is consensus that gender matters in understanding the differences in voting behavior between Latinas and Latinos and that those differences influence the messaging and outreach from the campaigns to different constituencies.

How Weaponized Gender and Racialized Messaging Widens the Latiné/x Gender Gap

Much like the 2020 election season, the 2024 campaign cycle was marked by a barrage of racialized, xenophobic, gendered, and transphobic messaging designed to overwhelm and exhaust opposition and ultimately exacerbate existing social and political differences in the population. The speed and frequency of these messages, coupled with the explosion of messaging platforms, meant that the flow of racism and sexism became normalized and even threats of violence or openly hostile and violent appeals became unexceptional. Moreover, objections to these were dismissed or undermined in a similarly gendered fashion as overly sensitive or needlessly attentive to insignificant feelings. This section examines the gendered and racialized messaging aimed at Latinos and Latinas and its effect.

Much as he did in both the 2016 and 2020 election seasons, Donald Trump regularly traded on racist and sexist messaging throughout the 2024 election cycle as a way to mobilize white male voters and fracture key constituencies in the Democratic Party. As Kelly Dittmar details in Chapter 1 of this volume, the Trump campaign itself was marked by a weaponization of gender and mobilization of masculinity that landed with younger men across racial and ethnic populations.

The weaponization of race and gender manifest in multiple different forms. Direct interpersonal attacks levied against Kamala Harris and her supporters – including surrogates, campaign staff, celebrities, and public figures such as Taylor Swift who endorsed Harris – are one example. These attacks employed overtly racist and sexist tropes intended to demean, belittle, and undermine Harris's position as the sitting vice president and former senator and extended the same diminution to Harris supporters, with the worst insults reserved for women and people of color. For example, Trump repeatedly mocked Harris's physical appearance, seeking to reduce her to clothing and physical features, with particular derision aimed at her laugh. He alternately complimented her beauty or chastised her for being "not that pretty." Trump's messages also frequently employed profane and hypersexualized stereotypes of women of color, describing Harris as a prostitute or suggesting she used sex to rise professionally.[24] When a rallygoer in North Carolina shouted that Harris

---

[24] Heather Knight and Shawn Hubler, Willie Brown to Donald Trump: Mention My Name Again and Get Sued, *New York Times*, August 17, 2024, https://tinyurl.com/svuy83ty

"worked on a corner," a crude reference to sex work, Trump responded, "this place is amazing."[25]

These direct interpersonal attacks persisted throughout the election cycle and were amplified by larger messaging campaigns that made use of television and radio commercials, podcast and livestream interviews, social media posts, and paid advertisements from both the official Trump campaign and organizations backing Trump. These overtly racist and sexist messages often became refrains chanted at rallies or printed on t-shirts and buttons. One of the most popular items at Trump rallies capitalized on the hypersexualized depictions of Harris with the phrase "Biden sucks, Harris swallows" and "Fuck Joe and the Hoe."[26]

Trump also regularly sought to use Harris's support for transgender persons as a strategic wedge and engaged in attacks that fueled transphobia and violence against the LGBTQ+ population. These translated into campaign messaging, such as the line that appeared regularly in his print and media campaigns: "Kamala Harris is for they/them; President Trump is for you."[27] Similarly, in the closing days of the campaign, a pro-Trump super PAC backed by Elon Musk released an ad calling Harris "a big ole c-word," labeling her a communist, but also making an obvious reference to a vulgar and offensive word used to demean women. Such messaging mirrored the calls to "lock her up" aimed at Hillary Clinton in 2016, calls that manifested in death threats aimed at Clinton and her staff and became the source of violent social media memes directed at Clinton.

Few issues dominated the campaign headlines more than immigration, and Trump repeatedly targeted Latiné/x immigrants in his speeches, rallies, and messaging. As a candidate, Trump repeatedly vowed to carry out the "largest deportation effort in American history" and cast that process in both gendered and racialized terms, maintaining that one of his first priorities upon taking office in January would be to make the border "strong and powerful."[28] When questioned about his campaign promise of mass deportations, Trump said his administration would have "no choice" but to carry them out, arguing that the absence of such drastic

---

[25] Hannah Knowles and Marianne LeVine, Trump Welcomes Rallygoer's Insult of Harris as a Prostitute, *New York Times*, November 3, 2024, https://tinyurl.com/3wyz5x9v

[26] Danielle Kurtzleben, When a Trump Rally T-Shirt Is More than Just a Shirt, *NPR Weekend Edition Saturday*, June 15, 2024, https://tinyurl.com/2rkdsbka

[27] Juan Williams, "Kamala Is for They-Them" – Trump's Trans Attacks Have Democrats Fighting Each Other, *The Hill*, November 18, 2024, https://tinyurl.com/43wn9z3u

[28] Laura Strickler, Didi Martinez, Chloe Atkins, and Julia Ainsley, How Would Mass Deportation of Migrants under Trump Actually Work?, *NBC News*, July 16, 2024, https://tinyurl.com/2h933snt

measures would leave the country looking "weak."[29] The repeated references to a "strong and powerful" immigration enforcement program invoked an aggressive masculine posture intent on unilaterally sealing a presumably porous US–Mexico border and patrolling that divide with an overwhelming show of strength. This messaging simultaneously casts alternative treatments of immigrants (particularly Democratic plans expanding access for asylum seekers) as uniformly gendered female and vulnerable. By extension, the border itself became gendered as feminine and open to penetration by racialized threats in the form of immigrants.

The aggressive targeting of Latiné/x immigrants went further, and in May 2023 Trump renewed his call to end the long-standing constitutional right of birthright citizenship in a campaign video replete with disinformation and loaded phrasing referencing an "invasion" by "floods" of "illegal aliens" and "criminals," and the scourge of "birthright tourism" where women "squat" in hotels during the final weeks of pregnancy presumably to take advantage of the United States.[30] In the video, Trump claims he would sign an executive order on the first day of his presidency that would ensure that children born to parents who do not have legal status in the United States will not be considered US citizens.[31] In subsequent videos, campaign speeches, and interviews Trump repeatedly returned to the stereotypical image of immigrant mothers as purveyors of an invasion on US life, whose very bodies bore the undoing of American privilege.

These openly hostile displays of aggressive masculinity and racist messaging centered on immigrants became even more vitriolic by the time of the first debate between Donald Trump and Vice President Harris in September 2024. Trump centered his debate strategy on trafficking in a long stream of racist stereotyping targeting Latiné/x immigrants, Arabs, Blacks, and – most notably – Haitian immigrants, with the most alarming and false claim from Trump that Haitian immigrants in Springfield, Ohio, were stealing residents' pets or taking wildlife from local parks to eat. "They're eating the dogs! The people that came in. They're eating the cats! They're eating, they're eating the pets of the people that live there," Trump said during the debate.[32] This false claim not only

---

[29] Kristen Welker and Alexandra Marquez, Trump Says There's "No Price Tag" for His Mass Deportation Plan, *NBC News*, November 7, 2024, https://tinyurl.com/uj4asr6a

[30] Trump War Room, X post, May 30, 2023, 6:25am, https://tinyurl.com/28fpkmk8

[31] KPIX/CBS News Bay Area, Trump Vows to End Birthright Citizenship, May 31, 2023, www.youtube.com/watch?v=09CFN_fro18

[32] Alexandra Ulmer, At Debate, Trump Shares Falsehoods about Pet-Eating, Infanticide, *Reuters*, September 11, 2024, https://tinyurl.com/5d6ph46z

dehumanized the large Haitian immigrant community in Ohio but also employed a long-standing stereotype of Asians and Asian immigrants as ruthless and foreign and extended the same connotations of savagery to a similarly vulnerable nonwhite community. Moreover, online memes engendered Trump as the country's savior, with AI images of him saving kittens and dogs.[33] The false claim about Haitian immigrants was quickly debunked by debate moderator David Muir, but the damage was done as residents of Springfield were forced to evacuate schools, city hall, and other buildings after threats poured into the community in the wake of Trump's remarks.[34] More importantly, the depiction of immigrant outsiders threatening to consume some essential American identity was already cemented in the campaign discourse and public imagination.

Trump regularly returned to these false claims throughout the campaign, both repeating and expanding on them, as he did in a rally in New Jersey when he likened immigrants to fictional serial killer and cannibal Hannibal Lecter from *The Silence of the Lambs*. After recounting stories of Lecter drawing in victims to consume them, he sought to draw parallels by claiming, "We have people that have been released into our country that we don't want in our country, and they're coming in totally unchecked, totally unvetted. And we can't let this happen. They're destroying our country, and we're sitting back, and we better damn well win this election, because if we don't, our country is going to be doomed. It's going to be doomed."[35]

This practice of dehumanizing and demonizing immigrants was a direct extension of Trump's strategic targeting of Mexican, Central American, Latin American, and other nonwhite immigrants in his 2016 campaign; however, as a recent survey of presidential speeches noted, by 2022 messages from Trump and the Republican Party became more targeted, vitriolic, and aggressive.[36] Moreover, the campaign continued to traffic in

[33] Jasmine Garsd, The Stereotype of Immigrants Eating Dogs and Cats Is Storied – and Vitriolic as Ever, *NPR*, September 11, 2024, https://tinyurl.com/yp5t56wa; Justine McDaniel, Anumita Kaur, María Luisa Paúl, and Samantha Chery, Trump's False Claim about Haitian Immigrants Eating Pets Invokes Racist Trope, *Washington Post*, September 14, 2024, https://tinyurl.com/2zf2ka9a

[34] Azi Paybarah and Amy B. Wang, Springfield Bomb Threat Used "Hateful" Language toward Migrants, Haitians, Mayor Says, *Washington Post*, September 12, 2024, https://tinyurl.com/mrywjbfd

[35] Michael Gold, Trump, Bashing Migrants, Likens Them to Hannibal Lecter, Movie Cannibal, *New York Times*, May 12, 2024, www.nytimes.com/2024/05/12/us/donald-trump-hannibal-lecter.html

[36] How Have Attitudes towards US Immigration Changed?, HAI Stanford University Human-Centered Artificial Intelligence, July 29, 2022, https://hai.stanford.edu/news/how-have-attitudes-towards-us-immigration-changed

false and criminalizing narratives regarding Venezuelan migrants, with the often repeated stereotype equating recently arrived Venezuelans with gang activity and violence.[37] These narratives played into existing ruptures dividing newly arrived Latin American migrants from established Latiné/x communities and laid the groundwork for his appeals to aggressive masculinity in the form of "massive deportations."

The dehumanizing depictions of immigrants and targeting of Latiné/x communities coupled with aggressive racism, hostile sexism, and masculinist appeals to take strong action intensified in the final days of the election, when the Trump campaign organized a rally at Madison Square Garden and employed a collection of surrogates to deliver messages steeped in racism, sexism, and xenophobia. Trump himself used the rally to reiterate his vilification of Venezuelan immigrants, claiming that a "savage Venezuelan prison gang" had "taken over Times Square." He reiterated his pledge to protect Americans from "the enemy within" with the "largest deportation program in American history."[38] Other Trump supporters carried similarly racialized and gendered messaging, including Tucker Carlson, who mocked Harris's racial identity; radio host Sid Rosenberg, who described Hillary Clinton as a "sick bastard" and claimed "the fucking illegals get everything they want"; and a childhood friend of Trump's, who literally demonized Harris as "the devil" and "the antichrist."[39] Arguably the most incendiary comments of the rally came from podcaster Tony Hinchcliffe, who delivered a misogynistic and racist tirade aimed squarely at Latiné/x communities including Puerto Ricans – who are citizens of the United States. In addition to calling Puerto Rico "a floating island of garbage," Hinchcliffe said, "These Latinos, they love making babies too, just know that they do. There's no pulling out. They don't do that. They come inside – just like they did to our country."[40]

The full impact of these messages on Latinas, Latinos, and gender politics within the Latiné/x community are still being dissected, but one compelling indicator of their effect can be seen in the distance between young

[37] Adrian Florido, Trump Calls Venezuelan Migrants Criminals. Some Venezuelans Agree, Others Fight Back, *NPR All Things Considered*, October 21, 2024, https://tinyurl.com/3kes8c5f

[38] NDTV, Donald Trump Full Speech at Madison Square Garden, October 29, 2024, www.youtube.com/watch?v=YuOeFaxyHr0

[39] Adam Gabbatt and Ed Pilkington, Trump Fills Madison Square Garden with Anger, Vitriol and Racist Threats, *The Guardian*, October 27, 2024, www.theguardian.com/us-news/2024/oct/27/trump-madison-square-garden-rally

[40] C-SPAN, Comedian Tony Hinchcliffe Full Remarks at Trump Rally at Madison Square Garden in New York, October 28, 2024, www.youtube.com/watch?v=GzjNeA6FPMk

Latino men and their older counterparts and the Democratic Party as a whole as well as Kamala Harris specifically. While the precise measure of Latino support for Trump is still in doubt, there is evidence that young Latinos, who were the frequent target of Trump's masculinist appeals, were the least receptive to the Democratic Party, the most receptive to Donald Trump and the Republican Party, and the most likely to view Harris's gender as a problem. Specifically, data from the 2024 American Electorate Poll, which provided the most comprehensive and detailed picture of Latino vote choice, documented that young Latino men were the least likely among all age groups and genders to view Democrats as capable of doing a better job on the issues important to them and the most likely to say that "Donald Trump and the Republican Party care a great deal about the Latino community." They were also the least likely to report voting for Kamala Harris, and the most likely to say they were supporting Donald Trump.[41] Even more daunting, when asked about the factors that went into their vote choice, 14 percent of young Latino men who voted for Trump said "That Harris is a woman contributed to my opposition," and an additional 8 percent reported "That Harris is a woman was a major reason I voted for Trump."[42] This data indicates a divide between young Latino men and the Democratic Party that goes beyond differences in policy choices and partisanship and is rooted in a fundamental opposition to gender. Whether this gendered opposition was already present and to what extent deserves further exploration, but there is little doubt that Trump and the Republican Party sought to fully exploit this opposition in the course of their aggressive appeals to masculinity.

LATINA CANDIDATES AND OFFICEHOLDERS

For Latinas, the 2022 and 2024 election cycles were a study in contrasts. In 2022 more Latinas ran for Congress than at any other point in US history, and their growing experience as candidates coupled with increases in political capacity and experience meant more Latinas were elected to Congress than ever before. This translated into greater representation of Latinas on congressional committees and in oversight functions, and a greater attention to issues of concern among Latina voters. It also brought with it an expanded network of mentors and advocates for Latinas in the

---

[41] BSP Research and African American Research Collaborative, 2024 American Electorate Voter Poll: Latino Voters, 2024, https://2024electionpoll.us/wp-content/uploads/2024/11/7.-Latino-crosstab.pdf
[42] Ibid.

national electoral pipeline. The growth of Latinas in national office had been building for decades within local and state-level offices and manifested nationally starting in 2018.

Gains in Elections 2018, 2020, and 2022

Latinas have a long history of political participation and activism in the United States, albeit for much of the nineteenth and twentieth centuries that work was concentrated in nonelectoral and nontraditional forms of participation, including organizing and mobilizing in community-based organizations, labor unions, and faith-based communities. Building upon the strategies and coalitions cultivated through nontraditional politics, Latinas began to form successful campaigns for candidates, initiatives, and policy change in more traditional political venues beginning in the 1980s. In particular, Latinas mobilized both Latiné/x and non-Latiné/x voters through registration drives, educational campaigns, and Get Out the Vote efforts, leading to a steady increase in the numbers of Latinas and Latinos taking part in political processes that had largely excluded them.

At the national level Latinas were largely excluded as congressional candidates until the late twentieth century. The first Latinas elected to Congress were Representative Barbara Vucanovich, a Republican from Nevada who served from 1983 to 1997, and Representative Ileana Ros-Lehtinen, a Republican from Florida who served from 1989 to 2019. Throughout the 1990s and 2000s, the number of Latinas elected to the House of Representatives grew, but those numbers remained in the single digits until 2016 and were concentrated in largely Democratic districts with large concentrations of Latiné/x voters in California and New York. Moreover, Senator Catherine Cortez Masto, a Democrat from Nevada who was elected to office in 2016, remains the only Latina to ever serve in the US Senate. As more Latinas were elected to office, they exerted greater influence on national issues. For example, in 2012 Representative Linda Sánchez of California became the first Latina to serve on the influential House Ways and Means Committee, and she has been an outspoken advocate and mentor for other Latinas pursuing elective office.

The midterm election of 2018 marked a key milestone for Latina congressional candidates, as many were drawn into the political process by an increasingly hostile political environment that targeted immigrants and Latiné/x communities with racialized rhetoric and restrictive policies. More Latinas ran successfully for national office in 2018 than in any prior general election. In total, twelve Latinas were elected (or reelected) to national office (out of a total of fifty-one Latinas who ran as major-party candidates). This included historic wins for Democrat Alexandria Ocasio-Cortez (NY-14), who became the youngest elected member of Congress, and Democrats Veronica Escobar (TX-16) and Sylvia Garcia (TX-29), who became the first Latinas elected to the US House of Representatives from Texas.

Latinas continued to play prominent roles in the 2020 and 2022 general elections as major-party candidates for political office, as political organizers, and as key portions of the electorate in states with competitive congressional and gubernatorial races. These election cycles continued to reshape the gender landscape of US elections, with significant increases in the volume and diversity of Latinas and other women of color who ran for national office as major-party candidates and won in each of these cycles.[43] A greater diversity of Latina congressional candidates also emerged in this period, drawing more opportunities for Afro-Latina candidates, first-time candidates, and Latina candidates from states that lacked a critical mass of Latiné/x voters. Specifically, seventy-five Latinas ran for national office in 2020 and thirteen won; and eighty-eight ran in the 2022 general election. At the beginning of the 118th congressional session in January 2023, nineteen Latinas were serving as voting members of Congress.[44] This included eighteen Latinas in the US House of Representatives (14D, 4R) and one US senator. Put another way, in just five years – between 2017 and 2023 – the number of Latina candidates for Congress grew by more than 50 percent and the number of Latinas elected to Congress as voting members nearly doubled from ten to nineteen.[45]

[43] Results for Women Congressional and Statewide Candidates in Election 2022, CAWP, 2022, https://tinyurl.com/2z9ep4ww; Kelly Dittmar, Unfinished Business: Women Running in 2018 and Beyond, CAWP, 2019, https://womenrun.rutgers.edu/2018-report/; Kelly Dittmar, Tracking Gender in the 2020 Presidential Election, CAWP, 2020, https://womenrun.rutgers.edu/2020-presidential/

[44] Republican Mayra Flores was elected to Congress from Texas during a special election in June 2022; however, she lost her reelection bid during regularly scheduled elections in November 2022. Thus, while there were twenty Latinas elected to Congress through both the general election and special cycles in 2022, there were nineteen voting members in office at the outset of the 118th Congressional session in 2023.

[45] Nicole Acevedo, Young Latinos Mobilized, Voted and Were Pivotal in 2020. Organizers Want to Keep It Going, *NBC News*, November 27, 2020, https://tinyurl.com/22ac49t9; Kelly Dittmar, What You Need to Know about the Record Numbers of Women Candidates in 2020, CAWP, 2020, https://cawp.rutgers.edu/election-analysis/record-numbers-women-candidates-2020; Jens Manuel Krogstad, Antonio Flores, and Mark Hugo Lopez, Key Takeaways about Latino Voters in the 2018 Midterm Elections, *Pew Research Center*, 2018, https://pewresearch.org/fact-tank/2018/11/09/how-latinos-voted-in-2018-midterms/; Anna Sampaio, Latinas Deliver in the 2018 Midterms. Gender Watch, 2018, https://cawp.rutgers.edu/blog/latinas-deliver-2018-midterms

The partisan diversity of Latina congressional candidates also grew in 2018, 2020, and 2022. While Latina congressional candidates continued to be concentrated in the Democratic Party, an increasing number of Latina Republicans ran for office and won in 2020 and 2022. The emergence of Latina Republican congressional candidates from Texas drew particular political attention in 2022 as their numbers more than doubled from six candidates in the previous midterm in 2018 to fourteen.[46] An especially bright spot within the Republican Party of Texas emerged in a special election in June 2022, when Mayra Flores became the first Latina Republican elected to Congress from Texas. Representative Flores, whose 34th congressional district seat was redistricted, lost her bid for reelection during the November 2022 general election to incumbent Democrat Vicente Gonzalez Jr. Despite Flores's defeat, two additional Latina Republican candidates won primaries in Texas in 2022 – Monica De La Cruz (TX-15) and Cassy Garcia (TX-28). De La Cruz won the general election in 2022, becoming the fourth Latina from Texas elected to the US House of Representatives and second Latina Republican elected from the state.

This growth of Latina candidates at the national level reflected decades of organizing among local, state, and national political parties and nonpartisan organizations dedicated to expanding the pool and competitiveness of Latinas and other women of color. It also reflected a broadening political capacity among Latinas, including more connection to financial resources, social networks, volunteers, and knowledge, and an increasing number of Latinas who possessed prior political experience and ran in districts with a large concentration of Latiné/x voters that made them highly competitive candidates.

Some of the opportunities that emerged for Latinas to become competitive in national races in 2018, 2020, and 2022 also came from retirements or departures among senior Latina and Latino congressional representatives. Beginning with US Representative Ileana Ros-Lehtinen's (FL-27) 2017 announcement that she would not seek reelection in 2018, there have been a handful of seats in Latiné/x-heavy districts that have drawn a highly competitive field of Latina candidates. While the seat previously

---

[46] Ronald Brownstein, Are Latinos Really Realigning toward Republicans?, *The Atlantic*, April 5, 2023, https://tinyurl.com/yn8h7c4j; Li Zhou, How 2022 Became the Year of the Latina Republican, *Vox*, September 12, 2022, https://tinyurl.com/5477v45y; Aaron Zitner and Bryan Mena, Latino Voters, Once Solidly Democratic, Split Along Economic Lines, *Wall Street Journal*, September 14, 2022, https://wsj.com/articles/latino-voters-republican-midterm-elections-11663166135

held by Ros-Lehtinen was initially won by Democrat Donna Shalala in 2018, the race to replace her drew six Latinas to the competition. This included Republican Maria Elvira Salazar, who narrowly lost to Shalala in 2018 but defeated her in 2020 and won reelection for the second time in 2024. More recently, the departure of Democrat Tony Cárdenas from California's 29th congressional district drew three Latinas to the open-seat contest in 2024 (Democrats Luz Maria Rivas and Angélica María Dueñas, and Republican Margarita Maria Carranza), resulting in the election of Democrat Luz Maria Rivas.

Stalled Progress in Election 2024

While the 2018, 2020, and 2022 elections generated consistent growth and electoral success for Latina candidates, this upward trajectory was disrupted in 2024. In particular, the number of Latinas running as major-party candidates for the US House of Representatives in 2024 decreased by more than 30 percent over the previous general election – from eighty-five in 2022 to fifty-nine in 2024. By the opening of the 119th session of Congress in January 2025, there were eighteen Latinas serving in the US House of Representatives and one Latina (Democrat Catherine Cortez Masto) serving in the US Senate. In addition, the diversity of Latina candidates and officeholders also changed during the 2024 election cycle, with no Afro-Latina candidates emerging from either major political party and fewer Latina candidates running from states without a high concentration of Latiné/x voters.

Changes in the diversity of Latina candidates were especially apparent in declines among Latina Republicans who ran successfully in 2024 as compared with 2020. Among the sixty-three Latina congressional candidates running in 2024, 38 percent ran as Republicans – a decline from the 45 percent of Latina candidates who ran as Republicans in 2020. As noted previously, the impact of this was especially apparent in Texas, where Latina Republican candidates have been concentrated and where outreach and recruitment of Latinas between 2018 and 2022 more than doubled the number of Latina Republicans running for Congress from six to fourteen. This outreach and recruitment yielded important successes for the Republican Party, including general election wins for Latina Republicans including Mayra Flores and Monica De La Cruz. While De La Cruz ran successfully for reelection in 2024, the political landscape for Latina Republicans in Texas had once again shifted by 2024 as the total number of Latina Republican congressional candidates receded from a high of fourteen in 2022 to seven in 2024.

Despite an overall decrease among Latina candidates vying for the US House of Representatives, there was a small uptick in the number of Latinas who ran for the US Senate from three in 2020 to four in 2024. This is particularly noteworthy given the increased competition from high-profile challengers and expenses associated with running a state-wide race for the US Senate. Reflecting the larger partisan imbalance in Latina candidates generally, all four of the US Senate candidates running in 2024 were Democrats: Debbie Mucarsel-Powell in Florida; Patricia Campos-Medina in New Jersey; and Heli Rodriguez Prilliman and Meri Gomez in Texas. Among these candidates, only Florida's Debbie Mucarsel-Powell, who previously served in the US House, was successful in the primary election. She drew significant national attention in her challenge to incumbent Republican Rick Scott. In the end, Mucarsel-Powell lost in the general election but laid the groundwork for the possibility of a future statewide campaign.

Outside of the national decrease in Latina candidates, another bright spot for Latina political participation in 2024 occurred in California, where Latina political power has been developed across multiple generations and jurisdictions. Defying the national trend, the number of Latinas running for Congress in California increased from fifteen in 2022 to seventeen in 2024, reflecting both growth among Democratic candidates and a loss among Republican Latina candidates. Moreover, while two long-standing Latina US representatives from California (Lucille Roybal-Allard and Grace F. Napolitano) retired in 2024, Californians elected a new Latina to the US House of Representatives – Democrat Luz Rivas from the 29th congressional district. She joined two other Latina newcomers – Democrat Emily Randall from Washington and Democrat Nellie Pou from New Jersey – in the 119th session of Congress (Table 5.4).

CONCLUSION

The Latiné/x electorate played an important role in the outcome of the 2024 presidential election, with both major political parties investing significant time, money, and effort into messaging and mobilizing key segments of the electorate. As in previous presidential elections, a majority of Latiné/x voters supported the Democratic nominee for president; however, there was a notable decline in Democratic support and an increase of Latiné/x votes for Trump that was concentrated among young Latino male voters. While the degree of Latino male support for Trump is still being debated, the diversification and divergences within

Table 5.4 Latinas in the 119th session of Congress (voting members)

State	Party Affiliation & District	Member of Congress
CA	Democrat (CD 29)	US Representative Luz Maria Rivas
–	Democrat (CD 35)	US Representative Norma Torres
–	Democrat (CD 38)	US Representative Linda T. Sánchez
–	Democrat (CD 44)	US Representative Nanette Diaz Barragán
FL	Republican (CD 13)	US Representative Anna Paulina Luna
–	Republican (CD 27)	US Representative María Elvira Salazar
IL	Democrat (CD 3)	US Representative Delia C. Ramirez
NV	Democrat	US Senator Catherine Cortez Masto
NJ	Democrat (CD 9)	US Representative Nellie Pou
NM	Democrat (CD 3)	US Representative Teresa Leger Fernández
NY	Democrat (CD 7)	US Representative Nydia M. Velázquez
–	Republican (CD 11)	US Representative Nicole Malliotakis
–	Democrat (CD 14)	US Representative Alexandria Ocasio-Cortez
OR	Democrat (CD 6)	US Representative Andrea Salinas
TX	Republican (CD 15)	US Representative Monica De La Cruz
–	Democrat (CD 16)	US Representative Veronica Escobar
–	Democrat (CD 29)	US Representative Sylvia R. Garcia
WA	Democrat (CD 3)	US Representative Marie Gluesenkamp Perez
–	Democrat (CD 6)	US Representative Emily Randall

Source: "Members of the U.S. Congress," Congress.gov; "Women Elected Officials by Position," Center for American Women and Politics.

the Latiné/x populations are noteworthy, particularly for how they manifested along gender and partisan lines. The ascension of Kamala Harris as the Democratic nominee set off a wave of energy and joy, particularly notable among women of color including Latinas, and helped to close the enthusiasm gap and the bleeding of young and nonwhite voters evident in the early months of the 2024 presidential campaign. This explosion of enthusiasm was evident in national polling among Latinas and Latinos and in polling data from key states. It was also reflected in the creativity and energy of Latina-led organizations such as PODER North Carolina, a statewide political organization led by Iréne Godinez, working to mobilize traditional and low-propensity Latiné/x voters in a battleground state where the community is often overlooked. Utilizing a mix of innovative outreach strategies, including telenovela-style voter education video series and their "Ballots y Belleza" events, providing information on ballot measures and candidates to potential voters who also enjoyed free beauty services, the presence of Kamala Harris as the Democratic presidential nominee and the potential to bring together voters around progressive alliances centered on racial and gender justice animated a new wave of Latina organizing.

At the same time, the lead-up to the election saw record numbers of Latinas and especially Latinos lend their time and support to Donald Trump's bid for reelection to the presidency. This support was clearly gendered – not only because of its concentration among Latino men but also because of the campaign messaging steeped in the language of strength, domination, and aggressive masculinity that formed its central appeal.

Ultimately, while the preponderance of Latiné/x voters continued to support Democratic candidates for president and Congress at the federal level, palpable shifts in voter outreach and messaging resulted in a more significant wave of Latiné/x support for Republican candidates than was observable in recent elections. Moreover, gender and race were openly weaponized in an election cycle that saw the first woman of color nominee for president from a major party and repeated attempts to discredit and undermine her candidacy. Finally, the increasing diversity and political polarization of the country along racial, ethnic, gendered, political, and ideological lines has manifested as well in significant changes and challenges within Latiné/x communities. In particular, as the Latiné/x population in general has grown, so too have the complexities, divergences, and intersectional differences within the Latiné/x electorate. While Latina voters in particular remain strongly Democratic voters, even their support has wavered as more younger voters refuse to associate with either party and outreach from the Republican Party reaches a larger percentage of the population.

The 2024 election also disrupted six years of significant increases among Latinas as congressional candidates and officeholders. Since 2018 there has been a steady expansion in the number of Latinas running for office within the major political parties and a virtual doubling of the number of Latinas elected to national office. This is particularly important because Congress holds plenary power on issues of central concern to Latiné/x communities such as immigration, admissions, deportation and detention policies, and border enforcement. In 2024 this progress was interrupted as fewer Latinas and fewer women of color in general pursued congressional office, and the total number of Latinas serving in Congress remained unchanged from the previous year. In many ways the election and its outcomes have already begun to impact Latiné/x communities across the country with increased raids and roundups, increased scrutiny of undocumented and documented immigrants, and increased fear leading to further marginalization. These circumstances mirror the forms of targeting and terror registered by Latinés/xs during the first Trump presidency, fears that drove several to pursue political office to effect change. Whether that same pattern will be replicated in the ensuing midterm election remains to be seen, but it is evident that the previous patterns of Latina and Latino politics are being challenged and are shifting, and that racial and gendered politics will continue to play a significant role in future outcomes.

6 LGBTQ+ Women in Politics

The Challenging Journey to Inclusion

At the beginning of 2025, 507 out LGBTQ+ (lesbian, gay, bisexual, transgender, queer) women served in elective office in the United States at any level of government, from neighborhood councils and school boards to Congress and governor's offices. Additionally, sixty-three elected officials nationwide openly identified as nonbinary, gender nonconforming, and genderqueer.[1] LGBTQ+ women, gender nonconforming, and nonbinary elected officials were present in all but seven states, from Maine to Texas, from Oregon to Georgia.

This was not always the case. Until 1974, no out LGBTQ+ woman had ever been elected to political office in the country. Still in the early 1990s, barely a few dozen out LGBTQ+ women were in office, mostly in progressive cities and blue states. And while today's numbers might seem impressive, in fact they highlight how LGBTQ+ women remain severely underrepresented. While 8.7 percent of women in the US population identify as LGBTQ+, LGBTQ+ women and nonbinary individuals represent only 0.1 percent of elected officials nationwide.

Who are the LGBTQ+ women and nonbinary individuals serving in office? How have their numbers evolved over time? What explains their increase? What challenges do LGBTQ+ women face in their campaigns? How do they overcome such challenges to win elections? And what impact do they have when they are in office?

To answer these questions, this chapter examines the experiences of LGBTQ+ women running for office. While this is still an emerging field

---

[1] Nonbinary refers to individuals whose gender identity does not fit within the traditional categories of male or female. Gender nonconforming refers to people whose gender expression differs from cultural expectations of masculinity and femininity. Genderqueer is an umbrella identity for people who reject conventional gender categories.

of inquiry with a limited number of politicians to study, the chapter can offer important insights. Tracing the historical evolution of these candidacies, the analysis shows how their number has increased over time and how the group has grown more diverse along gender identity, race, and ethnicity. The chapter then explores the challenges that LGBTQ+ women face when running for office, which are often magnified for transgender women (i.e., women whose gender identity differs from the sex they were assigned at birth) and LGBTQ+ women of color. The analysis also shows that, despite the obstacles, LGBTQ+ women tend to exhibit unusual political strengths that allow them to make up for the negative bias they encounter. In the end, the chapter offers a snapshot of the landscape of LGBTQ+ women in office at the beginning of 2025 and discusses their political and social impact.

LGBTQ+ WOMEN IN OFFICE OVER TIME

Famous gay activist Harvey Milk, who was elected in 1977 to the San Francisco Board of Supervisors, is often identified as the first LGBTQ+ person to be elected to public office. Milk was indeed the first openly LGBTQ+ elected official in California. But two LGBTQ+ women had won their races three years earlier in other states. Kathy Kozachenko was elected to the Ann Arbor (Michigan) City Council in April 1974, becoming the first openly LGBTQ+ person ever elected to public office in the United States. A few months later, in November of the same year, Elaine Noble was elected to the Massachusetts State House.

Kozachenko was a twenty-one-year-old student at the University of Michigan in 1974. She ran as an openly lesbian candidate at the height of the anti-Vietnam War activism for the Human Rights Party, a left-leaning organization championing racial justice, gay rights, and working-class policies, which had already won two seats on the Ann Arbor City Council two years before. Kozachenko ran a progressive campaign that proposed limits to landlord profits and to marijuana fines. Kozachenko's sexuality was not central in her campaign.[2] She explained there was no need to focus on her sexuality because Ann Arbor was a progressive town

---

[2] Sexuality is a broader term than sexual orientation. Sexual orientation usually refers to consistent patterns of a person's emotional, romantic, and/or sexual attraction to others. Sexuality includes sexual orientation but usually also encompasses other aspects, such as sexual desires, fantasies, expressions, and behaviors as well as attitudes and values related to sex.

that had already embraced gay rights. Indeed, before Kozachenko won the election, two other councilmembers had come out as LGBTQ+ after entering office. The City Council had also passed one of the first ordinances in the country against discrimination on the basis of sexual orientation in public accommodations.

In the end, Kozachenko defeated her Democratic opponent by only fifty-two votes. In her victory speech, she declared:

> This is the first time in the history of the US that someone has run openly as a gay person and been elected to public office. Gay liberation was not a major issue in the campaign – both candidates in this ward said they supported gay rights, but ten years ago, or even three years ago, lesbianism would have meant automatic defeat. This year we talked about rent control. We talked about the city's budget. We talked about police priorities, and we had a record of action to run on. Many people's attitudes about gayness are still far from healthy, but my campaign forced some people at least to re-examine their prejudices and stereotypes.[3]

LGBTQ+ Women Serving in City Councils and as Mayors

The year before Kozachenko was elected, Nancy Wechsler – who also served on the Ann Arbor City Council – came out as lesbian after winning her election. Wechsler became the first out LGBTQ+ member of a city council in the country along with fellow Ann Arbor councilman Jerry DeGrieck, who also came out as gay while in office. With Kozachenko joining, the Ann Arbor City Council had three LGBTQ+ members, an extreme rarity.

In the years that followed, out LGBTQ+ women elected to local office were few and far between. Among them, Tammy Baldwin was elected to the Dane County (WI) Board of Supervisors in 1986. Roberta Achtenberg and Carole Migden were elected to the San Francisco (CA) Board of Supervisors in 1990. Sherry Harris won her race for the Seattle (WA) City Council in 1991, becoming the first Black out lesbian elected official in the country. Also in 1991, Irene Rabinowitz was elected to the Provincetown (MA) Board of Selectmen. A few more successful elections followed in 1993, including Jackie Goldberg to the Los Angeles (CA) City Council, Christine Kehoe to the San Diego (CA) City Council, Katherine Triantafillou to the City Council of Cambridge, Massachusetts, Susan

---

[3] Steve Friess, The First Openly Gay Person to Win an Election in America Was Not Harvey Milk, *Bloomberg News*, December 11, 2015, www.bloomberg.com/politics/features/2015-12-11/the-first-openly-gay-person-to-win-an-election-in-america-was-not-harvey-milk

Hyde to the Hartford (CT) City Council, and Pam Cuthbert to the City Council of Ypsilanti City (MI).

However, it was only in the late 1990s and early 2000s that the number of out LGBTQ+ women in local office started to pick up. Some won prominent positions. Cathy Woolard was elected to the Atlanta (GA) City Council in 1998 and became president of the City Council after winning a city-wide race in 2002. Christine Quinn was elected to the New York (NY) City Council in 1999. Seven years later, in 2006, Quinn became speaker of the New York City Council, the first woman and the first openly LGBTQ+ person to hold the position. The speakership in New York City has often been a springboard for higher office, and this was no different for Quinn. Quinn ran for mayor of New York City in 2013 to succeed Michael Bloomberg. She was the early frontrunner in the Democratic primary, but she was ultimately defeated by Bill de Blasio.

Even though Christine Quinn did not win her race, other LGBTQ+ women have been elected mayor. The first openly lesbian mayor in the country was Valerie Terrigno, who became mayor of West Hollywood, California, in 1984. Judy Abdo became mayor of Santa Monica, California, in 1990. A few more were elected in the following decades, including in two of the largest US cities. The election of Annise Parker as mayor of Houston (TX) in 2009 was especially pathbreaking, as she became the first out LGBTQ+ mayor of one of the ten most populous cities in the country. Parker served three two-year terms and passed the Equal Rights Ordinance, which banned discrimination – including on the basis of sexual orientation and gender identity – in the workplace, housing, and public accommodations. The 2014 Equal Rights Ordinance was a trailblazing measure in Texas, even though voters would repeal it in a referendum the following year.

In 2019, Lori Lightfoot, who is Black and lesbian, was elected mayor of Chicago (IL), the third largest city in the United States. She was also the first Black woman, and only the second woman, to serve as mayor of Chicago. Three other LGBTQ+ women have been elected as mayors of top 100 cities: Mayor Jenny Durkan in Seattle, Washington (2017–21), Mayor Jane Castor in Tampa, Florida (2019–present), and Mayor Satya Rhodes-Conway in Madison, Wisconsin (2019–present). Austin Quinn-Davidson served as acting mayor of Anchorage, Alaska, in 2020–21 but chose not to run for reelection. Just outside the top 100 cities, Jackie Biskupski was mayor of Salt Lake City, Utah, from 2016 to 2020.

It took longer for transgender women and bisexual women to win local offices. About fifteen years after the first LGBTQ+ woman – Kathy

Kozachenko – had won her race, Joanne Conte became the first openly transgender person elected to office in the United States. She won a seat on the Arvada City Council in Colorado and served from 1991 to 1995. Twenty more years would go by before another notable first occurred. It was only in 2012 that the first openly bisexual woman was elected to a city council. This happened when Marlene Pray won a seat in Doylestown, Pennsylvania. One might be surprised by the delay in electing out bisexual women to office. But bisexual individuals continue to be underrepresented today. In 2023, while bisexual individuals constituted just over 57 percent of the LGBTQ+ community in the United States, they represented only about 12 percent of all LGBTQ+ elected officials.

Why are there so few openly bisexual individuals in office? On the one hand, there might be less urgency to publicly come out for someone who is bisexual and in a relationship with an opposite-sex individual. If this is the case, we might be undercounting the number of bisexual elected officials. On the other hand, bisexual individuals sometimes are misunderstood by both the straight and the LGBTQ+ communities. On this point, Kate Brown, the openly bisexual former governor of Oregon, explained what happened when she came out. Her parents told her it would have been easier if she were a lesbian, her gay friends called her half-queer, and her straight friends believed she could never make up her mind about anything.[4]

LGBTQ+ Women in State Legislatures

A few months after Kozachenko's victory in Michigan, another woman became the first out LGBTQ+ person elected to a state-level office. Elaine Noble won a seat in the Massachusetts House of Representatives in November 1974. She would go on to serve two terms (1975–79), representing a district that included parts of Boston. Before running for office, Noble had been a women's rights activist, cofounded the Massachusetts Women's Political Caucus, and served on the Governor's Commission on the Status of Women. She was also an LGBTQ+ activist, working with the local chapter of the Daughters of Bilitis, one of the oldest lesbian organizations in the country, founded in 1955 in San Francisco.

Noble's electoral run and service in office encapsulated some of the challenges and pressures that would emerge in the political campaigns and activities of future LGBTQ+ politicians. Noble faced both homophobia

---

[4] OutHistory, Kate Brown, Oregon, 1992, n.d., https://outhistory.org/exhibits/show/
    out-and-elected/1992/kate-brown

and criticism from within the LGBTQ+ community, in sectors unhappy with her work to desegregate schools. Before running, Noble also worried about whether voters would support an LGBTQ+ candidate, explaining, "We had helped form the Massachusetts Women's Political Caucus and at that time we were trying to find women to run. I said I don't know if I'm electable, being gay."[5] And yet she never thought about not running as an openly lesbian candidate. She said, "When I ran for political office, it was really important to me to be open about my gayness, even though I felt a lot of pressure from people telling me to either downplay it or not say anything about it at all."[6] If sexuality had not been an issue for Kozachenko in Michigan, it took center stage in Noble's campaign, and not only because of her choice. During the campaign, Noble faced prejudice and violence, which she attributed to the strong animosity against homosexuality then present in all sectors of society. In the end, Noble observed how she had been elected "in spite of being gay," a nod to the obstacles she had to overcome to win in what was still a largely Catholic Irish town. Once in office, new challenges arose. An eighty-five-year-old man called to her on her walk to the state House and spit on her. Her colleagues left feces at her desk. And she faced strong pressure and expectations from the LGBTQ+ community, being the only out LGBTQ+ person in office. Noble recalled, "The gay community expected me to be on call 24 hours a day. It was like they felt they owned me."[7] Noble won a second term in 1976 but decided not to run for a third term in the state House due to physical and emotional exhaustion. She left politics in 1979 after an unsuccessful run for US Senate.

After Elaine Noble, Karen Clark was elected to the Minnesota House of Representatives in 1980. She would remain in office until 2019, becoming the longest-serving openly lesbian member of a state legislature in the United States. But up until 1991, there was never more than one out LGBTQ+ woman at a time in state legislatures. The number started to take off in the 1990s, when more LGBTQ+ women were elected around the country. Among them, Deborah Glick was elected to the New York

---

[5] Larry Nichols, A Talk with Elaine Noble, *Philadelphia Gay*, October 10, 2007, https://windycitytimes.com/2007/10/10/a-talk-with-elaine-noble/

[6] Something Personal; A Woman's Place Is in the House: A Portrait of Elaine Noble, American Archive of Public Broadcasting, accessed December 27, 2024, https://americanarchive.org/catalog/cpb-aacip_15-33rv1gdz

[7] Sasha Gregory-Lewis, Interview with Elaine Noble, in *Long Road to Freedom: The Advocate History of the Gay and Lesbian Movement*, ed. Mark Thompson (New York: St. Martin's Press, 1994), pp. 96–99.

State Assembly in 1990; Liz Stefanics to the New Mexico State Senate, Kate Brown and Gail Shibley to the Oregon State Assembly, and Susan Farnsworth to the Maine House of Representatives in 1992; Sheila Kuehl to the California State Assembly in 1994; and Carole Migden to the California State Assembly in 1996. The numbers continued to grow in the following decades, as shown in Figure 6.1.

LGBTQ+ Women in Statewide Offices

So far, there have been three out LGBTQ+ women elected governors, including two from Oregon. Kate Brown became governor of Oregon in 2015. Brown, who was the first out LGBTQ+ person elected to state-wide office and the first to become governor in any US state, has had a long career in Oregon politics. She served in the Oregon House of Representatives from 1991 to 1997, in the Oregon Senate from 1997 to 2009 (being majority leader from 2003 to 2009), and as Oregon Secretary of State from 2009 to 2015. Brown became governor in 2015, replacing John Kitzhaber, who resigned under criminal investigation. She then won two full terms and remained in office until 2023. To this day, Brown is the only openly bisexual person to have served as governor in the country.

Two more LGBTQ+ women were elected governors in 2022 and took office the following year: Tina Kotek in Oregon and Maura Healey in Massachusetts. Similar to Brown, Kotek, who is openly lesbian, has

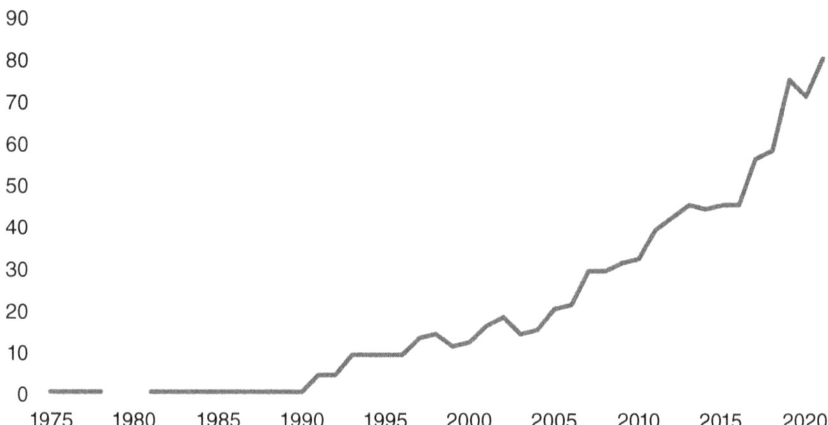

Figure 6.1 Out LGBTQ+ women in state legislatures have grown over time since 1974.
Source: Original data collected by Charles W. Gossett, Andrew Reynolds, and Gabriele Magni.

had a long career in Oregon politics. She served in the Oregon House of Representatives from 2007 to 2022, including as speaker of the House since 2013, when she became the first openly lesbian state House speaker in the country. Maura Healey, who also identifies as lesbian, served as Massachusetts attorney general from 2015 to 2023 before becoming governor. In 2015, Healey became the first out lesbian attorney general in the country and the first out LGBTQ+ person elected to statewide office in Massachusetts. Two more LGBTQ+ women have been elected attorneys general. Dana Nessel took office as attorney general of Michigan in 2019, and Kris Mayes became attorney general of Arizona in 2023.

LGBTQ+ Women in Congress
In November 1998, Tammy Baldwin, then a member of the Wisconsin State Assembly, won her race for the US House of Representatives. When she took office in January 1999, Baldwin became the first out LGBTQ+ woman to ever serve in the US Congress. Baldwin was the only LGBTQ+ woman in Congress for thirteen years until she was joined by Kyrsten Sinema, who was elected to the US House from Arizona. Sinema was the first bisexual member of Congress.

A few years later, the 2018 election was labeled the "rainbow wave" because of the unprecedented number of LGBTQ+ candidates elected to office. These included three new LGBTQ+ women in the House: Sharice Davids, a Native American woman from Kansas and the first openly LGBTQ+ woman of color in Congress; Angie Craig from Minnesota, the first nonincumbent LGBTQ+ parent elected to Congress; and Katie Hill, a bisexual woman from California. Becca Balint from Vermont was elected in 2022. In 2024, three new LGBTQ+ women won their races for Congress. Sarah McBride became the first openly transgender member of Congress, Emily Randall the first LGBTQ+ Latina in Congress, and Julie Johnson, elected from Texas, the first out LGBTQ+ congressmember from a southern state (see Table 6.1).

In 2013, Tammy Baldwin broke another ceiling when she became the first out LGBTQ+ woman elected to the US Senate. Five years later she was joined by Kyrsten Sinema, the first out bisexual senator. The number grew in 2023, when California Governor Gavin Newsom appointed openly lesbian Laphonza Butler to finish the term of the late Senator Dianne Feinstein. Butler, who is Black, was the first nonwhite LGBTQ+ senator, as well as the first Black LGBTQ+ woman in Congress. Both Sinema and Butler decided not to run for reelection in 2024, leaving Tammy Baldwin as the only out LGBTQ+ woman in the US Senate in 2025 (see Table 6.2).

Table 6.1 Out LGBTQ+ women elected to the US House of Representatives over time

Years	Number	LGBTQ+ Women in the US House
Before 1999	0	–
1999–2012	1	Tammy Baldwin (D-WI)
2013–18	1	Kyrsten Sinema (D-AZ)
2019	3	Angie Craig (D-MN), Sharice Davids (D-KS), Katie Hill (D-CA)
2020–22	2	Angie Craig (D-MN), Sharice Davids (D-KS)
2023–24	3	Angie Craig (D-MN), Sharice Davids (D-KS), Becca Balint (D-VT)
2025	6	Angie Craig (D-MN), Sharice Davids (D-KS), Becca Balint (D-VT), Julie Johnson (D-TX), Sarah McBride (D-DE), Emily Randall (D-WA)

Source: Author's own elaboration.

Table 6.2 Out LGBTQ+ women elected to the US Senate over time

Years	Number	LGBTQ+ Women in the US Senate
Before 2013	0	–
2013–18	1	Tammy Baldwin (D-WI)
2019–22	2	Tammy Baldwin (D-WI), Kyrsten Sinema (D-AZ)
2023–24	3	Tammy Baldwin (D-WI), Kyrsten Sinema (D-AZ), Laphonza Butler (D-CA)
2025	1	Tammy Baldwin (D-WI)

Source: Author's own elaboration.

The combined number of out LGBTQ+ women in the US House and Senate (Figure 6.2) reveals a steady increase over time, even though the overall number remains low. Between 1999 and 2012, Tammy Baldwin was the lone LGBTQ+ congresswoman. The number doubled to two between 2013 and 2018, when Baldwin (now in the Senate) was joined by Sinema in the House. The number increased to five in 2019, following the 2018 rainbow wave. After Katie Hill resigned that same year, the number decreased to four. In 2023, the number grew to six, with the election of Balint to the House and the appointment of Butler to the Senate. Following the 2024 election, the number of LGBTQ+ women in Congress further increased to seven. Figure 6.2 shows that there have never been

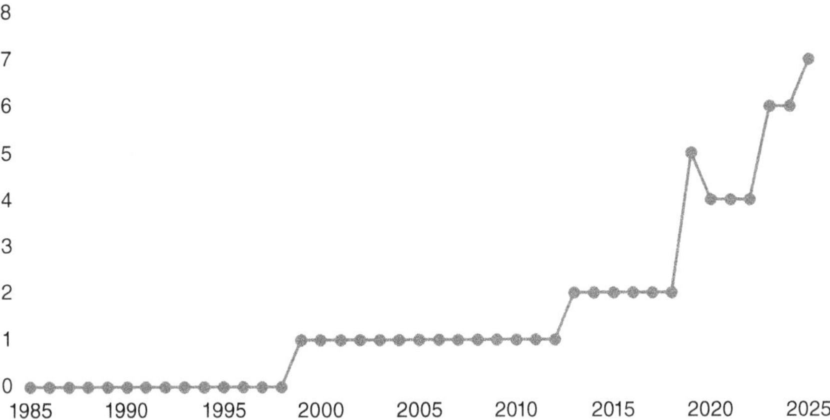

Figure 6.2 The number of out LGBTQ+ women in the US Congress has slowly grown over time.
Source: Original data collected by Gabriele Magni.

more than seven LGBTQ+ women in Congress at any one time. At this high, it only represents 1.3 percent of all members of Congress. This indicates that, despite progress, more LGBTQ+ women need to be elected to Congress to reach equitable representation.

In total, ten LGBTQ+ women have served so far in Congress, with two of them – Baldwin and Sinema – serving in both the House and the Senate. All of them have been elected (or appointed, in the case of Butler) as Democrats, even though Sinema switched to Independent during her last two years in office. Nine are ciswomen and one – McBride – is a trans woman. Six identify as lesbian, two as bisexual (Sinema and Hill), and two as queer (McBride and Randall). Seven are white, one Native American (Davids), one Black (Butler), and one Latina (Randall). California is the only state that has so far sent two LGBTQ+ women to Congress, one to the House (Hill) and one to the Senate (Butler). The other LGBTQ+ women in Congress have hailed from Arizona, Delaware, Kansas, Minnesota, Texas, Vermont, Washington, and Wisconsin.

EXPLAINING THE INCREASE IN LGBTQ+ WOMEN IN OFFICE

As we have seen, the number of LGBTQ+ women in local, state, and federal office started to take off in the 1990s, culminating with the election of the first lesbian congresswoman, and then grew more quickly in the 2000s. Various factors help explain why such growth happened at that time.

First, advances in LGBTQ+ rights in the previous two decades laid the foundation for the growing political power of the LGBTQ+ community and encouraged more LGBTQ+ individuals to run for office. In June 1969, gay, lesbian, and transgender patrons of the Stonewall Inn, a gay bar on Christopher Street in New York City, fought back against a homophobic police raid. What became known as the Stonewall Riots is considered the starting point of modern LGBTQ+ activism. Although gay life and gay organizations had existed even in the first half of the century and had grown in the 1950s, most notably with the Mattachine Society, the Stonewall Riots became the catalyst for future mobilization. The following year, the first Pride marches were organized in New York City, Los Angeles, and Chicago to commemorate the riots. New, emboldened gay and lesbian groups, often collectively described as the gay liberation movement, developed in the 1970s to fight for LGBTQ+ rights.

The HIV/AIDS crisis in the 1980s contributed to further LGBTQ+ mobilization. This culminated in the 1993 March on Washington for Lesbian, Gay, and Bi Equal Rights and Liberation, which revealed the growing political strength of the LGBTQ+ movement on the national stage. This mobilization provided gay men and lesbian women with fertile terrain on which to hone their political skills. This history of organizing and activism led to the development of political experiences and connections that would prove crucial for LGBTQ+ people to successfully run for office in the following years.

Second, the HIV/AIDS crisis of the 1980s and 1990s crucially contributed in another way to the rise of LGBTQ+ people, and in particular women, running for office. On the one hand, the crisis made even more urgent the need to have a seat at the table to shape public policy. At a time when rampant homophobia in society and in the government led to the failure to address a crisis that was claiming the lives of thousands of gay men and other marginalized groups, it was left to LGBTQ+ leaders to push for medical and political change. The HIV/AIDS epidemic made it clear that the presence of LGBTQ+ leaders in the halls of power, including elective office, was essential to address a crisis that was devastating the LGBTQ+ community. On the other hand, the HIV/AIDS crisis spurred many lesbian women to become more politically active. As HIV/AIDS predominantly decimated gay men, lesbian women often stepped up to help and lead in social and political contexts.

Third, in the 1990s the United States started to witness positive changes in public opinion toward LGBTQ+ people and rights. The change is documented by the General Social Survey, a sociological survey created in

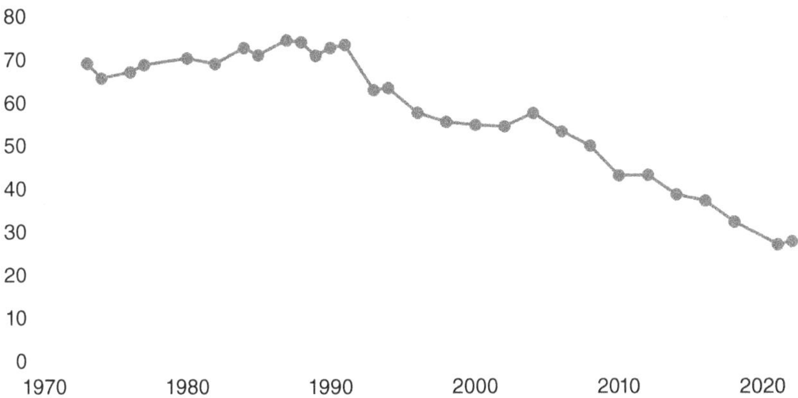

Figure 6.3 Percent of people who agree that sexual relations between two adults of the same sex are always wrong (1972–2024).
Source: General Social Survey.

1972 to collect public opinion data on a wide variety of social and political issues. Starting in 1973, one question asked respondents: "What about sexual relations between two adults of the same sex – do you think it is always wrong, almost always wrong, wrong only sometimes, or not wrong at all?" In 1973, 69 percent of respondents considered same-sex relationships always wrong, a share that had increased to 74 percent in 1991. Then, the trend started to reverse. By 2000, the share had decreased to 55 percent, and it would further decrease to 43 percent by 2010 (Figure 6.3). Decreased negative attitudes in society and among voters made possible the election of more LGBTQ+ politicians, initially in more progressive areas, such as cities with larger gay populations and college towns.

The 1990s and 2000s also saw an increase in sympathetic LGBTQ+ media representation, which positively affected public attitudes toward gays and lesbians. The TV show *Frasier* aired affirming episodes with gay characters in 1994. Ellen DeGeneres, then at the height of her popularity, publicly came out in 1997 in "The Puppy Episode" of the *Ellen* show. The episode was an enormous popular and critical success, with forty-two million viewers and earning two Emmy Awards and a Peabody Award. *Time Magazine* dedicated a cover to Ellen under the title "Yep, I'm Gay." Almost twenty years later, in 2016, DeGeneres would receive a Presidential Medal of Freedom from President Obama in part for her groundbreaking 1997 public coming out, which became a watershed moment for the LGBTQ+ community.

In 1998, NBC premiered *Will and Grace*, which centered on the relationship between a gay lawyer and his best friend. *Will and Grace* would become among the most successful TV shows ever, winning eighteen

Primetime Emmy Awards and remaining the highest-rated sitcom among adults eighteen to forty-nine from 2001 to 2005. The show was widely credited for normalizing LGBTQ+ people and issues in many American households, thus improving attitudes toward LGBTQ+ people. In 2012, then Vice President Joe Biden remarked that the show "probably did more to educate the American public" on LGBTQ+ issues "than almost anything anybody has ever done so far."[8]

The early 2000s also saw the first mainstream TV shows entirely focused on gay and lesbian characters. In 2000, Showtime aired *Queer as Folk*, a series that followed the lives of five gay men in Pittsburgh. Four years later, Showtime premiered *The L Word*, a TV show that lasted five years and chronicled the lives of a group of lesbian and bisexual women living in West Hollywood, California.

Fourth, LGBTQ+ organizations and women's rights organizations played an active and central role in supporting women LGBTQ+ candidates running for office. Two political action committees created in the late 1980s and early 1990s were of paramount importance. EMILY's List was founded in 1985 to help elect Democratic women running for office and promising to protect abortion rights. The Gay & Lesbian Victory Fund (later renamed the LGBTQ+ Victory Fund) was created as a nonpartisan political action committee in 1991.[9] The goal of the Victory Fund was to increase the number of LGBTQ+ people elected to office through fundraising.

The first candidate endorsed by the Victory Fund was Seattle (WA) City Council candidate Sherry Harris, who in 1991 defeated a twenty-four-year incumbent to become the first openly lesbian African American city council member in the country. The following year the Victory Fund supported more candidates, including Tammy Baldwin, who won her race for the Wisconsin State House. In 1994, twenty-eight candidates endorsed by the Victory Fund won their elections, including Sheila James Kuehl, who became the first out LGBTQ+ person elected to the California State Legislature. The number of LGBTQ+ women endorsed by the Victory Fund continued to grow in the second half of the 1990s, with the Victory Fund playing a pivotal role in Baldwin's election to Congress in 1999.

The fifth factor explaining the growing number of LGBTQ+ women in office in the 1990s and 2000s is the presence of LGBTQ+ trailblazers who had paved the way and won elections in the two previous decades.

---

[8] David Eldridge, Biden "Comfortable" with Gay Marriage, Cites "Will & Grace," *Washington Times*, May 6, 2012, https://tinyurl.com/33eb5pye

[9] LGBTQ+ Victory Fund, Our History, n.d., https://victoryfund.org/about/history/

LGBTQ+ pioneers such as Elaine Noble, Allan Spear, Harvey Milk, and Barney Frank proved that gay men and lesbian women could win, encouraging more LGBTQ+ women to run. Trailblazers winning elections generated confidence in LGBTQ+ women's ability to succeed, generating higher fundraising numbers and weakening opposition to their candidacies from party leaders.

CHALLENGES FOR LGBTQ+ WOMEN RUNNING FOR OFFICE

While a growing number of LGBTQ+ women have been elected to office in the last two decades, LGBTQ+ candidates have faced and continue to face obstacles that many cisgender (i.e., a person whose gender identity matches the sex they were assigned at birth) and straight candidates do not experience. Two challenges stand out: prejudice and electability concerns.

Prejudice: Homophobia and Transphobia

Homophobia and transphobia have long been present in society and remain rooted in large sectors. As mentioned earlier, until the 1990s, over 70 percent of Americans considered same-sex relationships wrong. Even though attitudes have improved significantly over the years, about 30 percent of Americans still considered same-sex relationships wrong in the 2020s. Prejudice at times leads to violence. Between 2017 and 2019, LGBT people experienced 6.6 violent hate crime victimizations per 1,000 persons, compared with 0.6 per 1,000 persons for non-LGBT people.[10] Recent years have also seen an increase in anti-LGBTQ+ bills and legislation around the country. In 2024, the American Civil Liberties Union counted 576 anti-LGBTQ+ bills introduced around the country.

People who dislike LGBTQ+ individuals are unlikely to support LGBTQ+ women running for office. Political science research has shown that voters, on average, tend to penalize LGBTQ+ candidates. A 2021 article found that gay and lesbian candidates in the United States faced an electoral penalty of over five percentage points, partly due to the outright discrimination and prejudice that voters displayed toward these candidates.[11] Indeed, lesbian women have faced prejudice among voters

---

[10] A. R. Flores, R. L. Stotzer, I. H. Meyer, and L. L. Langton, Hate Crimes Against LGBT People: National Crime Victimization Survey, 2017–2019, *PLoS One* 17(12) (2022): e0279363.

[11] Gabriele Magni and Andrew Reynolds, Voter Preferences and the Political Underrepresentation of Minority Groups: Lesbian, Gay, and Transgender Candidates in Advanced Democracies, *The Journal of Politics* 83(4) (2021): 1199–215.

since they first began to run for office. In an interview a few years after her election, Elaine Noble – the first out LGBTQ+ state legislator in the country – recalled the vitriol and the violence she endured during her 1974 run for office: "It was a very ugly campaign. Ugly. There was a lot of shooting through my windows, destroying my car, breaking windows at my campaign headquarters, serious harassment of people visiting my house and campaign office – it was really bad."[12]

Elaine Noble was the first but certainly not the last LGBTQ+ woman to experience prejudice on the campaign trail. No LGBTQ+ woman has been fully immune, even if attacks have become more subtle over time. As recently as 2024, two-term incumbent US Senator Tammy Baldwin, the highest-ranked LGBTQ+ elected official in the country, faced attacks for being in a same-sex relationship in a series of ads by her Republican opponent.

Trans women and nonbinary candidates often face greater prejudice, partly because transphobia is even stronger than homophobia in society. Many of the recent anti-LGBTQ+ bills have targeted transgender people and rights, focusing on banning gender-affirming care, trans women in sports, and bathroom access. This has led to a deterioration of attitudes toward transgender people and rights in recent years. Consequently, transgender women still face strong prejudice on the campaign trail, face opponents who intentionally misgender and dead name them (i.e., they call them by their birth name when they have changed their name as part of their gender transition), and experience harassment and violence on social media and in public spaces.

Electability Concerns

Electability concerns are another big challenge for LGBTQ+ candidates. Electability concerns refer to the doubts that a specific candidate will be able to gather enough voter support and win the election. Historically, women and racial minority candidates have faced electability concerns among voters, party leaders, the media, and potential financial support-ers. This is because such candidates departed from the norm of past elected officials, who, for a long time, have been white men. When Hillary Clinton ran for president in 2016, many wondered whether the country was ready for a female president. Eight years later, when Kamala Harris became the Democratic nominee, some doubted that the country would vote for a

12 OutHistory, Elaine Noble, Massachusetts, 1974, accessed December 27, 2024, https:// outhistory.org/exhibits/show/out-and-elected/1970s/elaine-noble

Black and South Asian woman for president. Indeed, it is hard for people to believe that something can be done until someone accomplishes it.

LGBTQ+ candidates have also faced many questions about their electability, partly because the vast majority of elected officials have historically been straight and cisgender. Thus, when Pete Buttigieg ran for president in the 2020 Democratic primaries, many doubted that the country would support a gay man. At the time, a Politico/Morning Consult poll revealed that only 40 percent of Americans believed that the country was ready for a gay president.[13]

It is therefore of little surprise that LGBTQ+ women have also faced severe electability concerns because of both their gender identity and their sexual orientation. Brianna Titone, one of the first trans women elected to a state legislature when she won her race for the Colorado House in 2018, faced doubts from party leaders. Even after she won her seat, many of her colleagues believed her time in the state House would be short-lived and refused to provide support. In an interview with the *Denver Post* after entering office, Titone recalled: "[They thought] well, you're probably not going to win again. That was the attitude when I first ran – well, she's probably not going to win, don't bother helping. So it became, she's not going to win again, let's not waste any positions that are going to help somebody get more experience."[14] Electability concerns are often magnified for LGBTQ+ women who are minoritized on more than one identity, such as LGBTQ+ women of color, LGBTQ+ Muslim women, and LGBTQ+ women with disabilities. Sherry Harris, who in the early 1990s became the first Black lesbian elected official when she joined the Seattle City Council, explained: "In 1991, I made history by becoming the first openly gay African American lesbian to be elected to public office in the country. I won a city-wide, at-large, non-partisan election in a mid-size American city when everyone had told me it would be impossible to win because of my triple minority status."[15]

Additional Challenges

LGBTQ+ women often face additional challenges, even compared with male LGBTQ+ candidates. These challenges are further magnified for

[13] Caitlin Oprysko, Poll: Voters Split on Whether Country Is Ready for a Gay President, *Politico*, October 30, 2019, https://politico.com/news/2019/10/30/pete-buttigieg-gay-president-poll-061350

[14] Alex Burness, Brianna Titone and the Weight of Being Colorado's First Out Transgender Lawmaker, *Denver Post*, January 24, 2022, https://denverpost.com/2022/01/24/brianna-titone-transgender-colorado-lawmaker/

[15] Out History, Sherry Harris, Washington, 1991, accessed January 17, 2025, https://outhistory.org/exhibits/show/out-and-elected/1991/sherry-harris

transgender women and nonbinary individuals, as well as for LGBTQ+ women of color. In 2023, I conducted a survey of LGBTQ+ candidates in partnership with the LGBTQ+ Victory Institute. An invitation to participate was distributed online to all out LGBTQ+ candidates who ran for office between 2018 and 2022. In total, 487 candidates completed the survey, which corresponds to nearly one in five of every out LGBTQ+ candidate in the country. This is the largest survey of LGBTQ+ candidates conducted to date. In the survey, I asked LGBTQ+ candidates about their subjective experiences, including the challenges they faced during their campaigns.

LGBTQ+ women were more likely than men to report that they had been *attacked for their appearance*. Four in ten LGBTQ+ women (40.1 percent) faced attacks based on their appearance or the way they dress, compared with 27.8 percent of gay and bisexual men. LGBTQ+ women also said they were attacked more frequently. Among them, 10.9 percent reported receiving attacks at least weekly, compared with 4.1 percent of gay and bisexual men. These attacks have a long tradition, as LGBTQ+ women running for office have often been criticized for being "too masculine" and "aggressive" in their appearance and demeanor. This was the case, for instance, with Lori Lightfoot, the former Black lesbian mayor of Chicago. Christine Quinn, the former lesbian speaker of the New York City Council who ran unsuccessfully for New York City mayor, was also ridiculed for her short hair and tailored suits, described as "unfeminine."

These attacks often go even further in the case of transgender women. For example, during the 2017 campaign that would lead to her becoming the first out trans state legislator in the country, Danica Roem faced repeated attacks on her gender identity in her opponent's ads. Her opponent, thirteen-term Republican incumbent Bob Marshall, proudly self-described himself as Virginia's "chief homophobe."

LGBTQ+ women were also more likely to report facing *gender-based violence* on the campaign trail. Among LGBTQ+ women, 5.4 percent said they had faced gender-based violence, compared with 1.9 percent of gay and bisexual men. The share is especially high for trans women, 7.1 percent of whom faced gender-based violence. But even cis women (lesbian, bisexual, and queer) faced significant more gender-based violence than gay and bisexual men: 5 percent vs. 1.9 percent. For instance, in 2018, after winning Vermont's Democratic gubernatorial primary, Christine Hallquist emerged as the first openly transgender person to receive a major party nomination for governor. As national attention enveloped her campaign, Hallquist became the target of about a dozen death threats and other attacks. This forced the Hallquist campaign to increase security measures, avoid providing advanced notice of public appearances, and avoid publicizing the location of the campaign headquarters.[16]

Attacks and violence against LGBTQ+ women cause damage not only to the candidates who endure them. They also have chilling effects among other LGBTQ+ women who are considering running. Women on the fence on whether to enter the race may worry about their personal lives being distorted, their dating lives being weaponized, and their safety – as well as the safety of their family – being threated. All these considerations might discourage some LGBTQ+ women from running, thereby complicating the path toward increased LGBTQ+ representation.

LGBTQ+ women also reported facing *greater difficulty in being taken seriously* as candidates than gay and bisexual men. Among LGBTQ+ women, 28.6 percent said they faced difficulty in being taken seriously compared with 21.4 percent of LGBTQ+ men. The challenge was especially acute for trans women, 32.1 percent of whom faced difficulty in being taken seriously. But even cis women (lesbian, bisexual, and queer) faced more difficulty than gay and bisexual men, 27.7 percent vs. 21.4 percent. Additionally, compared with gay and lesbian men, LGBTQ+ women were more likely to report having to face *media challenging their qualifications*. Among lesbian, bisexual, and queer cisgender women, 16 percent experienced media challenging their qualifications, compared with 10.5 percent of gay and bisexual men.

HOW LGBTQ+ WOMEN GET ELECTED

Despite the unique challenges they face, LGBTQ+ women running for office have been increasingly successful. Various factors help us understand why. First, LGBTQ+ women tend to have greater *political experience* than their opponents.[17] Before running for office, compared with men and straight women, many LGBTQ+ women often have a longer history of political organizing and activism, as well as greater experience in lower elective offices. This experience proves an important asset on the campaign trail. It helps LGBTQ+ women hone their political skills, equipping them with greater ability to oversee complex campaign tasks such as drafting campaign plans, fundraising, securing endorsements, and coordinating volunteers.

---

[16] Associated Press, Vermont's Transgender Gubernatorial Candidate Getting Death Threats, *NBC News*, August 22, 2018, https://tinyurl.com/635nmj95

[17] Gabriele Magni and Andrew Reynolds, The Preparation Gap and the Political Strength of LGBTQ+ Candidates: Evidence from a New Dataset of U.S. State Elections, Working paper, n.d.

The lengthy experience of LGBTQ+ women in politics and activism also creates a group of supporters over the years who can be mobilized for campaign volunteering, door-knocking, and financial contributions. Additionally, experience in lower offices provides LGBTQ+ women with evidence that they are indeed capable of winning elections, given that they have already done so. This crucially addresses some of the electability concerns that often hamstring LGBTQ+ candidates. When asked during her 2024 campaign whether voters were ready for the first transgender member of Congress, Sarah McBride, who was at the time a state senator in Delaware, referred to this point: "People asked that question when I ran for the state Senate, and we proved them wrong. With people's continued support, I'm optimistic we'll prove those naysayers and those cynical political observers wrong once again."[18]

Second, LGBTQ+ women running for office are often formidable *fundraisers*. A recent analysis has shown that, in the 2020 state elections, the mean campaign spending amount was $269,649 for lesbian candidates, $182,575 for gay male candidates, and $150,376 for straight candidates.[19] These numbers are confirmed by anecdotal evidence. During her historical 2017 run for the Virginia State Assembly, Danica Roem raised over $500,000, outpacing her thirteen-term incumbent opponent by a three-to-one margin. The bulk of donations came from LGBTQ+ supporters from all over the country eager to back the candidate who would become the first out trans state legislator in the United States.

This fundraising success is partly due to the still relatively low number of LGBTQ+ women running for office, who often attract outsized attention and campaign donations from outside their district. Organizations such as the LGBTQ+ Victory Institute, EMILY's List, Run for Something, Human Rights Campaign, and L-PAC often contribute to this fundraising success, playing a big role in raising funds for LGBTQ+ women candidates. But LGBTQ+ women's fundraising success is also linked to their greater political experience. Their history of organizing allows them to forge deep ties over the years with their communities, which in turn produces a robust network of potential donors to rely on when they run for office.

Third, LGBTQ+ women who emerge as candidates are stronger than the average candidate for public office because they have had to *overcome challenges and discrimination* just to make it onto the ballot. LGBTQ+

---

18   Orion Rummler, Sarah McBride Believes Voters Are Ready for the First Ever Transgender Member of Congress, *19th News*, December 12, 2023, https://tinyurl.com/4sndyemv
19   Magni and Reynolds, The Preparation Gap.

women have often had to overcome the prejudice they face and convince stakeholders, party leaders, and voters that they are indeed unusually strong candidates in order to secure their support and win the primaries. Additionally, past experiences with discrimination have equipped many LGBTQ+ women with a resilience that proves very useful in politics, where attacks happen frequently on the campaign and in office.

In many cases, these challenges have reinforced their commitment to public service. Trailblazers who have faced heightened discrimination, such as Annise Parker, the first openly lesbian mayor of a major US city, and Tammy Baldwin, the first out lesbian woman in Congress, have emphasized how the challenges they faced prompted them to work even harder to get elected. This point is especially true for LGBTQ+ women who are minoritized on more than one identity. US Representative Sharice Davids, who in 2018 became the first Native American LGBTQ+ person elected to the US Congress, has explained how her experiences with barriers and discrimination on the reservation have made her a stronger candidate.[20]

Fourth, LGBTQ+ women – and lesbian women in particular – running for office can to some extent benefit from *masculinity stereotypes*, especially compared with gay men and straight women. Voters often see lesbians as more masculine than heterosexual women.[21] To be clear, these stereotypes have been used to attack LGBTQ+ women, such as in the case of Lori Lightfoot, former Black and lesbian mayor of Chicago, who has been negatively described as too masculine and aggressive. But these perceptions of masculinity can sometimes lead to perceived higher competence of LGBTQ+ women among voters.[22] Because the lesbian stereotype and the traditional stereotype of a good politician – both based on masculinity and competence – overlap, stereotyped lesbian candidates may be evaluated relatively more positively by voters.[23]

The fifth point explaining the political strength of LGBTQ+ women relates to their media and candidate *communication strategy*. Some LGBTQ+

---

20 Isaac Stanley-Becker, Sharice Davids, Who Sees Past Discrimination as Her Asset, Could Become the First Gay Native American in Congress, *Washington Post*, August 14, 2018, https://tinyurl.com/y9n46bxh

21 A. J. Blashill and Kimberly K. Powlishta, Gay Stereotypes: The Use of Sexual Orientation as a Cue for Gender-Related Attributes, *Sex Roles* 61 (2009): 783–93.

22 Claudia Niedlich et al., Ironic Effects of Sexual Minority Group Membership: Are Lesbians Less Susceptible to Invoking Negative Female Stereotypes than Heterosexual Women?, *Archives of Sexual Behavior* (44) (2015): 1439–47.

23 Ewa A. Golebiowska, Group Stereotypes and Political Evaluation, *American Politics Research* 29(6) (2001): 535–65.

women have at times *downplayed their sexual orientation and/or gender identity*. This does not mean they have hidden their LGBTQ+ identity. But they have decided not to make it the center of their campaign, choosing instead to focus on issues deemed important for their constituents. This strategy serves at least two purposes. On the one hand, it shows that LGBTQ+ women are not single-issue candidates – that is, they are not focusing only on one political issue such as LGBTQ+ rights. They promise they will work on a variety of issues, and not only on LGBTQ+ rights. On the other hand, this strategy can help deflect possible attacks from opponents, who could otherwise highlight their LGBTQ+ identity to mobilize conservative voters. For instance, Danica Roem was always open about being transgender but in 2017 explained she did not want to make her campaign about her gender identity. Instead, she focused on an issue less headline-grabbing but important to voters in her district: traffic. In 2024, Sarah McBride's election to the US House made history as she became the first openly transgender member of Congress. While never shying away from her trans identity, and in fact acknowledging its historical importance, McBride focused her campaign on other issues important to her future constituents, including health care, childcare, and abortion rights.

THE 2024 ELECTIONS AND ATTACKS ON TRANSGENDER RIGHTS

While LGBTQ+ women have sometimes made the decision to focus their communication on issues other than their LGBTQ+ identity, this is not always possible when political opponents have targeted LGBTQ+ issues to mobilize homophobic and transphobic voters against LGBTQ+ and progressive candidates. This is the case with wedge issues – that is, divisive issues (often connected to questions of morality) that are used strategically to mobilize supporters. One of the most well-known examples of the use of wedge issues was the decision by the 2004 George W. Bush presidential campaign to focus on same-sex marriage to bring conservative voters to the polls on Election Day. More recently, in the 2024 election, transgender rights have become one of the most prominent wedge issues.

In 2024, the Republican Party spent a record $65 million on anti-trans ads, which focused mostly on three policies. The first was the promise to prohibit gender-affirming care, especially for minors. Gender-affirming care refers to a series of social, psychological, behavioral, and medical interventions that aim to support an individual's gender identity when such identity conflicts with the gender assigned at birth. The second issue was the promise to ban transgender women from competing in sports with cisgender women. The third was the prohibition on transgender women using bathrooms that do not correspond to their biological sex.

While the Harris campaign largely chose to ignore and not respond to anti-trans ads, LGBTQ+ women candidates usually addressed these attacks during the campaign. This is because those attacks directly targeted the community that LGBTQ+ women come from and represent. The link is clear for transgender women running for office, who are directly targeted by anti-transgender actions. For example, immediately after Sarah McBride was elected to Congress, South Carolina Republican Representative Nancy Mace pushed for banning Representative McBride from using the women's bathrooms in Congress. But campaign attacks also affected lesbian and bisexual women, who have often been among the major supporters of transgender rights in office.

Additionally, LGBTQ+ women also often emphasized the need to protect abortion rights during the 2024 campaign. This is not surprising if one considers that attacks on abortion rights often went hand in hand with attacks on women's bodies, including attacks on gender identity and gender-affirming care. As access to health care was often a campaign priority for LGBTQ+ women and especially trans women, the protection of abortion and reproductive rights also emerged as a key point.

LGBTQ+ WOMEN OFFICEHOLDERS IN 2025

What was the landscape of LGBTQ+ women in office at the beginning of 2025? The Out for America map by the LGBTQ+ Victory Institute shows that 507 out LGBTQ+ women served in office at any level of government in the United States. Additionally, sixty-three elected officials nationwide openly identified as nonbinary, gender nonconforming, and genderqueer. A total of 567 out LGBTQ+ women and nonbinary individuals were in office throughout the country.[24] While this might seem like a large number and certainly is a significant increase from only a couple of decades ago, out LGBTQ+ women and nonbinary individuals constituted only about one-tenth of 1 percent (0.11%) of all elected officials in the country. This clearly shows that they remain severely underrepresented, if one considers that, according to Gallup, 8.7 percent of women in the US population identify as LGBTQ+. The next pages offer a portrait of who the LGBTQ+ women and nonbinary individuals in office are.

[24] The total is 567 (rather than 570) because elected officials could select more than one label to describe their gender identity.

Table 6.3 Out LGBTQ+ women and nonbinary elected officials in 2025 by level of office

Office	Number
US Congress	7
Governor	2
Statewide office	5
Mayor	15
State Legislature	137
Local office	327
Judicial office	81

Source: LGBTQ+ Victory Institute tracking as of April 2025.

LGBTQ+ women and nonbinary elected officials served at most levels of government (Table 6.3). Six were in Congress, two were governors, and four served in statewide office. A large number served in state legislatures and an even larger number in local offices (319), including city councils, county boards, school boards, and neighborhood councils. Thirteen were mayors, while seventy-five served in judicial offices.

Gender Identity, Sexual Orientation, Race, and Ethnicity

A little over eight in ten of the out LGBTQ+ women in office in 2025 identified as cisgender, over 6 percent were transgender women, and about 3 percent each identified as nonbinary, gender nonconforming, and genderqueer (the total is greater than 100 because elected officials could select more than one option) (Table 6.4). The number of transgender women in office – thirty-six – is remarkable, especially if one considers that there were only nine transgender men in office nationwide. Sarah McBride, who in 2024 was a state senator in Delaware, won her race for the US Congress in November 2024. In 2025, there were seven trans women in state legislatures. Danica Roem served in the Virginia State Senate, Brianna Titone in the Colorado House of Representatives, Leigh Finke in the Minnesota House, Zooey Zephyr in the Montana House, Taylor Small in the Vermont House, Aime Wichtendahl in the Iowa House, and Kim Coco Iwamoto in the Hawaii House.

There were also four nonbinary elected officials in state legislatures. Among them, Izzy Smith-Wade-El, who is Black and bisexual, served in the Pennsylvania House of Representatives. There were three gender nonconforming state legislators, including Mike Simmons, who is Ethiopian American and in 2021 became the first openly gay state

Table 6.4 Out LGBTQ+ women and nonbinary elected officials in 2025 by gender identity, sexual orientation, race and ethnicity

Gender Identity

	Number	Percentage of LGBTQ+ women in office*
Cisgender woman	471	83.1%
Gender nonconforming	20	3.5%
Genderqueer	8	1.4%
Genderqueer/nonbinary	19	3.4%
Nonbinary	14	2.5%
Transgender nonbinary	2	0.4%
Transgender woman	36	6.4%

Sexual Orientation

	Number	Percentage of LGBTQ+ women in office*
Asexual[25]	2	0.4%
Bisexual	113	19.9%
Gay	14	2.5%
Heterosexual	2	0.4%
Lesbian	275	48.5%
Pansexual	32	5.6%
Queer	128	22.6%
Same-gender loving[26]	4	0.7%

Race and Ethnicity

	Number	Percentage of LGBTQ+ women in office*
Asian/Pacific Islander	18	3.2%
Black/African American/Afro-Caribbean	69	12.2%
Latinx/Hispanic	79	13.9%
Middle Eastern/Arab American	7	1.2%
Multiracial	29	5.1%
Native American/Alaska Native	7	1.2%
Native Hawaiian	0	0%
White/Caucasian	370	65.3%
Other	3	0.5%

* *The total is greater than 100 because elected officials could select more than one option.*

Source: LGBTQ+ Victory Institute tracking as of April 2025.

[25] A person who experiences little or no sexual attraction to others.
[26] A term sometimes used to describe same-sex attraction without using labels such as gay or lesbian.

senator in Illinois history. Among genderqueer/nonbinary elected officials, Liliana Bakhtiari served on the Atlanta (GA) City Council. Bakhtiari, who is Iranian American, became the first out queer Muslim elected official from Georgia in 2021 and one of the few elected officials who is in a non-monogamous relationship with two partners.

Regarding sexual orientation, among out LGBTQ+ women in office, almost one in two identified as lesbian, about one in five identified as bisexual, 22.6 percent identified as queer, and over 5 percent identified as pansexual – that is, they are attracted to people regardless of their gender identity (Table 6.4). When it comes to race and ethnicity, about two in three of the out LGBTQ+ women in office in 2025 were white (Table 6.4). Black LGBTQ+ women were about 12 percent and Latinx LGBTQ+ women about 14 percent, while Asian LGBTQ+ women were just over three percent of all LGBTQ+ women in office. Around 5 percent were multiracial.

States

Out LGBTQ+ women, gender nonconforming, and nonbinary elected officials were present in all but seven states in 2025. The states with the highest numbers of LGBTQ+ women and nonbinary individuals in office at the end of 2025 were California (sixty-four), Illinois (thirty-four), Pennsylvania (thirty-two), Washington (twenty-eight), Oregon (twenty-five), and Minnesota (twenty-five). There were no LGBTQ+ women or nonbinary individuals in office in Alabama, Idaho, Louisiana, Mississippi, North Dakota, South Carolina, and Wyoming (Figure 6.4).

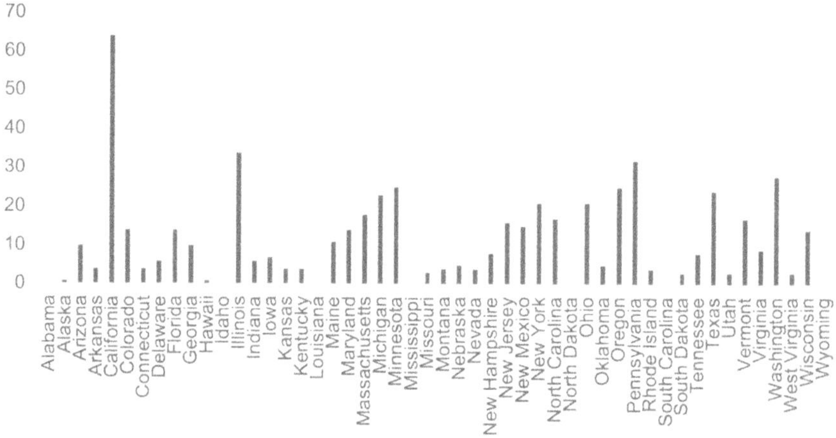

Figure 6.4 Out LGBTQ+ women and nonbinary elected officials in 2025 by state. *Source:* LGBTQ+ Victory Institute tracking as of April 2025.

These differences across states are in part due to varying state populations and the availability of elective offices. More populous states, such as California and Illinois, where a higher number of elected positions are available, tend to have more opportunities to elect LGBTQ+ women to office. But this is only part of the story, as some large states such as Texas and Florida are not at the top of the list. At the same time, states such as Oregon, Minnesota, and Washington, which are only the twenty-seventh, twenty-second, and thirteenth state by population, respectively, are in the top five when it comes to LGBTQ+ women in office as of 2025. How do we explain this?

Various factors account for the varying number of LGBTQ+ women in office. First, states that have traditionally been more progressive (such as Washington and Massachusetts) tend to have more LGBTQ+ women in office. Second, states with larger urban populations and cities with strong LGBTQ+ communities (including San Francisco, Los Angeles, New York, Chicago, Philadelphia, and Boston) tend to elect more LGBTQ+ officeholders. Third, states with stronger anti-discrimination laws, more inclusive policies, and stronger LGBTQ+ protections are on average more supportive of LGBTQ+ women running for office. Fourth, the effectiveness of candidate recruitment and support networks vary by state, which influences representation outcomes. Finally, states that have a longer history of electing LGBTQ+ women to office create a pipeline effect where earlier representation encourages more LGBTQ+ women to run for office and win elections.

IMPACT OF LGBTQ+ WOMEN IN OFFICE

Over 500 LGBTQ+ women were in office at the beginning of 2025. Why does it matter? LGBTQ+ women in office promote LGBTQ+ rights, improve attitudes toward LGBTQ+ people, and become role models for other LGBTQ+ women and youth. Let's expand on each of these points. The presence of LGBTQ+ elected officials has a positive effect on the passing of LGBTQ+ legislation and policies.[27] The presence of a few LGBTQ+ legislators can generate positive impact even in the absence of a critical mass sometimes needed for the promotion of other minority rights.[28] Why is this the case?

---

[27] Andrew Reynolds, *The Children of Harvey Milk: How LGBTQ Politicians Changed the World* (New York: Oxford University Press, 2018).

[28] Andrew Reynolds, Representation and Rights: The Impact of LGBT Legislators in Comparative Perspective, *American Political Science Review* 107(2) (2013): 259–74.

First, LGBTQ+ women can act as *legislative entrepreneurs* who advocate, set the agendas, and build alliances to support LGBTQ+-related bills. This is because LGBTQ+ women tend to have greater sensitivity toward LGBTQ+ issues, which impact them personally or impact members of their own community. For instance, lesbian and gay elected officials have taken the lead on same-sex marriage. In 2022, after the Supreme Court overturned *Roe v. Wade* and the constitutional right to abortion, many worried that the court could similarly reverse its earlier decision on marriage equality. Lesbian Senator Tammy Baldwin then spearheaded the efforts that led the US Senate to pass the Respect for Marriage Act to protect same-sex unions. Senator Baldwin spent months convincing Republican senators to come on board, eventually securing the support of twelve Republicans who proved crucial to reach the required sixty-member majority and enshrine marriage equality into law. Bisexual senator from Arizona Kyrsten Sinema also played an important role in convincing some of her Republican colleagues to support the bill.

This points to a second way in which LGBTQ+ women promote LGBTQ+ rights in office. They nurture *familiarity and acceptance* from their straight and cisgender colleagues, thereby *building alliances* to pass legislation. With their presence in office, they personalize LGBTQ+ issues, making it harder for their colleagues to deny rights to someone they know personally. Indeed, people who have LGBTQ+ friends and family members tend to have more positive attitudes toward LGBTQ+ people and rights. Senator Baldwin explained how knowing someone who is LGBTQ+ positively shaped the position of several senators: "I have so many colleagues who have friends, relatives, staff members who are gay and married. So, there are a lot more people based on those relationships who want to get to yes. And again, those were really moving conversations."[29] Carole Migden, who in 1996 was one of only three openly LGBTQ+ members of the California State Assembly, also emphasized the crucial role of LGBTQ+ legislators in forging alliances with their straight colleagues to pass LGBTQ+ legislation:

> Over the years, I've repeatedly witnessed the importance of forging alliances with my fair-minded straight colleagues. Rallying the support of straight members and advocates on behalf of my community's struggle for equal rights is a key component to many of my legislative

---

[29] Liz Goodwin, How a Bipartisan Group of Senators Got Same-Sex Marriage Protections Passed, *Washington Post*, November 30, 2022, https://washingtonpost.com/politics/2022/11/30/same-sex-marriage-vote/

successes. Having straight people stick up for gay people is a powerful way to open the minds and hearts of those who would otherwise be against us.[30]

Additionally, LGBTQ+ women in office often *break barriers and become role models*. This has several positive consequences. It sends the message to *LGBTQ+ youth* that they belong everywhere, including in the halls of political power. Deborah Glick, who is openly lesbian, was first elected to the New York State Assembly in 1990, and was still in office thirty-five years later, once explained: "And then there are young people who come in ... they're working in other fields, and when everybody is shaking hands and the lobby visit is over, they say, "and I just want to say on a personal note that you've been a role model."[31]

The presence of LGBTQ+ women in office also mobilizes and encourages *other LGBTQ+ women to run*, following in the footsteps of those who paved the way. Several trans women elected to office in recent years credited Danica Roem for their decision to run, after Roem became the first out trans state legislator in 2017. In this regard, Sean Meloy, the vice president of political programs at the LGBTQ+ Victory Fund, remarked in 2024: "I haven't talked to one trans person running for state legislature who hasn't said that [Roem] was an inspiration to them to step forward to fight for their community. Now that's being coupled by Sarah McBride."[32]

Finally, LGBTQ+ women in office can also contribute to *improving public attitudes toward LGBTQ+ people*. This is because individuals often project a feeling of familiarity onto their elected representatives, which mirrors the impact of a close friend or family member. LGBTQ+ women in office therefore nurture familiarity that can reduce stigma and prejudice against LGBTQ+ people.

CONCLUSION

This chapter has explored the experiences of LGBTQ+ women who run for, and are elected to, office. Over time, since the first out LGBTQ+ women were elected in 1974, their number has substantially increased.

---

[30] OutHistory, Carole Migden, California, 1990, accessed January 17, 2025, https://outhistory.org/exhibits/show/out-and-elected/1990/carole-migden

[31] Out History, Deborah Glick, New York, accessed January 17, 2025, https://outhistory.org/exhibits/show/out-and-elected/1990/deborah-glick

[32] Isabela Espadas Barros Leal, Trans Candidates Are Running on a Slew of Issues Besides Anti-LGBTQ Bills, *NBC News*, October 23, 2024, https://tinyurl.com/22cbw3j4

Yet LGBTQ+ women remain vastly underrepresented at any level of government. They also continue to face challenges on the campaign trail, such as prejudice, electability concerns, and double standards in media coverage. They are often able to overcome such disadvantages because of their political strengths, which include robust political experience and strong fundraising results. Once in office, LGBTQ+ women emerge as role models, play a pivotal role in the promotion of LGBTQ+ rights, and contribute to the improvement of LGBTQ+ public attitudes.

RICHARD L. FOX

7 Congressional Elections

Women's Candidacies and the Road to Gender Parity

The 2022 and 2024 congressional elections highlighted several of the trends that have dominated the bumpy road to gender parity in the United States Congress. Recent elections have shown progress, stagnation, partisan differences, and a host of electoral firsts. The 2022 election set a record, with a total of 151 women elected to serve in the US House and Senate, surpassing the 146 who served in the prior Congress. Even though female representation in American politics reached an all-time high in 2022, women still made up only 28.4 percent of the US Congress.[1] The slow march toward parity took a small step back in 2024 as only 150 women were elected to serve in the 119th Congress. Women's fortunes as congressional candidates continue to be deeply tied to the political parties, with more than two-thirds of women in Congress identifying as Democrats.

Because of the gap in numbers of women serving and the ideological differences between women in the Republican Party and their Democratic counterparts, much of the increase in ethnic and racial diversity among America's female representatives continues to be attributable to the Democratic Party. In fact, almost 90 percent of the women of color ever elected to Congress have been Democrats.[2] When the 119th Congress convened in January 2025, there were fifty-nine women of color – fifty-four of whom were Democrats. All twenty-nine Black women serving in the 119th Congress are Democratic representatives; out of the nineteen Hispanic representatives, fifteen of them are Democrats; eight out of the nine Asian American women, both of the Middle Eastern/North African

I would like to thank Emilie Olson and Kiana Karimi for assistance with data collection.

[1] Center for Women and Politics (CAWP), Current Congress and Temporary Records, November 12, 2024, https://tinyurl.com/4bwcbm8c

[2] CAWP Women Elected Officials Database, https://cawp.rutgers.edu/data/women-elected-officials-database.

women, and the lone Native woman in Congress are from the Democratic Party. The 2024 Senate elections saw a notable first. Democrats Angela Alsobrooks of Maryland and Lisa Blunt Rochester of Delaware are the first Black senators to represent their respective states in the chamber and also mark the first time two Black women have served simultaneously in the Senate.

While Democrats have led the way in adding a diverse group of women candidates to Congress, the Republican Party has continued to make progress in the advancement of female representation in terms of age and geography. As shown later in this chapter, fewer and fewer states have never sent a woman to Congress. Indeed, in 2023 Republican Katie Britt became the first woman to be sent to the US Senate from Alabama and, at forty-one years old, was the youngest Republican woman to be elected to the US Senate in the history of the GOP. Britt represents a cohort of conservative female politicians who are dedicated to conservative efforts that have typically not aligned with a women's rights agenda. Though Republican women in the general population tend to be more ideologically moderate than their male counterparts, in a highly polarized political environment such as the United States, moderate politicians have a hard time getting elected. Another case is the election of Anna Paulina Luna, elected to Florida's 13th district in 2022. She is young – thirty-four at the time of the election – a former member of the air force, a model, and an Instagram influencer. Luna self-identifies as a younger, more diverse MAGA candidate who called Donald Trump "the greatest president of our lifetime."[3]

Many of the increases in women's representation in the US political system over recent elections also represent an increase in social and political representation for the LGBTQ+ community. For example, in 2025, Sarah McBride made history when she became the first transgender woman to ever be elected to the United States House, serving as the US Representative from Delaware.[4] Laphonza Butler made history when California Governor Gavin Newsom appointed her to fill Dianne Feinstein's seat in the US Senate in 2023, after Senator Feinstein's death. Butler, who pledged not to run for reelection, became the first openly lesbian Black senator to ever serve in Congress.[5]

---

[3] Ruby Cramer, Anna Paulina Luna Throws a Coming-Out Party for New MAGA Generation, *Washington Post*, November 8, 2022, https://tinyurl.com/ymr45dzv

[4] Annie Karni, "A Bounty on My Head": Congress's First Transgender Member Faces the Trump Era, *New York Times*, January 23, 2025, https://tinyurl.com/2dwskbms

[5] Ece Yildirim, Laphonza Butler makes history as first Black openly lesbian U.S. Senator, CNBC, October 3, 2023, https://cnbc.com/2023/10/03/laphonza-butler-sworn-in-makes-history-as-first-black-openly-lesbian-us-senator.html

This chapter examines the evolution of women's candidacies for Congress and the role gender continues to play in congressional elections. Ultimately, I focus on one fundamental question: Why is the road to gender parity in Congress so slow? I explore the persistence of gender as a factor in congressional elections in three sections. In the first, I offer a brief historical overview of the role of gender in congressional elections. The second section compares male and female candidates' electoral performance and success in House and Senate races through the 2024 elections. The results of this analysis confirm that, when considered in the aggregate, the electoral playing field in general elections has become largely level for women and men. But if that is the case, why are there still so few women in Congress? In the final section of the chapter, I provide some answers, examining some of the subtler ways that gender continues to affect congressional elections. The combination of gendered geographic trends, women's presence in different types of congressional races, the scarcity of women running as Republicans, and the gender gap in political ambition suggests that gender continues to play an important role in congressional elections.

THE HISTORICAL EVOLUTION OF WOMEN'S CANDIDACIES
FOR CONGRESS

Throughout the 1990s, women made significant strides competing for and winning seats in the US Congress. The 1992 elections, often referred to as the "Year of the Woman," resulted not only in a historic increase in the numbers of women in both the House and the Senate, but also in the promise of movement toward some semblance of gender parity in our political institutions (see Table 7.1). After all, in the history of the US Congress, more than 12,000 men and only 441 women have served as voting members of Congress. Only sixty-four women have ever served in the US Senate, nineteen of whom either were appointed or won special elections.

The continued dearth of women in Congress suggests that a masculine ethos, ever present across the history of Congress, is still present in the congressional electoral environment. A host of interrelated factors – money, familiarity with power brokers, political experience, and support from the political parties – contributes to a winning campaign. Traditional candidates are members of the political or economic elite. Most emerge from lower-level elected offices or work in their communities, typically in law or business. They tend to receive encouragement to run for office from influential members of the community, party officials, or outgoing

Table 7.1 Over time, more Democratic women than Republican women have emerged as general election House candidates and winners

	1970	1980	1990	2000	2010	2020	2022	2024
General Election Candidates								
Democratic women candidates	15	27	40	81	91	204	178	191
Republican women candidates	10	25	29	42	47	94	82	68
Total women	25	52	69	123	138	298	260	259
General Election Winners								
Democratic women winners	10	11	20	41	48	89	91	94
Women as a percentage of all Democrats that won a House seat	3.9	4.5	7.1	19.4	29.0	40.3	43.7	43.7
Republican women winners	3	10	8	18	24	30	33	31
Women as a percentage of all Republicans that won a House seat	1.7	5.2	5.4	8.1	7.0	14.2	15.3	14.1

Note: Except where noted, entries represent the raw number of women candidates and winners for each year.

Source: Past Candidate Information, Center for American Women and Politics (CAWP), https://cawp.rutgers.edu/facts/elections/past_candidates, and New York Times listing of election results.

incumbents. And these same elites who encourage candidacies also contribute money to campaigns and political action committees (PACs) and hold fundraisers. This process has been in place for most of the recent history of congressional candidacies and, for obvious reasons, has served men well and women very poorly.

Because they have been excluded from their communities' economic and political elites throughout much of the twentieth century, women often take different paths to Congress. Widows of congressmen who died in office dominated the first wave of successful female candidates. Between 1916 and 1964, twenty-eight of the thirty-two widows nominated to fill their husbands' seats won their elections, for a victory rate of 88 percent. Across the same time period, only thirty-two of the 199 non-widows who garnered their parties' nominations were elected (a 14 percent victory rate).[6] Overall, roughly half the women who served in the House during this period were widows. Congressional widows were the one type of woman candidate that was readily acceptable to party leaders at this time.

The 1960s and 1970s marked the emergence of a second type of woman candidate – one who turned her attention from civic volunteerism to politics. Several women involved in grassroots community politics rode their activism to Washington. Notable figures (all Democrats) who pursued this path include Patsy Mink in Hawaii, elected in 1964; Shirley Chisholm in New York, elected in 1968; Bella Abzug in New York, elected in 1970; and Pat Schroeder in Colorado and Barbara Jordan in Texas, both elected in 1972. Mink was the first Asian American woman and Chisholm was the first Black woman elected to Congress.

We are currently in the third and possibly final stage of the evolution of women's candidacies. The prevailing model of running for Congress has become far less rigid. The combination of decreased political party power, the emergence of independent campaign funding networks (PACs and Super PACs), and growing media influence facilitates the emergence of a more diverse array of candidates competing successfully for their parties' nominations. In the first and second waves, the idea of a candidate like Democrat Alexandria Ocasio-Cortez – a twenty-nine-year-old political activist working as a bartender – knocking off a revered incumbent in the primary, as she did in 2018, would have been unthinkable. The same is true for Republican Lauren Boebert, a thirty-four-year-old restaurant owner and gun rights supporter who became an Internet sensation by challenging a Democratic presidential candidate on gun rights in 2020 and the notoriety she received propelled her to a seat in Congress. Converging with this less rigid path to Congress is an increase in the number of women who now fit the profile of a "conventional" candidate. Women's presence in fields such as business and law, from which candidates have often emerged, has increased dramatically. Further, the number of women serving in state legislatures, often a springboard to Congress, has roughly quadrupled since 1975 (for a thorough analysis of women's fluctuating success in running for state-level office, see Chapter 9 in this volume). Together, these developments help to explain why the eligibility pool of prospective women candidates has grown substantially since the 1990s.[7]

---

[6] Irwin N. Gertzog, *Congressional Women* (New York: Praeger, 1984), p. 18

[7] Danielle Thomsen and Aaron A. King, Women's Representation and the Gendered Pipeline to Power, *American Political Science Review* 114(4) (2020): 989–1000.

Despite growth in the number of eligible women who could run for Congress, women's progress has continued only in fits and starts in the most recent congressional election cycles. The 2024 elections marked the fourth time since 1990 that the results of a national election did not increase women's presence in the House. In the Senate, the growth in the number of women has been just as slow, with elections alternating between stagnation and modest increases.

Table 7.1 presents the numbers of women candidates who won their party nominations and ran in House general elections from 1970 through 2024. In 2020, the 298 women who secured their party's nomination to be the general election candidate was more than double the number of women nominees from a mere ten years earlier. The total number of general election House candidates in 2022 and 2024 dropped by more than 10 percent from this high in 2020. But to put these numbers into perspective, it is helpful to recognize that more than 500 male candidates garnered their parties' nominations to run as general election candidates in each of the three most recent elections.

Despite recent gains by Republican women, most notably in 2020, Table 7.1 illustrates the divergent paths of the Democratic and Republican parties. The Democrats have been on a steady path, continually increasing the number of women who run for Congress and eventual winners. The Republicans, in comparison, have put forward far fewer women over the past two decades. We are now at a point where roughly three times as many female Democrats as Republicans serve in Congress.

In the evolution of women's candidacies for Congress, the first election of Donald Trump as president in 2016 shocked many observers and caused a chain reaction that propelled more women to run for Congress.[8] After Donald Trump defeated Hillary Clinton, the first female major-party presidential candidate to make it to the general election, millions took to the streets for the Women's March and thousands looked into running for office. To many women (and men), Donald Trump's election was a setback to the cause of gender equality. After all, he was accused of sexual harassment and assault by more than a dozen women and had a history of making derogatory remarks about women. Yet he won despite all of this. Although there was some question as to whether Trump's presidency would actually motivate more women to seek office, the results

---

[8] Jacob Pramuk, The Number of Women Running for Office Is Rising: 7 First-Time House Candidates Explain Why They're Running in the Age of Trump, *CNBC*, April 4, 2018, https://cnb.cx/3iAxhBz

of the 2018 election were clear: more than twice as many Democratic women filed to run for Congress than had ever done so before.[9]

But this was not a one-time blip. The record number of Democratic women filing to run in 2018 was repeated in 2020. While Trump may have motivated a number of women to finally jump into the ring and run for office, the 2018 election motivated action by Republicans. In response to Democratic women's historic gains and after decades of stagnation in the number of candidates, the Republicans set a new record for women congressional candidates in 2020, roughly doubling their previous high. The trend lines for the 2022 and 2024 elections did not see the dramatic fluctuations of the previous cycles, but Democrats tended to maintain high numbers of congressional candidates while Republicans saw slippage, especially in 2024.

Overall, the historical evolution of women's success in winning congressional offices demonstrates that we are in a period of increasing opportunity for women candidates. An early assessment of the impact of Donald Trump regaining the presidency in 2025 does not suggest that it is having the same motivating effect among prospective women candidates, though it is too early to draw this conclusion. Regardless, at this point we can conclude that women's progress in pursuing parity in the US Congress remains slow and uncertain. Figure 7.1 highlights the uneven progress for winning election to the US Congress. Next, we turn our attention to the performance of women candidates in elections.

MEN AND WOMEN RUNNING FOR CONGRESS: THE GENERAL INDICATORS

In assessing why so few women serve in Congress, many researchers have turned to key election statistics and compared female and male congressional candidates. The research increasingly reveals little or no overt bias against women candidates. There is some research, relying on experimental methods in which participants are presented with hypothetical candidate match-ups between men and women, where researchers have identified clear bias against women candidates.[10] But studies that focus on

[9] Margaret Talbot, The Women Running in the Midterms during the Trump Era, *The New Yorker*, April 18, 2018, https://bit.ly/3xDwyU9

[10] For examples of experimental designs that identify voter bias, see Yoshikuni Ono and Barry C. Burden, The Contingent Effects of Candidate Sex on Voter Choice, *Political Behavior* (41) (2018): 583–607; Sara Saltzer and Mary C. McGrath, Voter Bias and the Partisan Gender-Gap in Office, *Political Behavior* (46) (2022): 473–500; Leonie Huddy and Nadya Terkildsen, Gender Stereotypes and the Perception of Male and Female Candidates, *American Journal of Political Science* 37 (1993): 119–47; Leonie Huddy and

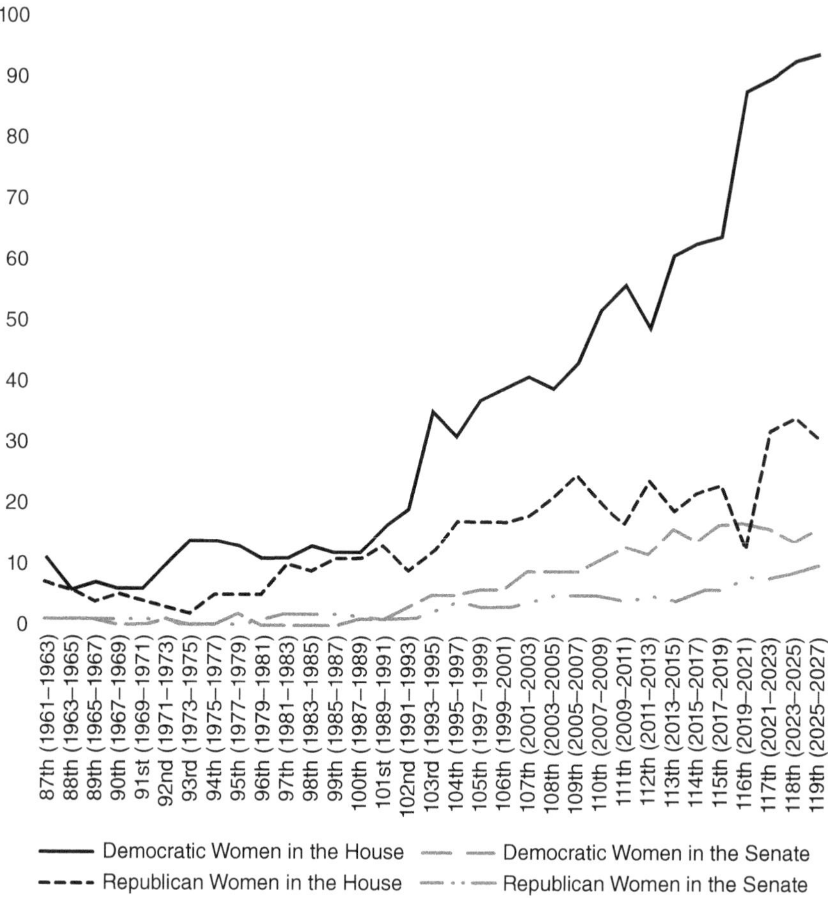

Figure 7.1 The slow path to gender parity in the House and Senate was highlighted in the 2022 and 2024 congressional elections.
Source: History of Women in the US Congress, CAWP, https://cawp.rutgers.edu/data/levels-office/congress#Historic. Values reflect the number of women serving at the end of each Congress with the exception of the 119th Congress, where values reflect the number at the start of the Congress.

actual vote totals and election outcomes fail to uncover evidence of systematic bias.[11] Barbara Burrell, in an early landmark study of vote totals,

Nadya Terkildsen, The Consequences of Gender Stereotypes for Women Candidates at Different Levels and Types of Office, *Political Research Quarterly* 46 (1993): 503–25; and Richard L. Fox and Eric R. A. N. Smith, The Role of Candidate Sex in Voter Decision-Making, *Political Psychology* 19 (1998): 405–19.

[11] Susanne Schwarz and Alexander Coppock, Meta-Analysis of Sixty-Seven Factorial Survey Experiments, *The Journal of Politics* 84(2) (2022): 655–68; Kathleen Dolan and Timothy Lynch, It Takes a Survey: Understanding Gender Stereotypes, *American Politics Research* 42(4) (2013): 656–756. For a comprehensive examination of vote totals through

concluded that candidates' sex accounts for less than 1 percent of the variation in the vote for House candidates from 1968 to 1992.[12] Kathy Dolan, who in 2004 carried out a comprehensive study of patterns in gender and voting, concluded that candidate sex is a relevant factor in deciding who wins and loses only in rare electoral circumstances.[13]

Jennifer Lawless and Kathryn Pearson, in an analysis of congressional primary elections between 1958 and 2004, found that women candidates are more likely to face more crowded and competitive primaries, but they did not find evidence of voter bias.[14] Examinations of more recent elections have also failed to find that women are more likely to compete in crowded primaries. A 2016 book by Jennifer Lawless and Danny Hayes relying on sophisticated survey data finds little evidence that voters choose or oppose a candidate based on sex.[15] The previous edition of this chapter, focusing on the 2018 and 2020 elections, also found no systematic evidence of voter bias in the results of the general elections.

If we look at the performance of men and women in general election House races in 2022 and 2024, we arrive at a similar conclusion. The data presented in Table 7.2 confirm that there is no widespread voter bias against women candidates in general elections. Voters still may use gender stereotypes to assess women candidates, but when it comes to casting ballots, candidate sex appears to matter little. In the most recent House races, women and men fared similarly in terms of mean vote share. The top half of Table 7.2 presents the results for Democrats, showing that the mean vote share across all types of candidates in both years is almost always the same. Democratic women running as incumbents, challengers, and open-seat candidates in 2022 and 2024 performed equally well with their Democratic male counterparts. Turning to the Republicans presented in the bottom half of Table 7.2, female congressional candidates tended to fare less well than their male counterparts in some categories. In 2022

the mid 1990s, see Richard A. Seltzer, Jody Newman, and M. Voorhees Leighton, *Sex as a Political Variable* (Boulder, CO: Lynne Reinner, 1997).

[12] Danielle M. Thomsen, Ideology and Gender in U.S. House Elections, *Political Behavior* 42(2) (2020): 415–42. See also Barbara C. Burrell, *A Woman's Place Is in the House* (Lansing: University of Michigan Press, 1994).

[13] Kathleen A. Dolan, *Voting for Women* (Boulder, CO: Westview Press, 2004).

[14] Jennifer Lawless and Kathryn Pearson, The Primary Reason for Women's Underrepresentation: Re-evaluating the Conventional Wisdom, *Journal of Politics* 70(1) (2008): 67–82.

[15] Danny Hayes and Jennifer Lawless, *Women on the Run: Gender, Media, and Political Campaigns in a Polarized Era* (New York: Cambridge University Press, 2016).

Table 7.2 Women and men general election House candidates have similar vote shares for 2022 and 2024

	2022		2024	
	Women (%)	**Men (%)**	**Women (%)**	**Men (%)**
Democrats				
Incumbents	63.7	64.6	65.0	65.3
	(77)	(106)	(81)	(105)
Challengers	35.0	35.9	36.2	36.2
	(72)	(95)	(83)	(96)
Open seats	49.2	50.9	48.9	46.6
	(28)	(37)	(27)	(27)
Republicans				
Incumbents	62.4	66.7	61.1	65.9
	(26)	(159)	(31)	(165)
Challengers	37.7	35.3	35.5	35.3
	(43)	(130)	(30)	(145)
Open seats	49.0	50.3	44.7	52.3
	(12)	(50)	(8)	(43)

Note: Entries indicate mean vote share won. Parentheses indicate the total number of candidates for each category. Congressional delegates not included in these totals.
Source: Compiled from *New York Times* listing of election results.

and 2024, male incumbent Republicans on average received roughly 4 percent higher vote shares then female incumbent Republicans. And in 2024, female Republican candidates running for open seats on average performed almost 9 percent worse than their male counterparts. These differences are certainly worth noting and monitoring going forward, but because of the small sample sizes they are not statistically significant differences. In the Senate, with a smaller number of races to consider, it is difficult to assess the vote totals meaningfully. Ultimately, though, general trends continue to reveal no clear evidence of bias for or against women Senate candidates in 2022 or 2024.

Turning to the second most important indicator of electoral success – fundraising – we see similar results. In the 1970s and 1980s, because so few women ran for office, many scholars assumed that women in electoral politics simply could not raise the amount of money necessary to mount competitive campaigns. Indeed, older research that focused on the few women candidates who did run concluded that women ran campaigns with lower levels of funding than did men. More systematic examinations of campaign receipts, however, have uncovered few sex differences in fundraising for similarly situated general election candidates. An early study of congressional candidates from 1972 to 1982 found only a "very weak" relationship between gender and the ability to raise campaign funds.[16] More recent research indicates that by the 1988 House elections, the disparity between men and women in campaign fundraising had completely disappeared.[17] In cases where women raised less money than men, the differences were accounted for by incumbency status: male incumbents generally held positions of greater political power and thus attracted larger contributions.[18] Since 1992, PACs such as EMILY's List have worked to make certain that viable general election women candidates suffer no disadvantage in fundraising (see Chapter 8 in this volume for a discussion of EMILY's List). This does not rule out the possibility that fewer women run because of lack of access to funds, but it does show that once in the race women raise as much money as their male counterparts.

If we examine fundraising totals of male and female general election House candidates in 2022 and 2024, we see a few notable gender differences but none that point to systematic bias against women (see Table 7.3). In fact, some of the discrepancies that do exist are often to the advantage of women candidates. Women incumbents in both parties, for instance, outraised their male counterparts in 2022 and 2024, and often by large margins. Female Republican challengers also outraised male Republican challengers in both cycles.[19] Fundraising for open seats was very volatile, with Democratic men significantly outraising Democratic women in open seat races in 2024; however, the sample size is relatively small, and this was driven by two male Democrats, Eugene Vindman (Virginia, CD7) and Adam Frisch (Colorado, CD3), who both raised over $17 million. Overall, one would be hard pressed to look at general election fundraising totals

---

[16] Lefteris Anastasopoulos, Estimating the Gender Penalty in House of Representatives Using a Regression Discontinuity Design, *Electoral Studies* 43 (2016): 150–57; Barbara Burrell, Women and Men's Campaigns for the US House of Representatives, 1972–1982: A Finance Gap?, *American Political Quarterly* 13(3) (1985): 251–72.

[17] Burrell, *A Woman's Place Is in the House*, p. 105.

[18] Chisun Lee, Gregory Clark, and Nirali Vyas, Small Donor Public Financing Could Advance Race and Gender Equity in Congress, Brennan Center for Justice, 2020, https://tinyurl .com/y2r6k8hr; Kira Sanbonmatsu, Money and Women Candidates, Political Parity, 2017, https://tinyurl.com/326cb3e8; Carole Jean Uhlaner and Kay Lehman Schlozman, Candidate Gender and Congressional Campaign Receipts, *Journal of Politics* 52(1) (1986): 391–409.

[19] Kira Sanbonmatsu, Women's Underrepresentation in Congress, *Daedalus, the Journal of American Academy of Arts & Sciences*, 149(1) (2020): 40–55.

Table 7.3 Women and men general election House candidates have similar fundraising patterns for 2022 and 2024

	2022		2024	
	Women	**Men**	**Women**	**Men**
Democrats				
Incumbents	$3,741,468 (77)	$2,920,198 (106)	$3,105,289 (81)	$3,026,250 (105)
Challengers	$470,228 (72)	$787,546 (95)	$1,107,919 (83)	$1,283,183 (96)
Open seats	$1,773,455 (28)	$2,097,598 (37)	$1,628,506 (27)	$3,274,127 (27)
Republicans				
Incumbents	$4,346,576 (26)	$2,429,250 (159)	$4,196,934 (31)	$3,055,736 (165)
Challengers	$1,415,406 (43)	$626,766 (130)	$834,108 (30)	$481,253 (145)
Open seats	$2,366,276 (13)	$1,793,477 (49)	$1,207,210 (11)	$1,691,323 (41)

Note: Entries indicate total money raised. Parentheses indicate the total number of candidates in each category. Congressional delegates not included in these totals.
Source: Compiled from Federal Election Commission (FEC) reports and fundraising totals listed in Opensecrets.org.

and conclude that women candidates are disadvantaged when it comes to the total amount of money raised.

For Senate races, the number of candidates is too small for statistical comparisons between women and men. In recent cycles, Senate elections have been ferocious battles to see which party can control the chamber in a heavily divided country. The 2022 and 2024 US Senate elections were no different. In 2022, the Democrats picked up one seat to give them a fifty-one to forty-nine majority in the 118th Congress. In 2024, the Republicans picked up four seats to give them a fifty-three to forty-seven majority in the Senate. Across the intense battle to control the Senate, fundraising totals show no evidence that women have trouble raising the money needed to compete in Senate races. In 2022, US Representative Val Demings took on incumbent Senator Marco Rubio in Florida. She lost the race quite badly (58% to 41%) but outraised Rubio by $30 million. In Nevada in that same year, incumbent Democratic Senator Catherine Cortez Masto was in a tough reelection battle with Adam Laxalt, the former attorney general of Nevada. Cortez Masto squeaked through (49% to 48%), but she outraised Laxalt $65 million to $18 million.

If we highlight a few races from 2024, the story is similar. Democrat Angela Alsobrooks, running against former Republican governor Larry Hogan for Maryland's open Senate seat, won the race 55 percent to 43 percent. Alsobrooks also outraised Hogan $30 million to $12 million. In a race the Republicans did not target in their quest to take over the US Senate, Republican Kari Lake lost to Democrat Ruben Gallego by less than three percentage points. Lake was outspent in the race $65 million to $24 million. The Republicans' decision to not focus on Lake's candidacy is typically attributed to her embrace of conspiracy theories and other controversial stances. Ultimately, while certain races might have unique circumstances that explain levels of fundraising, there appears to be no widespread gender bias in fundraising patterns among women and men general election Senate candidates.

With the mounting evidence that women fare just as well as men in general elections, we do not want to be too quick to completely dismiss the role of gender in congressional elections. Focusing only on general election outcomes can obscure some of the challenges women still face in making it to the general election. While it is fair to say that once women get to the general election they are at least as likely as their male counterparts to raise the money necessary to compete and win, it remains true that for many women candidates the journey is more diffi-cult. Recent research that has taken a more nuanced approach has found that women in the general election are often more "qualified" than their male counterparts – meaning that they are more likely to have experi-ence holding elective office.[20] This "performance premium" may help explain why women and men perform at equal rates when running for office.[21] The conclusion drawn by this research is that for women to do just as well as men, they need to be better candidates. A 2018 analysis of Democratic US Senate candidates found that women were about three times more likely to have held prior office than men seeking Democratic

<hr>

[20] Sarah A. Fulton and Kostanca Dhima, The Gendered Politics of Congressional Elections, *Political Behavior* 43 (2021): 1611–37; Mary Layton Atkinson and Jason Harold Windett, Gender Stereotypes and the Policy Priorities of Women in Congress, *Political Behavior* 41 (2019): 769–89

[21] Jeffrey Lazarus and Amy Steigerwalt, *Gendered Vulnerability: How Women Work Harder to Stay in Office* (Ann Arbor: University of Michigan Press, 2018); Kelly Dittmar, Unfinished Business: Women Running in 2018 and Beyond, CAWP, 2019, https://womenrun .rutgers.edu/

nominations for the Senate.[22] While one could certainly debate the notion of what makes someone qualified for elective office, women candidates for high elective office appear to run for office after amassing traditional credentials – such as serving in lower-level offices – while male candidates with varying levels of traditional qualifications feel free to throw their hats in the ring.

In terms of fundraising, there are some challenges remaining that a comparison of general election funding totals might not reveal. Women candidates perceive a much greater challenge in raising funds than their male counterparts.[23] Because of this, they may feel that they have to work harder to achieve the same results. Also, most of the support networks set up to assure that women have equal funding with male colleagues are on the Democratic side of the ledger, meaning there is less targeted support for female Republican candidates.[24] And studies of women of color running for Congress have found that they have not always been able to raise funds at levels similar to white women.[25] Finally, some research finds that women candidates are more reliant on small donors and less likely to self-fund than male candidates.[26] All of this is to say that differences in fundraising by gender and race may still be an impediment on the path to becoming a general election candidate.

Nevertheless, on the basis of vote and fundraising tallies presented earlier, we see what appears to be a relatively gender-neutral playing field in general elections. Women are slowly increasing their numbers in Congress, with substantial gains over time on the Democratic side of the aisle. The data certainly suggest that men have lost their stranglehold over the congressional election process and that women can now find

---

[22] Sarah Fulton and Kostanca Dhima, The Gendered Politics of Congressional Elections, *Political Behavior* 43 (2020): 1611–37.

[23] Sanbonmatsu, Money and Women Candidates; Susan J. Carroll and Kira Sanbonmatsu, *More Women Can Run: Gender and Pathways to the State Legislatures* (New York: Oxford University Press, 2013).

[24] Melody Crowder-Meyer and Rosalyn Cooperman, Can't Buy Them Love: How Party Culture among Donors Contributes to the Party Gap in Women's Representation, *The Journal of Politics* 80(4) (2018): 1211–24.

[25] Ashley Sorensen and Phil Chen, She Works Hard for the Money: Explaining Racial and Gender Disparities in Candidate Success in Primary Elections, *Politics, Groups, and Identities* 12(4) (2023): 806–25; Grace Haley and Sarah Bryner, Which Women Can Run? The Fundraising Gap in the 2020 Elections' Competitive Primaries, CAWP, 2021, https://opensecrets.org/news/reports/2020-gender-race; Philip Chen and Ashley Sorenson, Intersectionality in Campaign Finance and Elections, Paper presented at the annual meeting of the Southern Political Science Association, Austin, Texas, January 17–19, 2019.

[26] Women, Money, & Political Watch, The National View Congressional Elections, CAWP and OpenSecrets, 2024, https://tinyurl.com/whypd8pp

excellent political opportunities. But these broad statistical comparisons tell only part of the story.

ARE WOMEN MAKING GAINS EVERYWHERE? STATE AND REGIONAL VARIATION

Women have not been equally successful running for elective office in all parts of the United States. At the start of 2025, sixteen states had never elected a woman to the US Senate, while in four states both of the senators were women. Mississippi is the only state that has never elected a woman to the US House, though it has sent a woman to the Senate. Historically, California, Maryland, and Missouri were among the first to send multiple women to Congress, while Pennsylvania, Mississippi, and Kentucky have been very slow to elect women to Congress. But the resistance to women's candidacies in certain places in the United States seems to be diminishing. The election of Becca Balint to the lone House seat from Vermont in 2022 meant that all fifty states had sent at least one woman to Congress at some point in time. However, there are still discrepancies in the frequency with which states and regions have elected women to Congress.

As the results of the 2022 and 2024 elections suggest, women may still face some disadvantages when running for office in some parts of the United States. If we examine the prevalence of male and female House officeholders by region and state (Tables 7.4 and 7.5), we see that the broader inclusion of women in high-level politics has not been maintained or extended equally to all regions of the country. Table 7.4 tracks women's electoral success in House races since 1970, breaking the data down by four geographic regions. Data are shown in ten-year increments since 1970 but also include the pivotal 1992 Year of the Woman elections.

Before 1990, the Northeast had two and three times as many women House members as any other region in the country. The situation changed dramatically in 1992. The geographic breakdown in Table 7.4 puts the 1992 elections, as well as the modest increases in women's numbers in Congress since that time, into perspective. The 1992 gains were largely from the West and the South. The number of women winning election to Congress from western states more than doubled, and in the South the number more than tripled. Gains were much more modest in the Midwest and the Northeast. Since the late 1990s, the West is the one region that has led the way in electing women candidates and continues to show clear gains for women. A lot of the gains in the West can historically be

Table 7.4 The regional proportion of US representatives who are women continues to vary by region, though the differences are closing

	West (%)	South (%)	Midwest (%)	Northeast (%)
1970	3.9	0.0	2.5	4.9
1980	2.6	1.6	3.3	8.1
1990	8.2	2.3	6. 2	9.6
1992	17.2	7.9	6.7	12.4
2000	21.4	9.0	13.0	10.8
2010	27.4	9.0	18.0	15.3
2020	35.3	18.7	29.8	28.2
2022	39.4	23.2	30.8	28.9
2024	36.5	24.4	31.9	32.9
Net percentage change (1970 to 2024)	+32.6%	+24.4%	+29.4%	+28.4%

Note: Percentages reflect the proportion of House members who are women.
Source: Compiled by author from CAWP and *New York Times* listing of election results.

attributed to the high number of women from California holding House seats, but women also have strong records of success in other western states such as Wyoming, Nevada, and Washington.

If we go back to as recently as 2010, there were still dramatic variations across regions of the United States. The western states had almost three times the female representation of southern states and was approaching double the representation of northeastern states. But if we look at the last three election cycles – 2020, 2022, and 2024 – these gaps are closing, with only the southern region lagging behind. This can likely be explained by the domination of the Republican Party in the South, and the lower frequency of women running as Republican House candidates.

Looking beyond regional variation, there are also several striking differences among individual states. Consider, for example, that as a result of the 2024 election, nine states had no women representatives in the US House and six states had no women representatives in either the House or Senate. Table 7.5 identifies those states with no women in the US House, those approaching gender parity, and those that are currently achieving gender parity in their House delegations as of January 2025. Since the 2016 elections, women have made breakthroughs in large states that previously had no women serving in the House. Pennsylvania, with eighteen seats, elected four women representatives in 2020, and Georgia, with fourteen House seats, also elected four women that year. The state breakthroughs have largely held through the 2024 elections.

Table 7.5 also demonstrates that women congressional candidates have succeeded in a number of states with small and medium-sized populations. The right-hand column of Table 7.5 shows that fourteen states have House delegations made up of at least 50 percent women. This is particularly noteworthy in medium-sized states such as Washington, Minnesota, and Oregon. Women have fared well in high-population states such as California, Florida, and New York, though the numbers in California are down as a result of the 2024 election. For states with the largest delegations, we can assume that more political opportunities for women might lead to more women sent to Congress, but this would not explain women's lack of success in populous states such as Texas (where women currently hold seven out of thirty-eight House seats). Moreover, what explains women's success in states such as Missouri, where, for much of the 1990s and again in 2020, three of the state's eight House members were women? Missouri borders Kansas, which has never elected more than one woman at a time to the House. However, things can change

Table 7.5 Roughly 20 percent of the states had no women serving in the US House of Representatives as a result of the 2024 elections

States with No Women in the House of Representatives (alphabetical order)	States Approaching Gender Parity in the House of Representatives (between 25% and 49%)	States Currently Achieving Gender Parity in the House of Representatives (at least 50%)
Alaska (1)	Michigan (13) – 46%	Delaware (1) – 100%
Arkansas (4)	Connecticut (5) – 40%	North Dakota (1) – 100%
Idaho (2)	Colorado (8) – 38%	Vermont (1) – 100%
Kentucky (6)	Illinois (17) – 35%	Wyoming (1) – 100%
Mississippi (4)	Massachusetts (9) – 33%	Oregon (6) – 83%
Montana (1)	New Jersey (12) – 33%	New Mexico (3) – 67%
Nebraska (3)	Florida (28) – 32%	Minnesota (8) – 63%
Rhode Island (2)	New York (26) – 31%	Washington (10) – 60%
South Dakota (1)	California (52) – 29%	Hawaii (2) – 50%
–	North Carolina (14) – 29%	Iowa (4) – 50%
–	South Carolina (7) – 29%	Maine (2) – 50%
–	Ohio (15) – 27%	Nevada (4) – 50%
–	Utah (4) – 25%	New Hampshire (2) – 50%
–	Maryland (8) – 25%	West Virginia (2) – 50%
–	Kansas (4) – 25%	–

Note: Number in parentheses is the number of House seats in the state as of 2025.

Source: Compiled by author from CAWP and *New York Times* listing of election results.

quickly in some places once the political glass ceiling is shattered. Iowa had never sent a woman to Congress until Joni Ernst's US Senate victory in 2014. By 2020, three of four House members were women. In the matter of a few years Iowa transformed from a state that never elected women to Congress to one with a congressional delegation filled with women. In 2025, women are 50 percent of Iowa's congressional delegation.

Some political scientists argue that state political culture serves as an important determinant of women's ability to win elective office. The researchers Barbara Norrander and Clyde Wilcox have found considerable disparities in the progress of women's election to state legislatures across various states and regions. They explain the disparities by pointing to differences in state ideology and state culture.[27] States with conservative ideologies and "traditionalist or moralist" cultures are less likely to elect women.[28] Percentages of women in a state's legislature and its congressional delegation, however, are not always correlated.

Barbara Palmer and Dennis Simon, in their book *Breaking the Political Glass Ceiling: Women and Congressional Elections*, propose specific causes of regional and state differences in electing women US House members. Examining all congressional elections between 1972 and 2006, they introduce the idea of women-friendly districts. They find that several district characteristics are important predictors of the emergence and success of women candidates. For example, US House districts that are not heavily conservative, are urban, and are not in the South have higher levels of racial minorities, higher levels of education, and are much more likely to have a record of electing women candidates. Palmer and Simon's findings suggest that the manner in which gender manifests itself in the political systems and environments of individual states is an important part of the explanation for the paucity of women in Congress.[29] But things are changing quickly, and the elections of 2022 and 2024 suggest that the number of women-friendly districts and states is expanding.

[27] Barbara Norrander and Clyde Wilcox, Trends in the Geography of Women in the U.S. State Legislatures, in *Women and Elective Office* (3rd edn.), eds. Sue Thomas and Clyde Wilcox (New York: Oxford University Press, 2014), pp. 273–87.

[28] Christopher F. Karpowitz et al., Selecting for Masculinity: Women's Under-Representation in the Republican Party, *Political Science Review* 118(4) (2024): 1873–94; Kira Sanbonmatsu, Political Parties and the Recruitment of Women to State Legislatures, *Journal of Politics* 64(3) (2002): 791–809.

[29] Nicholas Pyeatt and Alixandra B. Yanus, It's All Relative: Understanding "Women Friendliness" Between and Within States, *Social Science Quarterly* 100(6) (2019): 2391–407; Barbara Palmer and Dennis Simon, *Breaking the Political Glass Ceiling: Women and Congressional Elections*, 2nd edn. (New York: Routledge, 2008).

ARE WOMEN RUNNING FOR BOTH PARTIES AND UNDER THE BEST CIRCUMSTANCES?

Most congressional elections feature hopeless challengers running against safely entrenched incumbents. The overwhelming majority of congressional elections are not competitive. A few months prior to the 2022 House elections, for instance, CNN's Election Center completed an analysis of all 435 US House races and concluded that only twenty out of 435 House seats were competitive.[30] Such numbers are typical. Even in more tumultuous election years, it is typical for only ten to fifteen percent of House races, or even fewer, to be competitive. In the 2024 House races, where the stakes could not have been higher as the Republicans began the cycle with a 222 to 213 edge, an early analysis from Sabato's Crystal Ball identified only nineteen (out of 435) House seats as true toss-ups.[31]

Political scientists often identify the incumbency advantage as one of the leading explanations for women's slow entry into electoral politics. Low turnover, a direct result of incumbency, provides few opportunities for women to increase their numbers in male-dominated legislative bodies. Further, when women are the incumbents, to maintain levels of representation they need to be replaced by a woman. Sixteen women incumbents, for instance, retired across the 2022 and 2024 House elections, adding more challenge to women maintaining their numbers in Congress. Between 1946 and 2002, only 8 percent of all challengers defeated incumbent members of the US House of Representatives.[32] In 2016 and 2018 combined, only 6 percent of incumbents were defeated. In 2024, 97 percent of House incumbents won reelection. Accordingly, as the congressional elections scholars Ronald Keith Gaddie and Charles Bullock state, "Open seats, not the defeat of incumbents, are the portal through which most legislators enter Congress."[33]

To begin to assess whether women are as likely as men to take advantage of the dynamics associated with an open-seat race, we can examine the presence of women in open-seat House contests. Table 7.6 compares Democratic and Republican women's presence in general election House

---

[30] CNN's Election Center, 2022 Race Ratings: House, *CNN*, November 14, 2022, https://cnn.com/election/2022/house-race-ratings

[31] Kyle Kondik, Five House Rating Changes as Overall Battle for Majority Remains Tight, *Sabato's Crystal Ball*, September 19, 2024, https://tinyurl.com/3n2rnx2s

[32] Gary C. Jacobson, *The Politics of Congressional Elections*, 6th edn. (New York: Longman, 2004), p. 23.

[33] Ronald Keith Gaddie and Charles S. Bullock III, *Elections to Open Seats in the US House* (Lanham, MD: Rowman & Littlefield, 2000), p. 1.

Table 7.6 Types of general election seats contested by women candidates in the US House vary by year and party

Type of seat	1980	1990	2000	2010	2020	2022	2024
Open seat	6	9	16	14	41	45	34
Democrats	4	8	11	10	28	32	26
Republicans	2	1	5	4	13	13	8
Challengers	31	36	55	54	161	107	113
Democrats	13	16	33	26	91	66	84
Republicans	18	20	22	28	70	41	29
Incumbents	15	24	52	70	96	106	112
Democrats	10	16	37	55	85	78	81
Republicans	5	8	15	15	11	28	31

Note: Entries indicate the raw number of all female candidates for that electoral category. *Source:* Compiled by author from Past Candidate and Election Information, CAWP, https://cawp.rutgers.edu/election-watch/past-candidate-and-election-information.

races by seat type and over time. As shown earlier, women were significantly more likely to run for office in the later eras, although the increase in women candidates is not constant across parties. In the 1980s, the parties were very similar in terms of the types of elections in which women ran. By the year 2000, however, the number of Democratic women running in all types of races had almost tripled, whereas the increases among Republicans were quite small. The disparities between the parties became even starker in more recent open-seat elections. In the 2010 election, Democrats put up ten women for open House seats, the Republicans just two. If open seats are one of the main "portals" to Congress, then Republican women would hardly stand a chance. Across the 2022 and 2024 elections, there were higher numbers of women candidates for open House seats in both parties, but Democrats were almost three times as likely as Republicans to put up women in these critical election opportunities.

Turning to challengers – those who take on incumbents – one of the biggest jumps in candidacies occurred with female Republican challengers in 2020. Republicans almost tripled the number of women running from 2018, and in an election year where Democrats lost a number of seats, the female challengers were able to achieve some success. Ten of the ninety-one female Republicans were able to knock off Democratic incumbents.

Beyond open-seat races, the Democrats have been much more likely than the Republicans to nominate women to run for all types of House seats. This carries serious long-term implications for the number of women serving in Congress. For them to achieve full parity in US political institutions, women must be fully represented in both parties and in the most advantageous electoral opportunities.

So, why are there so few Republican women running for office? A 2015 article by Danielle Thomsen summarizes decades of research trying to answer this question and asserts there are two main reasons for the lack of female representation in the GOP.[34] First, women as a group in the United States tend to be more liberal than their male counterparts, and thus less likely to find an ideological home in the Republican Party. Second, there are simply fewer Republican women in the candidate pipeline. Thomsen asserts the former reason is more important than the latter in explaining the gender gap between the parties. She notes that if women are (usually) more liberal than their male counterparts, and Republicans are looking for explicitly conservative representation, Republican women are the least likely to embody the values at the conservative pole. When applying the same trend to the Democratic Party, the opposite is true: The tendency to be more liberal than their male counterparts makes female nominees look more viable as candidates to the Democratic Party. This partisan divide is then heightened by structural differences, with many more organizations focused on recruiting, training, and supporting Democratic women candidates.

ARE MEN AND WOMEN EQUALLY AMBITIOUS TO RUN FOR CONGRESS?

The decision to run for office, particularly at the congressional level, is a critical area of inquiry for those interested in the role of gender in electoral politics. Examples abound of political women who report that they had some difficulty taking the plunge. Eleven-term Wisconsin Congresswoman Gwen Moore never thought of herself as someone who would run for office until she was coaxed to run for a state legislative seat in the 1990s.[35] Even former House Speaker Nancy Pelosi claims that she had never thought of running for office until she was encouraged to do so in 1987.[36]

---

[34] Danielle Thomsen, Why So Few (Republican) Women? Explaining the Partisan Imbalance of Women in the US Congress, *Legislative Studies Quarterly* 40(2) (2015): 295–323.

[35] Reluctant to Take the Plunge, *USA Today*, May 29, 2008, p. 10A.

[36] Dana Wilkey, From Political Roots to Political Leader, Pelosi Is the Real Thing, *Copley News Service*, November 13, 2002.

Only in the last twenty-five years has empirical research emerged that explores the initial decision to run for office. The rationale for focusing on the initial decision to run for office is that if the general election playing field is largely level, then gender differences in the candidate emergence process likely provide a crucial explanation for women's underrepresentation in Congress. In 2001, 2011, and 2021, Jennifer Lawless and I conducted separate waves of the Citizen Political Ambition Study. This series of surveys asks women and men working in the four professions most likely to precede a career in Congress (law, business, politics, and education) about their ambition to run for elective office someday. Table 7.7 shows results of the surveys, focusing on whether women and men have ever thought about running for office and whether they have taken steps that usually precede a candidacy, such as speaking with party officials and community leaders. On the critical question of interest in running for office, the results of the study highlighted a substantial gender gap in political ambition. The results of the most recent survey in 2021 reveal that there was almost no change in the gender gap between 2001 and 2021. In 2001, there was a sixteen percentage point gap, with men more likely than women to have thought about running for office. In 2011, the gap

Table 7.7 Among potential candidates, women are less interested than men in seeking elective office

	2001		2011		2021	
	Women (%)	Men (%)	Women (%)	Men (%)	Women (%)	Men (%)
Has thought about running for office	43	59	46	62	32	47
Discussed running with party leaders	4	8	25	32	5	9
Discussed running with friends and family	17	29	27	38	14	23
Investigated how to place your name on the ballot	4	10	13	21	8	16
Sample size	1,248	1,454	1,796	1,969	2,580	2,496

Note: Sample is composed of lawyers, business leaders and executives, and educators. Entries indicate percentage responding "yes." All differences between women and men are significant at $p < .05$.
Source: Adapted from Richard L. Fox and Jennifer L. Lawless, The Invincible Gender Gap in Political Ambition, *PS: Political Science & Politics* 57(2) (2024): 231–37.

again stood at sixteen percentage points, virtually unchanged. And in the 2021 survey, the gap was fifteen points. The gender gaps in terms of the actual steps that a potential candidate might take before running for office were also roughly unchanged between 2001 and 2021. Even though the empirical evidence shows that women who run for office do well, a much smaller number of women than men are likely to emerge as candidates because women are far less likely than men to consider running for office.

Further, when we consider male and female potential candidates' interest in running for Congress specifically, the gender gap in political ambition is amplified. Table 7.8 shows the interest of potential candidates in running for the US Congress in all three years. Potential candidates were asked to identify which offices they might ever be interested in seeking. Men were significantly more likely than women to express interest in running for Congress. Again, the gender gap in interest in congressional office persisted across all three time periods. The one notable change in 2021 from the previous two survey years was that both women and men expressed less interest in running for Congress overall, likely a result of the increasingly negative and partisan view of politics in Washington.

Three critical factors uncovered in the surveys of potential candidates explain the gender gap in ambition. First, women are significantly less likely than men to receive encouragement to run for office. This difference

Table 7.8 Among potential candidates, women are less interested than men in running for the US House or Senate

	2001		2011		2021	
	Women (%)	Men (%)	Women (%)	Men (%)	Women (%)	Men (%)
Interested in someday running for …						
US House of Representatives	15	27	9	19	11	20
US Senate	13	20	6	11	8	13
Sample size	816	1,022	1,766	1,484	2,580	2,496

Note: Sample is composed of lawyers, business leaders and executives, educators, and other potential candidates. Entries indicate percentage responding "yes." All differences between women and men are significant at $p < .05$.

Source: Adapted from the Citizen Political Ambition Study data. See Richard L. Fox and Jennifer L. Lawless, The Invincible Gender Gap in Political Ambition, *PS: Political Science & Politics* 57(2) (2024): 231–37.

is very important, because potential candidates are twice as likely to think about running for office when a party leader, elected official, or political activist attempts to recruit them as candidates. Second, women are significantly less likely than men to view themselves as qualified to run for office. In other words, even women in the top tier of professional accomplishment tend not to consider themselves qualified to run for political office, even when they have the same objective credentials and experiences as men. Third, even among this group of professionals, women were much more likely to state that they were responsible for the majority of childcare and household duties. Although many of the women in the study had blazed trails in the formerly male professions of law and business, they were still serving as the primary caretakers in their households. Although family roles and responsibilities were not significant predictors of political ambition, interviews with potential women candidates suggested that traditional family roles are still an impediment.[37] For all three of these factors, there has been very little change over the twenty-year period that these surveys took place. Though the first Trump presidency certainly motivated a group of progressive women to run for office, the fundamentals of the gap remain unchanged, even as more women successfully run for office.

CONCLUSION AND DISCUSSION

When researchers and political scientists in the late 1970s and early 1980s began to study the role of gender in electoral politics, concerns about basic fairness and political representation motivated many of their investigations. For many, the notion of governing bodies overwhelmingly dominated by men offends a sense of simple justice. In this vein, some researchers argue that the reality of a male-dominated government suggests to women citizens that the political system is not fully open to them. These concerns are as pertinent today as they were in the past. As Susan J. Carroll, Kelly Dittmar, and I noted in the Introduction to this volume, a large body of empirical research finds that a political system that does not allow for women's full inclusion in positions of political power increases the possibility that gender-salient issues will be overlooked. Ample research has shown that women are more likely than men to promote legislation geared toward ameliorating women's economic and

---

[37] Jennifer L. Lawless and Richard L. Fox, *It Still Takes a Candidate: Why Women Don't Run for Office* (New York: Cambridge University Press, 2010).

social status, especially concerning issues of health care, poverty, education, and gender equity. Despite the substantive and symbolic importance of women's full inclusion in the electoral arena, the number of women serving in elected bodies remains relatively low and the rate of increase can seem maddeningly slow. This chapter's overview of women's performance in congressional elections makes it clear that we need to adopt a more nuanced approach if we are to understand – and address – gender's evolving role in the electoral arena.

As to answering this chapter's central question – why is it taking so long to move to gender parity in the Congress – three broad findings emerge from the analysis. First, the road to gender parity is slow and bumpy. The elections of 2022 and 2024 showed both stasis and decline in the number of women candidates and officeholders. And even as gains are made for women in terms of numeric representation, the United States is not making progress in the election of women in relation to the rest of the world. In 2023, the United States ranked seventy-first in the world in the number of women serving in the national legislature. By 2025, the United States had fallen to seventy-eighth.

Second, on a more optimistic note, women now compete in US House and Senate races more successfully than at any previous time in history. Recent election cycles saw record numbers of women candidates seeking and winning major-party nominations. The key to increasing women's representation is to get more women to run for office. As the broad empirical indicators show, female general election candidates are not greatly impeded by the major indicators of electoral success: vote totals and fundraising. The evidence presented in this chapter continues to show that women and men perform similarly as general election candidates. On the basis of recent congressional election results, the findings presented in this chapter confirm, as a number of other studies have found, that there is no evidence of widespread gender bias among voters and financial contributors.

The third broad finding to emerge from this chapter, however, is that gender continues to play an important role in the electoral arena and in some cases works to keep the number of women running for Congress low. Notably, there are still state and regional differences in electing men and women to Congress. Women candidates cannot emerge in greater numbers until the candidacies of women are embraced throughout the entire United States and by both parties.

Additionally, women's full inclusion will not be possible if the overwhelming majority of women candidates continue to identify with the

Democratic Party. Though the 2020 elections suggested possible change in this regard, Republican women made little progress in the 2022 and 2024 elections. If the fortunes of women candidates are tied so heavily to one political party, women's movement toward parity in officeholding will prove illusory. Republican Speaker of the House Mike Johnson has not publicly made the case for electing more Republican women, and this does not seem to be a concern of current Republican leaders.[38]

Finally, gender differences in political ambition – particularly in the ambition to run for the US Congress – suggest that gender is exerting a strong influence at the earliest stages of the electoral process. Many women who would make ideal candidates never actually consider running for office. The notion of entering politics still appears not to be a socialized norm for women. A 2012 study of full-time college students aged eighteen to twenty-five reveals that women continue to show far less interest than their male counterparts in ever running for office.[39] These results highlight some of the long-term challenges in creating an environment where women and men are equally likely to be interested in pursuing a seat in the US Congress.

As these findings suggest, gender permeates the electoral environment in congressional elections in subtle and nuanced ways. Broad empirical analyses often tend to overlook these dynamics. Yet the reality is that these dynamics help explain why the road to parity is a slow one to travel.

---

[38] John Bresnahan and Melanie Zanona, McCarthy Heads into Next Congress with Eye on Speaker's Gavel, *Politico*, November 17, 2020, www.politico.com/news/2020/11/17/kevin-mccarthy-house-speaker-436907

[39] Richard L. Fox and Jennifer L. Lawless, Uncovering the Origins of the Gender Gap in Political Ambition, *American Political Science Review* 108(3) (2014): 499–519.

8 Running Up That Hill

How Political Parties, Women's Organizations, and Political Action Committees Shape Women's Political Campaigns

When now-Representative Erin Houchin (R-IN) first ran for office in 2014, she asked her party for support in the party primary. The party's response, Houchin recalled, was to declare neutrality in the contested primary and advise her to seek help from "other women." When Houchin eventually won her House seat, she credited early financial support from Republican women officeholders and Value in Electing Women (VIEW) political action committee (PAC) – but not the Republican Party or other Republican-friendly donor groups – for her primary win, which was the most competitive election for the safe Republican seat.[1] What Houchin has in common with other women candidates regardless of party affiliation is that their paths to office often look different from those of men, who remain the electoral default. To better understand women's continued underrepresentation, this chapter considers how political parties, women's organizations, and women's PACs influence women's campaigns for federal office. In many ways, the election cycles between 2016 and 2024 marked a transformative time for women's candidacy at the highest levels of US politics. Senator Hillary Clinton and Vice President Kamala Harris each ran as the Democratic Party's presidential nominee in 2016 and 2024, respectively. Republican women House members more than doubled their numbers after the 2020 congressional elections. A record number of women – 152 – served in Congress in 2024. And Representative Nancy Pelosi again served as speaker of the House from 2019 to 2023.

These developments emphasize some of the highlights women achieved at the national level but provide an incomplete picture of

---

[1] Ibid.

women's experiences seeking federal office. This chapter fills in that narrative by focusing on three specific themes regarding the relationship between gender, political parties, women's organizations, and PACs during this period. First, the party gap in representation – where Democratic women significantly outnumber their Republican counterparts, especially in the US House of Representatives – is also present in the structure of the Democratic and Republican campaign committees and in terms of how party leaders direct resources to women candidates who run under their party's label. This party gap in resources has important implications for women running as Republicans. Next, women of color prospective candidates experience barriers – particularly in their campaign finance networks – that some women's organizations that support women candidates have only begun to recognize. Identity-based women's organizations have emerged to address these concerns and work to close gaps in women's fundraising networks. Most of these efforts benefit Democratic, not Republican, women candidates of color, which may add further to the party gap in representation. Finally, women's organizations that demand women's representation organize around different issues depending on whether they are demanding more representation of women in the Democratic Party or the Republican Party. Groups that demand more representation of women in the Democratic Party organize almost exclusively around the issue of abortion and emphasize the importance of electing women officeholders to defend reproductive rights. By contrast, most groups that demand more representation of women in the Republican Party are silent on the issue of abortion and instead focus on traditionally masculine issues such as fiscal conservatism and strong national security. President Donald Trump, who has been the Republican Party's presidential nominee from 2016 to 2024, is not typically mentioned in messaging from these groups. Taken together, understanding these three developments in the relationship between women candidates, political parties, and women's organizations provides a more complete picture of the challenges and opportunities women encounter when running for federal office.

THE ROLE OF POLITICAL PARTIES IN US POLITICS

In making the case for the central role that political parties play in US politics, John Aldrich argues that parties organize political competition by mobilizing voters, regulating the number of candidates running for office, and simplifying how officeholders form governing majorities.[2] When candidates run for elected office, they do so under a political party label. With those candidates, political parties seek to capture or retain, if not expand, majority party status in the elected body where they serve. Political scientist V. O. Key identified political parties as having three distinct components: party in the electorate, party organization, and party in government.[3] Party in the electorate refers to voters, who ultimately select a party's candidate in party primaries and determine which candidate emerges victorious in general elections. Party organization refers to the internal structure of the political parties that organize the party apparatus at local, state, and national levels and the people active within those structures that provide a link between candidates for office and the people who vote for them. And party in government refers to elected and sometimes appointed individuals who serve or run for office under a given party label and occupy that position of power. Even before women earned the right to vote they fought to be included within the parties and their organizational structures. These early efforts were most successful after women gained the vote, when both the Democratic Party and the Republican Party worked to "bind fast the loyalty of women" to vote for their preferred party and also convince their spouses and fellow women partisans to do the same.[4] However, women have been less successful in occupying leadership positions within their respective party organizations or as party leaders in government, especially at the national level. Starting in the mid 1960s and continuing through to the current decade, women's organizations have formed as a counterweight to provide resources and support and to demand more opportunities for women in both the Democratic and Republican party structures, as candidates and party leaders.[5] While both the Democratic and Republican parties have extended opportunities for women's participation, they remain underrepresented and underresourced in both parties.

---

[2] John Aldrich, *Why Parties? The Origin and Transformation of Political Parties in America* (Chicago: University of Chicago Press, 1995).

[3] V. O. Key, *Politics, Parties, and Pressure Groups* (New York: Thomas Y. Crowell, 1942).

[4] Jo Freeman, *A Room at a Time: How Women Entered Party Politics* (Lanham, MD: Rowman & Littlefield, 2000), p. 80.

[5] Rosalyn Cooperman and Melody Crowder-Meyer, Standing on Their Shoulders: Suffragists, Women's PACs, and Demands for Women's Representation, *PS: Political Science & Politics* 53(3) 2020: 470–73.

WOMEN'S ABSENCE FROM NATIONAL PARTY ORGANIZATIONS AND THE PARTY GAP IN LEADERS' CONTRIBUTIONS TO WOMEN CANDIDATES

In federal elections from 2016 to 2024, the Democratic Party had two women, Senator Hillary Clinton and Vice President Kamala Harris, secure the party's nomination for president in 2016 and 2024, respectively. In 2020, former Vice President Joe Biden and then-Senator Kamala Harris were the Democratic Party's nominees for president and vice president. Donald Trump was the Republican Party's nominee for president in 2016, 2020, and 2024. During each of these elections, the nominees had their own campaigns to raise and spend money. These campaigns worked closely with their respective national party organizations, the Democratic National Committee (DNC) and the Republican National Committee (RNC), and party structures in each of the fifty states to help elect and raise money on their behalf. To oversee those efforts, each party selects a national party chair who typically serves through a presidential election cycle and may stay on in that position at the request of the party's presidential nominee. As a general rule, presidential nominees have great influence over who serves as national party chair. The national party chair is a position of significant prominence and responsibility. In addition to serving as the face of the party, fundraising, and promoting its candidates, the chair is also tasked with the less enjoyable task of frequently "tamping down squabbles" between internal party factions.[6]

Women's Absence from Party Leadership Positions in National Elections

To date, only four women – two from each party – have ever served as national party chair and led their party's strategy in presidential and congressional elections. Democratic strategist Donna Brazile served as acting DNC chair briefly in 2011 and again for several months in 2016 to 2017. Representative Debbie Wasserman Schultz (D-FL) served as DNC chair from 2011 to 2016. After securing his party's nomination in 2016, Donald Trump installed Ronna Romney McDaniel as RNC chair. McDaniel remained on as RNC chair, even after Trump lost in 2020. Once Trump

---

[6] Marjorie Randon Hershey, *Party Politics in America*, 18th edn. (New York: Routledge, 2021), p. 79.

again secured his party's nomination in 2024, he replaced McDaniel with two co-chairs, one of whom was Lara Trump, his daughter in-law.[7]

Women have not fared much better in leadership positions within their party's congressional committees. Both the DNC and RNC have "Hill committees" that have a separate organizational and campaign finance structure from their national parties and work to recruit and support party candidates in the House and Senate. Democrats have the Democratic Congressional Campaign Committee (DCCC) and the Democratic Senatorial Campaign Committee (DSCC), and Republicans have the National Republican Congressional Committee (NRCC) and National Republican Senatorial Committee (NRSC). These congressional campaign committees have tailored their organizations to best suit the needs of incumbent members and the prospective members in which they invest resources.[8] Each of these Hill committees names a chair, a current member of the House or Senate, who serves as the point person for his or her party's efforts to secure, retain, or expand the party's majority status. Chairs assemble a Hill leadership team to assist them with candidate recruitment and fundraising for their respective chambers, particularly for targeted races designed to protect vulnerable incumbents from the party or recruit promising candidates to win competitive open seats or defeat vulnerable incumbents from the opposing party. The NRCC protects vulnerable House Republican incumbents through its Patriot Program and targets party-competitive seats through its Young Guns Program. The DCCC has similar programs, with the Frontline program for vulnerable House Democrats and Red to Blue program for party-competitive seats it hopes to flip.

Since 2000, three women House Democrats have served as DCCC chair, and another three women Senate Democrats have served as DSCC chair.[9] To date, no woman House Republican has ever served as NRCC chair and only one Republican woman senator has served as NRSC chair.[10] Interestingly, since 2018, the NRCC has named

---

[7] Natalie Allison and Meridith McGraw, Loyalty Is a One-Way Street in Donald Trump's GOP. Just Ask Ronna McDaniel, *Politico*, February 2, 2024, www.politico.com/news/2024/02/08/ronna-mcdaniel-trump-step-down-00140291

[8] Robin Kolodny, *Pursuing Majorities: Congressional Campaign Committees in American Politics* (Norman, OK: University of Oklahoma Press, 1998).

[9] DCCC chairs Nita Lowey (NY), 2001–02; Cheri Bustos (IL), 2019–20. Suzan DelBene (OR) will serve as DCCC chair for the 2026 election cycle. DSCC chairs Patty Murray (WA), 2001–02 and 2011–12; Catherine Cortez Masto (NM), 2019–20. Kirsten Gillibrand (NY) will serve as DSCC chair for the 2026 election cycle. Master list of congressional committee leadership positions compiled by author from archival material from the Democratic National Committee (DNC) webpage.

[10] Senator Elizabeth Dole (NC) served as NRSC Committee Chair from 2005 to 2006.

four successive Republican women to serve as vice chair of recruitment under the direction of the NRCC chair.[11] Women have mounted successful campaigns for Congress and yet they have not often been invited to serve as key strategists for the party's electoral fortunes in the institution.

Women's Absence from Leadership Positions in Congress

Women officeholders' presence in party structures matters also in relation to who is selected for leadership positions within the chambers and where those leaders direct the vast resources they command. Just as the party committees have structures in place to direct resources to preferred party candidates, party leaders in Congress use their own PACs to support fellow party members' campaigns and insulate themselves from challenges to their positions. The decisions party committee and chamber leaders make as to who receives funding signals to other donors who the party believes is worthy of investment. From 2016 to 2024, very few women served in party leadership roles in Congress. As vice president, Kamala Harris served as president of the Senate in the 117th and 118th Congresses. Senator Patty Murray (D-WA) served as president pro-tempore of the Senate in the 118th Congress. To date, no woman from either party has served as Senate majority or minority leader. In the House, Representative Nancy Pelosi served as minority leader in the 115th Congress and then resumed her role as speaker in the 116th and 117th Congresses. Representative Katherine Clark (D-MA) has served as the Democratic whip in the 118th and 119th Congresses. No Republican woman has served as speaker, majority or minority leader, or whip. Since the 115th Congress, five different women have served as Republican House conference chair, whose role is to work with fellow party leaders to manage the day-to-day operations of their members.[12] Given the membership size of the House, party leadership positions are

---

[11] Representative Elise Stefanik (NY) served as the first woman recruitment chair for the NRCC in the 2018 cycle. Since then, Representatives Susan Brooks (IN), Carol Miller (WV), and Kat Cammack (FL) have each served as NRCC recruitment chair in successive election cycles from 2020 to 2024. Master list of congressional committee leadership positions compiled by author from archival material from the National Republican Congress Committee (NRCC) webpage.

[12] The following Republican women representatives have served as Republican House Conference chair: 115th Congress – Cathy McMorris Rodgers (WA); 116th and 117th Congresses – Liz Cheney (WY); 117th and 118th Congresses – Elise Stefanik (NY); 119th Congress – Lisa McClain (MI). See complete roster at https://clerk.house.gov/Members/ViewLeadership

especially important to help party members communicate with one another and be organized. The limited number of women serving as party leaders within Congress means there are fewer women who have institutional clout and also the agency to use their leadership positions and PACs to recruit and fund fellow women partisans.

Party Gaps for Women in Party Caucuses

Table 8.1 shows the number of women serving in the House following elections between 2016 and 2024 as well as the percentage of their party's chamber caucuses this number represents. Even as the number of Democratic and Republican women House members has improved during this period, with women Democratic representatives reaching nearly 45 percent of their party's caucus at the start of the 119th Congress, the electoral default for both parties is a man running for office. Stated another way, the continued underrepresentation of women as party candidates is also the overrepresentation of men in those positions.[13]

In addition to noting the persistent party gap in representation between Democratic and Republican women House members, Table 8.1 details women's presence in their respective party's caucus and whether their party held majority or minority status. During this period, the Democratic Party held a majority in the House following elections in 2018 and 2020 (116th–117th Congresses), and Democratic women accounted for about 40 percent of the party's caucus. With Democrats currently in the minority, the percentage of women Democrats in the party's caucus is nearly 45 percent. When Republicans held the majority in the House following elections in 2016, 2022, and 2024 (115th, 118th–119th Congresses), Republican women only accounted for about 15 percent – at best – of their party's caucus and typically less than that when Republicans were in the minority. Recall that the goals of political parties in any given election cycle are to stem losses and expand their numbers. Democratic women are an integral part of their party's caucus and therefore electoral fortunes in the House. By contrast, Republican women House members serve in numbers that put them on the periphery of their party's caucus and, by extension, its electoral fortunes.

---

[13] Sarah Childs and Melanie Hughes, Which Men? How an Intersectional Perspective on Men and Masculinities Help Explain Women's Political Underrepresentation, *Politics and Gender* 14(2) 2020: 282–87.

Table 8.1 Women House members as a percentage of their party's caucus (115th–119th Congresses)

Congress	Number of Women Elected to House *(Majority Party in Italics)*	Percent of Party Caucus
115th (2017–2019)	62 Democrats	32
	21 Republicans	*9*
116th (2019–2021)	*89 Democrats*	*38*
	13 Republicans	7
117th (2021–2023)	*89 Democrats*	*40*
	30 Republicans	14
118th (2023–2025)	91 Democrats	43
	33 Republicans	*15*
119th (2025–2027)	94 Democrats	44
	30 Republicans	*14*

Source: Number of women House members by party accessed from Center for American Women in Politics post-election press releases. Number of House members by party accessed from the official House of Representatives' website. Percentages of women House members in their party caucus compiled by author.

Women's Candidacy, Political Parties, and PACs

Women's presence – or lack thereof – in a party's caucus also impacts their ability to collectively and individually wield clout with fellow members, such as through distributing funds through their member PACs. The Center for Responsive Politics, a nonpartisan, independent, nonprofit organization that collects data on money in national politics, defines a PAC as a political committee that raises and spends money to elect or defeat candidates.[14] Their data also show that as the cost of running for Congress – now typically several million dollars per candidate depending on the competitiveness of the race – has increased steadily since 1990, PAC contributions serve as an important fundraising source for many candidates, especially incumbents running for reelection.[15] Research on congressional leadership PACs reveals that while these PACs have traditionally been used to satisfy members' party and personal goals, they are increasingly used by party leaders to attain and maintain majority party

---

[14] Money-in-Politics Glossary: PACs, OpenSecrets – Center for Responsive Politics, www.opensecrets.org/resources/learn/glossary#S

[15] Most Competitive House Races, 2024 Open Secrets – Center for Responsive Politics, www.opensecrets.org/elections-overview/hot-races

status.[16] By this logic, the Democratic and Republican party leaders interested in keeping, if not increasing, the number of fellow women partisans in their chamber should direct funds commensurate with their percentage in their party's caucus. Party leadership contributions to women partisans also signals to friendly donors that the candidate receiving these funds is part of the party's team and worthy of investment. The percentage of women partisans in their party's caucuses as noted in Table 8.1 suggests that Democratic leaders will direct a higher percentage of their funds to women compared with Republican leaders. Table 8.2 identifies the leadership PACs of Democratic and Republican party leaders in the most recent (2024) election cycle, how much money they raised and distributed to fellow members, and what percentage of those funds was allocated to women partisans.

As shown in Table 8.2, House leaders raise and distribute millions of dollars to fellow partisans, both incumbents and competitive candidates, who they believe can win their elections. Two additional findings are evident from this table. The more positive takeaway suggests that Democratic and Republican party leaders distribute funds to women candidates at a level that exceeds their presence in the party's caucus. Stated another way, party leaders are directing funds above women's numbers in their caucus, which suggests that party leaders are funding competitive women candidates running as challengers or in open seats. At the same time, no Democratic or Republican party leader directed a majority of funds raised to women candidates, which means that the men in the party continued to receive the majority of party leaders' funds. These contribution patterns also communicate to the party's friendly donors that men's campaigns are the norm. Party leadership PACs do fund women partisans, but they are more likely to direct those funds to the men in the party.

There are additional points that further contextualize the limitations of political parties as central to recruiting and funding women's campaigns and also emphasize the party gap in resources available to them. First, as will be elaborated on in the next section, women's organizations formed to counteract both the Democratic and Republican parties' perpetually lagging efforts to encourage women to run and provide tangible support

---

[16] Marian Currinder, Leadership PAC Contribution Strategies and House Member Ambitions, *Legislative Studies Quarterly* 28(4) 2003: 551–77; E. S. Heberlig and B. A. Larson, Congressional Parties and the Mobilization of Leadership PAC Contributions, *Party Politics* 16(4) 2010: 451–75.

Table 8.2 House party leadership PACs and contributions to women candidates, 2023–24

Party Leader Name, Position, and Leadership PAC	Total Receipts	Disbursements to Party Candidates	Percent Allocated to Women Party Candidates
Speaker, Kevin McCarthy (R-CA), *Majority Committee PAC*	$1,055,000	$1,025,000	25
Speaker, Mike Johnson, (R-LA), *American Revival PAC*	$1,273,000	$1,264,500	22
Majority Leader, Steve Scalise (R-LA), *Eye of the Tiger PAC*	$1,417,000	$1,382,000	21
Majority Whip, Tom Emmer (R-MN), *Electing Majority Making Effective Republicans*	$1,348,500	$1,361,000	21
Conference Chair, Elise Stefanik (R-NY), *Elevate PAC*	$865,000	$805,500	30
Minority Leader, Hakeem Jeffries (D-NY), *Jobs, Education, & Families First PAC*	$1,080,000	$1,000,000	49
Minority Whip, Katherine Clark (D-MA), *Fair Shot PAC*	$1,219,700	$1,211,700	49

Source: Campaign Finance reports for House members' leadership PACs accessed from Open Secrets. Disbursements to party candidates and percentage of disbursements allocated to women compiled by author.

for their candidacies. Party organizations, particularly Hill committees and member leadership PACs, play an important role in campaigns, especially when they target races and direct resources to party candidates in congressional districts or states. But targeted races comprise a fraction of federal elections in any given cycle, and individual candidates – incumbents, candidates for open seats with no incumbent running, and challengers alike – are expected to assemble their own organizational, communication, and fundraising teams. Women's organizations formed expressly to provide women candidates guidance and support. As these organizations have evolved, however, they have typically benefitted women who run as Democrats, not Republicans.

For Us, By Us: Women's Political Action Committees

The rationale for these leadership PACs underscores a fundamental challenge Republican women face, that is, a reluctance by party members and party-friendly groups to embrace the demand for more representation by Republican women. The example of Representative Elise Stefanik's leadership PAC, Elevate PAC (E-PAC), lays bare this conundrum. Following the 2018 congressional elections, when the incoming Republican first-year class included only one woman, Carol Miller (R-WV), Stefanik rebranded her leadership PAC to expressly support Republican women candidates, including in primary elections when they run against other Republicans to secure the party's nomination – and when the party's Hill committee does not make endorsements or provide funds to assist one partisan over another.[17] While E-PAC's website boasts a fundraising figure of over $3 million raised to "engage, empower, and elevate women,"[18] the actual percentage distribution of E-PAC funds to Republican women candidates has decreased since Stefanik was tapped to replace Liz Cheney to serve as House Republican Conference chair in the 117th Congress following Cheney's work on the House January 6th Committee. Indeed, in the 2024 election cycle, Stefanik raised $865,000 for E-PAC, but only 30 percent of those funds went to the campaigns of Republican women candidates. Stefanik may well have created her leadership PAC with the intention of supporting Republican women candidates. However, in her role as House Republican Conference chair, she prioritized defending her party's majority status by primarily funding

[17] Simone Pathe, Stefanik Launches PAC to Boost Female Candidates, Now with GOP Leadership Support, *Roll Call*, January 18, 2019, https://tinyurl.com/yymbvd84

[18] About Elevate PAC, 2025, https://elevate-pac.com/

the campaigns of Republican men. For Republican women, the party gap in representation will continue so long as their party committees and leaders direct the lion's share of their resources to Republican men. Looking to the other side of the aisle, Democratic women candidates can advocate for greater support from their party while recognizing that they can also gain substantive assistance from other sources not available to Republican women.

WOMEN'S CAMPAIGN GROUPS AND THE SPECIAL CHALLENGE OF BOOSTING THE CAMPAIGN FINANCE NETWORKS FOR WOMEN OF COLOR CANDIDATES

Women's campaign groups (WCGs) are an important part of women's paths to public office as they create an opportunity structure, sometimes within, but often outside of the Democratic and Republican parties. WCGs create spaces for women not just to visualize but also to build successful political campaigns as elections in the United States are candidate, not party, centered.[19] These groups identify and strengthen networks between women, political practitioners, the voters they seek to represent, and, in some instances, donors who will fund them. This section gives a brief overview of the two main types of WCGs: groups that train women to run successful campaigns, and women's PACs that provide financial and material support to the women they endorse. It also explores how training and funding strategies have evolved to recognize the unique challenges faced by different groups of women candidates. A central purpose of candidate training programs is to pull back the veil on campaigns and demonstrate what is needed for women to assemble a winning coalition. Updated research on the efficacy of these programs in flipping the switch that moves women from thinking about running for office to actually doing so has revealed their limitations. Specifically, a one-size-fits-all-women approach to candidate training downplays the challenges that many prospective women of color candidates face in raising funds, particularly when drawing on personal campaign finance networks to raise the seed money required to demonstrate their competitiveness as a candidate and secure a campaign endorsement. In response, identity-based WCGs have emerged to promote Black women, LGBTQ+ women, and Latina candidates and work

---

[19] Jamie Carson and Gary Jacobson, *The Politics of Congressional Elections*, 11th edn. (Lanham, MD: Rowman & Littlefield, 2023).

to close the gaps in their fundraising networks that typically limit their ability to fundraise. Women of color and LGBTQ+ women who run as Democrats are invariably the beneficiaries of these targeted efforts. By contrast, women who run as Republicans have fewer options available to them for training and support and for outside funding from women's PACs. Just as Republican women candidates must compete with the men for party resources, they must also often share party-specific candidate training programs and PAC funds.

Women's Campaign Groups as Policy Demanders for More Women's Representation

Table 8.3 provides a partial listing of the national WCGs that offer campaign training programs for women at any stage of the candidacy process. The groups on this list are identified by the Center for American Women and Politics (CAWP) and appear on its Women's Political Power Map. I divide them into two main categories, namely WCGs that provide training for partisans – progressives and/or Democrats, and conservatives and/or Republicans – and WCGs that identify themselves as nonpartisan and/or issue-neutral in their training programs. I focus on examples from each of these categories to highlight research findings from scholars about WCGs, their impact on women's political candidacy, and why WCGs are more likely to provide candidate training to women seeking elected office as Democrats.

The proliferation of WCGs over the last twenty years has prompted a renewed scholarly focus on their work. A census of these groups – their location, whom they serve, and the type of training they provide – and their inclusion in an easily navigable database such as the CAWP's National Political Power Map is a foundational contribution. WCGs exist at both the national and state levels. Research on WCGs in the states reveals more than 400 groups active in forty-eight states, with a majority of those groups providing candidate training that is nonpartisan or issue-neutral. Indeed, when looking at the list of national WCGs, we also see that the nonpartisan/issue-neutral groups are most abundant. However, at the state level the nonpartisan group identification is a nominal one as "nearly three-fourths of active WCGs in our sample have an abortion litmus test for which potential candidates they will support."[20] The national WCGs

---

[20] Rebecca Kreitzer and Tracy Osborn, Women Candidate Recruitment Groups in the States, in *Good Reasons to Run*, eds. Shauna Shames et al. (Philadelphia, PA: Temple University Press, 2020), pp. 183–92, p. 185.

Table 8.3 Partial listing of national women's campaign groups (WCGs)

WCGs for Progressive/ Democratic Women	Nonpartisan/Issue-neutral WCGs	WCGs for Conservative/ Republican Women
Emerge America	Campaign School at Yale University	National Federation of Republican Women, *Campaign Management School**
EMILY's List, *Training Center*	Center for American Women and Politics, *Ready to Run National Training Network*	
Jordan-Huerta Women's Leadership Program, *Young Elected Officials Network*	IGNITE, *Boss Ladies: Training for the Next Generation of Campaign Leaders*	Women's Public Leadership Network
	LBJ Women's Campaign School Run Vote Lead She Should Run Supermajority	

* *WCG provides training to eligible men and women candidates.*
Source: List compiled from Center for American Women in Politics Women's Political Power Map.

identified as "Nonpartisan/Issue-neutral" in Table 8.3 do not mention the issue of abortion or reproductive rights on their websites and instead focus their messaging on themes of women's underrepresentation, demystifying the campaign process, and the importance of giving women tools to become more involved as political and community leaders.

This work of educating prospective candidates about the mechanics of campaigns and the actual work officeholders perform is especially important for women considering a political candidacy. Research shows that women's political ambition increases when the pitch to run is focused on fixing problems and improving communities.[21] Similarly, WCG training sessions increase women's confidence in their leadership skills and boost their interest in running by emphasizing the communal goals associated with public service – that holding office is about helping people, not just

---

[21] Sue Thomas and Catherine Wineinger, Ambition for Office: Women and Policy-Making, in *Good Reasons to Run*, eds. Shauna Shames et al. (Philadelphia, PA: Temple University Press, 2020), pp. 75–92, p. 78.

attaining power.[22] In fact, in response to the Trump administration's overhaul of the federal bureaucracy that has resulted in mass layoffs and firings of federal workers, Emerge America has hosted information sessions via Zoom to support women in this group who want to run for elected office.[23]

In addition to messaging that is tailored to pique women's interest in running for office, WCGs vary widely in the depth and breadth of training they provide to candidates. In response to the COVID-19 pandemic, many training groups shifted their workshops to be delivered online, often with a "go at your own pace" series or self-directed workshops for women who had work or care responsibilities that would make it difficult to meet on a set schedule. Presently, WCGs provide prospective candidates with a wealth of online resources, often for free or a nominal cost. She Should Run, a nonpartisan training group, provides free access to its "Resource Center" that includes webinars, courses, interviews, and worksheets. One program, "Ask Her Anything," offers to connect She Should Run participants "with a woman who has previously run for office for a thirty-minute, one-on-one conversation." WCGs that provide partisan-focused training, such as EMILY's List Run to Win program for women Democrats and Women's Public Leadership Network for Republican women, offer similar online content to engage prospective candidates.

Party-Focused Perceptions and Other Challenges Faced by Women's Campaign Groups

The perception of whom WCGs are designed to assist is a challenge these groups face, and these challenges may be especially relevant for Republican women. While many of these groups – at both the national and state levels – identify as nonpartisan, research suggests that these training opportunities may benefit women Democrats more than Republicans. Perception is definitely a part of the problem. Many Republican women candidates assume that candidate training programs sponsored by women's groups are for progressive women candidates, even when the organization explicitly indicates they are nonpartisan

---

[22] Monica Schneider and Jennie Sweet-Cushman, Pieces of the Women's Political Ambition Puzzle: Changing Perceptions of a Political Career with Campaign Training, in *Good Reasons to Run*, eds. Shauna Shames et al. (Philadelphia, PA: Temple University Press, 2020), pp. 203–14, p. 203.

[23] Lauren Egan, Fired Govt Workers Are Pissed Off and Running for Office, *The Bulwark*, April 16, 2025.

and issue-neutral.[24] This erroneous assumption likely deters some prospective Republican women candidates who are interested in candidate programs, and so these nonpartisan trainings tend to be populated with a majority of prospective candidates who intend to run as Democrats. Another reason that WCGs may advantage Democratic women over Republican women candidates is based on the very practices of WCGs on the right. WCGs for conservative and Republican women extend these training opportunities to men. The Campaign Management School, sponsored by the National Federation of Republican Women (NFRW), offers a ten-part online campaign school with workshops that cover topics including fundraising via events, direct mail, and emails, and also voter contact through door knocking, phones, and earned media. These sessions are available free of charge to all NFRW members and for a nominal fee for nonmembers.[25] The inclusion of Republican men in the Campaign Management School is in keeping with a central objective of the organization to "recruit, train, and elect Republican candidates" instead of a more specific, group-based claim directed to aid Republican women. Again, instead of offering resources exclusively for Republican women candidates, these resources are available to Republican men and women. This practice is also reflective of attitudes among Republicans regarding women's political candidacy, as noted in a 2023 Pew Research Study that asked respondents to consider different reasons that might explain why there are fewer women than men in high political office. Compared with Democrats, Republicans were significantly less likely to agree that women in politics have to do more to prove themselves than men and that women get less support from party leaders.[26]

The Emergence of Women's Campaign Groups for Women of Color Candidates

A more recent development in the work of WCGs and women's PACs is a recognition that while men and women candidates often experience campaigns differently, different groups of women candidates encounter

---

[24] Malliga Och, Political Ambition, Structural Obstacles, and the Fate of Republican Women, in *Good Reasons to Run*, eds. Shauna Shames et al. (Philadelphia, PA: Temple University Press, 2020), pp. 41–55, p. 42.

[25] Campaign Management School, National Federation of Republican Women, www.nfrw .org/cms

[26] Juliana Menasche Horowitz and Isabel Goddard, Women and Political Leadership Ahead of the 2024 Election, *Pew Research Center*, September 27, 2023, https://tinyurl .com/527bj2ry

different barriers to candidacy that negatively impact their ability to compete effectively. Political candidacy, when considered through an intersectional lens, reveals campaign finance gaps both in terms of how women of color assess the strength and reach of their personal fundraising networks and also how donors of color have a culture of charitable, but not political, giving. Research demonstrates that women of color generally have more modest personal fundraising networks due to gender and race wage gaps as well as existing campaign finance structures that are similarly gendered and raced.[27] For example, the original donor network created by Ellen Malcolm, founder of EMILY's List, was based on her rolodex of personal and professional contacts that were primarily white, affluent women with a record of giving to feminist groups. Even as EMILY's List has intentionally highlighted the importance of electing Democratic pro-choice women of color candidates, researchers looking at campaign donations for House elections have found a relationship between a donor's gender and race and a candidate's gender and race. Similarly, when women of color candidates – specifically Latinas and Black women – consider the importance of fundraising, particularly in leaning on personal campaign finance networks for seed money to demonstrate their ability to fundraise, they recognize that their networks are underdeveloped in what they can provide, in part because women of color do not consider political giving – even to candidates that look like them – as similar to charitable giving.[28] The concerns that women of color express about the challenges of fundraising have been folded into the programming many WCGs provide during candidate training and also have prompted the creation of women's PACs designed specifically by women of color for women of color. And, as will be described in further detail, these PACs direct their resources to Democratic, not Republican, women of color.

Women's PACs are the second main type of WCG. They evolved from women's organizations that pushed for ratification of the Equal Rights Amendment (ERA) and reproductive rights. The three main women's

<hr>

[27] Nadia Brown, Chris Clark, and Anna Mahoney, Women of Color: Explaining Racial and Gender Disparities in Candidate Success in Primary Elections, *Politics, Groups, and Identities* 12(4) (2023): 806–25; Ashley Sorensen and Philip Chen, Identity in Campaign Finance and Elections: The Impact of Gender and Race on Money Raised in 2010–2018 U.S. House Elections, *Political Research Quarterly* 75(3) (2021): 738–53.

[28] Jamil Scott, Let's Talk about Money, in *Where and When They Enter*, Paper prepared for delivery at the 2024 Annual Meeting of the American Political Science Association; Kira Sanbonmatsu, Understanding Black Women's and Latinas' Perspectives About Political Giving, *P.S.: Political Science & Politics* 58(1) (2025): 1–6.

groups that emerged in the 1960s – the National Organization for Women (NOW), National Women's Political Caucus (NWPC), and Women's Campaign Fund (WCF) – adopted a pro-ERA stance and worked to bring women into positions of authority and leadership to serve as a counterweight to leaders in the Democratic and Republican parties who ignored them. NWPC co-founder Gloria Steinem identified the goal of the group as "to humanize society by bringing the values of women's culture into it, not simply to put individual women into men's politics."[29] NOW, NWPC, and WCF recruited and endorsed women who pledged support for issues including the ERA, federally subsidized childcare, and abortion rights. Collectively, these groups sought to normalize the idea of women running for elected office. They provided modest financial support to endorsed candidates from both parties regardless of their viability, as most were challengers running against incumbents.

Women's PACs: EMILY's List and Everybody Else

As women's political candidacy became more routine and less novel, PACs such as EMILY's List emerged to focus on candidate viability and make a party-specific demand for more women's representation. EMILY's List, which initially organized during the 1986 federal election cycle to help then-Representative Barbara Mikulski (D-MD) win a Senate seat, endorsed only pro-choice Democratic women candidates and helped them fundraise during the early, primary elections phase of their campaigns.[30] The group required women seeking an EMILY's List endorsement to affirm their competitiveness by reaching minimum fundraising thresholds to demonstrate their ability to independently fundraise. EMILY's List also innovated the use of bundling funds, that is, pulling together donations from their donor base and sending those donations in clusters to the campaigns of endorsed candidates. This innovation had the effect of introducing a new group of donors into congressional campaigns, progressive women who had not previously contributed to the Democratic Party but demanded more representation by supporting their preferred women candidates. EMILY's List is also distinct from other women's PACs

---

[29] David Dismore, Today in Feminist History: The National Women's Political Caucus (July 12, 1971), *Ms. Magazine*, July 12, 2020, https://msmagaine.com/2020/07/12/feministhistory-july-12/

[30] Jennifer Lawless and Kathryn Pearson, The Primary Reason for Women's Underrepresentation? Reevaluating Conventional Wisdom, *Journal of Politics* 70(1) (2008): 67–68; Jamie Pimlott, *Women and the Democratic Party: The Evolution of EMILY's List* (New York: Cambria Press, 2010).

that endorse and fund candidates in that they have expanded their network to assist viable pro-choice Democratic women at nearly every state of their candidacies. Its Run to Win program trains women candidates. Its Political Opportunity Project develops women's candidacies at local and state levels and in doing so creates a pipeline of quality Democratic women candidates for Congress. As previously noted, its traditional PAC endorses and funds Democratic women candidates at the early stages ahead of the party primary. And its Women Vote! super PAC raises and spends vast amounts of money in independent expenditures that help endorsed candidates facing competitive elections. Super PACs such as Women's Vote must abide by federal campaign finance regulations that allow these entities to raise and spend unlimited funds so long as they do not give money directly to candidates or coordinate their funds with those of a candidate's campaign.

The willingness of EMILY's List to fund graduates of women's candidate training programs other than its own is an additional practice that further benefits Democratic women candidates. On its website, the Campaign School at Yale University boasts of four former or current Democrat women members of Congress – Senator Kirsten Gillibrand (NY), Representatives Nikema Williams (GA-5) and Lauren Underwood (IL-14), and former Representative Gabrielle Giffords (AZ-8) – as graduates of its program. Each was endorsed and funded by EMILY's List. A similar practice is evidenced with Emerge America graduates, as noted in Table 8.4. Again, all Emerge alumna identified as current or former members of Congress – in this case fourteen Democratic women – all received endorsements and funds from EMILY's List. And, in the several instances where the Democratic woman member of Congress had previously served in their state legislature, they were also endorsed by EMILY's List Political Opportunity Project. Of course, it is intuitive that candidates who complete a candidate training program may wage a more successful campaign as that is the very purpose of such programs. Still, there appears to be no identified contemporary equivalent for Republican women candidates to move from being a WCG training graduate to a candidate endorsed by a women's PAC.

Other groups have sought to copy the EMILY's List playbook (and part of its name) in support of their own preferred candidates. In the early 1990s, two women's PACs formed in support of Republican women candidates. WISH List (Women in the Senate and House) formed to aid pro-choice Republican women but disbanded by 2010 as pro-choice Republican women retired from Congress and women who ran under

　　　　　　　　　　　　　　　　　　　　　　　　

Table 8.4 Building stronger candidates through campaign training, endorsements, and funding

**Women Officeholders Trained by Emerge America,
Endorsed and Funded by EMILY's List**

Emerge America, a WCG that trains Democratic women, identifies fourteen current or former (*) women members of Congress as alumna, including:

Yassamin Ansari (AZ-3)	*Becca Balint (VT-AL)*
Janelle Bynum (OR-5)	*Maxine Dexter (OR-3)*
Sarah Elfreth (MD-3)	*Deb Haaland* (NM-1)*
Val Hoyle (OR-4)	*Lucy McBath (GA-6)*
LaMonica McIver (NJ-10)	*Andrea Salinas (OR-6)*
Kim Schrier (WA-8)	*Lateefah Simon (CA-12)*
Melanie Stansbury (NM-1)	*Emilia Sykes (OH-13)*

All of these Democratic women members of Congress have also been endorsed and funded by EMILY's List.

Source: Emerge America, https://emergeamerica.org/alumnae/.

the Republican Party label identified as pro-life.[31] Susan B. Anthony List formed around the same time as WISH List with the goal of supporting pro-life Republican women to run for office. Susan B. Anthony List, the self-proclaimed "anti-EMILY's List," is still active as a PAC and endorses pro-life candidates, both men and women. Other women's PACs have emerged to recruit and fund Republican women candidates, including VIEW PAC (Value in Electing Women), Winning For Women, Maggie's List, and Elevate PAC. EMILY's List remains *the* main women's PAC for Democratic women candidates, and it raises and distributes funds to endorsed candidates at a level that is simply unmatched by all other women's PACs. Table 8.5 lists selected women's PACs that raised and spent money in the 2024 election cycle, their endorsement criteria, and the amount of contributions from the PAC to federal candidates. Recall that in 2024, Vice President Kamala Harris secured the Democratic nomination for president in July 2024 after then-President Joe Biden withdrew from the race. As such, EMILY's List raised funds for Harris, whom they endorsed immediately after she announced she was running, and endorsed pro-choice Democratic women congressional candidates.

---

[31] Melody Crowder-Meyer and Rosalyn Cooperman, Can't Buy Them Love: How Party Culture Contributes to the Party Gap in Women's Representation, *Journal of Politics* 80(4) (2018): 1211–24.

Table 8.5 Campaign finance activities for selected women's PACs, 2024 elections

Group	Endorsement criteria	Funds raised	Funds spent	Funds distributed to endorsed candidates
EMILY's List	Viable pro-choice Democratic women	$60,891,745	$59,388,413	$438, 500
Elevate PAC	Electable Republican (women) candidates*	$1,867,883	$1,789,143	$805,500
Higher Heights for America PAC	Progressive Black women running for federal, state, or mayoral office	$125,159	$113,165	$66,542
L PAC	LGBTQ+ women and nonbinary candidates who support a gender equality agenda	$716,341	$710,859	$64,500
Maggie's List	Conservative women running for federal office	$240,802	$238,004	$25,535
Poder PAC	Democratic pro-choice Latinas who demonstrate a commitment to the Latino community	$147,069	$205,592	$68,000
Susan B. Anthony List	Pro-life candidates for Congress and high state public office*	$765,175	$643,530	$250,782
VIEW PAC	Qualified, viable GOP women congressional candidates	$1,222,080	$1,219,581	$475,000
Winning For Women	Free-market conservative women running for federal office	$22,728	$27,526	$8,400

* Indicates the PAC endorses men and women candidates

Source: Endorsement criteria from PAC websites, campaign finance figures compiled by author from Open Secrets.

Campaign finance activity from selected women's PACs in 2024 confirms important differences in the breadth of resources available to Democratic and Republican women candidates. In the most recent election cycle, EMILY's List raised over $60 million and spent nearly all of that money to support Kamala Harris and Democratic women running for Congress. That figure does not include the more than $30 million that the EMILY's List super PAC WomenVote! raised in independent expenditures in 2024, unlimited funds used to support or oppose a candidate's campaign. Taken together, EMILY's List PAC and its WomenVote! super PAC raised nearly $100 million in 2024 to elect Democratic, pro-choice women. While campaign finance reports indicate that the group distributed a mere $438,500 directly to candidates, it is important to recall that EMILY's List collects and bundles campaign funds to endorsed candidates. In other words, an endorsed candidate can receive funds from EMILY's List PAC and also receive bundled funds EMILY's List collected on the campaign's behalf. EMILY's List counts the bundled funds as "spent" funds and funds from the PAC itself as funds distributed to candidates. And, of course, the only group of candidates that receives EMILY's List funds are Democratic, pro-choice women.

The Party Gap in Women's PACs

EMILY's List may not be the only source of funds for Democratic women candidates, particularly Democratic LGBTQ+ women and women of color candidates. As previously discussed regarding the campaign training work of WCGs, concerns expressed by women of color candidates about the fundraising challenges they face incentivized the creation of identity-specific women's PACs, including Higher Heights for America PAC, which funds progressive Black women running for office; Poder PAC, which funds Democratic, pro-choice Latina candidates; and L PAC, which funds LGBTQ+ women and nonbinary candidates. Poder PAC identifies EMILY's List as a campaign partner, which suggests that Latina candidates endorsed by Poder PAC may also be endorsed by EMILY's List, creating avenues of additional funding streams available for their campaigns. Indeed, an examination of the lists of endorsed candidates from each of these PACs affirms an endorsement overlap for many Democratic, pro-choice women of color, LGBTQ+ women, and Latina candidates. To date, there are no identity-specific women's PACs that endorse Republican women candidates of color.

To be sure, women's PACs that endorse conservative and/or Republican women candidates do provide these women with another stream of campaign funding, including bundled funds. One problem is that the amount of money raised and spent by these PACs is much more modest than that raised and spent by EMILY's List, even as campaigns are no less expensive for similarly situated Republican women candidates. In addition, recall that two of the right-of-center PACs, Susan B. Anthony List and E-PAC, also endorse and fund the campaigns of Republican men. The example of Susan B. Anthony List's campaign finance activity in the 2024 elections underscores this funding problem for Republican women. As shown in Table 8.5, Susan B. Anthony List's PAC raised over $765,000 in funds and spent nearly as much for endorsed, pro-life candidates. It also distributed a little more than $250,000 directly to congressional candidates, and based on a review of their campaign finance reports, Republican women House candidates received only 34 percent of those funds. Susan B. Anthony List's super PAC, Women Speak Out, which raises unlimited amounts of money for independent expenditures to support or oppose candidates, directed even less of their funds to support Republican women candidates. Women Speak Out raised and spent nearly $12 million in 2024, including about $7 million in independent expenditures to support or oppose competitive campaigns featuring endorsed pro-life candidates. Nearly $5 million of the $7 million total was spent on two races – the 2024 presidential election contest opposing Kamala Harris and the US Senate race in Ohio featuring two men running against each other. Stated plainly, Susan B. Anthony List's allocation of funds in 2024 was not directed to support pro-life Republican women candidates. Taken together, WCGs provide important services and resources to women candidates, but Democratic, not Republican, women candidates are the overwhelming beneficiaries of this attention. Whether the WCG primarily focuses on candidate training or raising money from PACs on behalf of endorsed candidates, their activities are designed to normalize the idea of women's political candidacy. The WCGs that provide training frame officeholding through a communal lens of helping others and solving problems. They are abundant at both national and state levels, and they offer training options that are accessible, affordable, and as basic or comprehensive as is desired by the trainee. The perception of WCG training groups among some women partisans is that they are geared to women Democrats. And the practice of right-leaning training groups of serving men and women further limits opportunities for Republican women to take part in candidate training that is tailored to them. Most WCGs functioning as PACs that direct funds to endorsed women candidates are organized to benefit Democratic women. Their demand for more women's representation is increasingly party-, issue-, and identity-specific and targets pro-choice Democratic women and women of color. Right-of-center PACs do endorse and fund Republican women candidates, but Republican women again come up short as they must compete with the men in their party to receive those funds.

REPRODUCTIVE RIGHTS, "CONSERVATIVE" ISSUES DRIVE DEMANDS FOR MORE REPRESENTATION OF DEMOCRATIC AND REPUBLICAN WOMEN

The third development of note in the relationship between women candidates, political parties, and women's organizations and PACs from 2016 to 2024 relates to messaging and party-specific demands for more women's representation. Women's groups that demand women's representation organize around different issues depending on whether they are demanding more representation of women in the Democratic Party or the Republican Party. Groups that demand more representation of women in the Democratic Party organize almost exclusively around the issue of abortion and emphasize the importance of electing pro-choice women officeholders to defend reproductive rights. Following the June 2022 US Supreme Court ruling in *Dobbs v. Jackson Women's Health Organization* that overturned *Roe v. Wade* and returned the regulation of abortion to the states and Congress, messaging by progressive women's groups expressed outrage at the ruling and identified Democratic women candidates as the strongest advocates to protect reproductive rights. By contrast, most groups that demand more representation of Republican women do not reference specific issues. Save for Susan B. Anthony List, a pro-life PAC, group demands are silent on the issue of abortion. When these groups do get specific, they reference traditionally masculine issues such as fiscal conservatism and strong national security.

An additional difference between groups pertains to whom they talk about in their messaging. Whereas Democratic presidential nominees Hillary Clinton and Kamala Harris were featured prominently in the "Democratic women as pro-choice defenders" messaging in the 2016 and 2024 cycles, President Trump, who has been the Republican Party's presidential nominee from 2016 to 2024, was largely absent in messaging from right-of-center women's groups. Susan B. Anthony List, which promotes pro-life men and women candidates, was the only conservative group to reference Trump. The messaging of WCGs for Democratic and Republican women candidates therefore emphasizes very different issues they associate with women party candidates. The issue of abortion and reproductive rights more broadly has become *the issue* that informs Democratic women's political candidacy and their portrayal as the ultimate champions to advocate for choice in the legislatures in which they serve. This line of messaging raises funds for progressive women's PACs and Democratic pro-choice women candidates, to be sure, but it has not resulted in wins at the top of the ticket.

Messaging for Republican women has its own challenges. The messaging on this side of the aisle demands more representation for Republican women who are "conservative" like the men in their party but different from the leader of their party, Donald Trump. Right-of-center WCGs have certainly fundraised off of this message but more modestly and with limited success in growing women's presence in the party, particularly when Republicans are in the majority in Congress. Even as party polarization has divided Democratic and Republican party candidates and voters from one another, both parties are at important crossroads in considering how they wish to move forward with the policies and people they embrace in forthcoming elections and the space that women candidates will occupy in those respective plans.

Party and Issue-Specific Demands from Women's Campaign Groups

The idea that WCGs are the main policy demanders for more representation from Democratic and Republican women candidates is a central theme of this chapter. As such, the issues that WCGs emphasize in their policy demands for women partisans bears consideration. WCG endorsement criteria, as noted earlier in this chapter, is an obvious signal from groups as to the issues they consider to be most important. While the original demand for more women's representation was both progressive and bipartisan, contemporary demands from WCGs are both issue- and party-specific. After the 2022 Supreme Court ruling on *Dobbs*, EMILY's List, a key policy demander for Democratic women, repeatedly referenced the assault on abortion rights in their fundraising appeals, as shown in the different images in Figure 8.1. In addition, the Democratic Party's 2024 presidential nominee, Vice President Kamala Harris, was also featured prominently in their fundraising appeals. In 2016, EMILY's List prominently featured Democratic presidential nominee Hillary Clinton in their fundraising appeals that cycle. To be sure, EMILY's List has always emphasized a pro-choice stance as *the* criterion that determines the group's endorsement. Since the *Dobbs* decision, however, EMILY's

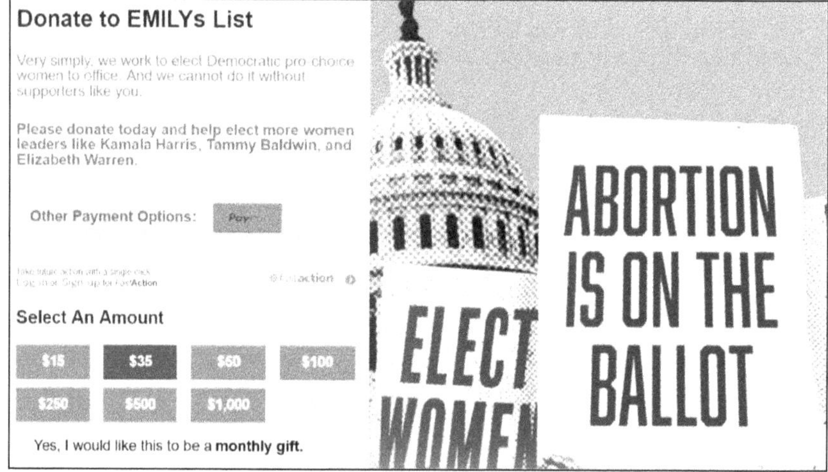

Figure 8.1 EMILY's List policy demands for more Democratic women focused on abortion.
Source: EMILY's List, https://emilyslist.org.

List has explicitly linked their demand for more women's representation with the election of Democratic women candidates – including the two women nominated for president – who will be the strongest advocates to champion abortion rights when elected. As noted in Figure 8.1, fundraising messages from EMILY's List remind donors of the perfidy of Republican Party officeholders and their nominees on the Supreme Court who dared to overturn *Roe* and strip women of their basic rights. EMILY's

List messages remind donors that "abortion is on the ballot" and ask them to "fight back" with their donation for Democratic women candidates, including those at the top of the ticket.

If abortion rights is the issue that informs the policy demands of progressive WCGs for more women Democrats, the policy demands from conservative WCGs for more Republican women are more diffuse. As noted earlier in this chapter, some women's PACs that endorse and fund Republican women candidates, including E-PAC, Maggie's List, and VIEW PAC, identify "conservative" as a requirement for endorsement without specifying exactly what "conservative" means. Recall that E-PAC also endorses and funds conservative Republican men despite their fundraising appeal to engage, empower, and elevate Republican women. Winning For Women provides the most detailed description of conservative women as determined by their support for free markets and a strong national defense. Figure 8.2 provides examples of several of these fundraising messages. Unsurprisingly, of the four images from the fundraising pages of conservative women's PACs in 2024, Susan B. Anthony List is the only group to specify a pro-life stance as a policy demand for electing more Republican women. However, as evidenced by whom they endorse and how they direct those funds, Susan B. Anthony List's abiding desire is to elect more pro-life legislators, both women and men. VIEW PAC, whose fundraising appeal image is not included, made only a generic demand to elect more Republican women. Finally, when looking at nearly all of the conservative women's PACs' webpages from the 2024 election cycle, it would not be evident that Donald Trump was the Republican Party's presidential nominee. Elect Republican women candidates – who will be as conservative as the men – but leave Trump out of the equation. Again, the messaging from right-of-center WCGs is in contrast to that of left-of-center WCGs, who specified that abortion was the defining issue and that the election of Kamala Harris and other Democratic women candidates was the path by which pro-choice interests would be most effectively defended.

The outcome of the respective messages from WCGs in 2024 as translated by electoral gains was mixed at best. Congressional Democrats came into the 2024 elections with Republican House and Senate majorities. Democratic women candidates added modestly to their numbers in both chambers, though the party remains in the minority. Democratic presidential nominee Kamala Harris lost both the popular and the electoral college vote to Republican nominee Donald Trump, despite her campaign having outraised his by more than double the funds and despite

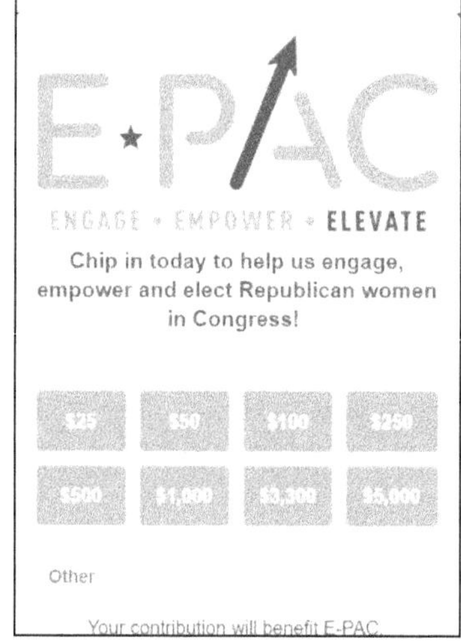

Figure 8.2 Conservative demands for more Republican women are varied and diffuse.
Source: Winning for Women, https://winningforwomen.com/about-us/; Maggie's List, https://web.archive.org/web/20241104152305/http://maggieslist.org/; EPAC, https://secure.winred.com/e-pac/pg-epac-donate.

Donald Trump's multiple felony convictions earlier in the year for falsifying business records in 2016 to cover up his affair with an adult entertainer. For their part, Republican women congressional candidates saw a net decrease in their numbers even as their party retained its majority status in both chambers.

CONCLUSION

This chapter began with an assertion that even as the campaign paths for women are often different from those of men, the election cycles between 2016 and 2024 were transformative for women running for federal office. In two distinct elections, the Democratic Party nominated a woman for president. In Congress, demands for more women's representation resulted in the most diverse group of Democratic and Republican women serving at their highest numbers in the two most recent Congresses. Women's campaign groups can point to these milestones as progress in their vital work to train women to run for office, fund them, and normalize the concept of women seeking elected office and leadership positions. That said, despite, or perhaps in spite of, these gains, women remain underrepresented in both party structures and leadership positions. The party gap in representation persists between Democratic and Republican women in Congress and further extends to the resources and opportunities political parties and women's training groups and PACs provide them. The issues that inform the demands for more Democratic and Republican women's representation from WCGs has also evolved and narrowed to a single issue – reproductive rights – for appeals from left-of-center groups even as right-of-center groups demand more representation from conservative women.

As the Democratic and Republican parties and WCGs all gear up for future elections, each will seek to make sense of what has transpired in recent elections to guide their strategies moving forward. To be sure, WCGs will continue to demand more women's representation, in some cases overall, but for many others based on women running as candidates under their preferred party label. Left-of-center groups will continue to organize and fund Democratic women candidates around the issue of abortion and reproductive rights, but they may also be well served to expand that message to highlight other issues salient to progressive voters and donors. Right-of-center groups will continue to organize and fund conservative Republican women candidates, but they may benefit from specifying the issue stances included in such a definition. Regardless of election cycle, the goal of political parties remains unchanged – parties want to win elections. For the Democratic Party, this means recognizing that Democratic women are a substantial portion of their party's congressional caucuses and providing them with requisite support and leadership opportunities. Determining the place of women in the Republican Party is more complicated. At the time of this writing, Republican women are on the periphery of a Republican administration and their legislative majorities in each chamber. Moving forward, both Democratic and Republican women – and the WCGs that support them – will continue their work to defend the value of their presence as candidates and officeholders and work to change the persistent electoral and representational default of male party candidate and officeholder.

9   Elections in the Fifty States

Why and Where States Matter to Women

Deliberations inside the Arizona state legislature attracted intense national scrutiny in 2024. Would the Arizona legislature overturn a law from the 1800s that prohibited abortion? The law, which predated the Civil War, became enforceable in the wake of the 2022 *Dobbs v. Jackson Women's Health Organization* decision that overturned *Roe v. Wade.* Other arcane state laws were thrust into the national spotlight in the 2022 and 2024 election cycles – the first elections after the stunning *Dobbs* decision that made possible abortion bans without exceptions.

Policy choices about health care, parental leave, voting rights, LGBTQ+ rights, immigration, and education differ depending on the state, as do emerging issues including the regulation of AI technologies. States are moving in dramatically different directions today depending on whether they are led by Democrats or Republicans. And states matter for political leadership, not just public policy: State legislative and statewide officeholders are a pool of potential candidates for federal offices including the presidency.

Understanding the role of women in state elections is central to understanding American politics. In the first half of this chapter, I analyze recent state legislative and statewide executive elections. Data from the Center for American Women and Politics (CAWP) show that women's state officeholding has reached historic highs in recent cycles. Notably, women constitute a *majority* of several state legislatures for the first time in US history. But women remain dramatically underrepresented in state offices compared with their presence in the population. In the second half of the chapter, I provide an overview of some key policy areas currently under debate in the states. For example, in the wake of *Dobbs*, differences across states in abortion policy are becoming more stark, with new controversies emerging. How women's experiences will be represented in these debates partly depends on the status of women candidates and officeholders state by state.

WOMEN IN STATE LEGISLATURES

The first women to serve in state legislatures did so in the 1800s. But the passage of time does not necessarily mean that more women will be elected: CAWP's comprehensive database of women state legislators shows that gains are not automatic.[1] Indeed, it was not until after the 2018 election that women became a *majority* of a state legislature, which happened in Nevada. Women remain underrepresented compared with their presence in the population in almost all state legislatures today. The persistence of women's underrepresentation in state legislative office is surprising because it is an entry-level rung on the political career ladder in many states.

Multiple factors help explain women's underrepresentation. Incumbency has been an institutional constraint given that the vast majority of state legislators have been men and incumbents are all but guaranteed reelection. Women are not always perceived to have the "right" credentials to run for state legislative office.[2] Favorable opportunities for winning state legislative office can also vary by women's racial/ethnic background due to intersectional barriers and the racial makeup of districts.[3] Political gatekeepers can restrict access to candidacy; historically, women have fared better in states with weaker party control over the nomination.[4]

Running effective campaigns takes resources. CAWP's in-depth analysis of campaign contributions found that women candidates are formidable fundraisers for state legislative races, raising similar amounts to men in similar types of electoral contests.[5] Yet, because women are underrepresented as state legislative candidates, we may only be analyzing the most successful women fundraisers when we analyze campaign finance data. We do not observe women potential candidates who declined to run due to fundraising difficulties.

In addition, CAWP's twenty-year analysis found that men out-give women in state elections by a factor of two to one (see Text Box 9.1). This means that women's voices – via their campaign contributions – are

[1] Center for American Women and Politics (CAWP), Elected Officials Database, n.d., https://cawp.rutgers.edu/data/women-elected-officials-database

[2] Kira Sanbonmatsu, *Where Women Run: Gender and Party in the American States* (Ann Arbor, MI: University of Michigan Press, 2006); Susan J. Carroll and Kira Sanbonmatsu, *More Women Can Run: Gender and Pathways to the State Legislatures* (New York: Oxford University Press, 2013).

[3] Christian Dyogi Phillips, *Nowhere to Run: Race, Gender, and Immigration in American Elections* (New York: Oxford University Press, 2021).

[4] Sanbonmatsu, *Where Women Run*.

[5] Kira Sanbonmatsu, The Donor Gap: Raising Women's Political Voices, A CAWP Women, Money, and Politics report, CAWP, 2023, www.cawp.rutgers.edu/donorgap

> **TEXT BOX 9.1 The Total Amount of Money Men Contribute to State Elections Exceeds the Amount Contributed by Women**
>
> - Men contributed two-thirds of all money to statewide executive and state legislative candidates (2019–22)
> - Men provided the majority of total funds contributed to state elections across states in 2022, including in abortion "battleground" states
> - The proportion of donors who are women is higher than the proportion of all funds that were contributed by women (2019–22)
> - Women give disproportionately to Democratic candidates and women candidates
>
> *Source:* Kira Sanbonmatsu, The Donor Gap: Raising Women's Political Voices, A CAWP Women, Money, and Politics report, CAWP, 2023, www.cawp.rutgers.edu/donorgap.

less likely to be heard in state policymaking to the same extent as men's. The candidates women support may lack the financial means to reach the ballot at all.[6] Because women disproportionately give to women candidates, the underrepresentation of women as political donors may deprive women candidates of valuable resources.

In 2022, CAWP found that a record number of women ran as nominees for state legislative seats (N = 3,621).[7] As in previous election cycles, women incumbents were more likely than other groups of women candidates to win their races in both 2022 and 2024. For example, most newly elected women ran in open-seat contests (see Table 9.1). Few women running as challengers won their races, whereas a majority of women running in open-seat contests won.

Racial identity shapes women's status as candidates and officeholders, including implications for fundraising.[8] The most recent US Census, conducted in 2020, reveals the increasing racial diversity of the country. But this diversity is not reflected in the composition of women state legislators.[9]

---

[6] Heather B. James, There's No Women's Mafia: Women's Donor Groups in State Legislative Elections, *Journal of Women, Politics & Policy* 43(4) (2022): 483–98.

[7] CAWP, 2024 Summary of Women Candidates, n.d., https://cawp.rutgers.edu/data/candidates-election-results-and-analysis-0/2024-summary-women-candidates#stleg

[8] Jamil Scott, It's All about the Money: Understanding How Black Women Fund Their Campaigns, *PS: Political Science & Politics* 55(2) (2022): 297–300.

[9] CAWP, Representativeness of Women State Legislators by Race/Ethnicity and State, October 2024, https://tinyurl.com/nun45xsf

Table 9.1 Women state legislative candidates are more likely to win their races as incumbents

	2022 (%)	2024 (%)
Incumbents		
Democrats	96.7 (1,050)	96.1 (1,094)
Republicans	94.4 (461)	97.3 (521)
Challengers		
Democrats	5.4 (502)	1.8 (770)
Republicans	4.7 (408)	8.1 (369)
Open seats		
Democrats	52.1 (756)	50.2 (454)
Republicans	56.6 (422)	61.1 (275)

Note: Cell entries are the success rate. N per cell appear in parentheses.
Source: Center for American Women and Politics (CAWP).

CAWP's database shows that women state legislators have become more racially diverse but still do not resemble the population at large. For example, 597 women serve in state senates and 1,873 serve as state representatives in 2025, according to CAWP. Yet women from historically underrepresented racial/ethnic groups remain underrepresented compared with their presence in the population. For example, 107 women state legislators identify as Asian American or Pacific Islander, 387 as Black, 208 as Latina, seventeen as Middle Eastern/North African, four as multiracial alone, and forty-one as Native American, Alaska Native, or Native Hawaiian, according to CAWP.[10] Women who self-identify as white total 1,510.[11]

Research finds dramatic differences across racial groups in access to state legislative office, with far fewer viable opportunities for women from historically marginalized groups.[12] In their analysis of the 2012 and 2014 elections, Paru Shah, Jamil Scott, and Eric Gonzalez Juenke concluded:

[10] Whereas Asian American or Pacific Islander women are 3.9 percent of the population, they are only 1.4 percent of state legislators; Black women are 7.8 percent of the population but 5.2 percent of state legislators; Latinas are 9.6 percent of the population but 2.8 percent of state legislators; and Native American, Alaska Native, or Native Hawaiian women are 1.1 percent of the population but 0.6 percent of state legislators. CAWP, Representativeness of Women State Legislators by Race/Ethnicity and State, updated March 2025, https://tinyurl.com/nun45xsf
[11] CAWP's racial/ethnic data were incomplete for about 250 women as of March 2025.
[12] Phillips, *Nowhere to Run.*

The data here suggest that racial/ethnic and gender representation is as much of a supply problem as it is a demand one. In other words, strategic minority women candidates run in places and elections where they believe their chances of winning are highest (such as uncontested elections and open seats, and seats in partisan-favorable environments), as do all candidates. But the racialized emergence in majority-white districts (white candidates) and majority–minority districts (minority candidates) is a lasting and formidable barrier to the growth of women of color in office. Put simply, underrepresentation will not change unless both parties recruit more women of color to run in majority-white districts.[13]

Political party is another crucial aspect of women's representation in the states. In 2025, women are 49 percent of all Democratic state legislators compared with only 21 percent of all Republican state legislators (see Figure 9.1). This dramatic party difference means that while women constitute about half of one party's state legislators, they remain a distinct minority within the opposing party. These party differences in women's state legislative representation mean that women are much more likely to hold leadership positions within Democratic Party caucuses than Republican Party ones. In 2025, women held just 29.6 percent of 345 state legislative leadership positions overall, according to CAWP.[14]

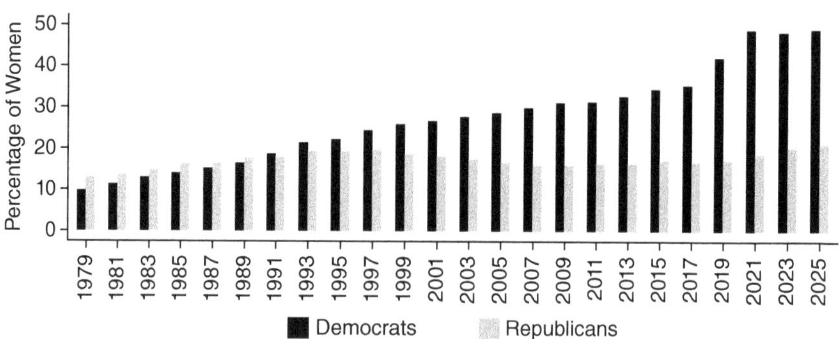

Figure 9.1 Democratic women, but not Republican women, are a growing share of their party's state legislators.
Source: Council of State Governments, National Conference of State Legislatures, and CAWP.

---

[13] Paru Shah, Jamil Scott, and Eric Gonzalez Juenke, Women of Color Candidates: Examining Emergence and Success in State Legislative Elections, *Politics, Groups, and Identities* 7(2) (2018): 429–43, p. 439.

[14] CAWP, Women in State Legislative Leadership 2025, 2025, https://cawp.rutgers.edu/data/levels-office/state-legislature?tab=StateLegislativeLeadership

There were only a few changes in party control of state legislative chambers following the 2024 election.[15] The relative stasis in party control at the state legislative level was a victory of sorts for the Democratic Party. As *The 19th* observed, the power that Democrats wield at the state level compares favorably with the federal level: "In a year where the electorate as a whole shifted to the right and Trump gained significant ground in blue states, Democrats' state-level wins were 'really remarkable,' said Lala Wu, co-founder and executive director of SisterDistrict, an organization focused on electing Democrats to state legislatures."[16] However, taking a national view of party competition, and taking the results of the 2024 state legislative elections into account, we can see that women legislators are especially underrepresented within the political party that dominates state policymaking: The Democratic Party controls thirty-nine state legislative chambers and the Republican Party fifty-eight chambers in 2025.[17]

Women's gains are partially attributed to conscious organizing to improve women's representation. Women's organizations recruit and train women and channel resources to candidates – grassroots activities that are themselves powered by resources.[18] For example, Emerge America, founded in 2002, is a national network that trains Democratic women to run for office; Vote Run Lead, founded in 2014, trains women to run at all levels of office; and Higher Heights for America, founded in 2011, is a national network of Black women in politics. To combat the underrepresentation of mothers in elected office, Vote Mama PAC (political action committee) supports Democratic candidates who are mothers. Meanwhile, the LGBTQ+ Victory Institute recruits and trains LGBTQ+ candidates.[19] Race and gender interact with LGBTQ+ identity,

---

[15] Wendy Underhill, 2024 State Elections by the Numbers, National Conference of State Legislatures, 2024, www.ncsl.org/state-legislatures-news/details/2024-state-elections-by-the-numbers

[16] Grace Panetta, Democrats Look to State Legislatures as Their Anti-Trump "Firewall," *The 19th*, December 18, 2024, https://19thnews.org/2024/12/democrats-state-legislatures-anti-trump-firewall/

[17] One chamber was tied. Nebraska is unicameral and elects senators on a nonpartisan basis. Underhill, 2024 State Elections by the Numbers.

[18] Rebecca Kreitzer and Tracy Osborn, Women Candidate Recruitment Groups in the States, in *Good Reasons to Run: Women and Political Candidacy*, eds. Shauna L. Shames et al. (Philadelphia, PA: Temple University Press, 2020), pp. 183–92, p. 183; Christina Bejarano and Wendy Smooth, Women of Color Mobilizing: Sistahs Are Doing It for Themselves from GOTV to Running Candidates for Political Office, *Journal of Women, Politics & Policy* 43(1) (2022): 8–24.

[19] The Experiences of LGBTQ+ Women Candidates: A Report from the When We Run Survey, LGBTQ+ Victory Institute, 2024, https://tinyurl.com/2sucsyj2; When We Run: The Motivations, Experiences and Challenges of LGBTQ+ Candidates in the United States, LGBTQ+ Victory Institute, 2023, https://tinyurl.com/3jj6byrp

creating a need for dedicated resources and strategies to overcome discrimination and secure scarce financial resources as well as party support.[20] According to the institute there are 245 state legislators who identify as LGBTQ+, reflecting growth in the diversity of elected officials nationally.[21]

To be successful, these types of activities must be ongoing across election cycles. Organizations tap women to run who might not have previously thought about entering electoral politics, connect them with resources, and build networks essential to successful campaigns. Conscious, targeted recruitment efforts can expand the number of women running for winnable open seats. And, to the extent that women are excluded from existing networks, trainings can give women information and expertise that they may not otherwise be able to access.

More organizations dedicated to electing women to office can be found on the Democratic side of the aisle than on the Republican side. With more women Democrats than women Republicans serving in state legislatures, the likelihood that more women who will be tapped to run takes on a partisan cast due to networks and recruitment activities. Even in open seats without incumbents, Republican women candidates are outnumbered by Democratic women (see Table 9.1).

When legislatures include higher proportions of women, more women are available to serve throughout the body in leadership roles. And with more women serving, a wider range of women's experiences can be captured in legislative deliberations.[22] For example, in Nevada, Nicole Cannizzaro (D) became the first woman to serve as majority leader of the state Senate – a position that she held during her pregnancy and after giving birth. She explained that she wanted to combat "this notion that maybe you don't belong, if what you're also doing in life is deciding to create a family."[23] Colorado state Representative Elizabeth Velasco (D), an Emerge alumna, described the perspective she brings to her legislature:

---

[20] Elliot Imse and Gabriele Magni, The Experiences of Black LGBTQ+ Candidates, A Report from the When We Run Survey, LGBTQ+ Victory Institute, 2024, https://tinyurl.com/27huxxm6

[21] LGBTQ+ Victory Institute, National Map, n.d., https://outforamerica.org/?office-level=State%20Legislature

[22] Nadia E. Brown, *Sisters in the Statehouse: Black Women and Legislative Decision Making.* (New York: Oxford University Press, 2014).

[23] Michelle Rindels, Senator Who Gave Birth during Session Hopes Motherhood No Longer Seen as "Disqualifying," *The Nevada Independent*, May 30, 2023, https://tinyurl.com/5ecay6dt

> I grew up low-income, living in mobile home parks in the Vail Valley, where I had to work multiple jobs to put myself through college and support my family. I know first-hand the realities that our working families face. I decided to run for office because for too long, too many of us have been left behind. We deserve leaders who take action and who put working families first.[24]

Velasco is the "first Mexican-born state representative in Colorado, the first Latina legislator from the western slope, and the first open LGBTQ legislator in western Colorado."[25]

National statistics mask uneven rates of progress for women by state. For example, in 2025, the state with the highest proportion of women is Nevada (see Table 9.2). Nevada boasts a legislature that is 61.9 percent women. The state with the lowest proportion of women is West Virginia; women are just 11.2 percent of the legislature.

Tables 9.2 and 9.3 show that multiple states – including Colorado and Nevada – have crossed the threshold into a gender parity situation or higher, with women comprising at least one-half of state legislators. But other states are far behind. Indeed, in five states women do not even comprise one-fifth of legislators (see Table 9.2).

Studies shed light on why women are more likely to hold office in some states than others. As the political parties forged alliances with different organized interests following women's rights activism in the 1970s, women candidates and officeholders became more likely to identify with the Democratic Party.[26] This means that states where the Democratic Party is more competitive are likely to have a higher proportion of women state legislators. Some states have term limits in which there are a maximum number of terms that state legislators are permitted to serve. Although term limits create more openings for new candidates, the presence of women running for these seats is not guaranteed. Women have fared best in states where service is low-paying and the length of legislative sessions is long.[27]

A recent CAWP study featuring case studies of five states offers valuable insights about the inner workings of states. States, according to the

---

[24] Elizabeth for Colorado, n.d., www.elizabethforcolorado.com

[25] Ibid.

[26] Carroll and Sanbonmatsu, *More Women Can Run*; Laurel Elder, *The Partisan Gap: Why Democratic Women Get Elected but Republican Women Don't* (New York: New York University Press, 2021).

[27] Kira Sanbonmatsu, Political Parties and the Recruitment of Women to State Legislatures, *The Journal of Politics* 64(3) (2002): 791–809.

Table 9.2 Women's representation varies across states

50% plus	40–49%	30–39%	20–29%	Under 20%
Nevada	California	Michigan	Utah	Alabama
New Mexico	Arizona	Delaware	Kentucky	Tennessee
Colorado	Oregon	South Dakota	Missouri	Mississippi
–	Washington	Minnesota	Nebraska	South Carolina
–	Illinois	New Hampshire	Idaho	West Virginia
–	Alaska	Virginia	Iowa	–
–	Vermont	Connecticut	Indiana	–
–	Florida	Georgia	Wyoming	–
–	Rhode Island	New York	North Dakota	–
–	Maryland	Ohio	Louisiana	–
–	Maine	Texas	Oklahoma	–
–	Hawaii	Montana	Arkansas	–
–	–	New Jersey	–	–
–	–	Wisconsin	–	–
–	–	Kansas	–	–
–	–	Pennsylvania	–	–
–	–	Massachusetts	–	–
–	–	North Carolina	–	–

Note: States are listed from high to low in each column for the percentage of women in state legislatures in 2025.
Source: CAWP.

Table 9.3 Majority-woman state legislatures and chambers, 2025

Overall Legislature	Senate Only	House/Assembly Only
Colorado	Arizona	Alaska
Nevada	California	Colorado
New Mexico	Nevada	Nevada
–	–	New Mexico

Source: Women in State Legislators, CAWP, https://cawp.rutgers.edu/facts/levels-office/state-legislature/women-state-legislatures-2025.

report's author Kelly Dittmar, are arguably unique "political ecosystems."[28] The report draws on nearly 200 interviews with current and former elected officials, party leaders, practitioners, and activists, showing how

[28] Kelly Dittmar, Rethinking Women's Political Power, CAWP, 2023, https://rethinkingpower.rutgers.edu/

> **TEXT BOX 9.2 Women Report Both Opportunities and Challenges in Their States (Excerpts from CAWP's "Rethinking Women's Political Power" Report)**
>
> **OPPORTUNITIES**
>
> I do believe that when women get [into political office], they want to bring other women along. … I think that it just kind of builds on itself.
> —Melinda Bush (D-IL), Former State Senator and Founder of Lake County Democratic Women
>
> One of the greatest things I love about being a legislator is that when I walk through the halls and there are youth in the building, how they get overwhelmed to see someone that looks like them and can relate to them.
> —Kim Schofield (D-GA), State Representative
>
> What I continue to hear is that people in our party are looking for a strong woman; they would like to see more strong Republican women running statewide for office. So I think there's just great opportunity for women who want to run statewide.
> —Kristin Phillips-Hill (R-PA), State Senator
>
> **CHALLENGES**
>
> There's higher expectations of [women of color in leadership spaces] because not only are they expected to fulfill the duties of that role, but they are also supposed to be the translator of our culture, right? … I think that that's also what we feel.
> —Selena Torres (D-NV), State Assemblywoman
>
> ---
>
> *Source:* Dittmar, Rethinking, Rethinking Women's Political Power, CAWP, https://rethinkingpower.rutgers.edu.

candidates emerge in different political settings and how and why women are underrepresented. Interviews revealed both the opportunities and importance of women's public service and the remaining challenges (see Text Box 9.2).

Women are only 23.5 percent of Oklahoma state legislators in 2025. In comparison, women made history in Nevada when they became a majority of the state legislature in 2018. But the Nevada case shows that equality for women in terms of numbers does not automatically yield political influence; Dittmar shows that the legislature is not perceived to be the most powerful office in the state.

Dittmar's study also reveals party differences in whether women's underrepresentation is perceived as a problem, and what can be done about it. Dittmar observes: "It is difficult to motivate action to address women's political underrepresentation without first articulating the need for intervention and acquiring buy-in from political influencers – party and organizational leaders, political professionals, and even donors and voters – in a state's political ecosystem."[29] As the interview subjects in Dittmar's research explained, women's organizations can help women see themselves as candidates and create networks to provide needed infrastructure for their campaigns. But infrastructure does not exist in all states, and the accessibility of that infrastructure may depend on women's racial and political party backgrounds.

WOMEN GOVERNORS AND OTHER STATEWIDE EXECUTIVES

All states elect governors. On this metric, women are only 24 percent of all governors in 2025. Women are 30.6 percent of all statewide executive offices including attorneys general and secretaries of state. Figure 9.2 shows that women's presence in statewide executive offices has hovered around 30 percent for some time; in contrast, the state legislative time series shows some evidence of recent growth.

The first women to ever serve as governors were usually widows – placeholders who were appointed to be governor after the death of their husbands. It was not until 1975 that a woman would serve as governor in her own right: Connecticut's Ella T. Grasso.[30] More Democratic than Republican women have ever served as governor. In 2025, women serve as governors in twelve states: Alabama, Arizona, Arkansas, Iowa, Kansas, Maine, Massachusetts, Michigan, New Hampshire, New Mexico, New York, and Oregon. These women took a variety of paths to the office. Massachusetts Governor Maura Healey (D) had been the state's attorney general. Arizona Governor Katie Hobbs (D) had served as a state legislator and state attorney general. Both Governor Kay Ivey (R-AL) and Governor Kathy Hochul (D-NY) were elevated to governor from the position of lieutenant governor when the sitting governor left office. Governor Kim Reynolds (R-IA) was appointed to the position after a vacancy and subsequently became the first woman to be elected governor of Iowa. Governor

---

[29] Kelly Dittmar, Partisan Differences in Identifying Barriers, Rethinking Women's Political Power, CAWP, 2023, https://tinyurl.com/4dksajxz

[30] History of Women Governors, CAWP, n.d., https://tinyurl.com/3w666zpf

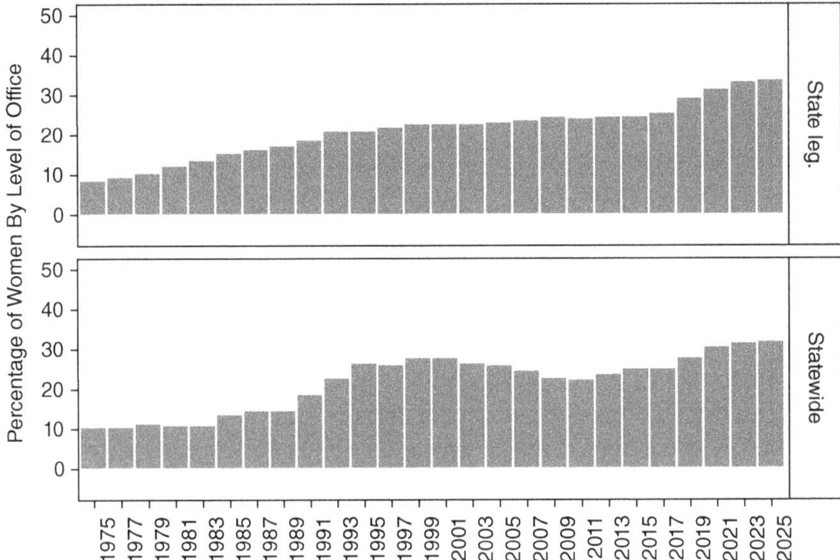

Figure 9.2 Women's officeholding in the states increased in recent elections. *Source:* CAWP.

Gretchen Whitmer (D-MI) had previously served in the state legislature, as had Governor Tina Kotek (D-OR) and Governor Laura Kelly (D-KS). Governor Sarah Huckabee Sanders (R-AR) served in the first Trump administration and is the daughter of a former governor.

Although women's state legislative representation trended upward with the 2022 and 2024 elections, the picture for women governors has been static. The pathways outlined for women governors show that some women happened to reach the office of governor via the lieutenant governor position. Just five new women became governor because they were elected in 2022 or 2024, including Governor Kelly Ayotte (R-NH), who previously served in the US Senate. Ayotte defeated former Manchester Mayor Joyce Craig (D). In Oregon, Tina Kotek (D), who previously made history as the country's first openly lesbian state House speaker, won election to the governor's office in 2022.[31]

For most states, having a woman governor is a recent experience if they have had women governors at all: Only thirty-two states have ever experienced a woman governor. No state has ever elected a Black, Native American, or Middle Eastern/North African woman to the office of governor.

[31] Milestones for Women in American Politics, CAWP, n.d., https://cawp.rutgers.edu/data?tab=Milestones

The expense of running for governor can limit the candidate pool. Financial gatekeepers may lack confidence in women candidates, making women's candidacies less likely. Women may not have the confidence of financial gatekeepers to run. CAWP's comprehensive study of campaign contributions in governors' races from 2000 to 2018 found that women and men candidates raised comparable amounts in similar types of races.[32] However, some important gender differences came to light in the CAWP study about women gubernatorial candidates: "women as a pool of candidates must be more qualified than their male competitors (as measured by prior officeholding) to raise comparable amounts. Democratic women are less likely than their male counterparts to self-finance, while both groups of women are more reliant on small contributors than are the men in their party."[33] The report found that women donors are underrepresented as a share of all donors and as a share of all money contributed – gaps that may diminish the financial resources available to potential women gubernatorial candidates. Women are also less likely to self-finance their gubernatorial campaigns.

One of the biggest obstacles to growing the number of women governors is that women are not running; one analysis found that "there were no women candidates in 71.7% of the gubernatorial primaries conducted between 1978 and 2022."[34] Voter expectations and stereotypes matter directly and indirectly, given that certain offices may align more with "feminine" or "masculine" traits.[35]

Types of statewide offices vary, though all states have governors and most states have an elected lieutenant governor, secretary of state, and treasurer. Historically, white women have been much better represented than women of color as statewide executive officials.[36] "Firsts" are often noted with each election cycle due to the historic underrepresentation of

---

[32] Kira Sanbonmatsu, Kathleen Rogers, and Claire Gothreau, The Money Hurdle in the Race for Governor: A CAWP Women, Money and Politics Report, CAWP, 2020, https://tinyurl.com/55v45fsz

[33] Ibid.

[34] Alana Jeydel and William R. Wilkerson, Why Aren't More Women on the Gubernatorial Ballot? *Politics, Groups, and Identities* 13(2) (2025): 346–67.

[35] Richard Fox and Zoe Oxley, Gender Stereotyping in State Executive Elections: Candidate Selection and Success, *The Journal of Politics* 65(3) (2003): 833–50; Jennie Sweet-Cushman, Legislative vs. Executive Political Offices: How Gender Stereotypes Can Disadvantage Women in Either Office, *Political Behavior* 44 (2022): 411–34.

[36] Kira Sanbonmatsu, Officeholding in the Fifty States: The Pathways Women of Color Take to Statewide Elective Executive Office, in *Distinct Identities: Minority Women in US Politics*, eds. Nadia E. Brown and Sarah Allen Gershon (New York: Routledge, 2020), pp. 171–86, p. 171.

women in these positions. For example, Letitia James (D) became New York's attorney general and the first Black woman to ever win statewide office in her state in 2019. Winsome Earle Sears (R) became the first Black woman to be lieutenant governor when she took her seat in 2022 in Virginia. When she was elected attorney general of Massachusetts, Maura Healey (D) became the first openly gay state attorney general and the first openly gay woman to be elected to any statewide office.[37] Whereas the office of secretary of state has often been held by a woman, the same cannot be said for the office of governor or attorney general.

The challenges facing women running for governor transcend party lines. But party divides women statewide executives from one another where policy is concerned. For example, while some Democratic governors including Governor Maura Healey vowed to resist President Trump's plans to deport undocumented immigrants in historic numbers,[38] all four Republican women governors joined a letter pledging their support: "Together, we will continue to defend the American people, uphold the rule of law, and ensure our nation remains safe and secure for future generations. We stand ready to utilize every tool at our disposal – whether through state law enforcement or the National Guard – to support President Trump in this vital mission."[39]

PUBLIC POLICY IN THE STATES

The *Dobbs* decision dramatically elevated states as policymakers on women's rights issues. Prior to *Dobbs*, some states had already enacted "trigger laws" that would ban abortion automatically in the event that *Roe* was overturned. By the end of 2022, abortion was prohibited in more than a dozen states, according to the Guttmacher Institute.[40] New anti-abortion legislation was introduced across the country and particularly in Republican-led "red states." Many of these restrictions were challenged in the courts, and as the Guttmacher Institute summarized: "Because the US Constitution no longer protects abortion rights, these cases are

---

[37] Milestones for Women in American Politics, CAWP, n.d., https://cawp.rutgers.edu/data?tab=Milestones

[38] Khaleda Rahman, Donald Trump's Deportation Plan Faces Rebellion from Democratic Governors, *Newsweek*, November 7, 2024, www.newsweek.com/trump-deportation-plan-faces-rebellion-1981970

[39] Republican Governors Join to Support President Trump's Immigration Policies, Republican Governors Association, December 11, 2024, https://tinyurl.com/689c9t87

[40] Elizabeth Nash and Peter Ephross, State Policy Trends 2022: In a Devastating Year, US Supreme Court's Decision to Overturn Roe Leads to Bans, Confusion and Chaos, *Guttmacher*, December 2022, https://tinyurl.com/2u2ur6zf

being heard in state courts rather than federal courts. Some of these bans have become entangled in a legal back and forth – with abortion being legal one day and illegal the next – and this chaos has had a yo-yo effect that has confused both providers and patients."[41] At the same time, so-called blue states, led by Democrats, moved in the opposite direction and worked to shore up protections for women seeking abortions. In one of the most closely watched debates, Arizona ultimately decided in 2024 to repeal the 1800s law that prohibited abortion; without the 1800s law, the state would return to its prohibition on abortion after fifteen weeks that was passed in 2022.

Women facing restrictions in their home state have had to travel out-of-state for abortion care. According to the *New York Times*, "Out-of-state travel for abortions – either to have a procedure or obtain abortion pills – more than doubled in 2023 compared with 2019 and made up nearly a fifth of recorded abortions."[42]

In addition to the flurry of litigation and legislative activity across states, activists took to ballot initiatives to change policy. For example, following the *Dobbs* decision, pro-choice advocates found success in state-wide ballot initiatives: An antiabortion state constitutional amendment was defeated in Kansas in 2022, and an effort to protect abortion rights in the state constitution of Ohio was successful in 2023.

The 2024 election saw ballot questions on abortion in ten states (see Table 9.4). Most, but not all, of the pro-choice ballot efforts were successful.

In a particularly significant defeat for pro-choice activists, a proposed constitutional amendment in Florida was defeated. In 2024, women seeking abortion in Florida after six weeks were prohibited from doing so, with rare exceptions. Because the ballot question took the form of a proposed amendment to the state constitution, it required a supermajority to pass. However, the question failed because it received 57 percent support from the electorate – just below the needed 60 percent. Governor Ron De Santis (R) played a central role in the amendment's defeat and argued that if it won, "we would become this major abortion tourist destination, which is not what we want for our state."[43]

---

[41] Ibid.

[42] Molly Cook Escobar, Amy Schoenfeld Walker, Allison McCann, Scott Reinhard, and Helmuth Rosales, 171,000 Traveled for Abortions Last Year. See Where They Went, *New York Times*, June 13, 2024, www.nytimes.com/interactive/2024/06/13/us/abortion-state-laws-ban-travel.html

[43] Travis Gibson and Scott Johnson, Gov. DeSantis: Florida Will Become "Major Abortion Tourist Destination" if Amendment 4 Passes, *News4Jax*, October 22, 2024, https://tinyurl.com/3c3jvhkt

Table 9.4 Most pro-choice ballot questions
passed in 2024

State	Outcome
Arizona	Won (61.6%)
Colorado	Won (62.0%)
Florida	Lost (57.2%)*
Maryland	Won (76.0%)
Missouri	Won (51.6%)
Montana	Won (57.8%)
Nebraska	Lost (49.0%)
Nevada	Won (64.4%)
New York	Won (62.0%)
South Dakota	Lost (41.4%)

Note: The percentage of the vote that was pro-choice
appears in parentheses.

* *In Florida, the amendment needed to pass a 60 percent
threshold.*

Source: Live Results: Abortion on the Ballot in 10 States,
Wall Street Journal, November 6, 2024, www.wsj.com/
politics/elections/abortion-results-ballot-2024-a4000fa4
(accessed March 1, 2025).

Pro-choice efforts also lost in Nebraska and South Dakota in 2024, while an antiabortion measure in Nebraska passed. But in most of the states with ballot questions, pro-choice activists found success. In 2024, New York State successfully voted to amend its state constitution in order to extend equal protection of the laws on the basis of "ethnicity, national origin, age, and disability" or "sex, including sexual orientation, gender identity, gender expression, pregnancy, pregnancy outcomes, and reproductive healthcare and autonomy."

As of late November 2024, nineteen states had very restrictive policies and seven very protective, with the remaining states falling in the middle.[44] With the return of Donald Trump to the White House, policymaking related to abortion rights remained in contention. Some Democratic governors including Maura Healey (MA), Kathy Hochul (NY), and Tina Kotek (OR) had stockpiled drugs for medication abortions. Governor Whitmer (MI) made headlines in October 2024 when

---

[44] Guttmacher, Interactive Map: US Abortion Policies and Access after Roe, Guttmacher.org, n.d., updated March 12, 2025, https://states.guttmacher.org/policies/

she announced that her state would distribute contraceptives for free, arguing: "Everyone, no matter how much money they make, deserves to make their own decisions about their own reproductive health and future."[45] In other states, conservatives were moving forward with efforts to ensure that abortion bans included restrictions on women's ability to travel across state lines to obtain abortion or receive abortion pills through the mail.[46]

One issue to watch is whether restrictive abortion policies harm women's health or even lead to deaths. During the 2024 presidential campaign, Vice President Kamala Harris drew attention to several cases identified by *Pro Publica* reporting in which women had died as a result of state abortion policies; they lacked access to medically necessary care out of hospitals' fear of violating state abortion laws.[47] In November 2024, the Texas agency tasked with overseeing statistics and research about maternal deaths decided to skip deaths that occurred during 2022 and 2023, ensuring that the abortion-related deaths that Harris highlighted during her campaign would not be investigated.[48]

Women state legislators do not speak with one voice on abortion, which is an extremely partisan issue; in fact, conservative women are often at the forefront of antiabortion policymaking.[49] At the same time, CAWP's data show that women state legislators disproportionately identify as Democrats rather than Republicans; this means that most women state legislators are pro-choice. Meanwhile, some women who have tried to moderate the Republican Party's abortion positions have lost their seats: Three Republican women state senators in South Carolina who had worked to moderate abortion policy in their state were defeated in their primaries in 2024.[50]

[45] Stephanie Akin, Michigan to Provide Free Contraception in November, *Pluribus News*, October 24, 2024, https://tinyurl.com/mrxw7dfp

[46] Naomi Cahn and Sonia Suter, Crossing State Lines to Get an Abortion Is a New Legal Minefield, with Courts to Decide if There's a Right to Travel, *The Conversation*, September 6, 2024, https://tinyurl.com/mrxhm8br

[47] Cassandra Jaramillo et al., Texas Lawmakers Push for New Exceptions to State's Strict Abortion Ban after the Deaths of Two Women, *Pro Publica*, November 20, 2024, www.propublica.org/article/texas-abortion-ban-exceptions-deaths

[48] Caroline Kitchener, Texas Committee Won't Examine Maternal Deaths in First Years after Abortion Ban, *Washington Post*, November 26, 2024, https://tinyurl.com/2usjsc76

[49] Beth Reingold, Rebecca Kreitzer, Tracy Osborn, and Michele Swers, Anti-Abortion Policymaking and Women's Representation, *Political Research Quarterly* 74(2) (2021): 403–20.

[50] Jeffrey Collins, GOP Women Who Helped Defeat a Near-Total Abortion Ban Are Losing Reelection in South Carolina, *AP*, June 12, 2024, https://tinyurl.com/4e9vvecs

Beyond abortion policy, states continue to be critical sites of policy-making in many areas. For example, states vary in parental leave policies. The federal Family and Medical Leave Act, enacted in 1993, provides leave to workers for the birth or adoption of a child and other situations, but most workers are not able to take the leave as it is unpaid and not all workers are eligible. According to the National Conference of State Legislatures, workers have access to *paid* leave in only thirteen states.[51]

Under the Biden administration, transgender students were protected from discrimination through federal guidelines. But the Trump administration is reversing Biden's policies. Meanwhile, in November 2024, Ohio adopted a new state law restricting bathroom use by K-12 and college students.[52] In so doing, Ohio joined other states that restrict bathroom usage to "sex assigned at birth." These policies, which opponents see as fundamental violations of civil rights, reveal the vulnerability of trans people in the face of legislative majorities and the increasingly partisan nature of the issue. Hundreds of anti-trans bills were introduced at the state legislative level in 2024.[53] One analysis found that despite the large amount of legislative attention, only a tiny number of transgender teenagers receive health care related to gender transitions.[54]

Prior to Trump's election in 2024, conservative attacks on diversity in education had taken root at the state level. Conservative women activists such as members of the group Moms for Liberty advocate for restrictions on education, including banning mention of gender identity or sexuality in schools. According to a *Washington Post* analysis, states saw over 100 policy adoptions between 2017 and 2024 in thirty-eight states that eliminate topics from the curriculum, banning the words "LGBTQ," "gender," and "diversity, equity, and inclusion."[55] According to the *Washington Post* analysis:

> Three-fourths of the nation's school-age students are now educated
> under state-level measures that either require more teaching on issues

---

[51] State Family and Medical Leave Laws, National Conference of State Legislators, accessed December 2, 2024, www.ncsl.org/labor-and-employment/state-family-and-medical-leave-laws

[52] Haley BeMiller, Ohio Gov. Mike DeWine Signs Transgender Bathroom Ban, *Columbus Dispatch*, November 27, 2024, https://tinyurl.com/bd93rya5

[53] Trans Legislation Home, Trans Legislation, accessed December 5, 2024, https://translegislation.com/

[54] Selena Simmons-Duffin, "A Very, Very Small Number" of Teens Receive Gender-Affirming Care, Study Finds, *NPR*, January 6, 2025, https://tinyurl.com/ss3nnazx

[55] Hannah Natanson, Lauren Tierney, and Clara Ence Morse, America Has Reshaped Education into Red and Blue Versions, *Washington Post*, April 4, 2024, www.washingtonpost.com/education/2024/04/04/education-laws-red-blue-divide/

like race, racism, history, sex and gender, or which sharply limit or fully forbid such lessons, according to a sweeping Post review of thousands of state laws, gubernatorial directives and state school board policies. The restrictive laws alone affect almost half of all Americans ages five to nineteen.[56]

In November 2024, the University of North Texas removed words including "gender" and "race" from hundreds of course titles proactively, anticipating scrutiny of its curriculum from the state.[57] The "anti-DEI" movement led to the termination of Oklahoma's nonpartisan leadership training program called "New Education for Women's (NEW) Leadership," which was part of CAWP's national NEW Leadership network, in response to Governor Kevin Stitt's (R) executive order. The state's NEW Leadership program had served 650 women from dozens of colleges and universities in Oklahoma over two decades. Women political leaders objected to the program's termination, with one arguing that the governor's executive order was an "embarrassment" for Oklahoma.[58] Meanwhile, Texas's program was discontinued at the University of Texas-Austin, and Texas Women's University subsequently decided to bring the program to their school.

Provisions related to the size and composition of the electorate and the conduct of elections are also at stake across the country. States have enormous discretion in how they conduct elections and whether they seek to make the right to vote more restrictive or expansive. Since the attack on the Capitol on January 6, 2021, states have moved in different directions on election security. Laws impact who is allowed to vote and how votes are counted, with implications for who runs and wins. Moreover, threats of violence against elected officials have increased in recent years. These threats can have a disproportionate impact on women legislators and especially women of color.[59] In one of the most dramatic incidents, law enforcement in 2020 thwarted an attempt to kidnap Governor Gretchen Whitmer (D-MI) – an attack that President Trump declined to condemn.[60]

---

[56] Ibid.

[57] Kate McGee, UNT Faculty Slam University for Removing References to Race and Equity in Course Names, *Texas Tribune*, November 19, 2024, www.texastribune.org/2024/11/19/texas-unt-dei-ban/

[58] Beth Wallis, OU Ends Women's Leadership Program to Comply with Stitt's Executive Order against DEI, *StateImpact Oklahoma*, May 6, 2024, https://tinyurl.com/2xxk3rwy

[59] Gowri Ramachandran et al., Intimidation of State and Local Officeholders, Brennan Center for Justice, 2024, https://tinyurl.com/yt3cst5b

[60] Mona Lena Krook, *Violence against Women in Politics* (New York: Oxford University Press, 2020); David D. Kirkpatrick and Mike McIntire, "Its Own Domestic Army": How the

CONCLUSION

States are pivotal players in policymaking on issues impacting women's daily lives. But women remain underrepresented as policymakers. Recent elections have seen a record number of women elected to state legislatures. At the same time, these gains have been uneven across states and parties. Women from historically underrepresented racial and ethnic groups remain underrepresented; the percentage of women state legislators still does not descriptively reflect the proportion of women in the US population.

Women lag behind men in statewide executive officeholding including as governors. The pool of potential candidates for the presidency and the US Congress remains disproportionately composed of men.[61] Public expectations of what a governor or an attorney general looks like continue to reproduce gendered patterns of underrepresentation. Meanwhile, women elected officials play a role in determining the policies that shape women candidates' experiences, including whether they can use campaign funds to pay for childcare expenses.[62]

While a majority of women did not get the woman president they voted for in 2016 or 2024, a number of current women state officeholders could launch a future presidential campaign. Indeed, Governor Whitmer (D-MI) is often mentioned as a potential 2028 presidential candidate. Meanwhile, women from both parties were vying to be governor of New Jersey and Virginia – the only two states with 2025 gubernatorial elections – and women were already preparing their 2026 statewide campaigns.

G.O.P. Allied Itself with Militants, *New York Times*, February 9, 2021, www.nytimes.com/2021/02/08/us/militias-republicans-michigan.html

[61] Danielle M. Thomsen and Aaron S. King, Women's Representation and the Gendered Pipeline to Power, *The American Political Science Review* 114(4) (2020): 989–1000.

[62] Vote Mama Foundation, Campaign Funds for Childcare, Vote Mama Foundation, 2024, www.votemamafoundation.org/reports/cfcc2024; Reid Wilson, Ariz., Okla. Allow Campaign Funds to Pay for Child Care, *Pluribus News*, September 19, 2024, https://tinyurl.com/3ppxyfn7

Index

For EU product safety concerns, contact us at Calle de José Abascal, 56–1°,
28003 Madrid, Spain or eugpsr@cambridge.org.